Write on Course

A Student Handbook for
WRITING, THINKING, and LEARNING

Written and Compiled by
**Patrick Sebranek, Dave Kemper,
and Verne Meyer**

Illustrated by
Chris Krenzke

WRITE SOURCE®

GREAT SOURCE,
a division of HOUGHTON MIFFLIN
HARCOURT COMPANY
www.greatsource.com
800-289-4490

Reviewers

Write Source: Steven J. Augustyn, April Barrons, Colleen Belmont, Chris Erickson, Mariellen Hanrahan, Dave Kemper, Tim Kemper, Rob King, Lois Krenzke, Mark Lalumondier, Jason C. Reynolds, Janae Sebranek, Lester Smith, Jean Varley

Great Source Editorial: Michele Order Litant

Great Source Design: Sara Noble

Printed in the United States of America

International Standard Book Number: 978-0-669-02401-2 (hardcover)

1 2 3 4 5 6 7 8 9 10 -RRD- 16 15 14 13 12 11 10

International Standard Book Number: 978-0-669-02405-0 (softcover)

1 2 3 4 5 6 7 8 9 10 -RRD- 16 15 14 13 12 11 10

Using the Handbook

The **Write on Course** handbook covers all of your communication needs—from learning about the traits of writing to participating in peer response groups, from writing persuasive essays to creating digital stories. The handbook is loaded with guidelines and samples that are (1) designed for easy use, (2) written in a friendly, supportive voice, and (3) enhanced by wonderful illustrations.

Write on Course will help you with other learning skills, too—including evaluating sources, using the Internet, study-reading, test taking, note taking, and making speeches. The "Student Almanac" in the back of the handbook contains tables, lists, maps, and charts covering everything from science to history. In other words, *Write on Course* can serve as your personal writing and learning guide in all of your classes.

Check our Web site
—**thewritesource.com**—
for more information,
including additional
writing topics and models.

Your Handbook Guide

You'll be able to quickly find information in the handbook using these guides:

The table of contents (starting on the next page) lists the five major sections in the handbook and the chapters found in each section. Use the table of contents when you're looking for a general topic such as *capitalization*.

The index in the back of the handbook (starting on page 580) lists all of the specific topics discussed in *Write on Course*. Use the index when you are looking for a specific piece of information.

The color coding used for the "Proofreader's Guide" (the pages are yellow) makes this important section easy to find. These pages contain rules for punctuation, capitalization, spelling, and grammar.

The special page references throughout the book tell you where to turn in the handbook for more information about a topic. Example: (See page 415.)

"The best effect of any book is that it excites the reader to self-activity."

—— Thomas Carlyle, writer and historian

Table of
Contents

The Process of Writing

The Forms of **Writing**

Poet Tree

The Tools of **Learning**

Proofreader's Guide

Student Almanac

Why Write?

Writing, like no other activity, helps you to learn, to understand, and to grow. And here's the good news: Writing is not that hard. In fact, it's really nothing more than thinking on paper. Here's some even better news: If you follow our advice, you will become a confident and skilled writer. Just give writing a chance, and it will help you in so many ways. Let's check in with a few middle school students to see how writing is helping them.

Writing to Explore

In study hall, Josie is writing in her journal about a conversation she had with her grandmother. She is writing to explore her feelings.

Writing to Share

Toshi is in a writing workshop, putting the finishing touches on a story. She is writing to share what she has created.

Writing to Learn

In science class, Lebron is writing in his learning log about a lab experiment. He is writing to learn more about his science work.

Writing to Show

Jason is busy responding to a prompt on a social studies test. He is writing to show what he has learned.

> **"A strange thing happens when you write: You discover what you truly think; you find out what your heart means."**
>
> —— Shirley Rousseau Murphy, author of the *Dragonbards Trilogy*

The Writing
Process

Understanding
Writing

The student writers on this page are ready for adventure. One student wants to revisit an important memory. Another student wants to write about something she saw on the way to school. You, on the other hand, may want to slip into the uncharted world of your imagination. Writing allows for all three types of adventures, plus many more.

Once the words start flowing, you'll find yourself asking, "Wow, where are these ideas taking me?" You won't know until your writing is complete *(that's what makes writing an adventure)*, but writing will certainly help you better understand yourself and the world around you *(that's what makes it so important)*.

What's Ahead

- Becoming a Student of Writing
- Previewing the Writing Process
- The Writing Process in Action
- The Writing Situation

> "What are the magic words
> for the would-be writers?
> Only two will really work the spell:
> 1. Write. 2. Read."
>
> — Ursula K. Le Guin, author of *The Farthest Shore*

Becoming a Student of Writing

To become a writer, you should think and act like one. Follow the tips below, and you will be headed in the right direction.

Write every day—same time, same place.
You set aside time to practice a musical instrument or an athletic skill. Do the same with your writing.

Become a regular reader.
Reading will help you see how effective stories and essays are put together. Read anything and everything—books, blogs, magazines, newspapers, even the backs of cereal boxes.

Write about subjects that truly interest you.
Or as Tamora Pierce, author of *The Song of the Lioness*, says, "Write about what makes you want to write more."

Write as well as you can . . . by your own standards.
Writing authority William Zinsser states, "Quality is its own reward." So set high standards for yourself.

Experiment with different forms of writing.
Stories, essays, poems, reports, blogs—they all have something special to teach you about writing.

Learn the craft of writing.
Know the traits of writing. (See pages 7–12.) Understand the difference between **description** and **narration**, between **anecdote** and **metaphor**, and so on.

Think of writing as a process, not as an end product.
Writing must go through a series of steps before it really begins to take shape.

Previewing the Writing Process

No two writers work in exactly the same way, but they all follow a process as they write. Here's how Thomas J. Dygard, author of *Running Scared*, writes: "[I go] as fast I can from start to finish on the first draft. Then I rewrite and rewrite. I'm lucky I enjoy every bit of the process."

You will personalize the writing process over time, but it generally includes these five steps.

Prewriting ■ At the start of a project, writers explore possible subjects before selecting a topic to write about. Then they collect details about their topic and make a writing plan.

Writing ■ Writers then complete a first draft using their plan as a general guide. This draft is their first look at a developing story or essay.

Revising ■ After reviewing their first draft, writers improve it by changing any parts that are not clear or complete. They may ask a peer to review the draft as well.

Editing ■ Writers then check their revised writing for conventions such as punctuation and capitalization to ensure that their work is error free. They proofread the final copy for errors, too.

Publishing ■ Publishing is to a writer what an exhibit is to an artist—an opportunity to share the finished work with others. This step makes all of the other ones worth completing.

Points to Remember

- **Writers' wishes, dreams, and experiences shape their work.** As Frank McCourt, author of *Angela's Ashes*, says, "You are your material. You'll never be bored again [if you truly connect with your writing]."

- **Writers move back and forth between the steps in the process.** For example, after completing a first draft, a writer may decide to collect more details before going any further.

- **Writing is both an individual and a shared activity.** Writers obviously form their ideas on their own, but they also need feedback from their peers to help them decide how well the writing works.

The Writing Process in Action

These two pages show how the writing process works. The graphic below shows that you can move back and forth between the steps in the process.

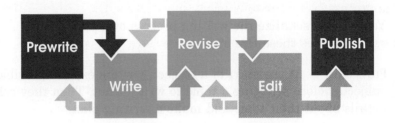

Prewriting ■ Choosing a Topic

1. To get started, search for a meaningful writing idea. If you need help, check out the selecting strategies listed in the handbook. (See pages 29–34.)
2. Choose a specific topic that truly interests you and meets the requirements of the assignment.

Gathering Details

1. Learn as much as you can about a topic before you write. If you need help, refer to the collecting strategies listed in the handbook. (See pages 35–37.)
2. Think of an important part of your subject to write about. This is your thesis or focus. (See page 38.)
3. Decide which details to include in your writing and how best to organize them.

Writing ■ Writing the First Draft

1. Write the first draft of your essay or story. Remember that this is a discovery draft, a first look at a writing idea.
2. Work in the details you've collected and add new ones that come to mind as you write.
3. Keep going until you get all of your ideas on paper. Your writing should include a beginning, a middle, and an ending.

Revising ■ Improving Your Writing

1. Review your first draft—but only after setting it aside for a while. Ask at least one other person to react to your writing.
2. Decide which parts need to be changed. One paragraph may be hard to follow. Another paragraph may need more details. Still another one may be in the wrong place.
3. Rewriting, reordering, adding, or cutting— these are the common revision strategies you will use.
4. Pay special attention to the beginning and ending parts. They should emphasize the importance of your thesis or focus. (See pages 41, 44, 112, and 115 for help.)

> Learning how to use a rubric helps you make meaningful changes in your writing as you go about revising your work.

Editing ■ Checking for Conventions

1. Check your revised writing for convention errors. Use your handbook (and the spell-checker and grammar guide if you are using a computer). Also ask a reliable classmate to check your work.
2. Prepare a neat final copy of your writing. Proofread this copy for errors.

Publishing ■ Sharing Your Writing

1. Share your finished work with your writing peers, friends, or other intended audience.
2. Decide if you are going to include the writing in your portfolio. (See pages 72–75.)
3. Consider submitting your work to a school publication, a writing contest, a blog site, and so on.

The Writing Situation

Writing for yourself in a personal notebook or journal is one thing. You can pretty much say what you want. Writing that you plan to share or publish is quite another thing. You must approach this type of writing with much more care and deliberation.

One of the first things to consider is the dynamics of the writing situation—your *subject*, your *purpose*, and your *audience*. The illustration shows how these elements work together.

What
Why
Who

Subject

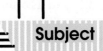

Purpose

Audience

▽ **Subject:**
   What will I write about?

▽ **Purpose:**
   Why am I writing?

▽ **Audience:**
   Who are my readers?

Helpful Hint

Your essays, articles, and stories will always be on track if you understand the writing situation.

Understanding the
Traits of Writing

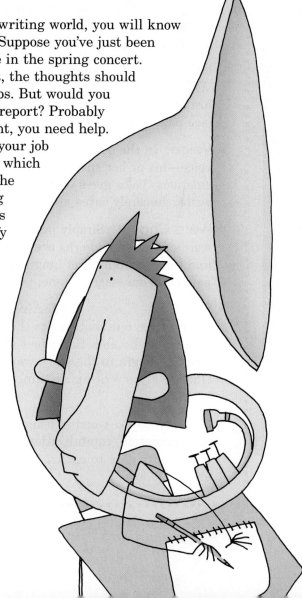

When all is right in your writing world, you will know exactly what you want to say. Suppose you've just been selected for a solo performance in the spring concert. When writing about this event, the thoughts should flow from your pen or fingertips. But would you work in this way for a science report? Probably not. For this type of assignment, you need help.

Two tools that will make your job easier are the writing process, which you already know about, and the **traits of writing**. The writing process provides you with steps to follow, and the traits identify key features to consider along the way.

What's Ahead

- Quick Guide: Traits
- The Traits in Action
- Connecting the Process and the Traits

Quick Guide ■ Traits

The traits listed below identify the main features you find in the best essays, reports, stories, and articles. If you write with these traits in mind, you—and your readers—will surely be pleased with the results.

- **Ideas:** Effective writing presents interesting and valuable information about a specific subject. It has a clear message or purpose. The ideas are thoroughly developed and hold the reader's attention.

- **Organization:** In terms of basic structure, good writing has a clearly developed beginning, middle, and ending. Within the text, each main point and the supporting details are arranged according to the best pattern of organization (see page 38).

- **Voice:** In the best writing, you can hear the writer's voice—his or her special way of expressing ideas and emotions. Voice gives writing personality; it shows that the writer sincerely cares about his or her subject and audience.

- **Word Choice:** Simply put, good writing contains good words. Nouns and verbs are specific; modifiers are colorful; and the overall level of language helps communicate a particular message or tone.

- **Sentence Fluency:** Effective writing flows smoothly and clearly from one sentence to the next. But it isn't, by any means, predictable. Sentences will vary in length, and they won't all begin in the same way. Sentence smoothness, or fluency, gives writing rhythm, which helps make it enjoyable to read.

- **Conventions:** Good writing follows the basic standards of punctuation, capitalization, spelling, and grammar. It is edited with care to ensure that the work is accurate and easy to follow.

The Traits in Action

On the next three pages, student writing examples illustrate the effective use of each trait.

Ideas

Discussion: In effective writing, the topic and supporting details hold the reader's interest from start to finish. In the following passage, John Kascinski shares many interesting ideas about his grandfather's favorite soup.

> When any family conversation turns to food, my grandfather, Ziggy, almost always mentions czarnina (pronounced chär nē′ nə). For those who don't know about czarnina, which would be about 99 percent of you, here's what it is: duck blood soup. That's right; my grandfather salivates whenever he talks about a soup made with blood. The weirdness continues with some of the other ingredients, including . . .

Discussion: John identifies his unusual topic, czarnina, in the beginning part. Then he provides specific details to describe it.

Organization

Good writing is easy to follow because it is organized from beginning to end. In the following passage, Anna Hernandez skillfully arranges the information about an Indian tribe's dying language.

> The Ho-Chunk language is fast approaching extinction. Linguist Joshua Fishman says that the language is at stage 7, meaning that it does have some speakers (3 percent of the tribal population), but they are all elderly. According to Fishman, these speakers must set up "learning nests" to teach the language to younger members of the tribe. Otherwise, the language will soon enter stage 8, the last stage before extinction. If, on the other hand, the language manages a rebirth, . . .

Discussion: Anna uses linking words and phrases, such as *otherwise, if,* and *on the other hand*, to help show the relationship between her ideas.

Voice

In the best writing, you can hear the writer's voice, or special way of saying things. In the following passage, Marcus Taylor's voice connects with his classmates, his intended audience.

> Football may be king in the United States; baseball may consume sports fans in Japan; but badminton dominates the sports scene in Indonesia. Badminton? That's right. The game Americans play at picnics is the national pastime in Indonesia. In fact, badminton has become so popular and so important in Indonesia that the country is now recognized as the superpower of the sport, . . .

Discussion: Marcus uses an engaging, almost conversational voice to share his information. (Factual writing does not have to be dry and dull.)

Word Choice

Good writing contains specific nouns, verbs, and modifiers. In the following passage, Guerdy Pierre discusses a special African headgear. As you will see, she pays special attention to the words that she uses.

> Headgear has always carried importance in many African cultures. Some types identify the wearer's valued trade, such as blacksmithing; other types signify royalty. Chiefs in the Kongo kingdom, for example, have adorned special caps (*ngunda* or *mpu*) to highlight their lofty status. To create these caps, Kongo artists traditionally worked with cotton thread or with threads carefully stripped from palm-leaf fibers. The artists wrapped or looped the threads in a spiral weave to form the cap. Then they used dyed thread to add a repeated geometric pattern around the cap . . .

Discussion: Note how Guerdy uses specific verbs—*identify, signify, adorned, stripped, wrapped,* and so on. Also note the effective use of adjectives—"*valued* trade," "*spiral* weave," "*dyed* thread," "*repeated geometric* pattern," and so on.

Sentence Fluency

Effective writing flows smoothly from sentence to sentence. In the following passage about rulers in Paraguay, Christina Sung pays special attention to sentence variety in order to achieve fluency.

> Many corrupt, ruthless leaders have made life miserable for the people of Paraguay. Francisco Solano Lopez may have been the worst. He involved Paraguay in three wars against three different neighbors—Brazil, Argentina, and Uruguay—all at the same time. These wars reduced the country's population from 525,000 to 221,000! What else needs to be said about this man? Then there is Dr. Francia, Paraguay's first president, who named himself Dictator for Life and ruled through ruthless suppression and random acts of terror. . . .

Discussion: Notice how Sung varies her sentence beginnings, types, and lengths. The longest sentence contains 24 words, and the shortest contains 6 words. (Names are counted as one word.)

Conventions

Good writing is carefully edited for conventions (punctuation, capitalization, spelling, and grammar) and presentation (arrangement on the page). In the following paragraph, Michael Curry pays careful attention to conventions.

> Scientists in Venezuela have discovered the remains of a buffalo-sized rodent that lived eight million years ago. The remains were found in Urumaco, a small town west of Caracas, the nation's capital. One scientist claims that during the late Miocene epoch, the Urumaco region was the land of giants. Along with "Guinea-zilla," huge turtles, crocodiles, and fish inhabited the area. . . .

Discussion: Notice how the well-placed commas control the flow of ideas. Also notice that all proper nouns are capitalized, and a special word, "Guinea-zilla," is set off by quotation marks.

Connecting the Process and the Traits

To make a pizza, you need a crust, sauce, cheese, and, perhaps, an additional topping or two. To develop a piece of writing, you need ingredients such as *ideas, organization, voice,* and so on. This chart shows you which traits to focus on during each of the steps in the writing process.

Process-Traits Chart

Prewriting

Ideas	What topic should I write about? What part of the topic should I focus on? What details should I include?
Organization	How should I organize my details? Which graphic organizer should I use for my planning?
Voice	What is my attitude about the topic?

Writing

Ideas	What do I want to say?
Organization	How do I want to arrange my ideas?
Voice	How do I want to sound?

Revising

Ideas	Are my ideas clear and complete?
Organization	Does each part work well?
Voice	Have I used the most appropriate voice?
Word Choice	Have I used specific nouns and active verbs?
Sentence Fluency	Are my sentences varied? Do they read smoothly?

Editing

Conventions	Have I used correct punctuation, capitalization, spelling, and grammar?

Publishing

All Traits	Have I used the traits effectively?
Presentation	Does my design make my ideas clear?

Using
Rubrics

Suppose you and your friend Jarrod are talking, and you happen to say, "I saw *Rocketeer II* over the weekend, and it was awesome."

Jarrod says, "Oh, yeah? What was so good about it?"

"Well," you reply, "it had a lot of action, and, ah . . ."

Not much for Jarrod to go on, is it? To give a better review, you would have to know which traits are used to evaluate movies—things like plot, characters, camera work, and so on.

You might have better luck reviewing a story or an article, because you know, or will soon learn, about the traits of effective writing. (See pages 7–12.) **Rubrics** are charts that help you evaluate writing according to these traits. This book contains traits-based rubrics for narrative, expository, persuasive, and workplace writing, as well as for responding to literature.

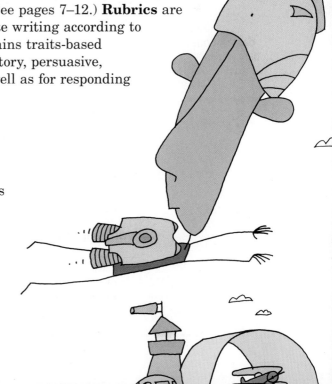

What's Ahead

- Understanding Rubrics
- Using a Rubric
- Assessing in Action
- Evaluating Tips

Understanding Rubrics

A rubric helps you make meaningful changes to your writing. The rubric for narrative writing (page 148) is shown below.

You can use a rubric to assess writing-in-progress or writing that is ready to publish.

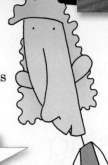

148

Rubric for Narrative Writing

Use the rubric that follows to assess your narrative writing.

The **main headings** list the traits.

Ideas

The writing . . .

—— focuses on a specific experience or time in the writer's life.

—— uses sensory details and dialogue to show rather than tell.

—— makes the reader want to know what happens next.

Organization

—— pulls the reader into the story.

—— includes a beginning, a middle, and an ending.

—— gives the events in an order that is easy to follow.

The **descriptions** help you know what to look for.

Voice

—— shows the writer's personality.

—— sounds honest and engaging.

Word Choice

—— contains specific nouns, vivid verbs, and colorful modifiers.

Sentence Fluency

—— flows smoothly from one idea to the next.

—— uses a variety of sentence lengths and beginnings.

Conventions

—— uses correct punctuation, capitalization, spelling, and grammar.

—— uses the format provided by the teacher or follows another effective design. (See pages 65–68.)

Using a Rubric

There are two ways in which a rubric can be used to assess your writing: the check-mark method and the numbering method.

Using Check Marks

You can put a check mark next to a description if the writing, for the most part, matches the description. Leaving a line unchecked indicates that there is still work to be done. In the sample assessment that follows, the writer feels that the narrative could use more dialogue and sensory details.

Ideas
The writing . . .
- ✓ focuses on one experience or time in the writer's life.
- ____ uses dialogue and sensory details.
- ✓ makes the reader want to know what happens next.

Using Numbers

You can also use numbers to rate the effectiveness of the writing for each description. Here is one rating scale that you could use.

| 6 Amazing | 5 Strong | 4 Good | 3 Okay | 2 Poor | 1 Incomplete |

In the sample assessment that follows, the number 3 indicates that the narrative contains some dialogue and sensory details, but it needs more of these elements. *Note:* The lower the number, the less the writing meets the description.

Ideas
The writing . . .
- 4 focuses on one experience or time in the writer's life.
- 3 uses dialogue and sensory details.
- 4 makes the reader want to know what happens next.

Assessing in Action

In the following narrative, Larisa, a student writer, shares a memorable experience, her first musical concert. As you read the narrative, pay special attention to parts that you like and parts that you have questions about. **(The writing does contain errors.)** Then on page 17, you can see how Larisa used the narrative rubric to assess her writing.

Narrative Essay

Musical Journey

I'll never forget my first concert. It was a muggy summer night in August, and my mom and I sat in the 18th row of a giant outdoor theater.

"What do you think of this place," my mom asked.

I turned around and saw row upon row of seats filled with people. In the distance, hundreds of people sat on blankets and lawn chairs along a wide grassy hill.

I said, "It's huge!"

The stage was dimly lit, and a stocky man with a long beard tested the micropone. Behind him a big drum set, a piano, and two guitars rested on the ground

"Test one. Test one, two, three," the man said.

After 30 minutes, the band still wasn't on stage and I stated getting antsy. That is, until I heard it—a single strum of an electric guitar. It was as loud as a reved-up motorcycle engine. Then a flash from a bright purple light illuminated the stage, and the band appeared.

The lead singer wore dark jeans, an un-tucked, white-buttoned shirt, and a pink tie. I thought he looked kind of goofy, but not as goofy as all the old people who started dancing and screaming.

My mom even danced. "Mom, stop that!" I insisted. But before I could say anything else, she grabbed my hands and twirled me around "Come on, Larisa, let me see your best moves," she said. I was embarrassed at first, but the more I danced, the more fun I had.

That night I feel asleep to memories of my mom and I laughing and dancing to the music.

Assessment

To evaluate her narrative (on the previous page), Larisa first made a response sheet on her own paper. Then she assessed her writing using the rubric on page 148 as a guide. She used numbers to rate her writing and added comments to explain some of her ratings.

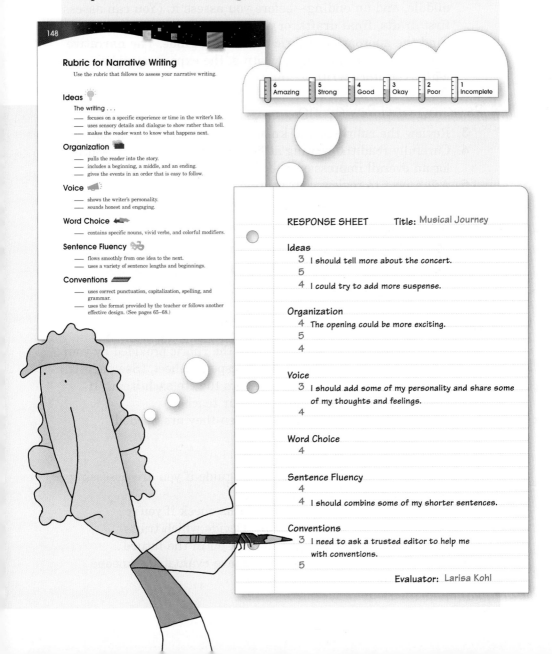

148

Rubric for Narrative Writing

Use the rubric that follows to assess your narrative writing.

Ideas

The writing . . .

— focuses on a specific experience or time in the writer's life.
— uses sensory details and dialogue to show rather than tell.
— makes the reader want to know what happens next.

Organization

— pulls the reader into the story.
— includes a beginning, a middle, and an ending.
— gives the events in an order that is easy to follow.

Voice

— shows the writer's personality.
— sounds honest and engaging.

Word Choice

— contains specific nouns, vivid verbs, and colorful modifiers.

Sentence Fluency

— flows smoothly from one idea to the next.
— uses a variety of sentence lengths and beginnings.

Conventions

— uses correct punctuation, capitalization, spelling, and grammar.
— uses the format provided by the teacher or follows another effective design. (See pages 65–68.)

| 6 Amazing | 5 Strong | 4 Good | 3 Okay | 2 Poor | 1 Incomplete |

RESPONSE SHEET   Title: Musical Journey

Ideas
3 I should tell more about the concert.
5
4 I could try to add more suspense.

Organization
4 The opening could be more exciting.
5
4

Voice
3 I should add some of my personality and share some of my thoughts and feelings.
4

Word Choice
4

Sentence Fluency
4
4 I should combine some of my shorter sentences.

Conventions
3 I need to ask a trusted editor to help me with conventions.
5

Evaluator: Larisa Kohl

Evaluating Tips

Review the following tips before you assess a piece of writing-in-progress. You can also use the same tips to evaluate a finished piece.

■ Getting Started

1. Make sure that the writing is complete—with a beginning, a middle, and an ending—before you assess it. (You can assess first drafts, final drafts, or anything in between.)
2. Find the appropriate rubric to use as a guide. The narrative rubric goes with narrative writing, the expository rubric goes with expository writing, and so on.

■ Reading and Reviewing

3. Review the rubric so you know what features to look for.
4. Carefully read the writing at least two or three times—once for an overall impression and the other times for specific traits.
5. Ask a peer to review your writing as well.

Helpful Hint

When you are assessing a classmate's work, comments should sound positive and helpful. Say "Could you tell more about the concert?" rather than "I can't picture the concert at all!"

■ Making Your Evaluation

6. Make your evaluation on a copy of the rubric provided by your teacher or on your own copy of a response sheet. (See page 17.)
7. Use either check marks or numbers to rate each item. (If you're not sure what to do, ask your teacher.)
8. Add comments to your ratings when they are needed.

■ Following Up

9. Use your evaluation as a revising guide if you are assessing your own work-in-progress.
10. Think of your evaluation as a status check if you're evaluating your own final copy. Decide which traits *(ideas, voice, . . .)* you need to work on in the future.
11. Be available for questions if you have evaluated someone else's writing.

One Writer's
Process

When it comes to the process of writing, most writers understand the importance of revising. Robert Lipsyte, author of *Yellow Flag*, says, "Writing is really rewriting—making the story better, clearer, truer." Student writer Emma Tobin says, "I've learned that no matter how good I think my first draft is, it can always be better."

What part or parts of the writing process are especially important to you? Do you enjoy drafting, getting all of your thoughts on paper? Or do you spend a lot of time revising? Of course, all of the steps are important. Yet, as you do more and more writing, you may find that one or more parts of the process will take on special importance for you. This chapter shows you how one student used the writing process to write a feature article.

What's Ahead

- Prewriting
- Writing
- Revising
- Editing
- Publishing

Prewriting—Selecting and Gathering

Selecting a Topic

Sayde Frey belongs to the journalism club, which publishes the school's online newsletter, *The Eagle News and Views*. Students, parents, and other community members read the newsletter. Sayde's job is to write feature stories about newsworthy people and happenings in the middle school.

After hearing about sixth grader Lamont Polk's heroics, Sayde knew that he would be the subject of her next story.

Gathering Details

Covering an Assembly

Sayde attended an all-school assembly honoring Lamont. She took accurate notes to collect important facts and details. Here are some of Sayde's notes:

Assembly Notes

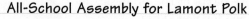

All-School Assembly for Lamont Polk   Feb. 15

Mr. M started assembly

— introduced L

— Mr. M described event

• happened on Wed., Feb. 13

• bus veered off Hwy. ES

• Ms. S fainted

• L used walkie-talkie

— Mr. M quote: "L did an incredibly mature thing. I'm awarding him a free pass to the front of the lunch line. It lasts the whole month."

Conducting Interviews

To find out more about the event, Sayde interviewed Lamont and Elicia Decker, a sixth grader on the bus. Sayde knew it was important to interview more than one person for her story. (See page 200 for more information about interviewing.) Here is part of Sayde's interview with Elicia:

Interview Notes

Interview with Elicia Decker   Feb. 18

Q. What caused Lamont to take charge?
- bus swerved off road
- Ms. S brought bus to stop
- Ms. S fainted

Q. What happened on the bus then?
- students scared—whole bus was in shock!

Creating a 5 W's Chart

Sayde then created a 5 W's chart to record all of the essential information for her story.

5 W's Chart

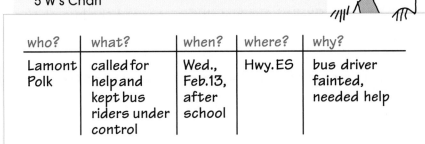

who?	what?	when?	where?	why?
Lamont Polk	called for help and kept bus riders under control	Wed., Feb.13, after school	Hwy. ES	bus driver fainted, needed help

Writing—Developing a First Draft

After she knew the facts, Sayde was ready to write the first draft of her feature story about Lamont. She wrote freely, incorporating facts and details she had collected. **(There are errors in Sayde's first draft.)**

> I tried to use a "friendly classmate" voice.

A Humble Hero

The lead paragraph hooks the reader.

Lamont Polk rocks! But this sixth grader isn't a show-off. He even gets embarrassed when people complement him. So he felt a little wierd when Benton's mayor called to thank him for saving a bus full of students. Lamont said "I was almost to nervous to talk!"

The middle paragraphs tell the story.

On Wed. afternoon, the school bus Lamont was on started to vear off the highway.

Ms Shelley, the bus driver, stopped the bus at the

Transition words like *then, later,* and *soon,* make the narrative easy to follow.

shoulder. Then fainted. We were all in shock—crying and everything!" said sixth grader Elicia Decker. Later the doctor said Ms. Shelley's diabetes had caused her to faint.

Quotations add interest to the story.

> Thats when Lamont acted like a hero. "My Dad taught me all about walkie talkies," he said. Lamontt asked for help on the buses' walkie-talkie. Then he went up and down the isle to tell everyone to stay seated. Help was on the way. "I was so scared," said Elicia.
>
> Soon a ambulance, a new bus, and a police officer came to help "Everyone cheered. We were even happier later when we found out that Ms. Shelley would be okay" Lamont said.

The ending paragraph adds a few finishing details.

> On Friday, Mr. Mathews held a school assembly. Ms. Shelley gave Lamont a hug and thanks him. The whole school clapped for Lamont and he got a free pass to go to the front of the lunch line for a month . . .

Good Thinking

A good thinker like Sayde does not try to get everything right in the first draft. Instead, she tries to get all her ideas on paper. This is her first look at a piece of writing-in-progress.

Revising—Improving Your Writing

Sayde took a break after drafting her story. Later, she read it over and made a few comments in the margin to guide her revising.

Sayde's Comments

First sentence too informal.

Use specific names and dates.

Need more action.

A Humble Hero

~~Lamont Polk rocks! But this~~ Lamont Polk sixth grader isn't
a show-off. He even gets embarrassed when people
complement him. So he felt a little wierd when
Benton's mayor ∧Mr. Becker∧ called to thank him for saving a
bus full of students. Lamont said "I was almost to
nervous to talk!"

On Wed. afternoon,∧February 13∧ the school bus Lamont
was on started to vear off ~~the~~ highway ES.
Everyone was screaming until
∧Ms Shelley, the bus driver, stopped the bus at the
shoulder. Then fainted. We were all in shock—crying
and everything!" said sixth grader Elicia Decker.
Later the doctor said Ms. Shelley's diabetes had
caused her to faint.

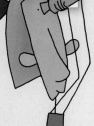

I also had a few trusted classmates review my first draft.

Use vivid verbs.

Thats when Lamont acted like a hero. "My Dad

taught me all about walkie talkies," he said. Lamontt

~~asked~~ *called* for help on the buses' walkie-talkie. Then he

~~went~~ *walked* up and down the isle to tell everyone to stay

but Lamont stayed calm and saved the day,

seated. Help was on the way. "I was so scared,"

Check notes for rest of Elicia's quotation.

said Elicia.

Soon a ambulance, a new bus, and a police

officer came to help "Everyone cheered. We were even

happier later when we found out that Ms. Shelley

would be okay" Lamont said.

Explain assembly better.

to tell us about Lamont's good deed.
On Friday, Mr. Mathews held a school assembly.

Ms. Shelley gave Lamont a hug and thanks him. The

whole school clapped for Lamont and he got a free

pass to go to the front of the lunch line for a

month . . .

Helpful Hint

Use the "Editing and Proofreading Marks," just as Sayde has done, to show your revising and editing changes. (See the inside back cover.)

Editing—Checking for Conventions

After making revisions, Sayde was ready to check her story for conventions—punctuation, capitalization, spelling, and grammar. She also asked a classmate to check her writing for conventions.

Spelling and usage errors are corrected.

Abbreviations are correctly spelled out or punctuated.

A subject is added to fix a fragment, and quotation marks enclose a speaker's words.

A Humble Hero

Sixth grader Lamont Polk isn't a show-off. He even gets embarrassed when people ~~complement~~ *compliment* him. So he felt a little ~~wierd~~ *weird* when Benton's mayor, Mr. Becker, called to thank him for saving a bus full of students. Lamont said, "I was almost ~~to~~ *too* nervous to talk!"

On ~~Wed.~~ *Wednesday* afternoon, February 13, the school bus Lamont was on started to ~~vear~~ *veer* off Highway ES. Everyone was screaming until Ms. Shelley, the bus driver, stopped the bus at the shoulder. Then *she* fainted. We were all in shock—crying and everything!" said sixth grader Elicia Decker. Later the doctor said Ms. Shelley's diabetes had caused her to faint.

I wanted my final version to be free of errors.

Apostrophes are correctly used in a contraction and to show possession.

That's when Lamont acted like a hero. "My Dad

taught me all about walkie-talkies," he said. Lamont's

bus's

called for help on the ~~buses~~ walkie-talkie. Then he

aisle

walked up and down the ~~isle~~ to tell everyone to stay

seated. Help was on the way. "I was so scared, but

Lamont stayed calm and saved the day," said Elicia.

A usage error is fixed and punctuation is added.

an

Soon, a ambulance, a new bus, and a police

officer came to help. "Everyone cheered. We were even

happier later when we found out that Ms. Shelley

would be okay," Lamont said.

On Friday, Mr. Mathews held a school assembly

to tell us about Lamont's good deed. Ms. Shelley

Verb tense is corrected.

thanked

gave Lamont a hug and ~~thanks~~ him. The whole

A comma is added in a compound sentence.

school clapped for Lamont, and he got a free pass to

the front of the lunch line for a month . . .

Publishing—Sharing Your Writing

Sayde submitted a carefully edited final copy of her feature story for publication in *The Eagle News and Views*, the school's online newspaper. Here is part of Sayde's story.

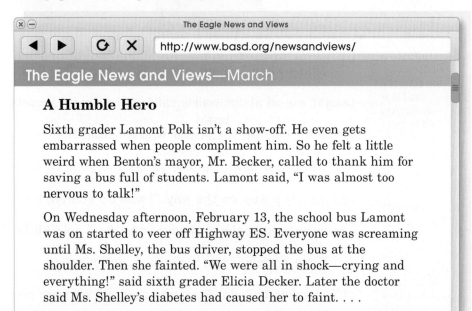

The Eagle News and Views

http://www.basd.org/newsandviews/

The Eagle News and Views—March

A Humble Hero

Sixth grader Lamont Polk isn't a show-off. He even gets embarrassed when people compliment him. So he felt a little weird when Benton's mayor, Mr. Becker, called to thank him for saving a bus full of students. Lamont said, "I was almost too nervous to talk!"

On Wednesday afternoon, February 13, the school bus Lamont was on started to veer off Highway ES. Everyone was screaming until Ms. Shelley, the bus driver, stopped the bus at the shoulder. Then she fainted. "We were all in shock—crying and everything!" said sixth grader Elicia Decker. Later the doctor said Ms. Shelley's diabetes had caused her to faint. . . .

Points to Remember

- **Do the necessary prewriting.** Sayde gathered all of the necessary facts about Lamont's heroics before she started her story. Thorough prewriting made the rest of her writing go smoothly.

- **Write with confidence.** Sayde knew she had a good story to tell, so she was able to write freely and do some of her best writing.

- **Expect to make changes.** She also knew that she had to make her story inviting and informative, so she carefully checked each part during revising. Her lead paragraph had to hook the reader, the middle paragraphs had to tell the story, and the ending paragraph had to bring the story to an effective close.

Prewriting

James Thurber, a famous short-story writer, once said, "To write about people, you have to know people, . . . to write about the Loch Ness Monster, you have to find out about it." In other words, before you try to write about people or monsters or anything else, do your fact finding. Information is to the writer what clay is to a sculptor: the raw material you work with.

Prewriting refers to the things you do at the beginning of a writing project so that you have enough "clay" to work with. During this step, you select a writing idea, gather details about it, and organize the details for writing. If you give the proper attention to prewriting, the rest of the process (*drafting, revising, editing*) usually goes smoothly.

What's Ahead

- Quick Guide: Prewriting
- Creating a Writing Resource
- Selecting a Topic
- A Closer Look at Freewriting
- Using Graphic Organizers
- Collecting Details
- Planning Your Writing

Quick Guide ■ Prewriting

Prewriting deals with all of the thinking, brainstorming, and collecting you do *early* in a writing project. But keep in mind that you may also do some prewriting activities *later* in the writing process. For example, once you review a first draft, you may decide to collect more details about your topic before moving on.

Consider the Writing Situation

To get started, think about your subject, purpose, and audience.

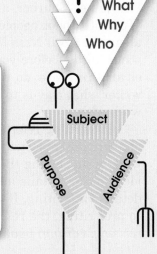

What
Why
Who

Subject

Purpose   Audience

 Subject:
What topic truly interests me?

 Purpose:
Why am I writing? To entertain, to inform, or to persuade?

 Audience:
Who are my readers?

Link to the Traits

When prewriting, pay special attention to three traits of writing: ideas, organization, and voice.

■ **Ideas:** Select a meaningful topic to write about. Then collect as much information about it as you can.

■ **Organization:** Decide on the best arrangement of the facts and details you have collected—a master plan that holds your ideas together.

■ **Voice:** To write with a personal, honest voice, you must truly care about your subject and your audience.

*"The secret to getting ideas really isn't a secret.
Open your mind and heart. Open your eyes
and your ears. Take risks."*

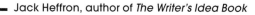

—— Jack Heffron, author of *The Writer's Idea Book*

Creating a Writing Resource

Writers are, in general, very curious people, observing and listening to everything around them. They also save every nugget of experience to use in their writing someday. The strategies that follow will help you develop your own resource of writing ideas.

■ Maintain a Writing Notebook or Folder

As you work on your writing in school, you will be thinking about and discussing new ideas often. Record these in your notebook.

■ Read Like a Writer

Reserve part of your notebook for ideas that you find as you read—intriguing names, surprising turns in a story, and so on.

■ Find Writing Ideas

Be alert for writing ideas you find unexpectedly—as you read, ride the bus, visit friends, or goof around. Add these ideas to your writing notebook.

> **Helpful Hint**
>
> Imagine, while walking home, you see a beautiful red geranium potted in an old coffee can. This solitary flower—on the rickety porch of a dilapidated house—is special because of its location. Such a scene inspires many writing ideas.

■ Get Involved

Get involved in your community. Visit museums, churches, parks, libraries, businesses, and so on. As you vary your experiences, you will naturally build a supply of writing ideas.

■ Search and Research

Explore the Internet for its wealth of information. Also scout around your school or community library for ideas.

Selecting a Topic

The following strategies will help you select specific topics that truly interest you. Try them all to learn which ones work best for you.

Journal Writing

Write on a regular basis in a journal or notebook, exploring your experiences and thoughts. Review your entries from time to time and underline ideas that you would like to explore. (See pages 131–136.)

Clustering

Begin a cluster with a nucleus word or phrase that is in some way related to your writing assignment. Circle it and then cluster words around it, as in the model below. After clustering for a few minutes, you will begin to sense an emerging writing idea.

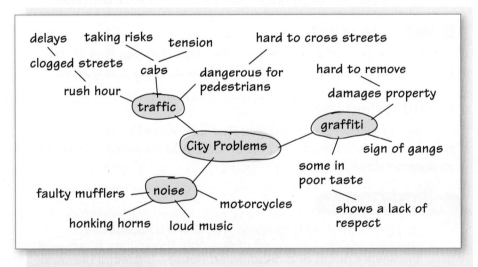

Helpful Hint

When you begin to sense an emerging writing idea, stop clustering, and freewrite for 5–8 minutes about the idea. (See pages 33–34.)

Listing

List ideas as you think about your writing assignment. Keep listing for as long as you can. Afterward, look for a possible subject.

Sentence Completions

Complete an open-ended sentence in as many ways as you can. Try to word your sentence so that it leads you to a subject for a particular writing assignment.

I wonder how . . .	I hope our school . . .	Television is . . .
Too many people . . .	I just learned . . .	Cars can be . . .
The good thing about . . .	One place I enjoy . . .	Grades are . . .

Review the Essentials of Life Checklist

The list below provides an endless variety of subject possibilities. Consider the category *energy*. You could write about . . .

- your uncle's hybrid car,
- wood-burning furnaces, or
- the five easiest things to do to conserve energy.

Essentials of Life Checklist

clothing	machines	rules/laws
housing	intelligence	tools/utensils
food	history/records	heat/fuel
communication	agriculture	natural resources
exercise	land/property	personality
education	work/occupation	recreation/hobby
family	community	trade/money
friends	science	literature/books
purpose/goals	plants/vegetation	health/medicine
love	freedom/rights	art/music
senses	energy	faith/religion

Freewriting

Write nonstop for 5–10 minutes to discover possible writing ideas. Begin writing with a particular thought in mind—one related to your assignment. Afterward, underline any ideas that might work as a specific subject. (See page 34.)

A Closer Look at Freewriting

Freewriting is an all-purpose writing tool that improves your writing fluency and unlocks some of your best thinking. It is especially helpful for finding writing topics.

The Process

- Write nonstop for at least 5–10 minutes, if possible.
- Begin writing with an idea in mind—perhaps something related to your writing assignment. Otherwise, start writing about the first thing that comes to mind. (Also see page 136 for writing ideas.)
- Do not stop to judge or edit your writing. You are writing for no one but yourself.
- Keep writing even when you are drawing a blank. Write "I'm stuck" until a new idea comes to mind.
- Stick with a certain topic for as long as you can, recording all the details that occur to you.

The Result

- Review your freewriting and underline ideas that you like. Some of these ideas may serve as topics for writing assignments.
- Team up with a partner to read and react to each other's writing.
- Continue freewriting about ideas you want to explore further.

Helpful Hint

Nonstop freewriting is an important skill to practice. It will make you feel more comfortable with generating thoughts and ideas on paper.

Using Graphic Organizers

Graphic organizers can help you gather and organize details for writing. This page lists organizers for many different types of writing.

Line Diagram

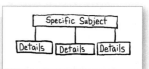

To collect and organize details for expository essays (See page 177.)

5 W's Chart

To collect the who? what? when? where? and why? details for news stories and narratives (See page 200.)

Venn Diagram

To collect details for a comparison of two subjects (See page 373.)

Cycle Diagram

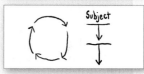

To collect details for science-related writing, such as "how flowering plants reproduce"

Sensory Chart

To collect details for descriptions and observation reports (See page 139.)

Cause-Effect Organizer

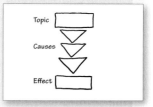

To collect details for cause-effect essays, such as "the causes and effects of metal detectors in school" (See page 377.)

Time Line

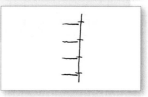

To collect details chronologically for narratives and essays (See page 375.)

Collecting Details

How much collecting should you do? When you know a lot about a topic, perhaps freewriting or listing will provide enough details. But when you know very little about a writing idea, you may need two or three collecting strategies. The next two pages list many of these strategies.

Gathering Your Thoughts

Focused Freewriting ■ Write freely for at least 5–10 minutes, exploring your topic from a number of different angles. (See page 34.) Or complete a freely written version of your actual paper. This will tell you how much you need to learn about the topic.

Listing ■ Jot down facts and details that you already know about your topic and also the questions you have about it. Keep listing for as long as you can.

Clustering ■ Create a cluster with your specific topic as the nucleus word. (See page 32.)

Covering the Basics ■ Answer the 5 W's—*who? what? when? where?* and *why?*—to identify basic information about your subject. Add *how?* to the list for even better coverage. (See page 21.)

Analyzing ■ Think carefully about a subject by answering these types of questions:

- What parts does my topic have? *(Break it down.)*
- What do I see, hear, or feel when I think about it? *(Describe it.)*
- What is it similar to? What is it different from? *(Compare it.)*
- What are its strengths and weaknesses? *(Evaluate it.)*
- What can I do with it? How can I use it? *(Apply it.)*

Good Thinking

Here's another way to think carefully about a topic: Keep asking the question *Why?* about your topic until you run out of answers. Then sum up what you've learned.

Imagining ■ Think creatively about a topic by writing and answering offbeat questions. Here are some examples:

Writing About a Person
- ■ What type of clothing is this person like?
- ■ What type of weather is she or he like?

Writing About an Important Issue
- ■ What sport would this issue participate in?
- ■ What food does this issue resemble?

Writing to Explain a Process
- ■ What television show is this process like?
- ■ Where in a hardware store would this process feel most at home?

Debating ■ Create a debate that explores your topic. You could be one of the debaters.

Researching

Searching ■ Explore the Internet for information about your topic. (See pages 301–308.)

Reading ■ Refer to nonfiction books, reference books, magazines, pamphlets, and newspapers for information about your topic.

Viewing ■ Watch television programs or movies about your topic.

Experiencing ■ Visit or watch your topic in action. If your topic involves an activity, participate in it.

Talking with Others

Interviewing ■ Interview an expert about your topic. Meet face-to-face, communicate via e-mail, or converse on the phone. (See page 200 for more on interviewing.)

Discussing ■ Talk with your classmates, family members, and community members to see what they have to say about the topic.

Planning Your Writing

Sooner or later, you need to identify a specific part of your topic to write about. This is called your *thesis*, or *focus*, and it helps you to organize your ideas.

Stating Your Thesis

To identify a thesis, decide what you want to emphasize about your topic—a specific part or a special feeling about it. (See page 110.)

Writing Assignment: **Essay about a key environmental issue**

Specific Subject: **Vanishing supply of fresh water**

Thesis Statement: **Homeowners need to conserve fresh water.**

Organizing Your Details

Next, you should select and arrange details that support your thesis. You can use a list, a cluster, an outline, or some other graphic organizer to arrange your ideas. (See page 111 for help with outlining.) Listed below are three basic methods of organization.

Methods of Organization

Chronological Order

You can arrange details in the order in which they happen (*first, then, next*).

Order of Importance

You can arrange details from the most important to the least—or from the least important to the most.

Logical Order

You can also arrange details in their logical or natural order—an order that simply makes sense.

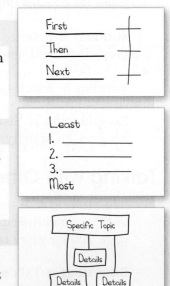

Writing

Most basketball coaches would tell you not to think too much when attempting a free throw. Instead, just step up to the line, take a deep breath, eye the rim, and shoot the ball. Worry about your mechanics, and there's a good chance you'll miss the shot.

In the same way, most professional writers would tell you not to think too much when writing a first draft. Instead, just review your prewriting and a few drafting basics (discussed in this chapter), sit down, and start writing. As author Bernard Malamud states, "The idea is to get the pencil moving quickly." Worry about every writing move, and you probably won't have much to show for your efforts.

What's Ahead

- Quick Guide: Writing
- Writing the Beginning
- Developing the Middle Part
- Bringing Your Writing to a Close

Quick Guide ■ Writing

Writing a first draft shows you how well you match up with your topic and sets in motion the actual development of your paper. You're ready to write a first draft once you've . . .

- gathered details about your topic,
- stated a thesis or focus for your writing, and
- decided on a basic pattern of organization.

Revisit the Writing Situation

Be sure to revisit the writing situation before starting your first draft.

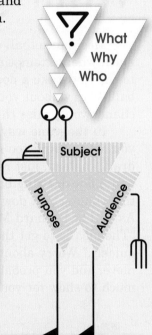

What
Why
Who

Subject

Purpose Audience

 Subject:
What topic truly interests me?

 Purpose:
Why am I writing? To entertain, to inform, or to persuade?

 Audience:
Who are my readers?

 Good Thinking

When writing a first draft, you are *synthesizing* information, or creating something new out of the details you have collected.

Link to the Traits

When drafting, keep in mind the following three traits of writing:

- **Ideas:** Work in the important ideas that you collected and include new ideas as they come to mind.
- **Organization:** Remember to include a beginning, a middle, and an ending in your writing. (See pages 41–44.)
- **Voice:** Speak honestly and naturally in your writing.

> "The best advice on writing I've ever received is 'Knock 'em dead with the lead sentence.'"
>
> ———————————— Whitney Balliett, acclaimed music critic

Writing the Beginning

The opening part of your writing should introduce the subject, gain the reader's attention, and identify the thesis of your writing. There are many ways to begin an opening paragraph. You might . . .

- share some interesting or important details,
- ask the reader a question,
- provide a thought-provoking quotation,
- reveal a personal connection with the subject, or
- identify the key points you plan to cover.

Beginning Paragraph

The following opening paragraph comes from student writer Michael Montgomery's biographical narrative about his grandmother. He begins this paragraph by making a personal connection with his subject. (The thesis statement is underlined.)

> She has shown me her love and support ever since I can remember. Whenever I visit her, she makes one of my favorite meals, like French toast and sausages. When I ask questions about her childhood, she entertains me with stories about growing up in England. She's always patient with me and responds to my problems in thoughtful ways. <u>She is Joan Capewell, my loving grandmother and role model.</u>

Helpful Hint

By all means, make your opening engaging, but, more importantly, make sure it expresses your true feelings. If you don't like your first attempt, try again. You'll know when you've got it right.

Developing the Middle Part

The middle part of your draft should support or explain your thesis. You can support a thesis with the following types of details. (Some of these types are used on the next page.)

Facts and **statistics** offer specific information that can be proven.

> The tsunami of 2004 was caused by an earthquake *(fact)* that measured 9.3 *(statistic)* on the Richter scale.

Examples illustrate a main point.

> Some dog owners do not take care of their pets. *(main point)*
> On my block, one owner never takes his dog for a walk. *(example)*

Anecdotes are brief stories that help make a point.

> My grandfather always found ways to entertain me. One day he placed two bowls at the end of his deck. One of the bowls was filled with water, and the other one with seeds. He then . . .

Quotations provide powerful supporting evidence.

> To live on a space station is to live on the edge. Astronaut Jerry Linenger, who spent 122 days on a space station, says, "There's something about it that makes you sure feel, 'Yeah, I'm on the frontier'" (Hoversten).

Definitions give the meanings of unfamiliar terms.

> A tsunami is a huge transfer of energy from the crust of the earth to a body of water.

Reasons answer the question "Why?"

> Esperanza and her mother decided to move from Mexico to the United States. With the father dead, they found themselves with no place to live.

Reflections reveal the writer's thoughts on a subject.

> I could only imagine how much the ship must have tossed on the high seas. The heat, the cramped quarters—it made me sick.

Middle Paragraphs

In the paragraphs that follow, Michael uses different types of details to support each main point in his narrative. In the first paragraph, he shares an **anecdote** to make a point about his subject.

> My grandmother often shares with me her affection for animals. I remember the first time she took me to Echo Park. After playing on the equipment, we raced down to the pond. I planned on throwing stones into the water, but my grandmother had other ideas. She told me to follow her. We stopped near some tall marsh grass where a family of ducks were paddling around. Grandma gave me two pieces of bread and told me to throw bits of it toward the ducks. I couldn't believe how they went after the bread and how much fun I had watching them, especially the little ducklings.

In the next paragraph, the writer **reflects** on the importance of this story about his grandmother.

> Up to that point, I hadn't really cared that much about wildlife in and around our city. I was too busy being a little kid—running around, playing games, watching TV. Feeding the ducks changed all that. I became much more interested in animals, especially about their welfare. This definitely made my grandmother happy because we started to enjoy animals together, including the cardinals and goldfinches in her backyard. I wonder if she knew this would happen.

In another paragraph, Michael gives **reasons** to support the paragraph's topic sentence.

> During many of my visits, we would make a trip to one of my grandmother's favorite places, the library. My grandmother reads all the time, so she has to exchange books every few days. She's the happiest when she finds a mystery or a historical novel about England that she hasn't already read. Of course, she expects me to check out at least one book, too. My grandmother claims that reading is one of life's great pleasures, and she wants to make sure that I become hooked on books.

Bringing Your Writing to a Close

A closing paragraph may not be necessary if your writing comes to an effective conclusion after the last main point is made. This often happens with a personal narrative. However, when a closing is needed, it should do one or more of these things:

- Answer any questions left unanswered in the middle paragraphs.
- Summarize the main points.
- Restate the thesis or primary message.
- Emphasize the importance of one main point.
- Reflect on the topic or the thesis.
- Leave the reader with a thought-provoking final idea.

Closing Paragraph

In the closing paragraph, Michael restates the thesis—that his grandmother has been a wonderful role model. He also reflects on the value of their relationship.

I don't spend as much time with my grandmother now as I did when I was in elementary school. I guess that's part of growing up. I still value my time with her, though, because she's so upbeat and positive. She doesn't tell me I need a haircut or I should eat more vegetables or I should get better grades. She just appreciates my company and enjoys the things we do together. I know I'm a better person because of her, and I only hope that I have helped make her life more enjoyable, too.

Good Thinking

When writing a first draft, take a few creative risks. Begin an essay with a brief dialogue, or end it with a few rhyming lines. Creative thinking, especially early in the drafting process, may help you produce your best writing. *Remember:* You can always try something else.

Revising

Writing a first draft can be a high-energy activity if your ideas are flowing. You don't want to stop (or you can't stop) until you get all of your thoughts on paper. Revising is a much slower, more deliberate process because you're deciding which parts of your first draft work and which parts need to be improved. Student writer Lee Barker understands the value of revising: "Revising is very important. It allows you to grow your writing to maturity."

Even experienced authors spend a lot of time revising. Ashley Bryan, author of many African folk tales, knows that revising is the key to his writing success: "By the time I reach a fifth version, [a book] usually begins to have its own voice." The first part of this chapter gives an overview of the revising process; the second part helps you revise for the traits.

What's Ahead

- Quick Guide: Revising
- Revising for the Traits
- Revising Checklist

Quick Guide ■ Revising

Revising helps you turn your early drafts into more polished pieces of writing. This step specifically deals with the changes you make by adding, cutting, rewriting, and reordering information. You're ready to revise, once you . . .

- complete your first draft,
- set it aside for a day or two, and
- review your writing.

Revisit the Writing Situation

Consider the writing situation before revising.

 Subject:
Do I still feel strongly about my writing idea?

 Purpose:
Does my writing entertain, inform, or persuade?

 Audience:
Does my writing speak to the reader?

Link to the Traits

Revise for the following traits. (Also see pages 47–52.)

- **Ideas:** Be sure your writing contains a thesis statement supported by different types of details.
- **Organization:** Determine if your writing forms a meaningful whole, with a beginning, a middle, and an ending.
- **Voice:** Decide if the real you comes through in your writing and if you sound interested in the topic.
- **Word Choice:** Consider the words you've used. Are they specific enough? Do they effectively communicate your ideas?
- **Sentence Fluency:** Decide if your sentences flow smoothly from one idea to the next.

Revising for the Traits

When revising, first focus on the ideas, organization, and voice in your writing. Then consider word choice and sentence fluency.

Revising for Ideas

The ideas are the most important feature in any piece of writing. Use these three questions as a guide to help you check for this critical trait:

- **Have I stated a specific thesis about my topic?**
- **Do all of the details support the thesis?**
- **Have I included enough details to make my ideas clear?**

Making Changes

This excerpt shows the changes the writer made in the *ideas* of a biographical story.

> Dr. Martin Luther King, Jr., and Rosa Parks are often recognized as civil rights icons. Not as many people know about Septima Poinsette Clark. *an important contributor to the civil rights movement.*
>
> **The thesis is made more specific.**
>
> Clark was born in 1898 in Charleston, South Carolina, so she experienced firsthand the racial hardships of the Jim Crow South. ~~Her father was a former slave, and her mother grew up in Haiti.~~ For example, after high school Clark wanted to teach in Charleston but wasn't allowed to. *because she was black.* In 1919 she became an active member in the National Association for the Advancement of Colored People (NAACP). ~~She helped them in many ways.~~ *Among other things, she petitioned for equal pay for black teachers.*
>
> **An unnecessary detail is cut.**
>
> In 1956 she lost her teaching position for refusing to leave the NAACP. She then helped establish ~~schools~~ *"citizenship schools"* to teach black adults to read. This was very important because many southern states required citizens to pass literacy tests . . .
>
> **Additional details make the ideas clearer.**

Revising for Organization

Ideas and organization work hand in hand. Your writing will be effective if, and only if, it contains plenty of information arranged in the best way. Use these four questions as a guide when you check your writing for organization:

- **Are my ideas properly organized, based on the purpose and form of my writing?**
- **Is my writing a meaningful whole, with effective beginning, middle, and ending parts?**
- **Have I used transitional words or phrases to connect my ideas?**
- **Do I need to reorder any information?**

Making Changes

This excerpt shows the *organization* changes the writer made in an article about Irish culture and history.

A seanachie (pronounced *shan-a-hee*) is the name given to a highly trained traditional Irish storyteller. Seanachie means "bearer of old lore." *and that's just what these men did—recite historical tales.*

> An added detail improves the beginning.

Seanachies were required to memorize 178 tales and sagas of common and royal history. The seanachies also learned the genealogies of great families. All tales were learned without the benefit of having anything written down; everything was done orally. An individual had to serve a 12-year apprenticeship before becoming an official seanachie.

> A sentence is reordered as a topic sentence.

A seanachie could be an itinerant, taking his skill from community to community in exchange for food and shelter. *Meanwhile,* Another storyteller could be based in a specific community. A seanachie would be a highly respected member of the town or village. . . .

> A transition word is added to connect ideas.

Revising for Voice

Voice gives writing personality, and it helps attract and hold the reader's interest. Use these two questions as a guide when you check your writing for voice:

- **Does my voice fit the writing situation *(subject, purpose, audience)*?**
- **Does my interest in the topic come through in my writing?**

Making Changes

This excerpt shows the changes the writer made in the *voice* of a travel pamphlet promoting Iceland.

> **An idea is reworded to fit the writing situation.**
>
> If you ever visit Iceland, be sure to page through a phone book. You will be amazed at ~~might be interested in~~ what you see. The entries are alphabetized by first names. That's because most people in Iceland do not have family last names such as Smith or Jones.
>
> **An idea is added to show the writer's interest.**
>
> Instead, most Icelanders' last names are a combination of their fathers', or sometimes their mothers', first names plus "son" or "dottir." So if an Icelander's first name is Adam, and his father's first name is Jon, then Adam's full name could be Adam Jonsson. If Jon has a daughter named Eva, her full name could be Eva Jonsdottir. How cool is that!
>
> **An idea is added to strengthen the voice in the writing.**
>
> The Icelandic naming tradition is one of many interesting facts about the country. Iceland is a small island nation (about the size of Kentucky) that sits east of Greenland in the North Atlantic. Just more than 300,000 people inhabit the island. If you like remote, out-of-the-way places, Iceland is the destination for you!

Revising for Word Choice ←▬▶

When checking for word choice, don't look for places to substitute flowery words for common ones. That would make your writing sound forced and unnatural. Instead, look for places to substitute better, specific words for those that are too general or inappropriate for the type of writing you are doing. Use these three questions as a guide when you revise your writing for word choice:

- **Do I use specific nouns and verbs?**
- **Do I use colorful modifiers when they are needed?**
- **Are my words well chosen for the writing situation (*subject, purpose, audience*)?**

Making Changes

This excerpt shows the changes the writer made in *word choice* for a science report about endangered animals.

A general verb is changed to a specific one.	The largest living primate, the mountain gorilla, roams ~~lives~~ high in the mountainous tropics of central Africa. Male mountain gorillas grow up to six feet tall and weigh between 350 and 500 pounds; the females reach five feet tall and weigh in the 215-pound range. Characteristic
Modifiers are added to enhance the image.	physical features include huge heads; bulging chests; thick, massive menacing dark hair; and long arms. Despite their size and look, mountain gorillas are docile unless threatened.
	The mountain gorilla is an endangered animal.
An informal expression is replaced to fit the writing situation.	Because of poaching, loss of habitat, and disease, only 700 mammals of these ~~big fellas~~ are still in existence. They populate the countries of Uganda, Rwanda, and the Republic of the Congo.
	Civil wars and corrupt governments in central Africa have put gorilla conservation efforts at risk, but . . .

Revising for Sentence Fluency

When checking your writing for sentence fluency, pay special attention to the sound and the flow of your ideas. Use these three questions when you revise your writing for sentence fluency:

- **Are my sentences clear and complete?**
- **Do my sentences flow smoothly?**
- **Have I varied my sentence beginnings and lengths?**

Making Changes

The excerpt shows the changes the writer made to improve the *sentence fluency* in a science report on preserving food.

Even before recorded history, ancient peoples preserved food by drying it. All types of food, including herbs, meat, fruits, and vegetables, have been dried. The drying process removes almost all of the water from the food. This ensures that it will be safe to eat, ~~.~~ because the Bacteria that causes food spoilage needs moisture to grow.

> Two sentences are combined for smoothness.

Food that has gone through the drying process contains more of its original nutrients than does the same type of food that has been canned or cooked. Dried Food ~~that has been dried~~ can be restored to its original condition by adding water. It can also be eaten dried. Common dried foods include raisins, prunes, sun-dried tomatoes, and beef jerky.

> A sentence beginning is changed for variety.

~~There are~~ three traditional methods for drying food. ~~They~~ include sun drying, air drying, and smoking. People that live in dry, warm climates have the best conditions for sun drying and air drying. Smoking adds flavor to the food by enfusing it with smoke. . . .

> Two sentences are combined for smoothness and clarity.

Revising Checklist ✔

Use this traits checklist as a guide when you revise your draft. Remember the four basic revising moves: *add* needed details, *cut* unneeded details, *rewrite* unclear parts, and *reorganize* anything that is out of order.

Revising Checklist

Ideas

____ Do I have a clear thesis, naming the topic and focusing on a specific part of it?

____ Do I support the thesis with a variety of interesting details?

Organization

____ Does my beginning grab the reader's attention and identify the topic?

____ Is my middle organized in a way that fits my purpose and the form of writing?

____ Does my ending revisit my thesis?

Voice

____ Does my voice fit my purpose (to entertain, to inform, to persuade)?

____ Does my voice connect to my audience?

Word Choice ◄►

____ Have I used specific nouns and active verbs?

____ Do my adjectives and adverbs clarify my writing?

Sentence Fluency

____ Do I use a variety of sentences with different beginnings and lengths?

____ Do my sentences flow smoothly from one to another?

Peer
Responding

In almost all sports, teamwork can make the difference between success and failure, between winning and losing. What chance would a soccer team have if they didn't set up an offense or help each other on defense? Not much. Or how successful would a baseball team be if they didn't work together to advance a runner or field a bunt? The best teams work together, period.

Believe it or not, writing is also a team game . . . at certain points. For much of the time, it's just you and your writing—one on one. However, sometimes you will need your teammates— your fellow writers—to get involved. Early on in a project, you may want to discuss a writing idea, or later on in the process, you may want to share your first draft. For situations like these, you and your classmates need to work together in peer-responding sessions.

What's Ahead

- Peer-Responding Guidelines
- Responding with Comments
- Responding with Questions
- Responding in Writing

Peer-Responding Guidelines

Some of you already may participate in peer-responding sessions, so you know the value of writers sharing their work. The following guidelines explain how you should prepare for peer responding.

Role of the Writer-Reader

> Respond to the writer's work, not the writer.

1. Come prepared with a complete piece of writing (first draft or revised writing). Make a copy for each group member if this is the usual practice.
2. Introduce your writing, but don't say too much about it and don't make excuses for it.
3. Read your copy out loud, and don't stop to make comments.
4. Listen and take notes as the group responds to your writing.
5. Share any special concerns you have. You may need help with the beginning, or you may wonder if the writing sounds like you.

Role of the Listener-Responder

1. Listen carefully as the writer reads. Take notes if necessary. Some groups just listen and complete a freewriting afterward. Other groups use a response sheet to record their comments. (See pages 57–58.)
2. Think of the intended purpose and audience. If the writing is a story intended to entertain young children, react to it accordingly.
3. Keep your comments positive and helpful. (See page 55.)
4. Ask questions of the author: *Why does the main character . . . ? What paragraph best supports the thesis?*
5. Listen to others' comments and add to them.

Good Thinking

Good thinkers ask questions that truly help the writer. They may even ask writers to reread certain parts to make sure of their thinking before responding. (See page 56.)

> "Comment on what you like in the writing.
> What you say must be honest, but you don't
> have to say everything you feel."

—— Ken Macrorie, author and teacher

Responding with Comments

Peer-responding sessions are meant to help you and your fellow writers develop effective pieces of writing. The information on this page will help you achieve this goal.

Making Focused Comments

The most useful responses are focused and specific. They compliment the writer or suggest ways to improve the writing. Here are some examples:

Compliments

- Your opening questions really got my attention.
- The phrase "snaking into the room" stuck in my mind. I can really picture that.
- I love the way you kept the ending a total surprise.

Suggestions

- It isn't quite clear to me why the tigers are endangered.
- I noticed that a lot of your sentences begin with "There is . . ."
- I couldn't hear your voice in the second and third paragraphs.

Using Tact

How do you get your thoughts across without hurting the writer's feelings?

- **Make sure that your comments are constructive.** For example, a comment such as "I wonder if the beginning could use a better grabber" is more constructive (and less hurtful) than "The beginning is totally boring."
- **Begin your comments with words other than "You" or "Your paper."** Comments that begin with "You" or "Your paper" often sound like criticisms, even when they are not meant that way.
- **Leave writing decisions to the writer.** Your job is to share your sincere, thoughtful responses.

Responding with Questions

Asking questions is an effective way to make suggestions. The best questions cannot be answered with a simple yes or no. Instead, they get a writer thinking about his or her work.

Forming Questions

If you have trouble forming effective questions, follow writer and teacher Nancie Atwell's advice. She suggests that you ask questions that help the writer do the following:

- Reflect on the purpose and audience.
    - What is the purpose of this writing?
    - What do you hope to accomplish in this essay?
    - Who will read this, and what do they need to know?

- Focus.
    - What is the thesis or main point of the writing?
    - How did you decide on this thesis?
    - What key ideas and details support the thesis?
    - In what order are these details arranged?
    - In what other way could these details be organized?

- Think about the information.
    - What do you know about the topic?
    - What else do you need to find out about it?
    - What parts of the writing could use more detail?

- Think about the opening and closing.
    - What does the opening accomplish?
    - How else could you start this essay?
    - What does the ending accomplish?
    - How do you want the reader to feel at the end?

- Take the next step.
    - What is your revising plan?
    - What is the single most important revision to make?
    - What could you do to make the essay flow more smoothly?
    - What parts could sound more interesting?

Responding in Writing

Use a response sheet like the one below or the one on the next page to respond to another person's writing. (Do not write on either response sheet in this book.)

Specific Response Sheet

This response sheet provides questions that you answer in response to a paper. It may work best when you are just starting out.

Response Sheet I

Responder's Name:
Writer's Name:
Title:

1. Which part seems the strongest—the beginning, the middle, or the ending? Why?

2. Which part seems the weakest? Why?

3. What is the thesis or main idea of the paper?

4. What important points support or explain the thesis?

5. What would you still like to know about the topic?

6. What could the writer do, if necessary, to sound more convincing or more interesting?

7. What could the writer do, if necessary, to better organize the paper?

General Response Sheet

This response sheet is open ended and allows you to decide what to comment on in a piece of writing. It may work best after you have gained some peer-responding experience.

Response Sheet II

Responder's Name:

Writer's Name:

Title:

What I liked about your writing:

Changes I would suggest:

Questions to consider:

Editing

English includes the most words of any modern language, and new words are being added all the time! So how is a young writer like you supposed to correctly use all of these words? For starters, you should gain a working knowledge of the conventions, or rules, for using the language. Then you should know where to turn for help when you have questions about usage and grammar—starting with your handbook and a dictionary.

The conventions, of course, become especially important when you are ready to edit your revised writing. When you edit, you check your writing line by line for errors, both at the sentence level and the word level. The first part of this chapter provides an overview of the editing process, and the second part identifies common errors to look for.

What's Ahead

- Quick Guide: Editing
- Editing in Action
- Common Mistakes
- Editing Checklist

Quick Guide 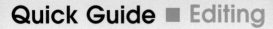 Editing

Editing helps you turn your revised writing into clear, accurate copy. It is your opportunity to find and correct any punctuation, capitalization, spelling, and grammar mistakes. You're ready to edit once you . . .

- revise your first draft,
- create a clean copy of your revised writing, and
- set your work aside for a day or two (if time permits).

Good Thinking

Editing requires that you analyze, or carefully examine, your revised writing for possible convention errors.

Carrying Out Your Editing

If you're working on a computer, do your editing on a printed copy of your revised writing. Then enter the changes on the computer. Save the edited copy so you have a record of the changes you've made.

If you're working with pen and paper, do your editing on a clean copy of your revised writing. Then recopy your work again, and save the edited copy for your records.

Helpful Hint

Try to focus on one convention (grammar, spelling, or so on) at a time. This will help you edit more thoroughly. Also have a classmate check your writing for conventions.

Link to the Traits

When editing, focus on the following trait:

- **Conventions:** Carefully check your writing for punctuation, capitalization, spelling, and grammar.

Use the "Proofreader's Guide" (pages 448–519) as you edit.

- Use the table of contents to find general subjects, such as *capitalization*.
- Use the index to find specific rules, such as *capitalizing geographical names*.

Editing in Action

Be sure to edit your writing with care. As student writer Katie Pringle says, "There is nothing worse than reading a final piece with a lot of errors." Use the following four questions to guide your editing. (See page 64 for a complete checklist.)

- Does each sentence have end punctuation?
- Does each sentence start with a capital letter?
- Have I checked for spelling errors?
- Do I use the correct forms of irregular verbs *(give, gave, given)*? (See page 511.)

Marking Changes

As you will see, the writer of the essay below used the editing and proofreading marks to show where changes are needed. (See the inside back cover of your handbook for these marks.)

An apostrophe is added to show ownership.	Taking a memorable picture—one worth a thousand words—is a hard thing to do. Margaret Bourke-White made it her lifes work.
A capital letter is added.	Bourke-White accomplished many historic firsts as a photographer. she became the first Western photographer allowed in the former Soviet Union and the first photojournalist hired by Life magazine.
A title is properly punctuated.	Her body of work includes lasting images of victims of the Dust Bowl during World War II, she was the first
A comma splice is corrected.	female war correspondent and the first woman allowed into combat zones. There she captured the valer and grief of American soldiers as well as the horror of Nazi
Spelling and punctuation errors are corrected.	concentration camps. Bourke-White believed if you "saturate yourself with your subject, the camera will all but take you by the hand. . . ."

Common Mistakes

Here are common errors to check for when you edit.

1. Missing Comma in a Compound Sentence

Use a comma between two independent clauses (complete sentences) joined by a coordinating conjunction—*and, but, or, nor, so, for,* or *yet.* (See page 454.)

> Sam finally learned how to swim‸but he still won't go to the quarry.
> (A comma is inserted before the conjunction *but.*)

2. Comma Splices

Do not use a comma to separate clauses that could stand alone as sentences. (See page 454.)

> Lynette always makes a PB and J sandwich for lunch‸Katelyn likes the school's salad bar.
> (Two complete thoughts are correctly separated with a period.)

3. Missing Commas in a Series

Use commas to separate three or more words, phrases, or clauses in a series. (See page 452.)

> Jasper hates storms, baths‸and vegetables.
> (A comma is inserted before the conjunction that precedes the last word in a series.)
> He rolls in the grass, fetches tennis balls‸and loves car rides.
> (A comma is inserted before the conjunction that precedes the last phrase in a series.)

4. Misusing *Its* and *It's*

Its is a possessive pronoun. *It's* is a contraction of "it is" or "it has." (See page 488.)

> My favorite team suffered ~~it's~~ its worst defeat. ~~Its~~ It's unbelievable!
> (The correct forms of *its* and *it's* have been substituted.)

5. Missing Apostrophe to Show Ownership

Use an apostrophe and *s* to show ownership. (See page 465.)

> Mr. Cosford's new rec room celebrates jazz music.
>
> (An apostrophe is added before the *s* to show singular ownership.)
>
> musicians'
> Jazz ~~musician's~~ unique skills include the ability to improvise.
>
> (An apostrophe is added after the *s* to show plural ownership.)

6. Pronoun-Antecedent Agreement Errors

A pronoun must agree in number with its antecedent—the word that the pronoun refers to. (See page 88.)

> his
> Everyone raised ~~their~~ hand when our football coach asked for volunteers.
>
> (*Everyone* is a singular antecedent, so the pronoun that refers to it, *his*, must also be singular.)

7. Missing Comma After Long Introductory Phrases

Place a comma after a long introductory phrase or phrases. (See page 454.)

> In the middle of the night, our street is very, very quiet.
>
> (A comma is inserted after the two introductory phrases.)

8. Subject-Verb Agreement Errors

A verb must agree in number with its subject. A singular subject takes a singular verb, and a plural subject takes a plural verb. (See pages 86–87.)

> feels
> Every contestant in the talent show ~~feel~~ nervous.
>
> (*Contestant* is a singular subject, so the verb, *feels*, must be singular as well.)
>
> use
> The judges ~~uses~~ a checklist to rate each contestant.
>
> (*Judges* is a plural subject, so the verb, *use*, must be plural as well.)

Editing Checklist ✔

Use this checklist as a guide when you edit and proofread your writing. Also refer to "Common Mistakes" on pages 62–63 for other errors to watch for. *Remember:* Carefully edit your writing only after you have revised it.

Editing Checklist

Conventions

Punctuation (See pages 449–465.)

—— Does each sentence have end punctuation?

—— Do I use commas correctly (in compound sentences, in a series, after introductory phrases, . . .)?

—— Do I use apostrophes correctly (in contractions, to show ownership, . . .)?

—— Do I punctuate dialogue correctly?

Capitalization (See pages 466–469.)

—— Does each sentence start with a capital letter?

—— Do I capitalize proper nouns?

Spelling (See pages 473–480.)

—— Have I checked for spelling errors (including those the spell-checker may have missed)?

Grammar and Usage (See pages 481–519.)

—— Do my subjects and verbs agree?

—— Have I used correct forms of plurals?

—— Do I use the correct forms of irregular verbs (**give, gave, given**)?

—— Do my pronouns agree with their antecedents?

—— Have I checked for commonly misused words (**your, you're**)?

Presentation

First impressions can be important. A good first impression, for example, can earn you a tryout for the volleyball team or a chance to run for student council. Of course, your appearance is a key factor when it comes to making a good first impression. You don't want to look like you just got out of bed, nor do you want to look like someone you're not—a junior executive, for instance. It's always best to present a clean and neat version of the real you.

First impressions are important in your writing, too. You don't want to turn in a piece of writing full of water stains, Day-Glo type, and oversized illustrations. Instead, keep your paper clean and neat, and its design simple and clear. That's effective presentation. This chapter covers the basic design principles for writing assignments.

What's Ahead

- Design Guidelines
- Effective Design in Action

Design Guidelines

Whenever you write, always focus on content first. Then consider the design of your writing, using the information below as a guide.

■ Typography

- Use an easy-to-read font for the body and the headings.
- Use an appropriate title and headings. A title sets the tone for your writing, and headings break the writing into smaller, more manageable units.

> Headings are especially helpful in longer pieces of writing, such as research papers and reports.

■ Spacing and Margins

- Double-space your writing and leave one-inch margins on all four sides of your paper.
- Indent the first line of every paragraph.
- Use one space after every period.
- Avoid awkward breaks between pages. For example, don't leave a heading or the first line of a paragraph at the bottom of a page.

■ Graphic Devices

- Create bulleted or numbered lists, where appropriate, to separate and highlight important points.
- Include a table, a chart, or an illustration if it can help make a point easier to follow.
- Keep each graphic small enough so that it doesn't dominate the page. Place larger graphics on separate pages.

Helpful Hint

These guidelines focus on academic writing—the essays, reports, and research papers that you turn in to your teachers. The design of your personal writing—stories, poems, blogs, and so on—is entirely up to you. Browse popular magazines and the Internet for ideas.

Effective Design in Action

The following two pages show a well-designed student essay. The side notes explain all of the design features.

Will Lee
Ms. Anderson/Language Arts
March 9, 2009

The title is 18-point and boldfaced.

Wake Up the Wild Side!

The main text is 12-point type.

"In each of you, there is a wild creature screaming to get out," Ms. Hillary tells the drama club at the start of each meeting. "It's the part of you that can be a star on this stage." Then she begins our warm-ups, which really get our bodies and minds in gear. They also help the group start working together. Some warm-ups are for individuals, and some are for partners. Ms. Hillary uses both types at every meeting.

Individual Warm-Ups

Every meeting begins with warm-ups to help individuals find their "centers." One is "Shake It Out," and the other is "Greet the Sun."

Margins are at least one inch all around.

- **Shake It Out:** In this warm-up, people stand on tiptoes with their hands stretched over their heads and shake out all the tension from their bodies. Everyone ends up completely loose and relaxed.
- **Greet the Sun:** Then everyone lies on the floor and rises like a plant, growing toward the sun. Everyone ends up with faces lifted and hands out like leaves.

Lee 2

Partner Warm-Ups

After "Shake It Out" and "Greet the Sun," everyone gets a partner. Ms. Hillary then leads one of the following warm-ups:

A bulleted list helps organize the essay.

- **Setting:** She shouts out a setting—optometrist's office, Niagara Falls, detention room, whatever—and the pairs must act out a scene in that location.
- **Character:** She names two characters—a pizza cook and a superhero, a dog and a salesperson, a genius and a child—and each partner must play one role and create a scene between the characters.
- **Conflict:** She calls out a conflict—an argument over a goat, a staring contest, two couch potatoes with two TV remotes—and partners have to act out a scene that shows that conflict.

Ready to Act

The headings are 14-point and boldfaced.

Once the individual and partner warm-ups are completed, the whole group is ready to act together. With everyone's wild side fully awake, it's time to hit the stage.

Publishing and
Portfolios

If asked how often you publish your writing, your response might be, "I've never published anything. I'm only 13 years old; only the pros publish their writing."

Now consider these questions: *Have you ever shared your writing with your classmates or with members of your family? Have you ever had an article or a poem printed in a school publication? Or have you ever posted a piece on the Internet?* There's a good chance that you'd answer yes to one or more of these questions, which means you have published your writing.

You are, in fact, publishing whenever you go public with your writing. In this chapter, you will learn all about the publishing process, from planning a portfolio to sending out your writing for publication.

What's Ahead

- Quick Guide: Publishing
- Publishing Ideas
- Understanding Portfolios
- Creating a Portfolio
- Sending Out Your Writing
- Places to Publish
- Publishing Online
- Publishing in a Blog

Quick Guide ■ Publishing

Publishing is the final step in the writing process, but it is also the driving force behind the first steps. It makes all of your writing, revising, and editing worth the effort. You're ready to publish a piece of writing once you . . .

- make all of the necessary improvements and corrections,
- prepare a neat final copy of your work, and
- proofread this copy before sharing it.

Review the Writing Situation

Revisit the writing situation before you publish.

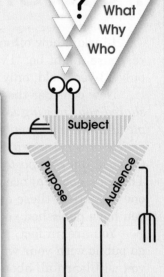

What
Why
Who

Subject

Purpose

Audience

 Subject:
Am I satisfied with my treatment of the topic?

 Purpose:
Does the writing effectively entertain, inform, or persuade?

 Audience:
Will the writing truly interest the intended reader?

Link to the Traits

Consider how well the writing addresses the traits.

- **Ideas:** Does the writing include meaningful information?
- **Organization:** Does the writing form a meaningful whole with a beginning, a middle, and an ending?
- **Voice:** Do you sound truly interested in and knowledgeable about the topic?
- **Word Choice:** Have you used the best words, especially specific nouns and action verbs?
- **Sentence Fluency:** Does the writing flow smoothly?
- **Conventions:** Is your writing correct and clear?

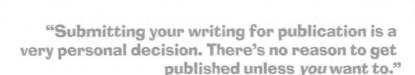

"Submitting your writing for publication is a very personal decision. There's no reason to get published unless you want to."

Janet E. Grant, author of
The Young Person's Guide to Becoming a Writer

Publishing Ideas

Publishing covers a lot of territory, as you will see in the ideas listed below. Some of these ideas are easy to carry out, such as sharing your writing with your classmates. Others are more adventurous and take some effort, such as entering a writing contest. Try a number of these ideas during the school year. Each new publishing experience will help you grow as a writer.

Performing

- Sharing with classmates
- Reading to other audiences
- Producing a video
- Performing onstage

Displaying

- Bulletin boards
- Display cases
- School or public library
- Business windows
- Clinic waiting rooms
- Literary/art fairs

Submitting (In School)

- School newspaper
- School Web site
- Literary magazine
- Classroom collection
- Writing portfolio
  (See pages 72–75.)

Self-Publishing

- Family newsletter
- Greeting cards
- Booklets
- Personal blog
  (See page 79.)

Submitting
(Outside of School)

- Community newspaper
- Local arts council
- Magazines and contests
- Young adult publishers
- Mainstream publishers
  (See pages 77–78.)

Understanding Portfolios

A writing portfolio is a collection of your writing during a school term. Four common types of portfolios include showcase portfolios, growth portfolios, personal portfolios, and electronic portfolios.

■ Showcase Portfolio

A showcase portfolio, which is the most common type of portfolio, presents your best writing. It is usually compiled for evaluation at the end of a grading period and may contain essays, articles, stories, poems, and letters.

■ Growth Portfolio

A growth portfolio shows how you are changing and developing as a writer. It contains assignments and pieces of writing that demonstrate your growth in various skills, including . . .

- writing beginnings and endings,
- using specific details and examples,
- developing dialogue, and
- varying sentence beginnings and lengths.

■ Personal Portfolio

A personal portfolio contains writing that you want to keep and share with others. Many professional writers, artists, and musicians keep personal portfolios. You can arrange a personal portfolio according to different types of writing, different themes, and so on.

■ Electronic Portfolio

An electronic portfolio is any type of portfolio that is available online or on a CD. In addition to written work, it may contain graphics, video, and sound. An electronic portfolio provides friends and family members with instant access to your writing—no matter where they live!

Creating a Portfolio

A showcase portfolio is the most common type of portfolio used in schools. It may contain the parts in the list that follows, but always check with your teacher for specific requirements.

- A **table of contents** listing the parts of your portfolio
- A **reflective essay or letter** discussing your portfolio story—how you compiled it, how you feel about it, what it means to you, and so on (See page 74.)
- A **number of finished pieces** representing your best work (Your teacher may require you to include all of your planning, drafting, and revising for some of these pieces.)
- A **best "other" piece** written in another class
- A **cover sheet** attached to each piece of writing, discussing the reason for its selection (See page 75.)
- **Evaluation sheets or checklists** charting the basic skills you have mastered as well as those you need to work on

Points to Remember

When compiling a portfolio, remember to do the following:

- **Make sure you understand the requirements for your portfolio.**

- **Keep track of all your work,** including prewriting notes and various drafts. Then, when you put together your portfolio, you will have everything that you need.

- **For storage, work with a pocket folder or computer file** to avoid dog-eared or ripped pages.

- **Keep on schedule.** Work on your portfolio throughout the term. Don't wait until the night before it's due!

- **Take pride in your work.** Your portfolio should reflect positively on you. Look your best!

Good Thinking

Before including a piece of writing in a portfolio, a good thinker would ask, *Does the writing show my progress? Does the writing fulfill its purpose? Does it speak to the reader?*

Portfolio Pages

On these two pages, you will find an opening letter for a complete portfolio and a cover sheet for a particular piece of writing. Reviewing them will help you develop similar pages for your own portfolio.

Opening Letter for a Portfolio

Beginning
In the beginning, the writer connects with the teacher and her approach.

Middle
The middle paragraphs (1) explain what the writer learned and (2) review the portfolio selections.

Ending
The ending paragraph looks to the future.

Dear Ms. Peterson,

    The way you had us work really helped me feel better about writing. I wasn't too crazy about it at first, though, especially when you said that we had to publish some of our writing. Then you gave us some options, like presenting a piece of writing as a gift. I thought that would be okay, and it was. I really liked writing workshop because it gave me time to concentrate on my writing. I used to rush through my writing and hand in any old thing.

    I learned a lot about writing this year, but one thing stands out: Good writing isn't automatic. It may take three or more rewrites before it sounds right.

    Overall, I'm happy with my selections. I'm especially proud of the biographical story about my cousin Nathan. That story came straight from my heart. I also like my article about playground basketball. It shows what it is like on the Lincoln Park courts. For my other pieces, I decided on my haiku poems because I like the descriptions I created. I also included my review of *Fast Sam, Cool Clyde, and Stuff* because it's one of my favorite books.

    I plan on writing in my journal over the summer so I stay in writing shape. I may even write a few poems, especially like the ones we wrote during National Poetry Month. I'll also be reading with the "writer's eye" that you always talk about.

                     Sincerely,
                     Ricky Lee

Cover Sheet for a Writing Selection

Beginning
The beginning identifies the writing selection.

Our assignment was to write a biographical story about someone who has made a difference. I wrote about one of my favorite people, my cousin Nathan.

Middle
The middle paragraphs discuss the process of writing the story.

Nathan looked after me for many years, so it wasn't easy to write just one story about him. But after doing a lot of thinking and freewriting, I decided to focus on the time he took me to City Pool. Somehow, he convinced me to swim across the deep end. He then got me jumping off the diving boards. I can still remember how good I felt about myself after our swim.

I did many things to re-create the experience. I included dialogue between Nathan and me. I also shared my thoughts and feelings before, during, and after my deep-water swim. I included some sensory details, but I could have included more. Most importantly, I explained how Nathan helped make it all happen.

Ending
The ending puts the assignment in perspective.

This writing assignment helped me remember the good times I had with Nathan. It got me thinking how Nathan was like a mentor to me. He kept me in line, he helped me grow up, and he gave me confidence. I'd sure like a chance to do the same for someone else.

Points to Remember

A cover sheet should do one or more of the following things:

- Explain why you chose the piece of writing.
- Tell the story of the piece—how you wrote it.
- Identify the writing's strong points and weak points.
- Reflect on its importance to you.

Sending Out Your Writing

The questions and answers listed below will help you submit your writing to publishers.

Q What types of writing can I submit?

A Newspapers are interested in articles, essays, and letters to the editor. Some magazines publish fiction, nonfiction, and poetry; others focus on nonfiction.

Q Where should I send my writing?

A Your chances of getting published are best close to home, so first consider local publications. If you're interested in submitting something to a national publication, turn to *Writer's Market* or *Children's Writer's & Illustrator's Market.*

Helpful Hint

Writer's Market comes in a print and an online subscription version. If your teacher or school library doesn't have access to this resource, your city library will. The print version is also available in major bookstores.

Q How should I submit my work?

A Check the publication's masthead for guidelines. The masthead is the small print on one of the opening pages identifying the publisher and editors. You should also visit its Web site for specific submissions guidelines. Most publications expect you to include . . .

- **a brief cover letter** identifying the title and form,
- **a neatly printed copy of your work** (formatted according to the guidelines) with your name and the title on each page, and
- **a SASE** (self-addressed stamped envelope) large enough to hold your writing so it can be returned after it has been read.

Q What should I expect?

A Expect to wait a long time for a reply. Also understand that your writing might not be accepted, and you may get no response. Just keep writing and submitting.

Places to Publish

Listed below are four publications that accept student submissions and four writing contests to enter. (For contests, be sure to check for deadlines.) Refer to *Writer's Market* for more places to publish.

Publications

Teen Ink (Grades 6–12)

Web site: www.teenink.com
Forms: Articles, fiction, poems, reviews, photos, art
Mail to: P.O. Box 30
     Newton, MA 02461
Or send to: www.teenink.com/
     submissions

Junior High School Writer (school needs subscription to submit)

Web site: www.writerpublications.com
Forms: Fiction, nonfiction, photos, artwork, letters to the editor
Mail to: The School Writer
     P.O. Box 718
     Grand Rapids, MN 55744

Skipping Stones: An International Multicultural Magazine (Ages 8–16)

Web site: www.skippingstones.org
Forms: Stories, articles, photos, art (any language)
Mail to: Managing Editor
     Skipping Stones
     P.O. Box 3939
     Eugene, OR 97403
Or e-mail to: editor@skippingstones.org

Stone Soup Magazine (Age 13 maximum)

Web site: www.stonesoup.com
Forms: Fiction, nonfiction, poetry, book reviews, artwork
Mail to: Stone Soup
     Submissions Dept.
     P.O. Box 83
     Santa Cruz, CA 95063

Contests

Merlyn's Pen

Web site: www.merlynspen.org
Forms: Fiction, nonfiction, sci-fi, poetry
Mail to: Merlyn's Pen
     11 South Angell St., Suite 301
     Providence, RI 02906
Or send to: www.merlynspen.org/write/
     submit.php

Scholastic Writing Awards (Grades 7–12)

Web site: www.artandwriting.org
Forms: Fiction, articles, poetry, essays
Mail to: Your regional address (look on the Web site)

Creative Communications Essay and Poetry Contests

Web site: www.poeticpower.com
Mail to: Essay Contest or Poets Contest
     Creative Communication
     1488 N 200 W. Logan
     Logan, UT 84341
Or send to: www.poeticpower.com

The America Library of Poetry: Student Poetry Contest (Grades 3–12)

Web site: www.libraryofpoetry.com
Forms: One poem of no more than 20 lines on any subject, and in any form
Mail to: Review Committee
     c/o The America Library of Poetry
     P.O. Box 978
     Houlton, ME 04730
Or send to: www.libraryofpoetry.com/
     student.asp

Publishing Online

The Internet offers many publishing opportunities, including online magazines and writing contests. The information that follows will help you submit your writing online.

Q What should I do first?

A Begin by checking with your teacher to see if your school has its own Web site where students can post their work. If not, suggest that one be started. Also ask your teachers about Web sites they know of that accept student submissions.

Q How should I begin my Web search?

A Use search engines to find places to publish. (See "Research Link" at www.thewritesource.com for a recommended list of search engines.) Refer to the search engine's index of topics, and look for an "education" topic; then click on the "K-12" subheading to find places to publish.

Q Does the Write Source Web site list places to publish?

A Yes, on our Web site—www.thewritesource.com—follow the "Publish It" link for suggestions.

Q How should I submit my work?

A Before you do anything, learn about the publishing guidelines for each publishing site and share this information with your parents. Get their approval before submitting online. Then follow these guidelines:
- Include a message explaining why you are contacting the site.
- Send your work following the site's requirements.
- With a parent's approval, provide the publisher with correct information for contacting you.

Q What should I expect?

A Within a week or so of your submission, you should receive a note from the publisher stating that your work has been received. It may take longer for the publisher to make a decision about your writing.

Publishing in a Blog

One surefire way to publish online is to post your work on your own blog. Whether you have a stand-alone blog or a social networking page (see 403–408), you can share your work with friends online. Remember these tips:

- **Date your postings.** Blog readers want to know when you posted your work. A date helps them find the most current postings but also track back to favorite posts.
- **Create a strong title.** Online readers are notorious skimmers. To get them to slow down and read, you need a title that grabs their attention.
- **Post pieces with strong voice.** Since a blog is a form of journal writing, pieces that let your voice shine through are best for blog posting.
- **Add links.** Connect your writing to other Web pages. For example, if you post something about whale song, link the words to a site that offers recorded audio clips of the sound.
- **Post regularly.** To keep readers returning to your blog, add new material on a regular basis.

Blog Posting

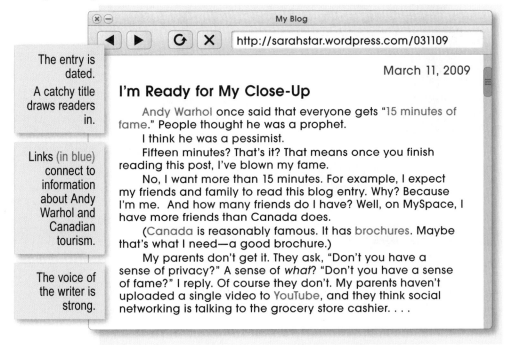

The entry is dated.

A catchy title draws readers in.

Links (in blue) connect to information about Andy Warhol and Canadian tourism.

The voice of the writer is strong.

My Blog

http://sarahstar.wordpress.com/031109

March 11, 2009

I'm Ready for My Close-Up

Andy Warhol once said that everyone gets "15 minutes of fame." People thought he was a prophet.

I think he was a pessimist.

Fifteen minutes? That's it? That means once you finish reading this post, I've blown my fame.

No, I want more than 15 minutes. For example, I expect my friends and family to read this blog entry. Why? Because I'm me. And how many friends do I have? Well, on MySpace, I have more friends than Canada does.

(Canada is reasonably famous. It has brochures. Maybe that's what I need—a good brochure.)

My parents don't get it. They ask, "Don't you have a sense of privacy?" A sense of *what*? "Don't you have a sense of fame?" I reply. Of course they don't. My parents haven't uploaded a single video to YouTube, and they think social networking is talking to the grocery store cashier. . . .

The Basic Elements
of Writing

Creating
Sentences

The physical part of writing has gone through many changes. Among other things, writers have used quill pens, ballpoint pens, pencil stubs, manual typewriters, electric typewriters, and personal computers. The mental part of writing, however, has not changed. Writers today still express themselves in sentences. As one writer has said, "Writers think sentences." They craft each one and string them all together to make meaning.

This chapter will help you understand the sentence basics, from writing complete sentences to combining short sentences. However, you'll discover the most about sentences through regular reading and writing. All elements of writing—from forming effective sentences to developing strong essays—are best learned by engaging in the language.

What's Ahead

- Understanding the Basic Patterns
- Using Different Types of Sentences
- Writing Correct Sentences
- Writing Sentences That Agree
- Writing Clear Sentences
- Combining Sentences
- Sentence Checklist

Understanding the Basic Patterns

Simple sentences in the English language follow five basic patterns.

1. Subject + Verb

S	V

Bianca sprints.

Some verbs, like *sprints,* are intransitive. Intransitive verbs do not need a noun (direct object) to express a complete thought. (See 512.)

2. Subject + Verb + Direct Object

S	V	DO

Parnell throws the shot put.

Some verbs, like *throws,* are transitive. Transitive verbs do need a noun (direct object) to express a complete thought. (See 512.)

3. Subject + Verb + Indirect Object + Direct Object

S	V	IO	DO

Thea handed her teammate the baton.

A direct object names who or what receives the action; the indirect object names to whom or for whom the action was done.

4. Subject + Verb + Direct Object + Object Complement

S	V	DO	OC

The track coach named Ethan captain of the team.

The object complement renames or describes the direct object.

5. Subject + Linking Verb + Predicate Noun or Predicate Adjective

S	LV	PN

Fara is a hurdler.

S	LV	PA

Fara is very competitive.

Inverted Order

In most sentences, the subject comes before the verb. In a few sentences, however, the subject comes after the verb.

LV	S	PN

Is Max a sprinter?   (a question)

LV	S

There will be a track meet tomorrow.   (a sentence beginning with *there*)

Using Different Types of Sentences

Sentences come in all shapes and sizes, from very short simple sentences to long and involved compound-complex sentences. Listed here are the four basic types of sentences. (See pages 499–500 for more examples.)

- **Simple sentences** contain a subject and a verb and express a complete thought:

  Todd read. Katie and Larisa text-messaged each other.

- **Compound sentences** include two or more simple sentences that are joined by a coordinating conjunction *(and, but, or, nor, for, so, yet)*, punctuation, or both:

  Yvonne poured herself a glass of orange juice, and Guerdy cut two pieces of bread for a sandwich.

- **Complex sentences** include one independent clause (simple sentence) and one or more dependent clauses (beginning with *because, when, while, who,* and so on):

  While Tim watched TV *(dependent clause)*, Cody checked for e-mail messages on his laptop *(independent clause)*.

- **Compound-complex sentences** contain two or more independent clauses and one or more dependent clauses.

  Since it was so nice outside, Robert wanted to shoot some hoops, but Philip was more interested in running.

Additional Types

These two types of sentences can add style to writing. Watch for them when you read, and use them in your own writing.

- A **loose sentence** expresses the main idea near the beginning and adds additional ideas as needed.

  "Wil nodded to himself and slipped away *(main idea)*, softly as a mouse, toward the back of the house where tourists were never taken *(additional ideas)*."

  —from "A Room Full of Leaves" by Joan Aiken

- A **balanced sentence** includes two or more equal parts. (The equal or parallel parts are underlined below.)

  "He <u>goes out onto his baseball field</u>, <u>spins around second base</u>, and <u>looks back at the academy</u>."

  —from *The Headmaster* by John McPhee

Writing Correct Sentences

Use complete, correct sentences in your writing so that the reader can easily follow your ideas. Sentence fragments, comma splices, and run-on sentences are errors that you should avoid. Also avoid rambling or wordy sentences.

Sentence Fragment

A *sentence fragment* may look and sound like a sentence, but it isn't. It is a group of words that is missing either a subject, a verb, or both. A sentence fragment does not express a complete thought.

- **Sentence fragment:** The subject is missing.
  Loves playing the trumpet.

  Complete sentence: A subject has been added.
  My big brother loves playing the trumpet.

- **Sentence fragment:** The verb is missing.
  Every Saturday morning, he and his friends in our garage.

  Complete sentence: A verb has been added.
  Every Saturday morning, he and his friends jam in our garage.

- **Sentence fragment:** The subject and verb are missing.
  Not my cat's favorite sound.

  Complete sentence: A subject and a verb have been added.
  The trumpet's blare is not my cat's favorite sound.

Comma Splice

A *comma splice* is an error made when you connect two simple sentences with a comma instead of a semicolon or end punctuation.

- **Comma splice:** A comma is used incorrectly to connect, or splice, the two sentences.
  Jason thought about his favorite things to do, he listed soccer, swimming, and video games.

  Corrected sentences: A period is used in place of the comma, and the first word in the second sentence is capitalized.
  Jason thought about his favorite things to do. He listed soccer, swimming, and video games.

Run-On Sentence

A *run-on sentence* occurs when two simple sentences are joined without punctuation or a connecting word.

- **Run-on sentence:** Punctuation is needed.

    I had an awesome day at the beach we swam and played sand volleyball.

    Corrected sentences: A period is added, and the first word in the second sentence is capitalized.

    I had an awesome day at the beach. We swam and played sand volleyball.

Rambling Sentence

A *rambling sentence* occurs when you connect too many ideas with the word "and."

- **Rambling sentence:** Too many *and*'s are used.

    Zeus is the most powerful god in Greek mythology and his emblems are the thunderbolt and the shield and he rules supreme over the pantheon of gods who live on Mount Olympus.

    Corrected sentences: Unnecessary *and*'s are omitted, and two sentences are formed.

    Zeus, whose emblems are the thunderbolt and the shield, is the most powerful god in Greek mythology. He rules supreme over the pantheon of gods who live on Mount Olympus.

Wordy Sentence

A *wordy sentence* occurs when you repeat words (or their synonyms) unnecessarily. The result is a sentence that sounds awkward.

- **Wordy sentence:**

    Elissa and I met together at 3:30 p.m. in the afternoon and we decided to go ride our bikes over to the new movie theater, but first we decided to ask for our parents' permission before we left.

    Corrected sentence:

    Elissa and I met at 3:30 p.m. and decided to ride our bikes to the new movie theater, but first we asked for our parents' permission.

Writing Sentences That Agree

The subjects and verbs in your sentences must agree in *number*. If you use a singular subject, use a singular verb. (*John likes* pizza.) Then again, if you use a plural subject, use a plural verb. (*We like* pizza.) Be especially careful of agreement mistakes in the following types of situations.

Compound Subjects

- Compound subjects connected by *and* need a plural verb.

  Amy and Dequan love playing board games.

- In sentences with compound subjects connected by *or* or *nor*, the verb must agree with the subject that is nearer the verb.

  Neither Dequan nor his friend plays card games.
  (Use a singular verb because the subject nearer the verb—*friend*—is singular.)

  Neither Amy nor her friends play video games.
  (Use a plural verb because the subject nearer the verb—*friends*—is plural.)

Unusual Word Order

- When the subject is separated from the verb by words or phrases, you must check carefully to see that the subject agrees with the verb.

  Ettie, as well as Kisha and Estelle, shows horses.
  (*Ettie*, not *Kisha* and *Estelle*, is the subject, so the singular verb *shows* agrees with the singular subject *Ettie*.)

- When the subject comes after the verb in a sentence, you must check carefully to see that the true subject agrees with the verb.

  On the obstacle course are many gates and ditches.
  (The plural compound subject *gates* and *ditches* agrees with the plural verb *are*.)

  Next in line is the show horse that my grandpa owns.
  (The singular subject *horse* agrees with the singular verb *is*.)

  Has Kisha seen my new purple helmet?
  (The singular subject *Kisha* agrees with the singular helping verb *has*.)

Indefinite Pronouns

- In sentences with a singular indefinite pronoun as the subject, use a singular verb. (Use singular verbs with these indefinite pronouns: *each, either, neither, one, everyone, everybody, everything, someone, somebody, anything, nobody,* and *another.*)

  Each of my best friends loves my horse.

- Some indefinite pronouns *(all, any, most, none, some)* can be either singular or plural.

  Most of my grandpa's pets are farm animals.
  (Use a plural verb when the noun in the prepositional phrase that follows one of these indefinite pronouns is also plural. In the example sentence, the noun *pets* is plural.)

  Most of my grandpa's backyard is a garden.
  (Use a singular verb if the noun in the prepositional phrase is also singular. In the example sentence, the noun *backyard* is singular.)

Collective Nouns

- When a collective noun is the subject of a sentence, it can be either singular or plural. (A collective noun names a group or unit: *faculty, committee, team, congress, species, crowd, army, pair.*)

  The team is hoping it wins the championship.
  (The collective noun *team* is singular because it refers to the team as one group. As a result, the singular helping verb *is* is required.)

  The math faculty are asked to meet in the conference room.
  (The collective noun *faculty* is plural because it refers to the faculty as individuals. As a result, the plural helping verb *are* is required.)

Helpful Hint

There is additional information on indefinite pronouns, compound subjects, collective nouns, and subject-verb agreement in the "Proofreader's Guide." (Consult the index.)

Writing Clear Sentences

Create sentences that are clear and to the point. The next two pages identify problems that can lead to confusing sentences.

Problems with Pronouns

Avoid sentences in which a pronoun does not agree with its antecedent. An *antecedent* is the word the pronoun refers to.

- **Agreement problem:**

    Everyone on the team must perform at their peak.

    Corrected sentence: A pronoun must agree in number—singular or plural—with its antecedent. The antecedent *everyone* is singular, as is *his* or *her*.

    Everyone on the team must perform at his or her peak.

Avoid sentences with a confusing pronoun reference.

- **Confusing pronoun reference:**

    As he pulled up his car to the service window, it made a strange rattling sound.

    Corrected sentence: It is unclear in the first sentence which noun—*car* or *window*—the pronoun *it* refers to. Rewording has clarified this.

    His car made a strange rattling sound as he pulled it up to the service window.

Avoid sentences in which a pronoun is used immediately after the subject. The result is usually a double subject.

- **Double subject:**

    My grandma she always spoils me.

- **Corrected sentence:**

    My grandma always spoils me.

Misplaced Modifiers

Make sure that your modifiers, especially the descriptive phrases you use, are located as close as possible to the words they modify. Otherwise the sentence can become very confusing.

- **Misplaced phrase**: In the following sentence, the phrase *After . . . movie* appears to modify the *space creatures*.

  After seeing the movie, the **space creatures** seemed more believable than ever to all of us.

  Corrected sentence: Now the phrase *After . . . movie* correctly modifies *all*.

  After seeing the movie, all of us felt the space creatures were more believable than ever.

Nonstandard Language

Avoid sentences that include a double negative.

- **Double negative**:

  Never let no one convince you that you lack creativity.

  Corrected sentence: *No* was changed to *any* because *never* is a negative word. Do not include two negative words (such as *never* and *no*) in the same phrase, unless you understand how they change the phrase's meaning.

  Never let anyone convince you that you lack creativity.

Do not use *hardly, barely,* or *scarcely* with a negative word; the result is a double negative.

- **Double negative**:

  I don't hardly know what to do.

  Corrected sentence:

  I don't know what to do. (or) I hardly know what to do.

Avoid sentences that incorrectly use *of* for *have.*

- **Incorrect usage**:

  I would of liked to see my neighbor's art gallery.

  Corrected sentence:

  I would have liked to see my neighbor's art gallery.

Combining Sentences

Sentence combining is the act of making one smoother, more detailed sentence out of two or more short, choppy sentences. When used effectively, sentence combining can improve the flow of your writing.

Combining with Key Words

Moving a *key word* from one sentence to the other sentence can combine ideas from shorter sentences.

- **Short sentences:**
  The cat jumped on the couch. The cat was fat.

  Combined sentence using an adjective:
  The **fat** cat jumped on the couch.

- **Short sentences:**
  The snowboarder sliced down the slope. It was the expert-level slope.

  Combined sentence using a compound adjective:
  The snowboarder sliced down the **expert-level** slope.

- **Short sentences:**
  My family is leaving for a vacation in Puerto Rico. We are leaving tomorrow.

  Combined sentence using an adverb:
  My family is leaving **tomorrow** for a vacation in Puerto Rico.

Combining with a Series of Words or Phrases

Ideas from shorter sentences can be combined into one sentence using *a series* of words or phrases. All of the words or phrases you use in a series should be *parallel,* or stated in the same way.

- **Short sentences:**
  The train station is loud. The train station is chaotic. It is smelly.

  Combined sentence using a series of words:
  The train station is **loud, chaotic,** and **smelly.**

Combining with Phrases

Ideas from shorter sentences can be combined into one sentence using *appositive, infinitive,* and *participial phrases.*

- **Short sentences:**

    Yesterday, Cortney served meals at Hope House. Hope House is a local homeless shelter.

    Combined sentence using an appositive:

    Yesterday, Cortney served meals at Hope House, a local homeless shelter.

- **Short sentences:**

    Cortney was studying for a science test. She checked her notes, reread two chapters, and answered review questions.

    Combined sentence using an infinitive phrase:

    To study for a science test, Cortney checked her notes, reread two chapters, and answered review questions.

- **Short sentences:**

    Andre carefully examined the microorganisms. He adjusted the microscope.

    Combined sentence using a participial phrase:

    Andre, adjusting the microscope, carefully examined the microorganisms.

Combining with Compound Subjects and Verbs

Ideas from shorter sentences can be combined using compound subjects and compound verbs (predicates).

- **Short sentences:**

    Chang plays the saxophone. Nelle plays the saxophone, too.

    Combined sentence using a compound subject:

    Chang and Nelle play the saxophone.

- **Short sentences:**

    Mandy baked cookies. She sold them at the festival.

    Combined sentence using a compound verb:

    Mandy baked cookies and sold them at the festival.

Sentence Checklist ✔

Use this checklist as a guide when you revise and edit your writing for sentence correctness and sentence fluency.

Sentence Checklist

—— Are my sentences complete?

- Are there any fragments (incomplete thoughts) to correct?
- Are there any comma splices, run-ons, rambling sentences, or wordy sentences to change?

—— Do my subjects and verbs agree in number (singular or plural)?

- Are there any compound subjects connected with *and, or,* or *nor*?
- Are indefinite pronouns (*everyone, each, all,* . . .) or collective nouns (*team, crown,* . . .) used as subjects?
- Do any sentences use an unusual word order?

—— Are my sentences clear and concise?

- Are there problems with pronoun-antecedent agreement? Confusing pronoun reference?
- Are there any misplaced modifiers?
- Are there any examples of nonstandard language?

—— Do I practice sentence fluency?

- Do my sentences begin in different ways?
- Do my sentences vary in length?
- Are items in my sentences parallel (worded similarly)?
- Do I avoid sets of short, choppy sentences by combining ideas?
- Do my sentences read smoothly?

Building
Paragraphs

Think of language as a series of concentric rings around Planet Word. Words are the core element of the language: With them, we form sentences; then with sentences, we form paragraphs; and with paragraphs, we form essays.

This illustration helps you see how paragraphs fit into the scheme of things. They have more substance than sentences, but less than essays and reports. Writer Donald Hall rightly identifies paragraphs as both "maxi-sentences" and "mini-essays." In this chapter, you will learn how to write strong paragraphs, a skill that will help you with all of your academic writing.

What's Ahead

- The Parts of a Paragraph
- Types of Paragraphs
- Writing Guidelines
- Creating Unity
- Establishing Coherence
- Using Transitions
- Paragraph Checklist

The Parts of a Paragraph

Most paragraphs begin with a **topic sentence** that states the topic of the writing. The sentences in the **body** of the paragraph support or explain the topic, while the **closing sentence** brings the paragraph to a logical stopping point.

Topic Sentence

Body

Closing Sentence

Cultural Cuisine

Topic Sentence

Food says a lot about a person's culture. As a famous food scientist once said, "Tell me what you eat, and I'll tell you who you are." For some people, food preparation is very important in their culture. Many Jewish families eat only kosher foods, or foods prepared according to Jewish scripture. For example, meat and poultry have to be slaughtered in a certain way to be kosher. The kosher laws also identify foods that cannot be eaten together, such

Body

as meat and dairy products. For most people, their food choices have deep historical roots. Cheese has always been an important part of the American diet, probably because of this country's strong European roots. The Chinese eat foods like chicken feet and birds' nests because of their ancient belief in the wholeness of things. Modern Egyptians still love *fasieekh*, a dried fish that is preserved just as it was

Closing Sentence

thousands of years ago. Food certainly provides nourishment and enjoyment, but it also tells us something about the people who prepare and eat it.

Specific details make paragraphs interesting!

Good Thinking

When selecting details, a good thinker keeps the purpose of the paragraph clearly in mind. The purpose of this paragraph is to inform.

A Closer Look at the Parts

◼ Topic Sentence

The **topic sentence** tells your reader what the paragraph is about. It also helps you keep your writing under control. Here is a formula for writing good topic sentences.

Topic Sentence Formula

An interesting topic	**+**	A specific feeling about it	**=**	A good topic sentence
Food		*says a lot about a person's culture*		*Food says a lot about a person's culture.*

Helpful Hint

A sentence like *Food is found in grocery stores* would not make a good topic sentence because it does not express a specific feeling about the topic. It expresses a fact.

◼ Body

The **body** is the main part of the paragraph. In this part, you give the reader the information she or he needs to understand the topic. The sentences in the body should include specific details that support the topic sentence.

Details can be facts, statistics, reasons, examples, quotations, sensory descriptions, and so on. (See page 42.) They can come from your personal knowledge of the topic or from other sources.

Organize your details so that the reader can easily follow them. The details in "Cultural Cuisine" are organized logically by categories: food preparation first, then the historical significance of food.

◼ Closing Sentence

The **closing sentence** comes after all of the details have been included in the body of the paragraph. This sentence should remind the reader of the topic and keep him or her thinking about it.

> *Food certainly provides nourishment and enjoyment, but it also tells us something about the people who prepare and eat it.*

Types of Paragraphs

There are four basic types of paragraphs: narrative, descriptive, expository, and persuasive. Each one requires a different kind of thinking and planning.

Narrative Paragraph

A **narrative paragraph** tells the story of a memorable event or experience. The details in a narrative paragraph should answer the 5 W's (who? what? when? where? and why?) about your topic.

> This paragraph is organized chronologically (by time).

Five-Alarm Food

Topic Sentence

When you eat Cajun food for the first time, ask for an extra glass of water before digging in. I found this out the hard way. My family and I were on vacation in New Orleans, and we stopped for lunch at a Cajun restaurant. I ordered jambalaya because I thought the word sounded cool. The dish contained meat and vegetables in a red sauce served over rice. I thought the sauce would taste like spaghetti sauce, so I shoveled in a big spoonful of the stuff. Big mistake. My mouth felt like it was on fire, and I started sweating all over. While I sucked down some water, my dad dared me to add more hot sauce to my dish. I opted for more water because I hadn't yet put out the fire. As you might guess, my next spoonful was light on the red sauce, and heavy on the rice.

Body

Closing Sentence

Good Thinking

A good thinker knows that the voice depends on the purpose of the paragraph. The purpose of "Five-Alarm Food" is to entertain, so the writer used an engaging, conversational voice.

Descriptive Paragraph

A **descriptive paragraph** gives a clear, detailed picture of a person, a place, a thing, or an event. Descriptive paragraphs often contain many sensory details (sights, sounds, smells, taste, and touch).

"The sweet smell of carrots and peas" is an example of a sensory detail.

Soup's On

Topic Sentence

One Friday night, my family helped at a local soup kitchen. By the time we arrived, the kitchen was filled with noisy people doing all sorts of things. Across the room beside the sink, some people were washing vegetables, while others were peeling and chopping. Several people gathered around the stove that was in the middle of the kitchen. They

Body

added chopped vegetables to the steaming soup pots. Soon the sweet smell of carrots and peas filled the room. On the counter between the kitchen and the dining area, another group worked like an assembly line putting together huge stacks of ham and cheese sandwiches. I set the paper plates, salt-and-pepper shakers, and butter plates on the tables.

Closing Sentence

Finally, a stream of hungry people arrived. They seemed to really enjoy the meal and thanked us for everything.

Helpful Hint

Descriptive paragraphs are often organized spatially, or by location. The writer of "Soup's On" generally organized the details from far away ("across the room") to closer by ("the dining area").

Expository Paragraph

An **expository paragraph** informs or explains. Expository writing shares information about a topic, gives directions, or shows how to do something.

> Whenever possible, provide an illustration or a chart with directions.

Chopstick Primer

Topic Sentence

Chopsticks are the preferred eating utensils in many Asian cultures. The origin of chopsticks goes back 5,000 years, when men in China would use small sticks or branches to retrieve meat from fires. Later, the Chinese philosopher Confucius called chopsticks the most moral eating utensils, because an "honorable and upright man allows no knives on his table."

Body

To use chopsticks, position the first stick so that the thicker part rests at the base of your right thumb, and the thinner part rests on the underside of the middle fingertip. In the same hand, hold the other chopstick as you would a pencil.

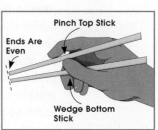

Pinch Top Stick

Ends Are Even

Wedge Bottom Stick

Then place pressure on the top chopstick so that it pivots (moves) on your index finger and thumb. This will make the tips of the sticks touch each other. Next, repeat this motion to pick up rice or noodles.

Closing Sentence

Eating with chopsticks will seem awkward at first, but with a little practice you will enjoy using them.

Persuasive Paragraph

A **persuasive paragraph** presents an opinion (or a strong feeling) about a topic. An effective persuasive paragraph convinces the reader that the opinion is worthy of her or his consideration.

> To be persuasive, a writer should sound confident, sincere, and knowledgeable.

New Taste Sensations

Topic Sentence

Trying new foods is a great way to add excitement to your life. Sure, fast food tastes great, and so do the blueberry pancakes at the local sit-down restaurant. But you haven't lived until you've tried calamari (squid) or tandoori chicken. Sushi is great, too. Eat one bite-sized sushi roll, and you'll experience a new taste sensation, raw fish and all. By the way, many forms of sushi contain only cooked

Body

ingredients. Trying different foods shows that you are open minded and willing to take risks. It also helps you to understand and enjoy different cultures. You may not like every new food you try, but surely you'll find at least one tasty treat that will prompt you to keep experimenting. So

Closing Sentence

how about some fried green tomatoes or matzo ball soup for your next food adventure?

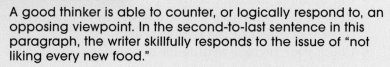

Good Thinking

A good thinker is able to counter, or logically respond to, an opposing viewpoint. In the second-to-last sentence in this paragraph, the writer skillfully responds to the issue of "not liking every new food."

Writing Guidelines

Remember that a paragraph focuses on one specific topic that can be developed in the form of a narrative, a description, an explanation, or an opinion. To be effective, a paragraph must give the reader a clear and interesting picture of the topic. Use the guidelines that follow to help you write paragraphs.

Prewriting—Choosing a Topic

- Explore the general subject area provided by your teacher. (See pages 32–33 for selecting strategies.)
- Select a specific topic that truly interests you and meets the requirements of the assignment.

Gathering Details

- Collect facts, examples, and ideas about your topic.
- Write a topic sentence that expresses a specific feeling about the topic of your paragraph. (See page 95.)
- Plan the rest of the paragraph. Which details will you include? How will you organize them?

Writing—Writing the First Draft

- Start your paragraph with the topic sentence, which tells the reader what your paragraph is about.
- Follow with sentences that support your topic with interesting details. Arrange these sentences in the best order.
- Use transitions, when needed, to connect your ideas. (See page 103.)
- End with a sentence that reminds the reader about the topic or leaves him or her with a final thought.

Revising and Editing—Improving the Writing

- Add information if you need to say more about the topic.
- Cut unimportant details. (See page 101.)
- Rewrite any sentences that are not clear or complete; move those that aren't in the correct order.
- Check your revised writing for conventions.
- Write a neat final copy of your paragraph and proofread it.

Creating Unity

In a well-written paragraph, each detail supports the topic. If a detail does not tell something about the topic, it breaks the *unity* of the paragraph.

In the following paragraph, the details in bold print disrupt the unity and should be cut.

World-Class Event

Topic Sentence

The performances in the 2008 Summer Olympics in Beijing, China, were truly world class. During the games, 10,500 athletes competed in 302 events in 28 different sports, ranging from gymnastics and basketball to table tennis and fencing. **The scoring in fencing is a mystery.** The number of record-breaking performances in the events thrilled the large crowds. Participants shattered 43

Body

world records and 132 Olympic records. Swimmer Michael Phelps of the United States became the first athlete to win 8 gold medals in one Olympics. **No one will ever do better.** The host nation, China, won 51 gold medals, the most of any country, and the United States won the most medals overall—110. Surprisingly, athletes from 87 countries brought home medals. The athletes in the next

Closing Sentence

Summer Olympics will have to work very hard to top the performances in the Beijing Olympics.

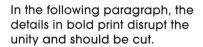 **Helpful Hint**

A unified paragraph forms a meaningful whole. All of the information follows logically and supports the topic sentence.

Establishing Coherence

A strong paragraph reads smoothly from start to finish. A paragraph has *coherence* when all of the details are effectively tied together. One way to make your writing coherent is to use transitions. In the following paragraph, the transitions highlighted in bold print help tie the details together.

Puppet Magic

Topic Sentence

Jim Henson used puppets to revolutionize children's television. **When** Henson was a college freshman, he created his first puppet show called *Sam and Friends*. The five-minute show appeared on a local television station and introduced the world to characters like Kermit the Frog. **Between** 1960 and 1975, Henson and his Muppets appeared on many television specials, talk shows, and commercials. **During** this time, Henson also became part of the *Sesame Street* team, which introduced the world to

Body

the likes of Oscar the Grouch, Bert, and Ernie. **Then**, in 1976, *The Muppet Show* premiered on national television. The show was an immediate success and led to a number of movies, which made stars out of Miss Piggy and Fozzie Bear. **When** the 1980s rolled in, Henson introduced the world to *Fraggle Rock*, a children's show promoting cross-cultural understanding, and *The Jim Henson Hour*, known for its use of computer-generated characters. Henson died unexpectedly

Closing Sentence

in 1990, but his innovative and creative legacy will live on forever.

Good Thinking

Use your best judgment with transitions. Writing that contains too many of them may sound awkward or unnatural. The selective, and effective, use of transitions should be your goal.

Using Transitions

Transitions connect one sentence to another sentence or one paragraph to another within an essay or a report. The chart below lists types of transitional words and phrases.

Transitional Words and Phrases

Words used to show location:

above	behind	by	into	outside
across	below	down	near	over
along	beneath	in back of	off	under
among	beside	in front of	on top of	
around	between	inside		

Words used to show time:

after	finally	next week	suddenly	until
at	first	now	third	when
before	later	second	then	while
during	next	soon	today	yesterday

Words used to compare two things:

also	in the same way	likewise	while
as	like	similarly	

Words used to contrast things (show differences):

although	even though	on the other hand	still
but	however	otherwise	yet

Words used to emphasize a point:

again	for this reason	to emphasize	truly
especially	in fact	to repeat	

Words used to conclude or summarize:

all in all	because	in conclusion	therefore
as a result	finally	lastly	to sum up

Words used to add information:

additionally	and	finally	moreover
again	another	for example	next
along with	as well	for instance	other
also	besides	in addition	

Words used to clarify:

for instance	in other words	that is

Paragraph Checklist ✔

Use this traits checklist as a guide when you revise and edit your paragraphs.

Paragraph Checklist

Ideas
—— Does my paragraph focus on one interesting topic?
—— Do I include enough specific supporting details?

Organization
—— Does my topic sentence identify the topic and express a feeling about it?
—— Have I organized the details in the body in the best order?
—— Does the closing sentence remind the reader about the topic?

Voice
—— Do I show interest in—and knowledge of—my topic?
—— Does my voice fit my topic? My purpose? My audience?

Word Choice
—— Do I use specific nouns and active verbs?
—— Do I explain any unfamiliar terms?

Sentence Fluency
—— Have I used clear and complete sentences?
—— Do I vary my sentence beginnings and lengths?

Conventions
—— Do I use correct punctuation, capitalization, spelling, and grammar?

Writing
Essays

Writing an essay is a journey of discovery. An effective essay begins with your genuine interest in a topic, and it ends with a written piece that shares what you have learned. What happens in between is the planning, drafting, and revising you do to produce an effective finished product.

Most essays follow the thesis statement-plus-support structure. That is, a successful essay includes a clear thesis statement (identifying an important feature of a topic) supported by convincing details (facts, examples, quotations, and so on). This chapter provides the direction you'll need to develop essay topics in meaningful and engaging ways.

What's Ahead

- Understanding Essays
- Writing Guidelines

Understanding Essays

You can say much more in an essay than you can in a paragraph because an essay contains many paragraphs. This chart shows how the working parts of a paragraph relate to the parts of an essay.

The Working Parts

Paragraph		Essay
Topic sentence	⸱⸱⸱⸱⸱⸱⸱▶	Beginning paragraph with thesis statement
Body	⸱⸱⸱⸱⸱⸱⸱⸱⸱⸱⸱⸱⸱⸱⸱▶	Middle paragraphs
Closing sentence	⸱⸱⸱⸱⸱⸱▶	Ending paragraph

From a Paragraph to an Essay

The examples on these two pages shows how a paragraph about types of armor compares to a classification essay on the same topic.

Paragraph

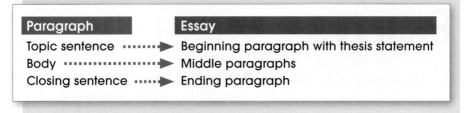

Topic sentence

Body

Closing sentence

From chain mail to steel suits to Kevlar vests, armor has protected people for centuries. Even though armor has been around for more than 2,500 years, the first important change in armor took place around 1000 C.E. when soldiers began wearing chain mail draped around their bodies. The next type of armor, the steel suits worn by knights in the 1400s, was a step up from chain mail. The heavy steel suit covered the knight from head to toe. Today, the newest armor is made of plastic and man-made fibers. One of these is Kevlar, a strong, lightweight fiber invented in the 1970s. People have always needed to protect themselves in battle, and through the years, they have found newer and better ways to do it.

Good Thinking

A good thinker understands that each paragraph in an essay must (1) stand on its own as a meaningful unit of thought and (2) connect to the paragraphs that come before and after it.

Essay

Centuries of Protection

Officer T. J. Cosford, a guest speaker at Cooper School, showed students a bulletproof vest that once saved his partner's life. Protective gear of all types has a long history, especially in the field of battle. While the need for armor has always been there, the materials used to make it have changed a great deal over time. From chain mail to steel suits to Kevlar vests, armor has protected people for centuries.

Even though armor has been around for more than 2,500 years, the first important change occurred around 1000 C.E. when soldiers began wearing chain mail. Chain mail was made of thousands of little metal rings hooked together. The thin rings formed a kind of metal cloth that could be draped around the soldier's body. It was lighter than a metal plate and could cover large areas of the body. However, chain mail was not perfect. It did very little to stop the impact of a blow from a sword, so the chain mail wearer still could be injured or killed.

The next type of armor, the steel suit worn by knights in the 1400s, was a step up from chain mail. A complete suit had the following parts: a breastplate, a back plate, flexible arm and leg covers, gloves, shoes, and a helmet with a hinged door that protected the face. Besides being extremely heavy, the armored suits were expensive to make. Only the rich could afford to wear them. A knight needed people to help him get dressed and mount his horse for battle. Although these steel suits offered excellent protection from weapons, they made movement very awkward. If he was knocked from his horse, a soldier in a suit of armor was as good as dead.

Today, the newest armor is made of plastics and man-made fabrics. One of these is Kevlar, invented in the 1970s. Kevlar is a lightweight fiber that is stronger than steel and more flexible than chain mail. With enough layers, Kevlar can stop a speeding bullet. The protective clothing items—helmets, jackets, vests, and boots—worn by today's soldiers contain Kevlar.

People have always needed to protect themselves in battle, and through the years, they have found newer and better ways to do it. Types of protection have evolved from chain mail and metal suits to man-made materials. Battle armor will continue to evolve as long as it is needed, and someday people may be protected by invisible force fields. In the meantime, individuals like Mr. Cosford will continue to rely on the latest forms of armor.

Writing Guidelines

Use these general guidelines whenever you have a question about selecting a topic, forming a thesis statement, and so on.

Prewriting—Selecting a Topic

The first step in the essay-writing process is to select a meaningful topic. Always keep the writing situation in mind when you work through the selecting process: *What topics truly interest you and meet the requirements of the assignment? What is your purpose for writing? Who is your audience?*

From General to Specific

This graphic shows how the selecting process should work. In most cases, your teacher will provide a general subject. It's your job to narrow the subject down until you identify a specific topic that is appropriate for the assignment.

General Subject Area
Subject of Interest
Specific Topic

The Selecting Process in Action

These examples show the selecting process in action.

General subject area ····▶	Development of artifacts
Subject of interest ····▶	Battle armor
Specific topic ····▶	Three basic types of armor: chain mail, steel suits, Kevlar

General subject area ····▶	The green movement
Subject of interest ····▶	Transportation
Specific topic ····▶	Using biodiesel fuels

Good Thinking

A good thinker makes sure that a topic is neither too general nor too specific. For example, *battle armor* is too general for an essay, while *steel helmets* is too specific. A topic such as *three basic types of battle armor* has the right depth.

Gathering Details

Once you select a specific topic, your next job is to collect facts and details about it. Start by freewriting or listing to see what you already know about your topic. Then talk with other people and explore the Internet, books, magazines, and newspapers for information. Remember to use sources that are reliable and accurate. (See pages 298–299.)

Using Graphic Organizers

Use these graphic organizers to help collect and organize the details that you collect.

5 W's & H Chart

Use this chart to collect the who? what? when? where? why? and how? details for personal essays and news stories.

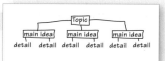

Line Diagram

Use a line diagram to collect and order details for essays that explain or inform.

Time Line

Use a time line when you are explaining how a process works or how to do or make something.

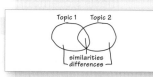

Venn Diagram

Use a Venn diagram to collect details for comparison essays.

Sensory Chart

Use a sensory chart to collect details for descriptive essays.

Helpful Hint

See "The Forms of Writing" section in this book for more specialized graphic organizers. For example, page 377 includes a graphic organizer to use when planning a cause-effect essay.

Prewriting—Writing a Thesis Statement

You should be ready to form a thesis statement for your essay after you have gathered your own thoughts and collected details from a variety of sources.

Using a Formula

A thesis statement usually expresses a specific feeling about, or feature of, a topic. The following formula can be used to form thesis statements:

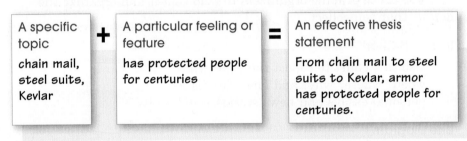

A specific topic	+	A particular feeling or feature	=	An effective thesis statement
chain mail, steel suits, Kevlar		has protected people for centuries		From chain mail to steel suits to Kevlar, armor has protected people for centuries.

Thesis Statements

Subject of interest: Ho-Chunk Nation
Specific topic: The dying Ho-Chunk language
Thesis statement: The Ho-Chunk language is fast approaching extinction *(specific topic)*, but there may still be time to save it *(particular feeling)*.

Subject of interest: Transportation in the green movement
Specific topic: Using biodiesel fuel
Thesis statement: Biodiesel fuel makes sense *(specific topic)* because it is easy to use, safe, and clean *(particular features)*.

Subject of interest: The role of women during World War II
Specific topic: Working mothers
Thesis statement: Working mothers *(specific topic)* played a key role in equipping U.S. soldiers for war *(particular feeling)*.

Organizing Your Information

With a thesis statement in place, you're almost ready to write. But first you need to organize the details for your middle paragraphs. (See page 113.)

Using an Outline

You can use a graphic organizer such as a line diagram (page 109) to organize your ideas. Or you can complete an **outline**, listing information in a general-to-specific pattern.

Topic outlines use words and phrases instead of sentences.

Sentence Outline

Thesis: From chain mail to steel suits to Kevlar vests, armor has protected people for centuries.

Main ideas come after Roman numerals.

I. The first important change in armor came in 1000 C.E. when soldiers began wearing chain mail.
   A. Chain mail was made of thousands of little metal rings hooked together.
   B. It was lighter than a metal plate and could cover large areas of a soldier's body.
   C. Chain mail did little to stop the impact of a blow from a sword.
II. The steel suit worn by knights in the 1400s was a step up from chain mail.
   A. A complete suit had many parts.

Supporting details come after capital letters.

   B. Steel suits were extremely heavy and expensive to make.
   C. They offered excellent protection, but they made movement very awkward.
III. The newest armor, such as Kevlar, is made of plastics and man-made fabrics.
   A. Kevlar is stronger than steel and more flexible than chain mail.
   B. With enough layers, Kevlar can stop a speeding bullet.
   C. The protective clothing of today's soldiers contains Kevlar.

Writing—Writing Great Beginnings

The beginning paragraph of an essay should grab the reader's attention, introduce the topic, and state your thesis. To grab your reader's attention, try one of these strategies:

- Start with an interesting or surprising fact.

  > The Ho-Chunk language is fast approaching extinction.

- Ask an interesting question.

  > How did World War II change the role of women in the workplace?

- Open with a thought-provoking quotation.

  > In 1912, Rudolph Diesel said, "The use of vegetable oils for engines may seem insignificant now, but it could become as important as the petroleum products of the present time."

- Share a brief story. (See the **first sentence** below.)

Using a Beginning Strategy

Use this strategy for strong opening paragraphs.

First sentence: Grab the reader's attention.

> Officer T. J. Cosford, a guest speaker at Cooper School, showed students a bulletproof vest that once saved his partner's life.

Second sentence: Give some background information.

> Protective gear of all types has a long history, especially in the field of battle.

Third sentence: Introduce the specific topic of the essay.

> While the need for armor has always been there, the materials used to make it have changed a great deal over time.

Fourth sentence: Give the thesis statement.

> From chain mail to steel suits to Kevlar vests, armor has protected people for centuries.

Helpful Hint

This strategy shows one way to write a beginning. For additional ideas, review other essays in this book.

Developing the Middle Part

The middle paragraphs in an essay provide information that supports or develops the thesis. These paragraphs should be arranged according to your planning or outlining. Most essays follow one of these patterns of organization:

Patterns of Organization

- **Chronological order:** This method of organization works well when you are presenting information that is time based.

- **Order of importance:** This method of organization works well when you are arguing for or against something. Writers often save their most important point for last.

- **Logical order:** This method of organization works well when you are informing your reader.

- **Spatial order:** This method works well when you are trying to describe something: top to bottom, left to right, and so on.

Middle Paragraphs

Use your outline as an organizing guide. Each middle paragraph should cover one main point (I) and supporting details (A, B, C).

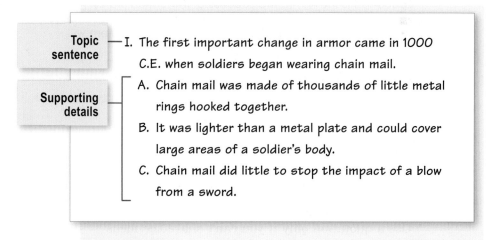

Topic sentence —I. The first important change in armor came in 1000 C.E. when soldiers began wearing chain mail.

Supporting details —
A. Chain mail was made of thousands of little metal rings hooked together.

B. It was lighter than a metal plate and could cover large areas of a soldier's body.

C. Chain mail did little to stop the impact of a blow from a sword.

Helpful Hint

The outline above lists just the key supporting details (A, B, C). The writer expands or completes these details with additional facts and explanations. (See page 107.)

Writing—Integrating Quotations

Quotations, the exact words of other people, especially authorities or experts, can provide an effective level of support in your writing. Always choose quotations that reinforce or enhance your own ideas about a topic. Use quotation marks to set off exact words of others.

Guidelines for Using Quotations

- Use quotations to lend authority to your writing.

  Linguist William Pierce, who studies Native American languages, says, "The Ho-Chunk language is in stage seven, which means it is in trouble. The remaining speakers must be prepared to teach the language to younger members of the tribe." There are a few tribal leaders who are doing just that.

- Use quotations that are clear and to the point.

  To lure women into the workforce, the government launched the "Rosie the Riveter" campaign. Historian Barbara Smalings states, "The campaign was an immediate success because many women joined the wartime effort." Yet one large group of women, stay-at-home mothers, didn't respond to the initial call.

- Use quotations to support your own thoughts.

  Education is the key to the success of the United States. As Benjamin Franklin stated, "An investment in knowledge always pays the best interest." A well-funded education system will greatly benefit and enrich this country.

Avoiding Quotation Problems

- **Don't plagiarize.**
  Cite the sources for quotations.

- **Don't use long quotations.**
  Keep quotations brief and to the point.

- **Don't overuse quotations.**
  Use a quotation only if you can't share the ideas as powerfully or effectively in another way.

- **Don't use quotations as the final word.**
  In most cases, your own thoughts should follow the quotations.

Writing Great Endings

A closing paragraph typically revisits the thesis and leaves the reader with a thoughtful final idea. Consider the following strategies for writing your closing.

- Review your main points.
- Emphasize the special importance of one main point.
- Tie up any loose ends.
- Draw a conclusion and put the information in perspective.
- Present one last idea that solidifies your thesis.

Using an Ending Strategy

If you have trouble coming up with an effective closing paragraph, follow this step-by-step example.

First sentence: Revisit the thesis.

> People have always needed to protect themselves in battle, and through the years, they found newer and better ways to do it.

Second sentence: Add a related idea.

> Types of protection have evolved from chain mail and metal suits to man-made materials.

Third sentence: Expand on the idea or add something new.

> Battle armor will continue to evolve, and someday people may be protected by invisible force fields.

Fourth sentence: Leave the reader with something to think about.

> In the meantime, individuals like Mr. Cosford will continue to rely on the latest forms of armor.

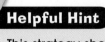

Helpful Hint

This strategy shows one way to write a closing. For additional ideas, review other essays in this book.

Revising and Editing—Improving Your Writing

Provided below are two key revising tips that you can apply to any essay-writing situation. (For help with revising and editing specific types of essays, see specific essays in this book.)

Ideas: Include Completing Details

If your essay does not provide clear and complete explanations, you may have to add more details. Notice how the new details (in red) complete the explanation about chain mail.

Even though armor has been around for more than 2,500

years, the first important change occurred around 1000 C.E.

when soldiers started wearing chain mail. Chain mail was made

The thin rings formed a kind of metal cloth that could be draped
of thousands of little metal rings hooked together. It was lighter
around a soldier's body.
than a metal plate and could cover large areas of the soldier's body.

However, chain mail was not perfect.
It did very little to stop the impact of a blow from a sword, so the

chain mail wearer still could be injured or killed.

Organization: Connecting Paragraphs

If your essay does not read smoothly from paragraph to paragraph, you may need to add transitions. (See page 103.) In the following excerpt, the transitions are shown in red.

. . . From chain mail to steel suits to Kevlar vests, armor has protected people for centuries.

Even though armor has been around for more than 2,500 years, the first important change occurred around 1000 CE when soldiers began wearing chain mail. Chain mail was made of thousands of little metal rings hooked together. . . .

The next type of armor, the steel suit worn by knights in the 1400s, was a step up from chain mail. A complete suit had the following parts: a breastplate, a back plate, flexible arm and leg covers, . . .

Writing
Techniques
and Terms

Just as you need tools in a shop class, you need a special vocabulary for writing. For example, you will learn what it means to write with *sensory details*. You will, in time, also discover the difference between *exposition* and *persuasion*, between *symbol* and *simile*, between *puns* and *personification*, and so on.

You'll find this chapter very helpful because it explains many important techniques and terms associated with writing—including the seven italicized above. Understanding these expressions is important because your teachers will use them in writing assignments, and your writing peers will use them in peer-editing sessions.

What's Ahead

- Writing Techniques
- Writing Terms

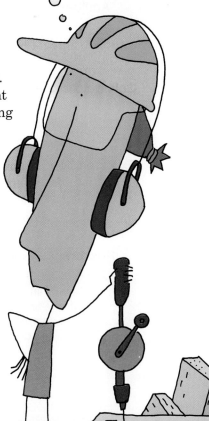

Writing Techniques

Writers use different techniques to add interest and details in their stories, essays, and articles. Review the following techniques and then experiment with some of them in your own writing. (Also see pages 288–289 for poetic techniques.)

Allusion	A reference to a well-known person, place, thing, or event
	With the strength of Hercules, Hector lifted one end of the cabinet.
Analogy	A comparison suggesting that two things that don't seem alike actually have some things in common
	Reading is like traveling. Both take you far away and show you how much there is to learn.
Anecdote	A brief story used to illustrate or make a point
	Abe Lincoln walked two miles to return several pennies he had overcharged a customer. (This anecdote shows Lincoln's honesty.)
Antithesis	Using opposite ideas in the same thought or sentence
	"Mankind must put an end to war or war will put an end to mankind."
	—President John F. Kennedy
Colloquialism	A common word or phrase used regionally in everyday speech but not in formal speech or writing
	I was liked to boil over with rage.
Exaggeration	An overstatement or a stretching of the truth to emphasize a point (See *hyperbole* and *overstatement.*)
	We opened up the boat's engine and raced along at a million miles an hour.
Flashback	A technique in which a writer interrupts a story to go back to an earlier event
	In *The Outsiders,* readers first meet Ponyboy as he leaves a movie theater and is jumped by gang members. Later, the author explains Ponyboy's background.

Foreshadowing Hints or clues about what will happen next in a story
As Mai explained why she had to break their date, she noticed Luke looking past her. Turning, she saw Meg smiling—at Luke.

Hyperbole Exaggeration used to emphasize a point
My brother exploded when he saw the damage to his car.

Irony An expression in which the author says one thing but means just the opposite
I was thrilled when my dentist appointment arrived.

Juxtaposition Putting two ideas, words, or pictures together to create a new, often ironic meaning
Ah, the joy of winter blizzards!

Loaded words Words that have strong emotion connected to them. (Persuasive writing, such as advertising, often uses loaded words.)
If you care about liberty, equality, and justice vote for _____.
Oh, sweetie, you'll make an utterly cosmic statement in that dress.

Local color The use of details that are common in a certain place.
Friday nights in Wisconsin feature two types of food: boiled fish and fried fish.

Metaphor A figure of speech that compares two things without using the word *like* or *as*
The sheep were dense, dancing clouds scuttling across the road.

Overstatement An exaggeration or a stretching of the truth (See *exaggeration* and *hyperbole*.)
We screamed until our eyes bugged out.

Oxymoron Connecting two words with opposite meanings
controlled chaos, small fortune, old news

Paradox A true statement that says two opposite things
The more free time you have, the less you get done.

Parallelism	Repeating similar grammatical structures (words, phrases, or sentences) to give writing rhythm The doctor took her temperature, checked her heartbeat, and tested her reflexes.
Personification	A figure of speech in which a nonhuman thing (an idea, object, or animal) is given human characteristics The clouds shouldered past the mountains.
Pun	A phrase that uses words in a way that gives them a humorous effect That story about a rabbit wasn't much of a hare raiser. (*Hare*, another word for rabbit, is used instead of *hair*. A *hair-raiser* is a scary story.)
Sarcasm	Insincere praise used as a "put-down" "That was a graceful move!" he said, as I tripped.
Sensory details	Specific details that are usually perceived through the senses (Sensory details help the reader to see, feel, smell, taste, and/or hear what is being described.) As Derrick spoke, his teeth chattered and his breath made little clouds in the icy cold air.
Simile	A figure of speech that compares two things using the word *like* or *as* The alley dog danced "like loose litter in the wind." —Anne-Marie Oomen
Slang	Informal words or phrases used by particular groups of people cool it all good peeps munchies
Symbol	A concrete or real object used to represent an idea. For example, the *dove*, a gentle bird that coos softly, is used as a *symbol of love and peace*.
Synecdoche	The use of part of something to represent the whole "Let me borrow your wheels." (*Wheels* represents the whole car.)
Understatement	The opposite of *exaggeration*; using very calm language to call attention to an object or idea These hot peppers may make your mouth tingle a bit.

Writing Terms

Here is a glossary of terms describing many aspects of writing. Turn here whenever you are unsure of the difference between *topic sentences* and *thesis statements*, *diction* and *dialogue*, or so on.

Argumentation Writing or speaking that uses reasoning, debate, and logic to make a point

Arrangement The order in which details are organized in a piece of writing

Audience Those people who read or hear what you have written

Balance Arranging words and phrases in a way to give them equal importance

Beginning The opening part in a piece of writing

Body The main part in a piece of writing, containing details that support a topic sentence or thesis statement

Brainstorming Collecting ideas by thinking freely about all the possibilities; used most often with groups

Central idea The main point of a piece of writing, often stated in a thesis statement or topic sentence

Cliche An overused word or phrase that is no longer an effective way of saying something—as in "flat as a pancake"

Closing The summary or final part in a piece of writing; the last sentence in a paragraph or the final paragraph in an essay

Coherence The logical arrangement of ideas in writing

Description Writing that creates a colorful picture of a person, a place, a thing, or an idea

Details The words used to describe a person, persuade an audience, explain a process, or in some way support the main idea

Dialogue Conversation between two or more people in stories, narratives, or essays

Diction A writer's level of language: slang, colloquial, formal, and so on

Drafting The actual writing that follows prewriting

Editing Checking writing for the standard conventions of the language

Essay Writing in which ideas on a single topic are explained, argued for, or described

Exposition Writing that explains

Extended definition Writing that goes beyond a simple definition of a term

Figurative language Language that goes beyond the normal meaning of the words used

Fluency The ability to express yourself freely and naturally

Focus The specific part of a topic emphasized

Freewriting Writing openly and freely on any topic

Generalization A general statement that gives a broad view

Grammar The rules that govern the standard structures of the language

Idiom A phrase or an expression that means something different from what the words actually say

> That answer was really out in left field.

Jargon The technical language of a particular group (musicians, computer programmers, and so on)

Journal A daily record of thoughts, impressions, and autobiographical information

Limiting the subject Narrowing the subject to a specific topic suitable for writing

General Subject	Area of Interest	Specific Topic
swimming →	different strokes →	mastering the butterfly

Literal The actual dictionary meaning of a word; language that means exactly what it appears to mean

Logic Correctly using reasons, facts, and examples to support a point

Modifiers Words, phrases, or clauses that describe another word or phrase

Narration Writing that tells a story or recounts an event

Objective Writing that gives factual information without adding feelings or opinions

Persuasion Writing that is meant to influence or change the way the reader thinks

Point of view The position or angle from which a story is told (See page 243.)

Prewriting The planning that comes before the actual writing

Prose Writing or speaking in standard sentence form

Purpose The specific reason a person has for writing; the goal of writing

Revision Changing a first draft to improve it

Sensory words Words for sights, sounds, smells, and so on

Style How authors write (the choice and arrangement of words)

Subjective Writing that includes personal feelings, attitudes, and opinions

Supporting details Details used to prove, explain, or describe a topic (examples, anecdotes, facts)

Syntax The order and relationship of words in a sentence

Theme The central idea in a piece of writing

Thesis statement A statement that gives the focus of an essay

Tone The writer's attitude toward a subject (A writer's tone can be serious, humorous, and so on.)

Topic The specific subject of a piece of writing

Topic sentence The sentence that identifies the topic of a paragraph

Traits of writing The basic elements of writing: *ideas, organization, voice, word choice, sentence fluency,* and *conventions*

Transitions Words or phrases that connect or tie ideas together (See page 103.)

Unity A sense of oneness in writing (All of the sentences work together.)

Usage The way in which people use language, usually either standard (formal and informal) or nonstandard

Voice A writer's distinctive tone and style

Writing situation Considering the *subject*, the *purpose*, and the *audience* for a particular writing situation

The Forms
of Writing

Choosing the
Best Form

On March 10, 1876, a new form of communication was born: the telephone. It carried a very simple message: "Mr. Watson—come here. I want to see you!" That was the very first phone call, made by Alexander Graham Bell to his assistant.

Nowadays, we have many new forms of communication, including texting, e-mailing, blogging, and microblogging. In addition, we still have the tried-and-true forms, such as journals, letters, essays, stories, poems, plays, and reports.

With all of these options, how is a person supposed to choose the best form of communication? This chapter will help you find the right form to use in any situation.

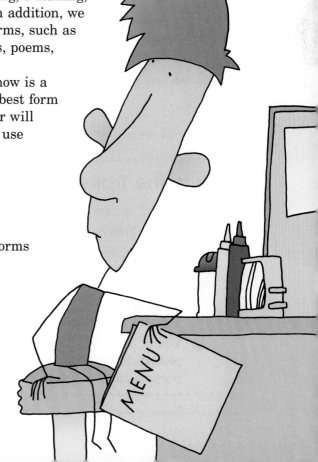

What's Ahead

- Quick Guide: Choosing Forms
- Analyzing the Situation
- Communication Options
- Levels of Language

Quick Guide ■ Choosing Forms

Every time you communicate, you have a message (subject) you are trying to get across to another person (audience) for a specific reason (purpose). When you understand those three parts of each communication situation, you can choose the best form to use.

Consider the Communication Situation

Ask yourself the following questions.

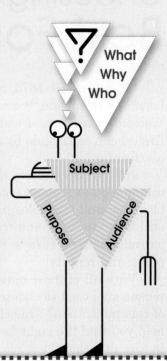

What
Why
Who

 Subject:
What do I want to say?

 Purpose:
Why do I want to say it?

 Audience:
Who will be listening
(or reading)?

Subject

Purpose

Audience

Link to the Traits

Each form of communication relies on these three traits:

■ **Ideas:** Your message is all about ideas. Perhaps you want to communicate ideas about your life, about a new technology, about politics, or about books.

■ **Organization:** The organization of your ideas makes them easy—or hard—for your audience to understand. Different messages need to be organized differently.

■ **Voice:** The voice you use not only reveals your personality but also reflects your grasp of the subject, purpose, and audience of your message.

Analyzing the Situation

Whenever you have a message to communicate, quickly think about the subject, purpose, and audience. Then decide what form your communication should take. Here are analyses of common communication situations.

Situation	You and some friends have formed a band, and you've arranged a Saturday concert in the school gym. Now you need to get the word out.
Analysis	**Subject:** Concert **Purpose:** To get people to come **Audience:** Friends, family, and general public
Forms	**Face-to-face conversations** with friends and family can be backed up with **e-mails** that remind them about the details. Also, a **flier** could be distributed to everyone at school and **posters** hung in local businesses. You can also **blog** about the concert.

Situation	Your grandmother, who had been sick with cancer for a long time, has died, and you want to write about what she meant to you.
Analysis	**Subject:** What your grandmother meant to you **Purpose:** To honor her **Audience:** Not sure yet
Forms	For a private reflection, write in your **journal**. To honor your grandmother at her funeral, write a **poem** or **biographical narrative** to share. For a wider audience, **blog** on your network page.

Situation	Congress is trying to decide how to vote on a health-care reform package, and you want to make sure your voice gets heard.
Analysis	**Subject:** Health-care reform **Purpose:** To get your opinion across **Audience:** Your congresspeople
Forms	A **phone call**, an **e-mail**, or a **letter** to the offices of your senators and representatives will communicate your position. For really serious issues, a **letter to the editor** can alert voters. For a less serious issue, a **pet peeve essay** submitted to a local newspaper may be appropriate.

Communication Options

Not all forms of communication are created equal. Some forms are spontaneous and informal. Others are more deliberate and formal. The following chart gives an overview of these differences.

The Continuum of Communication

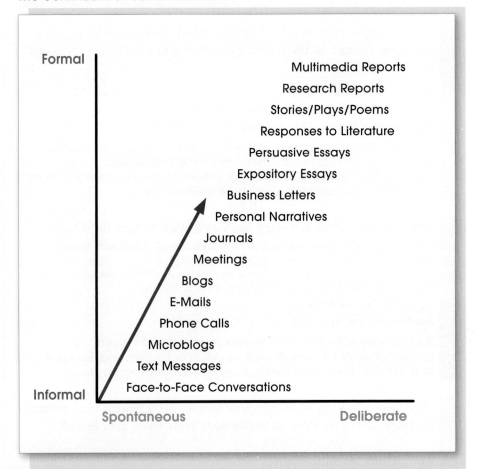

Formal

Multimedia Reports
Research Reports
Stories/Plays/Poems
Responses to Literature
Persuasive Essays
Expository Essays
Business Letters
Personal Narratives
Journals
Meetings
Blogs
E-Mails
Phone Calls
Microblogs
Text Messages
Face-to-Face Conversations

Informal

Spontaneous   Deliberate

Helpful Hint

When deciding on a form of communication, consider the importance of your message and the time you have to communicate it. Do you want a lasting record of the communication? Finally, think about your audience and how they may respond to whatever form you choose.

Levels of Language

Language is like clothing: It can be extremely casual, extremely formal—or somewhere in between. You wouldn't wear a swimsuit to a formal dance or a tuxedo to the beach. In the same way, you wouldn't use text-speak in an essay or transitions such as "furthermore" in a text message. The chart below shows the different levels of language.

Level	Features	Example	Forms
Formal	Carefully constructed language using Standard English, few personal pronouns, and few contractions	A seaweed commonly used to beautify fish tanks has overrun the Mediterranean Sea. The algae species *Caulerpa taxifolia* spreads rapidly and chokes out native plants, destroying habitats.	Multimedia reports Research reports Responses to literature Persuasive essays Expository essays Business letters (Some stories, plays, and poems)
Semi-formal	Conversational, natural-sounding language using mostly Standard English, with occasional colloquialisms or figures of speech used for effect	I woke up and looked at Gill McFin, my fish. Well, really, I looked at where he should've been because I couldn't see anything inside the aquarium except pea soup. "Gill! I got to get you out of there!"	Personal narratives Journals Meetings Blogs E-mails (Some stories, plays, and poems)
Informal	Everyday language often using personal pronouns (*I, you, we, he, she*), slang expressions, text abbreviations, emoticons, and other ways of connecting to a close friend	**Spoken:** Hey, what's with the green stuff in your fish tank, dude? Time to clean it, yeah? Gross! **Text Message:** R U going 2 buy fsh tnk clnr?	Phone calls Microblogs Text messages Face-to-face conversations (Some stories, plays, and poems)

Personal Writing

Making a
Personal
Connection

Biographer Catherine Drinker Bowen once said, "Writing is not a part of living. Writing is a kind of double living." Writer and diarist Anaïs Nis added, "Writing allows you to live life twice." Both writers make an important point: Writing allows you to relive experiences, explore your deepest thoughts, and figure out where you're headed. No other activity so effectively allows you to do these things.

In this chapter, you will learn all about personal writing in journals and blogs, and you will also find a list of personal-writing topics.

What's Ahead

- Journal Writing
- Personal Journal Entry
- Blog Entry
- Types of Journals
- Personal-Writing Topics

Journal Writing

Journals have two basic forms—personal journals that are "for your eyes only" and online journals, or blogs, that are shared with the world. Use your journal to reflect on your days and explore the inner landscape of your thoughts. To get started, follow these steps:

1. **Collect the proper tools.** For a personal journal, all you need is a notebook and a supply of pens or pencils. For an online journal, you'll need a computer, an Internet connection, and a place to post. (See page 134 for a sample blog entry.)

2. **Choose a regular time to write.** If you're an early bird, write when you get up. If you're a night owl, write before going to bed. Also, find a comfortable place to write—a place where you can concentrate.

3. **Write often.** Try to write for at least 5–10 minutes at a time. Write as freely as you can. If you plan to post your writing in a blog, check it for clarity and correctness before posting.

4. **Write about ideas and feelings that are important to you.** Here are some topics to get you started: (Also see page 136.)
   - interesting things you see and hear
   - personal thoughts and feelings
   - daily happenings
   - important events (personal or global)
   - books you've read
   - ideas for stories and poems
   - subjects you are studying

5. **Keep track of your writing.** Date your journal entries and read them from time to time. Mark ideas that you would like to write more about in the future.

Let past journal entries inspire future ones.

Helpful Hint

If you regularly write for the same amount of time—let's say 10 minutes—count the number of words you produce. The number should increase over time, which means you are gaining fluency as a writer.

Personal Journal Entry

Here is a journal entry written by student Phil Zahn about his first football practice. He dates the entry, and his language is casual.

Journal Entry

The writer explores his thoughts and feelings.

> August 21, 2009
>
> Today was our first football practice of the new season, and it did not go so well. Our new coach is a real drill sergeant. He made us do sprints over and over and over again. We never got to scrimmage. In fact, we didn't even get to pick up a ball. All we did was run and get yelled at.
>
> I miss Coach Bill from last year. Those practices were fun. Jimmy and I could have throwing and punting contests. We only ran at the beginning. Why did Coach Bill have to move?
>
> When I got home from practice, I collapsed on the couch. My muscles ached in places that I never knew existed before. I told my dad I wanted to quit, and he told me no way. I had to stick it out. He said the harder you work, the better you'll play. We didn't win a game last year, so he's probably right. But right now, it feels better just to complain.
>
> Well, I'm off to finish some homework. Nothing completes a bad day better than a set of math problems. I sure hope tomorrow is better.

A Closer Look at Journal Writing

Journal writing works best when you reflect on your experiences and feelings. *Reflecting* means to think carefully about something. Asking questions and wondering are two ways to reflect in your writing.

Ask questions ■ As you write, ask yourself questions: *What was fun or interesting about this experience? How do I feel about it now? Why does this matter to me?* Then try to discover some answers.

Wonder ■ Think about what you have learned from an experience. Compare it to other experiences you've had. Let yourself wonder what you could have done differently, or predict what the experience will mean to you in the future.

Blog Entry

The following entry comes from student Terry Miller's blog. As you will see, his writing is part recollection and part reflection.

Blog Entry

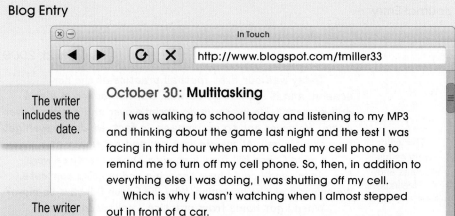

The writer includes the date.

The writer writes freely and naturally.

One thought leads to the next in an exploration of ideas.

In Touch

http://www.blogspot.com/tmiller33

October 30: Multitasking

I was walking to school today and listening to my MP3 and thinking about the game last night and the test I was facing in third hour when mom called my cell phone to remind me to turn off my cell phone. So, then, in addition to everything else I was doing, I was shutting off my cell.

Which is why I wasn't watching when I almost stepped out in front of a car.

It screeched, trying to stop, but it wouldn't have stopped in time if I had stepped out, and the woman behind the wheel was staring bug-eyed at me while stomping on the brake and talking on her cell, too.

The rest of the way to school, I was looking in every windshield and counting the number of people driving and talking on their phones. It was about 50 percent. Some of them were eating breakfast, too.

That's called multitasking. Mom says multitasking means being able to accomplish many things at once. Dad says it means not doing anything well.

So, still walking, I thought, "Is that what we do? We go through our whole lives doing everything but nothing well?"

I'd like, sometimes, to just do one thing, but it doesn't seem like I can. I mean, right now, I'm writing this and listening to my MP3 and IMing my buddy. Sometimes I think it'd be nice to be one thing—simple—to ring like a bell instead of jangling like a set of keys.

Helpful Hint

If you post your writing in a blog, use common sense about the things you write about. Don't reveal private information. Also read through your writing to make sure it is ready to be seen.

Types of Journals

You may want to keep other types of journals as well.

■ Diary

A diary is similar to a personal journal. It usually contains a writer's record of daily events, experiences, and observations, with some reflection on personal relationships and concerns. A diary often contains more specific and exact details than a personal journal that explores ideas and feelings.

■ Dialogue Journal

In a dialogue journal, two individuals (a teacher and a student, two friends, a parent and a child, and so on.) carry on a written conversation. A dialogue journal can help the writers get to know each other better, work through a problem, or share a common interest.

■ Learning Log

A learning log (classroom journal) gives students the opportunity to explore concepts, facts, and ideas covered in a specific class. Learning logs are very helpful in math and science classes, especially when the material is difficult or challenging.

■ Reader Response Journal

A response journal is a kind of learning log. In it students write about their feelings and reactions to the books they are reading.

■ Specialized Journal

When writers devote a journal to a specific event or experience, they are writing in a specialized journal. They may want to explore their thoughts and feelings while at summer camp, while participating in a team sport, while acting in a school production, or while working on a group project.

■ Travel Log

In a travel log, writers simply explore their thoughts and feelings while vacationing or traveling. It's a way to preserve memories . . . and a way to pass the time while waiting in lines and stations!

Personal-Writing Topics

What follows are possible topics for your personal writing.

Best and Worst, First and Last

My worst day
My craziest restaurant experience
An unforgettable dream
The hardest thing I've ever done
My first time home alone
The worst thing to wait for
My best kitchen creation

Deep in Thought

What word defines you as a friend?
What car are you like and why?
What duties make a good citizen?

As My World Turns

A day in the life of my pet
My secret snacks
The last time I went shopping
When I played the rebel
Wheezing and sneezing
_____ caused a lump in my throat.
When I'm in charge

What If . . . and How About . . .

Where do I draw the line?
What should everyone know?
Here is my wish list.
Why do people like to go fast?
What if I never forgot?

It could only happen to me!

It sounds crazy, but . . .
Putting my foot in my mouth
Guess what I just heard?
Creepy, crawly things
I looked everywhere for it.
Whatever happened to my . . .
I got so mad when . . .

Inside Education

My best class ever
Here's a look at the next episode of
   "As the School Swings."
Dear bulletin board,
Finally, a good assembly!
I memorized every word.
A student I really looked up to

Starter Sayings

"Almost anything in life is easier to get into than out of."
"It's time for a change."
"My interest is in the future because I'm going to spend the
   rest of my life there."
"Goofing off is a lost art."
"Everybody is ignorant, only in different subjects."

Descriptive
Writing

The great American poet Emily Dickinson once compared a book to a ship that can "take us Lands away." Descriptive writing does that. It transports us to faraway lands. It creates worlds in the air and introduces us to people who are long dead or who maybe were never born.

If you can effectively describe a person, a place, or a thing, you can make your subject real to your reader. What you see in your mind becomes what the reader sees in her or his mind. So practice descriptive writing, and take your reader "Lands away."

What's Ahead

- Descriptive Essay
- Writing Guidelines

Descriptive Essay

An effective description uses sensory details to set a scene, create a portrait, or describe an object. In the description below, student writer Pedro Martinez describes one of his favorite places.

Isla Luna

Beginning
The beginning introduces the topic.

Near my home, a forgotten trestle spans the Fox River. Trains don't cross the bridge anymore. The tracks were pried up and hauled away long ago, probably melted down and poured into some car chassis somewhere. The fat black ties are splintery and decaying. The metal cable that was supposed to be a handrail for foot traffic is now rusted and broken through in spots, with little wires splayed like fierce claws.

Middle
Sensory details make the description come alive.

This is one of my favorite spots—not so much because of the bridge, but what's under it. The bridge is held up by a cement post on an island in the river. An old rebar ladder runs down the post, which means I can climb down on the island, and suddenly, I'm Cortez in the Caribbean.

Details are arranged from general to specific.

The island is long and narrow, jutting upstream and then curving to the right to form a breakwater against the current. I call it "Isla Luna," or "Isle of the Moon," because it's the shape of the crescent moon. Saplings and shrubs and sprays of wildflowers huddle together on the island, their leaves overhanging the milk-chocolate river as it rolls past. Tangled piles of driftwood lie where the river dumped them when it was high. Footpaths from kids lead to handmade bridges over little rivulets.

Ending
The ending provides a final thought.

The murmur of water is everywhere, but it's the only sound except the sound of my feet. It's the only sound when I stand still.

Patterns of Organization

Follow one of these organization plans for your description.

General	Near	Left	Outside	Front
⬇	⬇	⬇	⬇	⬇
Specific	Far	Right	Inside	Back

Writing Guidelines

Prewriting—Selecting a Topic

A successful description begins with a strong topic—a person, place, or thing that you know well and would like to describe. Pedro used listing to think of possible topics for his description.

Listing

Favorite People	Favorite Places	Favorite Things
Grandpa Frank	my room	my guitar
Joey	the basketball court	the old VW
Michelle	Isla Luna*	

Gathering Details

Once you have selected a strong topic, you need to gather details about it. By using sensory details, you help your reader see, hear, smell, taste, and touch what you are describing. Here is a sensory chart that Pedro created to gather details for his description.

Sensory Chart

See	Hear	Smell	Taste	Touch
fat, black ties	water gurgling	wild flowers	water colored like chocolate	splintery
brown water	murmuring	musty		rusted
narrow island	wind	fish		old rebar
crescent-shaped	birds			
bushes huddling	footsteps			
leaf reflections				
footpaths				
rivulets				

Writing—Developing Your Description

Beginning ■ Grab your reader's attention and introduce your topic.

Middle ■ Provide sensory details in the best order. Move from general to specific, near to far, left to right, outside to inside, front to back, or some other sensible order. Think of the way a camera moves through a scene in a movie, revealing a location, an object, or a person in a smooth way.

Ending ■ Wrap up your description by providing the reader with a final thought.

Revising and Editing—Improving the Writing

Use the following checklist to revise and edit your description.

____ **Ideas** Have I chosen an interesting topic to describe? Do I include a variety of sensory details?

____ **Organization** Do my beginning and ending work well? Does my description follow a sensible order?

____ **Voice** Does my voice show my interest in the topic?

____ **Word Choice** Have I used strong nouns, active verbs, and effective adjectives?

____ **Sentence Fluency** Do my sentences read smoothly?

____ **Conventions** Have I carefully checked punctuation, capitalization, spelling, and grammar?

A Closer Look at Revising: Word Choice

Word choice can make or break a description. Note the difference between careless and strong word choice in the following sentence.

Careless: Plants are on the island, their leaves sticking out over the river as it goes past.

Strong: Saplings and shrubs and sprays of wildflowers huddle together on the island, their leaves overhanging the milk-chocolate river as it rolls past.

Narrative
Writing

> **"Tell us the one about when the computer caught on fire."**

We all know hundreds of funny or amazing personal stories, and for each story, we probably know one person who can tell it best. "Let Sarah tell this one." A good narrator knows just what details to include, how to build suspense, and how to make the story mean something.

This chapter guides you through writing a personal narrative, beginning with the simple invitation, "Tell us the one about . . ."

What's Ahead

- Personal Narrative
- Quick Guide: Narrative Writing
- Writing Guidelines
- Rubric for Narrative Writing

Personal Narrative

In the following personal narrative, student Stacey Gleason shares a memorable experience at the local Humane Society.

Beginning
The writer starts in the middle of the action.

Middle
Dialogue helps the story seem real.

Ending
The ending brings the story to a close in a humorous manner.

Top Dog

Before entering the Wolfe County Humane Society, my mom said for the seventeenth time, "Remember, Stacey, we are *just* looking." At the same time, she squeezed my hand to remind me that she was serious.

A volunteer led us into a room that looked like an animal warehouse. Metal cages housing abandoned dogs were stacked like boxes along the walls, and we were greeted with a cacophony of barks, yelps, and whimpers.

"Wow, look at all these dogs. They're so cute," I yelled.

"They smell," Mom said, holding her nose.

I grabbed her hand, and we began our tour. I recognized a few big Labs and tiny Malteses, but mostly there were row upon row of mixed breeds of all shapes and sizes. I just wished that I could open all the cages and lead each one of them to a happy home.

We made our way around most of the room when one dog stopped me in my tracks. He was the saddest-looking beagle you ever saw. Unlike most of the other dogs, he lay silent in his cage. A portion of his right ear was nipped, and his black, droopy eyes stared straight through me.

The volunteer let us take him out of the cage to hold. He just curled up in my arms. She told us that his name was Monty, and that he was a nice dog who had been at the shelter for a few months.

"Mom, can we please get him?" I pleaded.

"Absolutely not. I told you we are just . . ." Something stopped her, and I looked down to see Monty nuzzling his head against her hand. She paused for a moment, and said, "Oh, who am I kidding. I want this dog, too!"

So the volunteer had us complete some paperwork, and told us we could take Monty home in three days after his vet visit. Leaving him there was one of the hardest things I ever had to do.

On our way out, I said, "Mom, what are you thinking?"

She turned to me and said, "How I'm supposed to explain this to your father."

Quick Guide ■ Narrative Writing

Someone once said that writing is too much fun to be left to writers (as in the pros). And this is especially true with narrative writing. You can make discoveries and ask questions. You can dream and laugh and remember. Narrative writing is intended to share with those you care about.

Consider the Writing Situation

When you intend to go public with your narrative writing, consider the writing situation.

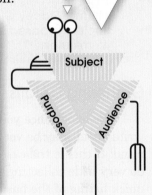

 Subject: What topic (experience) am I really interested in sharing?

 Purpose: Why am I writing? To inform, to entertain, or to do both?

 Audience: Who will be interested in this topic?

Link to the Traits

When writing, pay special attention to the traits of ideas, organization, and voice.

- **Ideas:** Select a topic that you really want to share. Include specific details that make the topic come alive for the reader.
- **Organization:** Organize the details in chronological order if you are sharing an experience. Otherwise, consider logical order or order of importance.
- **Voice:** Speak in a voice that connects with the reader— honest, sincere, and engaging.

Writing Guidelines

Prewriting—Choosing a Topic

Any event that you find hard to forget is a good topic for a personal narrative. This event doesn't have to be big and important (a trip to China). In fact, something much smaller in scale (the first dinner you made) may make a far better narrative.

Helpful Hint

Think of events that took place within a fairly short period of time. Stacey Gleason's story about a visit to the Humane Society is based on an experience that probably lasted only 45 minutes.

Gathering Details

The experience you choose to write about may be very clear in your mind. If this is the case, you may do very little collecting. A simple, quick listing of the basic facts may be enough. Just jot down things as they happened. Or you may want to use a 5 W's chart to collect this information. (See page 35.)

Once you finish your list, review all of the details you've included, using the following points as a general guide:

- Get rid of any information that is not that important.
- Move things around if they're not in the right order.
- Add important details you forgot.
- Use your list to begin your rough draft.

Quick List

~~We drove to the Humane Society.~~

My mom reminded me we were just "looking."

We toured a room full of caged dogs.

We held one dog, Monty.

My mom agreed to get him.

My mom worried what Dad would say.

We completed the paperwork.

Using Sensory Details

One way to make a narrative come to life is to use sensory details. Sensory details let the reader *see, hear, smell, taste,* and *touch* the experience—that is, live it. Stacey created this sensory chart.

Sensory Chart

See	Hear	Smell	Taste	Touch
metal cages	barks	dog smell		squeezed
big Labs	yelps			hand
tiny Maltese	whimpers			curled up in
nipped ear				arms
black eyes				nuzzling
droopy eyes				hand

Different sensory details have different effects on the reader.
- **Seeing is believing:** Stacey didn't just *tell* the reader that Monty was "the saddest looking beagle you ever saw," but *showed* him lying silent in the pen, his ear nipped and his black eyes drooping.
- **Hearing is communicating:** Hearing conveys what other people (or dogs) think or feel. In Stacey's story, the "cacophony of barks, yelps, and whimpers" communicates how the dogs feel about Stacey's arrival.
- **Touching is feeling:** Some touch words, such as *rough, sharp, blunt,* and *hard,* create negative emotions. Other touch words, such as *smooth, soft, warm,* and *solid,* create positive emotions. Stacey uses the word *nuzzling* to describe how Monty melted her mother's heart.
- **Smelling is evaluating:** People use their sense of smell to decide if something is good or bad: Is the milk fresh or sour? Are the clothes clean or dirty? A sweet smell will comfort your reader, but a rank one will set the reader on edge. Stacey's mother shows her resistance to getting a dog by saying, "They smell."
- **Tasting is desiring:** Taste words such as *tangy, sweet, ripe,* and *juicy* can make readers desire what they are connected to. Think about a *sweet* bike or a *juicy* offer. Other taste words such as *bland, bitter, acidic,* and *stale* can remove desire. Think about an *acidic* comment or a *stale* idea.

Writing—Developing the First Draft

As you write your narrative, focus on the **people** involved, the **place** and **time** of the event, what **happened**, and what people **said**. Use the following basic tools to write your narrative:

1. **Action:** Use active verbs so the reader can experience what is happening.

   > Something <u>stopped</u> her, and I <u>looked</u> down to see Monty <u>nuzzling</u> his head against her hand.

2. **Dialogue:** Capture the unique voice of different people involved in the situation. Use quotation marks around their words, and tell who said what.

   > "Wow, look at all these dogs. They're so cute," I yelled.
   > "They smell," Mom said, holding her nose.

3. **Description:** Use sensory details to describe people, places, and things.

   > A portion of his right ear was nipped, and his black, droopy eyes stared straight through me.

Beginning ■ Stacey Gleason's narrative jumps right into the thick of the action. In the opening scene, she and her mom are ready to enter the Humane Society. Try the same approach. Quickly indicate the setting, name the people, and have them do or say something. Then provide description along the way.

Middle ■ Organize your details in the order that they happened (chronologically). This way, the reader gets to experience the event along with you. Use transition words to connect your ideas. Also remember to use description, action, and dialogue to tell your story. Build up to the most exciting point. In Stacey's narrative, the most exciting point is deciding to adopt Monty.

Good Thinking

Remember to write down only the important parts of the event. As novelist Elmore Leonard says, "I try to leave out the parts that people skip." Imagine telling the story to a friend, and whenever the friend would say, "Get on with it," well, get on with it!

Ending ■ After the most exciting part, bring your narrative quickly to a close. Show how life changed for you after the event.

Revising and Editing—Improving Your Writing

Use the following checklist to revise and edit your narrative.

____ **Ideas** Do I focus on one experience? Do I include action and dialogue? Do I use sensory details in my descriptions?

____ **Organization** Do my beginning and ending work well? Are my details in time order?

____ **Voice** Is my storytelling voice engaging?

____ **Word Choice** Have I used specific nouns, active verbs, and descriptive modifiers?

____ **Sentence Fluency** Does my narrative read smoothly?

____ **Conventions** Have I checked punctuation (see below), capitalization, spelling, and grammar?

A Closer Look at Editing: Quotations Marks

As you edit your narrative, make sure you correctly use quotation marks and other punctuation around quotation marks. Follow these rules:

- Put quotation marks before and after the words spoken by someone.

    "Remember, Stacey, we are just looking."

- When a period or comma follows the quotation, place the period or comma *before* the quotation mark.

    "They smell," she said, holding her nose.

- When a question mark or exclamation point follows the quotation, put the punctuation before the quotation mark if it belongs with the quotation. Otherwise, put it after.

    "Mom, can we please get him?" I pleaded.
    Did my mother really mean it when she said, "We are just looking"?

- When a semicolon or colon follows the quotation, place it after the quotation mark.

    Her lips said, "Absolutely not"; however, her eyes were saying, "Most likely."

Helpful Hint

For more rules about using quotation marks, see 461.1–462.3.

Rubric for Narrative Writing

Use the rubric that follows to assess your narrative writing.

Ideas

The writing . . .

___ focuses on a specific experience or time in the writer's life.

___ uses sensory details and dialogue to show rather than tell.

___ makes the reader want to know what happens next.

Organization

___ pulls the reader into the story.

___ includes a beginning, a middle, and an ending.

___ gives the events in an order that is easy to follow.

Voice

___ shows the writer's personality.

___ sounds honest and engaging.

Word Choice

___ contains specific nouns, vivid verbs, and colorful modifiers.

Sentence Fluency

___ flows smoothly from one idea to the next.

___ uses a variety of sentence lengths and beginnings.

Conventions

___ uses correct punctuation, capitalization, spelling, and grammar.

___ uses the format provided by the teacher or follows another effective design. (See pages 65–68.)

Other Forms of
Narrative Writing

It is said in jest that extended families are a lot like fudge—mostly sweet with a few nuts. Just think of the last family reunion you may have attended. Perhaps one of your aunts pinched your cheeks as if you were a three-year-old? Or maybe a great-grandparent shared the same far-fetched stories that you heard the last time you were together? Family reunions can be fun— and a little crazy—because of the things people say and do.

Writing narratives (stories) about surprising experiences and interesting people can be fun, too. This chapter will explain how to write two different forms of narratives—a phase autobiography and a biographical story. A phase autobiography focuses on an extended period of time, or phase, in your own life. A biographical story tells about a person you find interesting (besides yourself).

What's Ahead

- Phase Autobiography
- Writing Guidelines
- Biographical Story
- Writing Guidelines
- Digital Story
- Writing Guidelines

Phase Autobiography

A phase autobiography is a special type of writing that focuses on an extended period of time, or phase, in the writer's life. In the following phase autobiography, Billy Stewart writes about his summer at Camp Dakota.

At Camp Dakota

Beginning
The beginning grabs the reader's attention and introduces the topic.

So you think *you* had a crazy summer? Try spending three weeks away from home without air conditioning, television, or your mom's cooking. It's hard to believe, but that is exactly what I did. The King of the Couch went to summer camp. And, boy, I never could have predicted how this adventure would turn out.

The first night at Camp Dakota was the worst. The staff put us in bunkhouses that looked like military barracks and felt like mosquito-infested saunas. I nabbed a top bunk above a kid named George, whom I quickly discovered had a snoring problem. As I lay in my bunk that first night, dripping with sweat and listening to the soundtrack of George's snoring, I was sure it was going to be a very, very long three weeks.

Middle
The middle establishes a personal tone, which helps the reader feel comfortable with the story.

Things only got worse during the next couple days. To begin with, I had to wake up at 7:30 every morning, which is way too early for any teenager to have to wake up in the summer. Next, the food was gross. (The Camp Dakota cooks are widely known for being the masters of mystery meat, and I now know that to be true.) Finally, I was not making any friends, because everyone in my cabin already knew each other from last year. They even called themselves the Camp Dakota Veterans. Meanwhile, I thought of myself as a depressed Camp Dakota Rookie.

Camp Dakota got so bad that I called my mom. "This place stinks," I complained. She recommended—in her sternest mom voice—that I at least *try* having fun instead of sulking all the time. "Billy, you're just going to have to stick this one out," she said. After I hung up the phone, I realized I had a choice to make. Either I could continue pouting, or I could try to make some friends. I decided to try the friends idea.

The action builds and reaches a critical moment.

I started by acting the same way I do with my friends at home. I told a joke to the person I knew best, my snoring bunkmate, George. He loved it, and we started sharing all kinds of jokes. Before long, we had the whole cabin laughing at our comedy routines.

My fortune continued to change during the Camp Dakota Soccer Cup. My team made it to the championship match. With the score tied 2-2, George kicked the ball toward the goal, and it ricocheted off my head and into the net for the win. "That was the best header I've ever seen," George said. If he only knew I didn't even see the ball coming. I just got lucky.

The soccer tournament wasn't the only fun experience I had. I also went canoeing, hiking, and rock climbing. George even convinced me to be in the camp play. I had to show my mom the DVD before she believed that I actually did it.

Ending

The ending shows what the writer learned from the phase.

I learned a lot from my three weeks at camp. It's okay to feel nervous in a new situation, but that doesn't mean you should act like a grouch. Just be yourself and join in the activities. Before camp I was known as the King of the Couch. Now I go by Camp Dakota Veteran.

Pattern of Organization

Use the graphic below to help organize your phase autobiography.

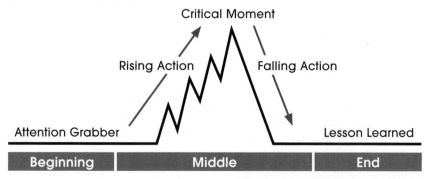

Writing Guidelines

Prewriting—Choosing a Topic

Think about the important phases, or stages, of your life. Then choose an important phase to write about. Billy created a life map to examine the phases in his own life. (A life map recalls the stages in a person's life, from birth to the present. Billy's map also rates the events.)

Life Map

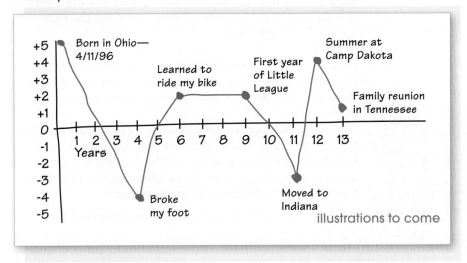

illustrations to come

Gathering Details

After choosing a topic, list the key actions or events related to the phase. Billy thought back to his summer at Camp Dakota and made a time line of key events.

Time Line (first part)

1.	Mom dropped me off. I was in a bad mood.
2.	Couldn't sleep. George was snoring like crazy.
3.	Asked my mom if I could go home.
4.	Became friends with George!

Writing—Writing the First Draft

Beginning ■ The beginning of your phase autobiography should accomplish three things, each of which is demonstrated in Billy's opening paragraph:

- ■ **Grab your reader's attention.**
  So you think you had a crazy summer?
- ■ **Include necessary background information.**
  Try spending three weeks away from home without . . .
- ■ **State the topic or phase that you will write about.**
  The King of the Couch went to summer camp.

Middle ■ Once you have introduced your phase, develop your story, working in the most important events of the phase. The action should intensify until it reaches a high point, or critical moment, where the story turns. (See "Pattern of Organization" on page 151.) At the critical moment in Billy's story, he chooses to make friends.

Ending ■ In the ending, explain the lesson you learned and show how the phase changed you.

Revising and Editing—Improving Your Writing

Revise and edit your first draft using the following checklist as a guide.

_____ Ideas Have I focused on the key details of the phase?

_____ Organization Is my narrative in chronological order?

_____ Voice Does my personality come through in my story?

_____ Word Choice Have I taken special care to use colorful words in my story?

_____ Sentence Fluency Are my sentences smooth and varied?

_____ Conventions Do I use proper punctuation, capitalization, spelling, and grammar?

Examples of Effective Word Choice

Descriptive:
  mosquito-infested sauna

Conversational:
  I _nabbed_ a top bunk.

Alliterative:
  masters of mystery meat

Biographical Story

Student Meg Doshan shares the accomplishments of a famous person in the following biographical story. To gather information, Meg researched her subject on the Internet and at the library.

Take It to the Summit

Beginning
The writer draws the reader in by creating a descriptive scene.

Standing on top of the highest mountain in the world, Stacey Allison proudly holds an American flag against her puffy red parka. Her cheeks are red from windburn, and she tries her best to crack a smile in the frigid weather. The photograph shows Allison becoming the first American female to reach the top of Mount Everest. Her accomplishment took hard work, determination, and a belief in herself, qualities she teaches others today.

Allison began serious mountain climbing at age 21. Her first important feat was climbing Mount McKinley in Alaska. From there, she traveled to Nepal and Russia to climb taller mountains. In 1987, at age 29, Allison attempted to climb Everest for the first time. But when she was 6,000 feet from the top, she got caught in a blizzard and had to spend five days in a snow cave. The storm forced her climbing team to turn around ("Allison").

Middle
Important details highlight the subject's life.

But Allison didn't give up. Just a year after her first attempt, she was back on Everest. Again, adversity struck. This time, two of the Sherpas who helped guide the team up the mountain got scared and turned back. They took two reserve oxygen tanks with them, meaning only one climber and one Sherpa could make the rest of the trek up the mountain. That climber was Allison. And on her 29th day on the mountain, she became the first American woman to reach the summit (Franks 25–28).

Since her climb up Mount Everest, Allison has traveled the United States as a motivational speaker. She talks about facing challenges and dealing with adversity. She has also written two books and owns a construction company.

Ending
The writer reflects on the subject's life.

Allison believes that people should challenge themselves to achieve their dreams. This philosophy has served her well, and she is an inspiration to many people.

Note: The works-cited page is not shown.

Writing Guidelines

Prewriting—Choosing a Topic

Finding a subject for a biographical story should be easy because you probably know, or have heard of, a lot of interesting people. Here are three ways to search for a subject:

1. Think about people who have had a big influence in your life. (*Meg thought of her mother, sister, best friend.*)
2. Think of people close to you that you want to know more about. (*Meg listed her grandfather, neighbor, teacher.*)
3. Think of interesting people you have learned about. (*Meg considered Amelia Earhart, Candice Parker, Stacey Allison.*)

Gathering Details

Gathering the best details for your writing may or may not be easy. It all depends on your subject. Meg chose to write about a person she admired but didn't know much about. She had to do a lot of research before she was ready to write. Here is a chart that can help you collect details.

Levels of Knowledge Chart

Knowledge Level	Examples	Source of Information
Well-known subject	best friend, mother, brother	Search your memory for ideas. Talk with your subject.
Somewhat-known subject	teacher, uncle, cousin	Search your memory. Interview your subject. Watch and take notes.
Little-known subject	dentist, firefighter, restaurant owner	Interview your subject. Watch and take notes. Read any related information.
Famous person	historical figure, author, athlete	Search the Internet. Read books, magazines, and newspapers. Listen to radio or television interviews.

Writing—Developing the First Draft

Beginning ■ In the beginning, spark your reader's interest in your subject: Ask a thought-provoking question, begin with an intriguing quotation, or establish a scene. Meg's beginning uses physical (sensory) details to describe an important scene in her subject's life.

Middle ■ In the middle, include specific details that help tell your story and answer the 5 W's (who? what? where? when? and why?). Meg's middle paragraphs describe her subject's most significant accomplishments.

Ending ■ In the ending, explain one final important detail about your subject and reflect upon the person's life. Meg's ending describes one of her subject's closely held beliefs.

Revising and Editing—Improving Your Writing

Use the checklist below to revise and edit your biographical story.

_____ **Ideas** Have I chosen an interesting subject and described an important event in the person's life? Do I include details that make the event come alive?

_____ **Organization** Do my beginning and ending work well? Have I answered all of the 5 W's about the person and the situation?

_____ **Voice** Does my voice sound knowledgeable and respectful?

_____ **Word Choice** Have I used specific nouns and active verbs?

_____ **Sentence Fluency** Do I use a variety of sentence lengths and beginnings?

_____ **Conventions** Have I checked punctuation, capitalization, spelling, and grammar?

A Closer Look at Revising: Voice

Your voice should fit your subject, purpose, and audience.

■ **Subject:** Sound knowledgeable, interested, and enthusiastic.
■ **Purpose:** Sound enlightening, entertaining, and informative.
■ **Audience:** Sound welcoming, respectful, and engaging.

Digital Story

Digital stories combine music, pictures, and recorded audio to produce a multimedia computer presentation. After Meg Doshan finished writing her biographical narrative, she turned it into a digital story. Below are the first two frames of her storyboard.

Digital Story Storyboard

Frame	Date: Feb. 8, 2009	Project Name: Take It to the Summit	Author: Meg Doshan

In the frame, Meg pastes a picture of her story's subject.

1

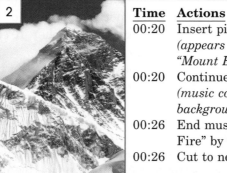

Time   Actions
00:00   Insert picture: "Allison."
00:00   Begin music: "Courage Under Fire" by the T-Bots.
00:05   Begin narrative audio *(music continues in the background)*.
00:20   Cut to next frame *(when narrator says "top of...").*

Meg includes the story portion she will record.

Narration: Standing on top of the highest mountain in the world, Stacey Allison proudly holds an American flag against her puffy red parka. The year was 1988, and Allison had just become the first American woman to reach the top of . . .

2

Meg inserts directions in italics.

Time   Actions
00:20   Insert picture: "Everest" *(appears when narrator says "Mount Everest").*
00:20   Continue narrative *(music continues in the background).*
00:26   End music: "Courage Under Fire" by the T-Bots.
00:26   Cut to next frame.

Narration: Mount Everest. Her accomplishment took hard work, determination, and a belief in herself—qualities she teaches others today.

Writing Guidelines

Prewriting—Choosing a Topic

If you have already written a narrative, you're all set to plan your digital story. If you are starting from scratch or want a new topic, refer to one of the narrative forms mentioned earlier in the handbook and follow the writing process to produce the narration for your digital story.

Gathering Details

The gathering process for digital stories is primarily done on the Internet. Meg searched for pictures, quotations, and music that related to her topic. You may also use your own digital pictures or video for your story.

Writing—Creating a Storyboard

Once you have gathered the necessary visuals for your digital story, you should draft a storyboard. The storyboard is a frame-by-frame outline of your digital story. Here you will decide which pictures and music will go with each frame of the story. Meg's storyboard includes the following three elements:

- **Frame:** Inside the "frame" box, Meg pasted a picture that appears at that particular time in her story.
- **Time/Action:** This box includes the length of time per frame, what music the listener will hear, and what image the viewer will see. Meg also included her director comments in *italics* in this section.
- **Narration:** Here Meg wrote out what part of the story she would record for each frame.

Revising and Editing

Revising and editing digital stories is a bit like working on a jigsaw puzzle—the pictures, music, and narrative must all fit together smoothly. Most of the revising and editing is done as you produce your story on the computer. There are a number of computer programs you can use to produce and edit digital stories. Ask your school or community librarian about them.

Feature
Stories

The goal of a feature writer is simple: Tell a great story. Features appear in newspapers every day, but their subjects and structure are different from those of straight news stories. Features are generally longer and more in-depth, and they do not deliver breaking news.

To understand the difference, pretend you are a feature reporter searching for a story at the scene of a massive flood. News reporters are looking at the big picture, focusing on the 5 W's because they are on a tight deadline. But your focus is narrower. As a feature writer, you are looking for a unique flood story. Your deadline is three days away. Then you see a police officer rescuing a stranded resident. Bingo! There's your story—what it's like to be involved in a rescue mission.

What's Ahead

- Feature Story
- Writing Guidelines

Feature Story

In the following feature article, student journalist Darius Miller hooks the reader by setting up a dramatic scene. This story appeared in the education section of the community newspaper.

Crunch! Invasion of the Sumo 'Bots

Beginning

The writer leads with a dramatic scene.

Janie Schrock's robot was on the brink of defeat. Each clanking collision pushed the shoebox-sized robot closer to the edge of the circular battleground.

As the opposing robot barreled forward for what surely would be a winning blow, Schrock, an eighth grader, swiftly maneuvered her metallic robot to the side. And the opponent zoomed outside of the circular boundary, giving Schrock the victory.

This type of drama is common at the annual Junior Gateway Tech Robotics Competition. It's an event in which students from area middle schools build their own remote-controlled robots and compete in various robotics challenges.

Middle

The news thread, or thesis, (underlined) gives the story focus.

Robot-Sumo is one of the most popular challenges in which two robots attempt to push each other off a circular piece of plywood in a similar fashion to the sport of sumo wrestling. "Robot-Sumo is definitely the coolest competition. What's not to like about slamming robots into each other?" asked Schrock.

Students learn the basics of engineering and design while spending months on their robot designs in their technology class. "We hope that the robotics competitions get the students excited about the possibilities in an engineering career," said Mr. Caldwell, the robotics adviser for Parkview Middle School.

The rules of the competition state that the length and width of the robot cannot exceed one foot. "You can't just be smart when you design a robot. You have to be creative, too," said Schrock.

Ending

The writer ends by quoting the subject of his lead.

Schrock plans to defend her Robot-Sumo title next year. "I have a lot of hard work ahead of me. Someday I hope I can build larger robots that can help people do everyday things like cooking and cleaning," she said.

Writing Guidelines

Prewriting—Selecting a Topic

The best features leave the reader thinking, "I'm really glad I read that story." Search for a story idea you think your audience ought to know about. Features can be about people, places, or things, so you can find topics just about anywhere. Here are some types of features to consider.

- **Personality Profile** Personality profiles help the reader get closer to a person by providing an in-depth story about the person's life or personality. Remember, everyone has a story worth sharing.

  Example: Describe the personality of a favorite cafeteria cook.

- **Human Interest** Human interest stories appeal to the reader's emotions by describing the drama of human experiences. Often times they focus on an exciting or unusual event in a person's life.

  Example: Write about the time a squirrel was loose in the school cafeteria and what a group of students did to remove it.

- **Informational Feature** These features give detailed accounts of historic or timely events. They inform rather than entertain, and they require extensive research and interviews.

  Example: Write about a historic snowstorm that caused the cafeteria roof to buckle and required students to eat in the gym.

- **Trend Story** Trend stories describe the evolution of trends that impact daily life.

  Example: Report how cafeteria food has changed in the last 10 years.

> "Ultimately, people will want to read about people, making the feature story increasingly important whether the context is entertainment, the arts, politics, technology . . ."

— Roy Peter Clark, author of *Coaching Writers*

Prewriting—Gathering Details

Anytime you write for the public, as you would in a newspaper, gathering background information and interviewing are essential. The quality of your writing will depend on the quality of your reporting.

Interviewing

Use the following quick guide for interviews. (Also see page 200.)

- **Pre-interview.** Begin by setting up the interview. Compile a list of questions and star the ones that you definitely need answered.
- **Interview.** During the interview, stay engaged by nodding your head or saying "I see" or "okay." Take notes of key details, such as the correct spelling of names.
- **Post-interview.** After the interview, review your notes.

Details. Details. Details.

Journalist Roy Peter Clark urges reporters to "Get the name of the dog" when gathering details. That is, make sure to collect specific details. Student writer Darius Miller uses specific sensory details to describe the action at the Robot-Sumo competition (page 160).

> "Each clanking collision pushed the shoebox-sized robot closer to the edge of the circular battleground."

Checking Your Reporting

To make sure you have the information needed for a feature story, use the following checklist.

Gathering Checklist

_____ Have I collected the 5 W's and H?
_____ Have I interviewed at least two people?
_____ Have I collected enough details?
_____ Am I clear about the chronology of specific actions?

Writing—Writing the First Draft

An effective feature story has a houselike structure (see below). The lead begins the story, building to the news thread (thesis) in the body. Additional details explain the news thread, and the story is brought to a satisfying close.

Lead   Feature leads are generally between two and three short paragraphs long. Try to be creative, set a mood, or spark the reader's interest with an intriguing scene, as Darius does on page 160. Take extra time on your lead in order to compel the reader to read on.

Body news thread   The first paragraph in the body of the story should include the news thread, a statement that serves the same purpose as the thesis statement of an essay. The news thread reveals the main idea or focus of the story. Use the rest of the body to fill in important details, using quotations to add color and human interest to the story.

Ending   Reward your audience with a lively ending. Share an interview quotation that sums up the story or makes the reader think. Tying the ending to the beginning is also an effective way to conclude a story.

Revising and Editing—Improving Your Writing

As you revise and edit your story, ask yourself if your work demonstrates the traits of effective writing.

____ **Ideas** Does the lead hook the reader?

____ **Organization** Have I explained my news thread?

____ **Voice** Is my writing lively and conversational but objective?

____ **Word Choice** Do I include enough specific details?

____ **Sentence Fluency** Do I use short, smooth-reading sentences and short paragraphs?

____ **Conventions** Does my writing follow the rules of punctuation, capitalization, spelling, and grammar?

Expository
Writing

Thinking
Academically

The tough thing about being in middle school is, well . . . being in the middle. You've put away your toys, but you don't have the car keys yet. You've outgrown your kid clothes, but you're not ready to dress like an adult. You realize there's a big world out there, but you're not quite part of it.

Thinking academically can help you take hold of the world. From childhood on, you've been acquiring thinking skills that help you learn new things and utilize what you already know. But the more you practice these skills, the better you'll get at figuring out what goes on around you—and the farther you'll go in life.

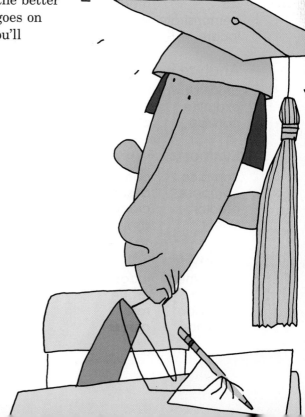

What's Ahead

- Basic Thinking Moves
- Recalling
- Understanding
- Applying
- Analyzing
- Synthesizing
- Evaluating
- Creative Thinking

Basic Thinking Moves

Different academic assignments call for the different "thinking moves" shown in the chart below. (**Hint:** Watch for these **key words** in assignments and on tests.)

When asked to . . .   ## Be ready to . . .

Recall ···············➤ Remember what you have learned.

underline	circle
list	match
name	label
cluster	define

- collect information
- list details
- identify or define key terms
- remember main points

Understand ···············➤ Explain what you have learned.

explain	review
summarize	restate
describe	cite

- give examples
- restate important details
- explain how something works

Apply ···············➤ Use what you have learned.

change	illustrate
do	model
demonstrate	show
locate	organize

- select the most important details
- organize information
- explain a process
- demonstrate a process

Analyze ···············➤ Break information down.

break down	rank
examine	compare
contrast	classify

- carefully examine a subject
- break it down into categories
- make connections and comparisons

Synthesize ···············➤ Reshape information into a new form.

combine	connect
compose	design
predict	create
invent	develop

- invent a better way of doing something
- blend the old with the new
- predict or hypothesize (make an educated guess)

Evaluate ···············➤ Judge the worth of information.

recommend	judge
criticize	argue
persuade	rate
convince	assess

- point out a subject's strengths and weaknesses
- evaluate its clarity, accuracy, value, and so on
- convince others of its value/worth

Recalling

The most basic type of thinking you use in school is **recalling**: remembering and repeating information you have learned. Multiple-choice, matching, fill-in-the-blanks, and short-answer questions ask you to recall information, as in the following test about the Mexican-American War. (Note: The name *Nueces* is pronounced nōo-ā′-sĭs.)

Directions: Fill in the blanks to correctly complete the sentences below.

1. President __James Polk__ called for war on Mexico in __1846__.

2. The U.S. and Mexico disputed land between the __Nueces__ and __Rio Grande__ Rivers.

3. The countries disagreed about which river was the southern border of the state of __Texas__.

Directions: Write three sentences about the start of the Mexican-American War.

1. _President Polk sent Zachary Taylor and 3,000 troops to cross the Nueces River and march to the Rio Grande._

2. _Mexican troops won a battle against a small group of American troops._

3. _President Polk said Mexican troops had "shed American blood on American soil."_

Strategies for Recalling

- Listen and read carefully in class.
- Take notes and draw pictures.
- Involve as many senses as possible.
- Use memory aids, such as rhymes. (See the example.)

Memory Aid

> Polk sent out Taylor
> From the Nueces River
> To make a stand
> At the Rio Grande.

Understanding

The next level of thinking is **understanding**: explaining a subject, telling how something works, or discussing what something means. You can show understanding by writing a paragraph, as one student did to explain "Manifest Destiny."

Assignment: Explain "Manifest Destiny" and how it led to the Mexican-American War.

Manifest Destiny was a belief in the 1800s that the United States was destined to expand westward to the Pacific. First, President Jefferson bought the Louisiana Territory from France, but that wasn't enough. Then Texas broke away from Mexico and joined the United States, but that wasn't enough. President Polk tried to buy the northern Mexico territories of California and New Mexico for $30 million, but Mexico refused. Then Polk pushed a disagreement over the boundary of Texas to set off the Mexican-American War. Once the war started, people in California broke from Mexico, too, and the U.S. took over that area. That still wasn't enough. In the end, the U.S. got all the territory it tried to buy, but for half the price. Manifest Destiny expanded the country through trade and war until it stretched from sea to sea. Because of the belief in Manifest Destiny, the United States flexed its territorial muscles for the first time.

Strategies for Understanding

- Use study-reading and note-taking strategies. (See pages 366–367 and 397–402.)
- Explain what you know to someone.
- Write down what you know.
- Use a graphic organizer to chart what you know. (See example.)

Time Line

1803	Louisiana Purchase
1845	Offered to buy northern Mexico
1848	Got northern Mexico by War

Applying

Once you understand something, you can **apply** or use the knowledge in a real-world way. In the following paragraph, a student defines the word *secession* and applies it to his classroom.

Assignment: What does *secession* mean? Apply your definition to a modern situation.

The word "secession" means "to break away from a group." When Texas seceded from Mexico, the people in Texas said they were not part of the bigger country. People may feel they have the right to secede, to decide what they're part of. But secession can cause big problems. What if five or six students in American History decide to secede? Maybe they want to start their own class. Mr. Hastings couldn't allow this to happen. He'd have to keep control or send the students to the principal's office. If he didn't, other people might secede, too, and soon there'd be no class. That's what happened in the Mexican-American War. After Texas seceded from Mexico, so did California. If Mexico hadn't fought, maybe more areas would have seceded. In the Civil War, when some states seceded from the U.S., more followed. If Lincoln had just let them go, the whole country could have fallen apart. So although people may have the right to break away from a group, they need to know that the group leaders will try to stop them.

Strategies for Applying

- Select an important idea.
- Apply the idea to a real-world situation.
- Explore how the idea works or doesn't work.
- Draw the results. (See the example.)

Drawing

Secession in Mr. Hastings' Class

☐ ☐ ☐ ☐ ☐ Loyalists
☐ ☐ ☐ ☐ ☐
☐ ☐ ☐ ☐ ☐
☐ ☐ ☐ ☐ ☐ Rebels

Analyzing

The next level of thought is **analyzing**: breaking a topic down into parts, comparing the parts, and showing how they fit together again. This paragraph breaks the Mexican-American War into different campaigns.

Assignment: In a paragraph, analyze the three major campaigns of the Mexican-American War.

The Mexican-American War stretched from Texas to California and down to Mexico City. The war began in the northeast corner of Mexico, in a dispute over the border of Texas. President Polk sent General Zachary Taylor and an army of 3,000 men to march from the Nueces River to the Rio Grande River, taking over the disputed territory. In 1846, Taylor crossed the Rio Grande to invade Mexico. Meanwhile, in northern Mexico, General Kearny marched to take what is now New Mexico and Arizona. He swept to the west, where John C. Fremont had led the Bear Flag Revolt. Kearny joined forces with him and the navy to take California. The final march in the war began in central Mexico under General Winfield Scott. He landed 10,000 troops at Veracruz. Then he marched westward, cutting a swath to Mexico City, which fell on September 14, 1847. These three campaigns combined to spell victory for the U.S.

Strategies for Analyzing

- Identify the important parts.
- Decide how the parts fit together.
- Diagram or map the parts.
  (See example.)

Map

Synthesizing

An even more challenging form of thought is **synthesizing**: using information to create something new. Below, one student has created a journal entry by Antonio López de Santa Anna, president of Mexico, on the day that Mexico City fell.

Assignment: Create a journal entry about an important day in the life of someone involved in the Mexican-American War.

September 14, 1847: Look how the Americanos come, those loping coyotes! That is how they have fought, like coyotes, not like men of honor. The U.S. has hungered for our lands and has disregarded all fences. They waded the Rio Grande and ran in packs through the north and joined with the wild bears in the west and came on snarling. We fought them everywhere. Yesterday, at the castle of Chapultepec, even our young boys fought like men—Los Niños Héroes—but the coyotes killed them.

And today, the first Americano marches into Mexico City! Who is that? Division Four Commander Quitman? What sort of slinking name is "Quitman"? And see how he comes, missing a shoe as he marches into our capital, into proud Mexico City! How have our people been brought low by such curs?

My army is gone, but I have one last surprise. The prison holds 30,000 men. I will release them and see what harm they can do to these coyotes!

Strategies for Synthesizing

- Express ideas creatively.
- Combine two ideas that haven't been combined before.
- Experiment with forms. (See sample.)

Experimental Form (Lune)

> Coyote Congress
> Declares war
> On a herd of sheep

Evaluating

The highest level of thinking is **evaluating**: deciding on the value of something—what is good about it and what is not so good. Below, one student evaluates the Mexican-American War.

Assignment: Evaluate the Mexican-American War, indicating whether it was good or bad for our country and why.

Though the Mexican-American War added many states to our country, the war was an unjust land grab. President Polk wanted everything from West Texas to California, and when he couldn't buy it, he used the dispute over Texas's border to pick a fight with Mexico. The secession of Texas led to the secession of California, and the U.S. military snatched up the rest. In 1885, Ulysses S. Grant, who had fought under Taylor, wrote in his memoirs, "For myself, I was bitterly opposed to the measure, and to this day regard the war, which resulted, as one of the most unjust ever waged by a stronger against a weaker nation." Later, Grant even wrote that the Mexican-American War was one cause of the Civil War: "The Southern rebellion was largely the outgrowth of the Mexican War. Nations, like individuals, are punished for their transgressions." Although the war added land to our country, it did so in an unjust way, and we've paid for it since then.

Strategies for Evaluating

- Learn as much as you can about the subject.
- Decide on standards for judging.
- Present evidence to support your evaluation.
- Use a graphic organizer to chart details that give support.

Table Diagram

U.S.-Mexican War was unjust.		
Tried to buy land.	Took land by force.	Grant: "most unjust war"

Creative Thinking

The best academic thinking can also be creative thinking. In *Writing with Power*, Peter Elbow suggests the following ways to use creative thinking in academic assignments:

Become the person whose ideas you are reading or writing about. Get inside his or her mind, and write as if you were the person.

> As president of the United States, I can't allow my people to crowd closer and closer when there are millions of square miles of wilderness waiting in the west.

Approach the subject of your writing as if you were dangerous, scandalous, or controversial.

> People say we should build a wall between Mexico and the U.S. This sounds like a fine idea to me. Let's just make sure the wall follows the 1845 border.

Live in your writing. Close your eyes to imagine the colors and shapes you are describing. Let textures tickle your fingertips; let sounds swell in your ears.

> The whole hot week, we marched through clouds of dust. Grit caked our sweaty faces, and the sun baked it into adobe masks.

Summarize what you are trying to say in your writing. If the summary is a better expression of your thoughts, add it to your writing.

> Though the war with Mexico added many states to our country, it was unjust—nothing more than ~~unfair in so many ways. Taking what~~ a land grab. ~~another country owns is wrong.~~

Explain your subject by using metaphors. (A metaphor equates two things that are different.) Equate your subject with something and then supply details that support the equation.

> Look how the Americanos come, those loping coyotes! . . . They waded the Rio Grande and ran in packs through the north and joined with the wild bears in the west and came on snarling. . . .

Experiment with words. Write in an unusual form or try using a literary technique. (See pages 240–243.) In the sample, a rifle is used as a symbol of Juan's war experience.

> Juan Marquez had taken his father's best farm rifle when he joined Santa Anna's army. He'd meant to keep the gun cleaned and oiled, but after four battles, it was dirty and scarred and prone to misfire.

Explore uncharted territory. Take a detour or travel in a new direction. The journey can enliven the piece you're working on or give you an entirely new writing idea.

> Though the U.S. Army defeated the California Lancers, their ghosts remain. You can see them riding across the desert in swirling dust devils. You can hear them calling on the wind: "Take back the land!"

Ask offbeat questions about your subject and develop creative answers. You'll be surprised where your thinking might lead.

> What type of weather was each U.S. general like?
> - Taylor was like a drought, relentless and scorching.
> - Kearny was like a tornado sweeping across the desert.
> - Scott was like a hurricane, arriving from the sea with unstoppable force.

Expository Essays

Imagine you've been assigned to help an exchange student adjust to life in the United States. You'll probably hear a lot of questions: "What is sales tax? Why is the Fourth of July important? What's in a hot dog?" As you try to explain, you may be surprised at how much you know—and how much you have left to learn.

When you write to explain something or demonstrate how something works, you are involved in expository writing. Your goal in expository writing is to help the reader understand and appreciate the information that you present

What's Ahead

Expository Essay

Student writer Candace Denoon loves Japanese pop culture—from *manga* (comic books) to *anime* (cartoons) to *bento boxes* (portable lunches). She wrote the following expository essay to explain bento boxes.

A Delicious Present

For most students, lunch comes in two types—hot and cold. Hot lunch provides variety, but the food comes from a big can and is plopped onto plastic trays. Cold lunch is homemade, but it's often the same every day. If only there were a third option! In Japan, there is. <u>A bento box is a meal specially packed up like a present.</u>

A bento box has many layers. The outside layer is a decorative cloth called a *furoshiki*. It holds everything else and is laid out on the table like a mini picnic blanket. Inside the furoshiki is a set of chopsticks and the bento box itself. Traditional boxes are lacquered wood, though modern boxes are plastic or metal. Some boxes look rich and royal, and others have anime characters all over them, but all bento boxes are supposed to look inviting and exciting. Within the box is the real present—food carefully prepared and arranged for color, texture, and smell. Often the food sits in little cubbies in the box, but sometimes it is separated by lettuce leaves or plastic grass. Some bento boxes have trays inside, with multiple layers of treats!

The food inside a bento box should be surprising. Most boxes include rice, but it is often pressed together into fun shapes such as circles, triangles, squares, or even animals. This pressed rice is called *onigiri*. Traditional bento

boxes also include some meat or fish, curry, and vegetables or fruits. Each item is carefully prepared. For example, cocktail sausages might be cut to look like octopuses, apple wedges like a fan, and broccoli like little *bonsai* trees.

The writer elaborates with a variety of details.

Of course, packing a bento box takes time. Few parents want to get up half an hour earlier to cook all the ingredients and arrange them thoughtfully. That's why most school bento boxes contain leftovers from the night before—popcorn chicken or a fish fillet or stir fried veggies. But parents aren't the only ones who make up bento boxes. Often, girls will prepare special bento boxes to give to boys they are interested in. These boxes are created like little works of art.

Bento boxes have also gone commercial. Grocery stores have whole cases full of bento boxes for every occasion— from a fancy dinner to a quick snack. Railway stations have *ekiben*, takeaway bento boxes that passengers eat on trips. According to bentoriffic.com, "Bento boxes are such a commercial success because they embody Japanese culture: traditional, beautiful, innovative, well designed, and practical." Actually, though, bento boxes have had a commercial side for over 300 years. When people went to see *kabuki* theater, the shows were very long, and so bento boxes gave people a meal between acts.

Ending

The ending connects the topic to the reader's everyday experience.

Imagine what a stir it would make to sit down with a beautifully prepared bento box among all those cafeteria trays and sack lunches. Imagine the jealous eyes, the questions, and the requests to trade food. That's part of the fun of bento boxes, too. They make even a simple meal an event.

Note: The bibliography page is not shown.

Pattern of Organization

Use this graphic to help organize the body of expository writing that explains or shares information.

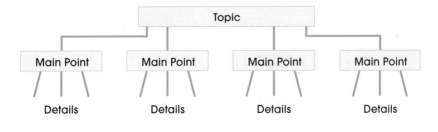

Quick Guide ■ Expository Writing

Expository writing should be chock full of interesting information. It's all about the details. Dive into your topic and search for the most interesting information about it. Then think about your reader—what does the person already know, and what would she or he like to find out?

Consider the Writing Situation

To get started, think about your subject, purpose, and audience.

What
Why
Who

 Subject:
What topic am I really interested in?

 Purpose:
How can I provide the reader with the most interesting information?

 Audience:
Who is the reader? What does the reader know and need to know?

Subject

Purpose

Audience

Link to the Traits

Pay special attention to ideas, organization, and voice.

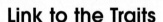

■ **Ideas:** Select a topic that really interests you. Create a clear thesis statement and provide a variety of interesting details.

■ **Organization:** Organize the details in the most informative way—time order, place order, order of importance, or logical order.

■ **Voice:** Use a voice that connects to your topic, showing your knowledge and interest, and connects to your reader, showing enthusiasm to share what you know.

Expository Writing Ideas

Expository writing is all about ideas. Once you identify a topic that really interests you, you'll have fun learning about it and sharing what you know. You can find great topic ideas in the books you read, in your classroom, and out in the world. Here's a list of other possible expository writing topics:

All about . . .
aquifers, hot springs, glaciers, oil wells, salt mines, mud slides, forest fires, the Vietnam Veterans Memorial, Martin Luther King Jr., video games, dirt bikes, computer-generated animation, horses, cheerleading

Definition of . . .
a good time, a conservative, soul, a grandparent, loyalty, one type of music, advice, courage, hope, strength, fun, freedom, pride, arrogance, success

Kinds of . . .
weather, games, personalities, music, clothing, crowds, friends, commercials, dreams, neighbors, pains, joys, heroes, chores, homework, frustration, workouts, extreme sports, diets

How-to . . .
skateboard, snowboard, surf, stand on your head, saddle a horse, show a dog, lift weights, recognize constellations, do origami, build a radio, make a favorite food, get from one place to another

Causes and effects of . . .
sunburn, acne, hiccups, tornadoes, dropouts, rust, computer viruses, arguments, droughts, climate change, war, recessions, booms, earthquakes, racism, sunspots

Comparing and contrasting . . .
soccer to football, rural life to city life, summer to fall, different types of heroes, new fashions to old, types of jobs, political parties, books, types of great apes, farming techniques, Aztecs to Egyptians

Helpful Hint

To write an essay based on any of the ideas in the first three categories, use the models and guidelines in this chapter. To write a how-to essay, a cause-effect essay, or a comparison-contrast essay, see the models and guidelines in the next chapter. For more help selecting a topic, see the next page.

Writing Guidelines

Prewriting—Selecting a Topic

The best expository essays start with a fascinating topic. Candace reviewed the Essentials of Life Checklist. She chose the category "food," and then listed types of food until she found a topic that interested her.

Essentials of Life Checklist

Foods			
Burgers	clothing	machines	rules/laws
Pizza	housing	intelligence	tools/utensils
Sushi	food	history/records	heat/fuel
Kobe steak	communication	agriculture	natural resources
Bento boxes*	exercise	land/property	personality/identity
– chopsticks	education	work/occupation	recreation/hobby
– rice	family	community	trade/money
– meat/fish	friends	science	literature/books
	purpose/goals	plants/vegetation	health/medicine
	love	freedom/rights	art/music
	senses	energy	faith/religion

Gathering Details

Once you've chosen a topic that interests you, find out as much as you can about it. Candace created a KWL chart listing what she knew, wondered about, and learned through research.

KWL Chart

Know	Wonder	Learn
Girls in Japan make up bento boxes for cute guys. People buy them to eat on trains. Usually there's rice in them and fish or meat, and it's all arranged like art.	1. I wonder why bento boxes got so popular. 2. I wonder if people actually make them in their homes anymore.	1. Bento boxes got popular 300 years ago because of long kabuki plays. 2. People still make them in their homes. Moms kind of compete.

Using Different Types of Details

The most effective expository writing overflows with wonderful details. As you gather details for your essay, remember that different types of details have different effects on the reader.

Types of Details Chart

Purpose	Type of Detail	Example
To sound well informed . . .	use facts and statistics.	Bento boxes have had a commercial side for over 300 years. When people went to see kabuki theater, the shows were very long, and so bento boxes gave people a meal between acts.
To explain words . . .	use definitions.	Railway stations have *ekiben*, takeaway bento boxes that passengers eat on trips.
To explain concepts . . .	use examples.	For example, cocktail sausages might be cut to look like octopuses, apple wedges like a fan, and broccoli like little bonsai trees.
To engage the reader . . .	use sensory details.	Within the box is the real present—food carefully prepared and arranged for color, texture, and smell.
To connect to life . . .	use anecdotes.	Often, girls will prepare special bento boxes to give to boys they are interested in.
To appeal to authority . . .	use quotations.	According to bentoriffic.com, "Bento boxes are such a commercial success because they embody Japanese culture: traditional, beautiful, innovative, well designed, and practical."
To imagine the future . . .	use predictions.	Imagine what a stir it would make to sit down with a beautifully prepared bento box among all those cafeteria trays and sack lunches.

Writing—Developing the First Draft

Carefully develop each part of your essay, following these guidelines.

Beginning ■ The beginning should grab your reader's attention and state your thesis. Try one of the attention-getting ideas that follow to begin your essay. Then write your thesis statement using the formula below as a guide.

- Connect to the reader's life:
  For most students, lunch comes in one of two types, hot lunch or cold lunch.
- Start with an intriguing question:
  How would you like to open a special present every lunch hour?
- Start with an interesting fact:
  Food is the one art form that involves all five senses.

Thesis Statement Formula

Your topic		A special thought or feeling		A strong thesis statement
bento boxes	**+**	a meal packed up like a present	**=**	A bento box is a meal specially packed up like a present.

Middle ■ The middle should include main points that support your thesis. Each paragraph should develop a separate main point. Use different types of details to elaborate on each main point. (See page 181.)

Ending ■ The ending paragraph should wrap up your essay in a thoughtful way. Try one of the following strategies:

- Restate your thesis:
  The bento box is a present that you can eat.
- Fire the reader's imagination:
  Imagine what a stir it would make to sit down with a beautifully prepared bento box among all those cafeteria trays and sack lunches.
- Provide an interesting quotation:
  According to bentoboxbuilder.com, "Bento boxes are thoroughly Japanese—beautiful, practical, compact, and well designed."

Revising—Improving Your Writing

When you revise your expository essay, you add, cut, move, and rework ideas to make your writing stronger. Here's a quick checklist to guide your revising:

Revising Checklist

____ **Ideas** Is my thesis statement clear and supported by a variety of details?

____ **Organization** Do my beginning, middle, and ending work well?

____ **Voice** Do I sound knowledgeable and interested?

____ **Word Choice** Do I define any special terms? (See below.)

____ **Sentence Fluency** Do my sentences read smoothly?

A Closer Look at Revising: Word Choice

If your essay contains special terms that may be unfamiliar to readers, you should provide definitions. Here are three ways:

- **Provide an actual definition:** A bento box is a meal specially packed up like a present.
- **Rename the word with an appositive:** Railway stations have ekiben, takeaway bento boxes that passengers eat on trips. (The appositive is the part of the sentence that follows the comma, and it renames *ekiben*.)
- **Provide word clues:** When people went to see kabuki theater, the shows were very long, and so bento boxes gave people a meal between acts. (Here, words like *see, theater, shows,* and *acts* help the reader know what *kabuki* refers to.)

Editing—Checking for Conventions

When you edit your expository essay, you polish its punctuation, capitalization, spelling, and grammar. Here is a quick checklist to guide your editing.

Editing Checklist

Conventions

____ Do I use end punctuation and commas correctly?

____ Do I correctly capitalize first words and proper nouns?

____ Do I avoid spelling errors?

____ Do I correctly use easily confused words (*there, they're, their*)?

Rubric for Expository Writing

Use the rubric that follows to assess your expository writing.

Ideas

The writing . . .

—— includes a clear, effective thesis statement.

—— provides a variety of interesting details to support it.

Organization

—— begins by capturing the reader's interest and providing the thesis statement.

—— has an effectively organized middle.

—— focuses on one main point for each middle paragraph.

—— ends by summarizing the ideas and giving the reader a final thought.

Voice

—— has a voice that shows knowledge of the topic.

—— has a voice that engages the reader.

Word Choice

—— uses precise nouns and active verbs.

Sentence Fluency

—— uses a variety of sentence lengths and beginnings.

—— flows smoothly from one sentence to another.

Conventions

—— uses end punctuation and commas correctly.

—— correctly capitalizes first words and proper nouns.

—— avoids spelling errors.

—— correctly uses words (*there, they're, their*).

Other Forms of
Expository Writing

Suppose that your friend says the second *Star Wars* trilogy is better than the first one. "No way," you respond. But as you compare the movies, you begin to understand that each film has its own strengths and weaknesses. Besides that, you realize that the old and the new movies are more alike than you had thought.

By comparing and contrasting two subjects, you learn more about each of them. By tracing causes and effects, you learn how events are connected. This chapter will help you write comparison-contrast essays and cause-effect essays. It starts, though, with a simpler form —the how-to essay.

What's Ahead

- How-To Essay
- Writing Guidelines
- Comparison-Contrast Essay
- Writing Guidelines
- Cause-Effect Essay
- Writing Guidelines

How-To Essay

A how-to essay describes a process. This type of essay is organized chronologically (*first, next, then* . . .). How-to essays tend to use command sentences, telling the reader what to do at each step. In the following essay, Joaquin tells how to change a tire.

How to Change a Tire

Nothing's worse than sitting on the side of a road with a flat. With the right tools and a little muscle, though, just about anybody can change a flat tire.

To change a flat tire, you need to have the right equipment. First, you need a tire iron. It looks like a crowbar, but at one end it has a socket, and at the other end, a wedge. Next, you need a jack, the little machine that lifts the car. Look in the trunk, maybe in a special compartment. Last, and certainly not least, you need a spare tire. That also should be in the car—in the trunk or hung underneath it.

Start by jacking up the car. Make sure the car is in a hard, level place, away from traffic. Also set the parking brake and use wood or rocks to block the good tires. Then position the jack under the frame, with its top in the little slot near the tire well. Use the tire iron to pump the jack until it holds firm but hasn't lifted the car off the ground.

Next, you need to get the flat tire loose. If there's a hubcap, pry it off with the wedge end of the tire iron. Then use the cupped end to fit to the lug nuts. Turn the iron counterclockwise to loosen the nuts, and make sure to put them someplace safe. Once the flat is loose, jack the car up until it clears the ground. Slide the flat off.

Finally, you need to put the new tire on. Slide it onto the bolts and hand-tighten the lug nuts. Lower the car before tightening them the rest of the way. Give a clockwise turn to each nut, and then go to the opposite nut to turn it. That way, you make sure the rim is even. When all the nuts are tight, stow the iron, jack, and flat in the back. Most spares are for short distances—so get a full-sized tire on soon.

These days, most things on a car are too complicated for home mechanics, but everybody should know how to change a flat. That's a little knowledge that can take you places.

Writing Guidelines

Prewriting—Selecting a Topic and Gathering Details

Think of things you know how to do well—or things you would like to learn how to do. Select a topic that you can cover in an essay. Then list all the tools, equipment, or supplies that you need. Make a separate list of the steps to take. Conduct research to fill in any gaps.

Focusing Your Essay

Write a thesis statement that names your topic and encourages your reader to try the process:

> With the right tools and a little muscle, anyone can change a flat tire.

Writing—Connecting Your Ideas

As you write your first draft, imagine explaining the equipment and the steps of the process to a friend. Think of what the person knows and needs to know. Use command sentences and sound encouraging.

Revising—Improving Your How-To Essay

Use this checklist to revise your essay.
- ____ Do I explain an interesting process and include the correct steps in the correct order?
- ____ Does my beginning introduce the topic and state my thesis?
- ____ Do the steps in the middle appear in time order?
- ____ Do I use command sentences and define important terms?
- ____ Does my ending effectively wrap up my writing?

Editing and Proofreading—Checking for Conventions

Use this checklist to polish your essay.
- ____ Have I checked end punctuation and commas?
- ____ Have I correctly capitalized first words and proper nouns?
- ____ Have I checked spelling and easily confused words?

Comparison-Contrast Essay

In the following essay, student writer Alayna Zents writes a point-by-point comparison of American football and Australian football.

Football "Down Under"

Football is the most popular sport in the world. But the hard-hitting game America watches on fall Sundays is only one of many forms of football. For example, most people around the world think of soccer as football. Australians play yet another version of football. It's known as Australian football, or "footy," a hard-hitting game in its own right. American and Australian football both involve a lot of running and tackling, but the playing field, scoring, and pace are quite different.

Even though both games are played on grass surfaces, the playing fields do not look alike. The oval-shaped Australian field is longer and wider than the traditional rectangular American field. Another difference is the number of goalposts. An American football field features one goalpost with two uprights at each end of the field.  On the other hand, an Australian field features four vertical uprights at each end of the field. The two middle uprights are called goalposts, and the two shorter outer posts are known as behind posts. (See the diagram.)

The object of both games is to score more points than the opposing team. Nevertheless, the methods of scoring are unalike. American football teams primarily score by running or passing the ball into an opponent's end zone for touchdowns (six points) or by kicking field goals through the goalpost (three points). The only way to score in Australian football is by kicking the ball between the goalposts (six points) or between the behind posts (one point). In American football, the final score is written as the winning team's points versus the losing team's points. For example, a typical score could be Green Bay 27, Denver 20. An Australian football score shows the number of goals and behinds with the total points in parentheses. A final score could look like this: St. Kilda 15.11 (101), Sydney 8.10 (58). St. Kilda made 15 goals and 11 behinds for 101 points, while Sydney made 8 goals and 10 behinds for 58 points.

The next paragraphs address the pace of play.

The pace of play in American football is characterized by a series of starts and stops. To advance the ball, the 11-player offense has four attempts to move 10 yards by running or passing. Play stops after each attempt, giving the offense time to pick a new play and set up a formation. If the offense fails to advance 10 yards in four plays, the defense gains possession of the ball. An American football game might take two and a half to three hours to complete. There is no action during a large portion of that time.

In contrast, the pace is much quicker in Australian "footy." Play continues without stopping until a team scores or earns a free kick. Players on both teams can roam freely as the 9-player offense tries to advance the ball by kicking, running, or handpassing. Handpassing involves punching the ball out of one hand with the palm or fist of the other. The defense regains possession by tackling the player with the ball or intercepting a kick or handpass. A typical Australian football game lasts two hours, without many breaks.

Ending
The ending revisits the beginning.

Despite the major differences between American and Australian football, both games involve physical play, intensity, speed, and strength. That may be why football, no matter which version, packs thousands of crazed fans into stadiums from Dallas to Sydney.

Patterns of Organization

Use the graphics below to help organize the body of your comparison-contrast essay.

Point-by-Point

Beginning

Point 1	
Subject 1	Subject 2

Point 2	
Subject 1	Subject 2

Point 3	
Subject 1	Subject 2

Ending

Subject-to-Subject

Beginning

Subject 1

Subject 2

Ending

Similarities-Differences

Beginning

Similarities

Differences

Ending

Writing Guidelines

Prewriting—Choosing a Topic

You will need to select two related topics for your comparison-contrast essay. Alayna wanted to write about something that really interested her, so she brainstormed ideas using a cluster. "My Interests" is the nucleus of her cluster.

Clustering

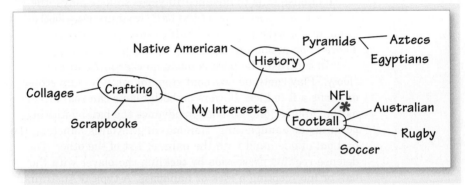

Alayna's cluster generated more than one possible writing idea, but she decided to compare American and Australian football.

Gathering Details

You will next need to collect and organize details about each topic. Alayna collected details from Web sites, books, and encyclopedias; and she used a gathering grid to track her research.

Gathering Grid (first part)

Playing Fields		
Question	American Football	Australian Football
What is the surface made of?	– Grass or artificial turf	– Grass or artificial turf
What shape is it?	– Rectangle	– Oval
What are the scoring areas?	– End zones, goalposts	– Goalposts, behind posts
How many goalposts are there?	– Two goalposts	– Four goalposts and four behind posts (shorter)

Writing—Writing the First Draft

Beginning ■ The beginning should introduce the two topics in an interesting way and lead up to the thesis statement. Alayna began her first draft by highlighting the popularity of football. Next, she used the formula below to write her **thesis statement**.

Thesis Statement Formula

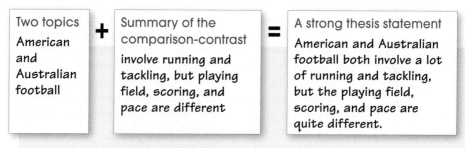

Two topics		Summary of the comparison-contrast		A strong thesis statement
American and Australian football	**+**	involve running and tackling, but playing field, scoring, and pace are different	**=**	American and Australian football both involve a lot of running and tackling, but the playing field, scoring, and pace are quite different.

Middle ■ After forming your thesis statement, you should write the middle part of your essay following one of the organization patterns on page 189. Alayna used the point-by-point organization pattern. Each middle paragraph focused on a different point of comparison between American football and Australian football. (See page 189.)

Ending ■ Your ending should leave the reader with something to remember about the topic. You can emphasize a key point, share one more insight, or refer back to the beginning. Alayna tied her essay's ending to the beginning by writing about the popularity of football.

Revising and Editing—Improving the Writing

During the revising process, consider, among other things, the organization of your writing. (See page 196 for a complete checklist.)

____ Does the essay follow one of the organization patterns on page 189?

____ Do I use appropriate transitions? (See below.)

Comparison		Contrast	
In the same way	One way	On the other hand	Although
Also	Another way	Even though	Yet
Similarly	Both	Nevertheless	Still
		However	In contrast

Cause-Effect Essay

In the following essay, student writer Coy Greenburg writes about the causes and effects of today's fast-food culture.

Beginning
The beginning introduces the topic and states the thesis (underlined).

Middle
The first middle paragraph explains the causes.

MLA citations credit sources.

The next middle paragraphs focus on the effects.

Fast-Food Frenzy

Do you know what comes in a kid's meal? Have you ever ordered from a value menu? If you answered yes to either of these questions, you probably know more about fast food than your grandparents or even your parents did at your age. In fact, the term "fast food" wasn't even listed in the dictionary until 1951 (Anderson). In today's world, fast food is a huge industry that has influenced the United States' economy, family habits, and health.

The fast-food industry started after the Great Depression when automobiles became more affordable. By the 1940s and 1950s, drive-in restaurants opened across the country, and eating in the car was a social activity for young people. In the 1960s, the demand for fast food prompted some restaurants to build national chains. Due to the thriving economy of the '60s and '70s and an increase in women in the workforce, families began spending more time on leisure activities and less time eating at home. These factors resulted in a greater demand for fast food.

Today, the multibillion-dollar fast-food industry is a major part of the country's economy. With more and more people eating out, the fast-food industry is cashing in. Consumers spent $110 billion on fast food in 2000, compared to $6 billion in 1970. Experts say the fast-food industry made $156 billion in profits in 2006 (National Restaurant Association). In addition, the industry employs about 3.5 million people, many of them working for minimum wage (Frey).

The fast-food industry has influenced changes in family habits, too. Adults are involved in more after-work activities, and young people are involved in more extracurricular activities. As a result, families don't eat an evening meal together at home as much as they used to. Instead, they grab burgers on the go one night, tacos the next, and pizza another night. The average person eats out five times a week (Frey). Fast food is perfect for a hectic lifestyle because it is quick, cheap, and convenient.

The health impact of fast food has many people worried. Experts blame fast food for increased levels of childhood obesity. Trans fat was, until recently, commonly found in fast food, and it has been linked to weight gain and increased risk of diabetes. In addition, many fast foods are packed with sugar, sodium, and calories, which can lead to high levels of cholesterol. Since today's children eat fast food five times more often than they did in the 1970s, these health issues are being taken very seriously (Center for Disease Control).

Fast food has caused changes in America's economy, culture, and health, and the industry will continue to do so in the future. However, fast-food businesses have shown they are willing to change to meet their customers' demands. With the rising rate of childhood and adult obesity, fast-food restaurants have begun to offer healthy options such as salad, fruit, and yogurt. Chains are promoting food without trans fat, too. Whatever your opinion is of fast food, one thing is clear: Fast food is here to stay, and its impact won't end any time soon.

Note: The works-cited page is not shown.

Sources of information are cited.

Ending
The ending reflects thoughtfully on the causes and effects.

Patterns of Organization

Use the graphics below to help organize the body of your cause-effect essay.

Cause-Focused	Effect-Focused
Beginning	Beginning
Cause	Cause(s)
Cause	Effect
Cause	Effect
Effect(s)	Effect
Ending	Ending

Writing Guidelines

Prewriting—Choosing a Topic

Keep the word *change* in mind as you begin thinking of cause-effect topics. Change is always *caused* by something, and every change, even a small one, can produce a number of *effects*. For your essay, consider changes that have affected people locally, nationally, or globally.

Coy started his topic search by thinking about significant changes in American culture. To narrow his focus, he made a topics chart with three categories. He starred the topic that interested him most.

Topics Chart

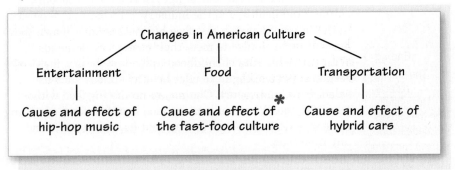

Changes in American Culture

Entertainment   Food   Transportation

Cause and effect of   Cause and effect of   Cause and effect of
hip-hop music   the fast-food culture   hybrid cars

Gathering Details

To write an effective cause-effect essay, you will need to research your topic. If your topic involves your school or community, you'll be able to interview people who are knowledgeable about it.

Coy used note cards to keep track of the information he collected.

Note Card

What is the economic impact of fast food?
- Americans spent $110 billion on fast food in 2000
- Americans spent $6 billion in 1970
- 3.5 million people work in fast food
  "21st Century Fast Food Culture"
                    Frey 57

Writing—Writing the First Draft

Beginning ■ In your first paragraph, capture the reader's interest and state your thesis. Coy introduced his topic with two questions. He then wrote his thesis statement following the formula below. The thesis statement gave Coy a focus for the remainder of his essay.

Thesis Statement Formula

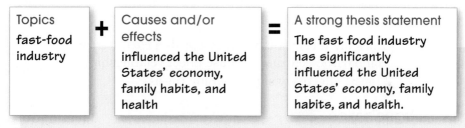

Topics		Causes and/or effects		A strong thesis statement
fast-food industry	**+**	influenced the United States' economy, family habits, and health	**=**	The fast food industry has significantly influenced the United States' economy, family habits, and health.

Middle ■ Select an appropriate pattern of organization for your essay. (See page 193.) Then develop the middle part of your essay. Be sure to expand on the key ideas with specific details—facts, quotations, and so on. Coy focused on the effects of fast food in his essay. He described the main causes in the first middle paragraph and then discussed a different effect in each of the remaining middle paragraphs.

Ending ■ The ending paragraph should tie all the information together and close with a memorable final sentence. Coy accomplished this by summarizing the importance of his topic.

Revising and Editing—Improving the Writing

During the revising process, pay special attention to the organization of your essay. (Also refer to the checklist on the next page.)

_____ Does the essay follow one of the organization patterns on page 193?

_____ Do I use appropriate transitions? (See below.)

To show cause and effect:		
Because	Also	More importantly
As a result	Usually	In addition
Due to	Though	Afterward

Revising and Editing Checklist ✔

Use the checklist below as a guide when you revise and edit your two-part expository essays.

Two-Part Expository Essay Checklist

Ideas
____ Does my thesis statement establish a clear, strong comparison-contrast or cause-effect relationship?
____ Have I effectively supported my thesis?

Organization
____ Does the beginning capture the reader's interest?
____ Are the middle and ending parts effective?
____ Does my essay follow an appropriate organizational pattern? (See pages 189 and 193.)
____ Have I used appropriate transition words? (See pages 191 and 195.)

Voice
____ Does my voice sound knowledgeable?
____ Is my voice appropriate for the audience?

Word Choice
____ Do I explain difficult or specialized terms?

Sentence Fluency
____ Are my sentences active and forward moving?
____ Have I avoided short, choppy sentences?

Conventions
____ Do I use proper punctuation, capitalization, spelling, and grammar?
____ Have I correctly cited my sources?

News
Stories

Think of all the news out there. It's in newspapers, on televisions, and all over the Internet. You simply can't avoid it. Now imagine a world without news. Sure, a few days without celebrity updates wouldn't be so bad, but how would you learn about the presidential candidates, the weather, or the results of an important baseball game?

To write your own news stories, you must first do the reporting *(interviewing, researching)*. The more reporting you do, the easier it will be to write your story. You can find story ideas just about anywhere, so put on your reporter's hat, find a story, and report on it. Oh, and remember: Pay attention to every detail.

What's Ahead

- News Story
- Writing Guidelines

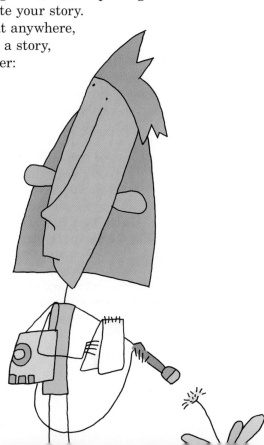

News Story

In the following news story, Hui Nguyen reports on her middle school's fund-raiser for cancer research. This story appeared in the school newspaper, the *Panther Press*.

Students surpass fund-raising goal

By Hui Nguyen

Beginning
The reporter includes the 5 W's in the lead.

Pittsfield Middle School students raised $2,400 for cancer research at the first Pittsfield Mini Relay for Life event last Friday. "I'm very proud of the students for rallying around such a great cause. They went above and beyond what the teachers asked them to do, and their success is certainly a reflection of their hard work," said our principal, Ms. Gabriella.

The students began fund-raising for the American Cancer Society three months ago, with a goal of raising $1,500. To earn the money, students asked for pledges from family and friends for every lap they walked at the relay event. For example, Jerry Overbeck received a $1 pledge for every lap he walked. He earned $22. Students also had bake sales and book sales to raise money. Mrs. Kelly's sixth-grade homeroom raised the most money of any classroom by collecting $463.

Middle
The body follows with additional facts.

Students also sent business letters to important community members to ask for pledges. They received pledges from all kinds of businesses. "It was great to see so many people willing to get involved. The mayor even donated some money," said seventh grader Brianna Yeakley.

Pittsfield Middle School presented the American Cancer Society with the money at the Mini Relay for Life event. The event took place at the school track. Each classroom formed a relay team, and at least one student from each room had to be walking on the track at all times.

Ending
The story ends with the least important information.

When students were not walking, they could enjoy art contests, obstacle courses, and other activities. There were also snacks and drinks provided for the participants. "I had an awesome time at Relay for Life. I hope we do it again next year and raise even more money," said Brianna.

Writing Guidelines

Prewriting—Choosing a Topic

To choose a topic, investigate what's happening in your school or community. Consider what your audience (classmates, teachers, and parents) needs to know about. Once you've gathered some ideas, decide if they are newsworthy or not. Your art teacher's vacation may not be news, but this teacher's retirement certainly is. Below are some factors that will help you determine the newsworthiness of a topic:

Timeliness ■ Current events are almost always more newsworthy than past events. Your audience wants to know about what's happening now.

Importance ■ The best news stories directly impact your audience. Before you begin writing, ask yourself if your audience wants or needs to know about this story.

Local angle ■ A story describing a statewide or nationwide trend may be newsworthy, but it needs to have local impact to be newsworthy.

Human interest ■ Stories about people who have defied odds, won awards, or done extraordinary things are popular among news readers. These stories should be entertaining and thought provoking.

Relay team headed to state . . .

School board mandates dress code . . .

PTA pushes wellness classes . . .

Students volunteer in Africa . . .

Prewriting—Gathering Details

To make sure you have the basic information to write your story, create a 5 W's chart. The example below was created for the news story on page 198.

5 W's Chart

Who?	What?	When?	Where?	Why?
Pittsfield students	raised $2,400 in Mini Relay for Life event	last Friday (the relay)	Pittsfield Middle School track	to support cancer research

Interviewing

One of the best ways to gather information for news stories is to interview people. If possible, interview more than one person for your story. Here are some tips that will help you conduct your interviews.

Before... Be prepared. Schedule a time for either an in-person, online, or telephone interview. Write a list of open-ended questions you want to ask. Put stars next to questions that you *must* have answered.

During... Listen attentively. Look the person in the eye. Use facial expressions or nod your head to show you are listening. (If you are conducting a phone interview, give feedback, such as "Yes" or "Okay.")

Take notes. Write down only the important details. If the person is talking too fast, politely ask him or her to slow down or repeat what was just said. Remember to thank the interviewee after you are finished. If you plan on using a tape recorder, first ask for permission.

After... Review your notes. The best time to review your notes is immediately after the interview. Then you'll know if you covered all of your questions or if you need to ask follow-up questions. When you complete your story, send a copy of it, along with a thank-you note, to the person you interviewed.

Writing—Writing the First Draft

Parts of a News Story

There are two main parts of a news story: the lead paragraph and the body.

Lead: The lead, or beginning paragraph, is the most important section of a news story. It must grab the reader's attention and summarize the main point of the story in just a few sentences. Most of the 5 W's should appear in your lead.

Body: The body fills in the rest of the news story with details and important facts that were not covered in the lead. (See below.)

Who?
What?
When?
Where?
Why?

Most important
information

Lead

Body

Least important
information

Organizing a Story

The facts and details in news stories are organized by order of importance. The most important information is placed at the beginning of the story, while subsequent information is written in descending order of importance. This top-heavy style is called the *inverted pyramid*.

The reason news stories are organized in this way is twofold: First, it allows busy readers to understand the essence of the story within the first few lines or paragraphs. Second, the essential information will not be lost if an editor has to cut the last paragraphs

Helpful Hint

Don't include your own thoughts and opinions in a news story. But do include quotations that express your interviewees' opinions. Use these quotations to complement the facts in your story.

Writing—Creating Headlines and Taking Photos

Glance at a newspaper and note the first thing that catches your eye. It's probably a headline or picture. Studies show that headlines and pictures draw readers to newspaper stories. Therefore, it is important to know how to effectively write headlines and take photographs.

Writing Headlines

Use these tips when you write a headline for your news story.

- **Reread your story.** Jot down key nouns that reoccur. They can provide a good subject for a headline.
- **Use the active voice.** Writing headlines in the active voice gives the story a sense of immediacy.

> Remember, a headline is active when the subject is doing the action.

> Passive: Fund-raising goal **surpassed** by students (The subject, *goal,* receives the action.)
>
> Active: Students **surpass** fund-raising goal (The subject, *students,* performs the action.)

- **Choose strong verbs.** If you are having trouble thinking of a strong verb, check your thesaurus.

> Weak: Students **better** fund-raising goal
>
> Strong: Students **surpass** fund-raising goal

Taking News Photographs

As the old saying goes, "A picture is worth a thousand words." It sounds a bit cliche, but in truth, a quality picture really can tell a story. Follow the tips below for taking news photos.

- **Know your story.** Think about the important 5 W's when you set off to take pictures. Where can you find a picture that will capture the essence of the story?
- **Get your knees dirty.** Hold your camera at your subject's eye level. This may mean you need to crouch or crane.
- **Think creatively.** Instead of having your subject pose for a picture, capture the person in an action shot.

Revising and Editing   Checklist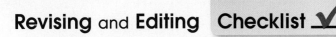

Use this traits-based checklist as a guide when you review and revise your news story and when you edit it for accuracy.

News Story Checklist

Ideas

—— Does the lead hook the reader and identify the topic?
—— Have I covered the main points in the lead and the body?

Organization

—— Does my story follow the inverted pyramid arrangement?
—— Do I use transitional words and phrases to connect my ideas?

Voice

—— Is my writing fair and balanced?
—— Is it also free of my opinion?

Word Choice

—— Do I use specific nouns and verbs?
—— Do I explain any unusual terms?

Sentence Fluency

—— Do I use smooth-reading sentences and short paragraphs?
—— Do I vary the sentence beginnings and sentence lengths?

Conventions

—— Have I checked my writing for correct punctuation, capitalization, spelling, and grammar?

Persuasive
Writing

Making an
Argument

You probably have arguments with your friends. You definitely have arguments with your siblings. In fact, if you have any contact with any other human being, you'll eventually find yourself in an argument.

But arguments aren't all bad. An argument is an attempt to persuade another person to come around to your way of thinking. To be convincing, you need to be logical, reasonable, reliable, and believable.

This chapter will help you understand the basics of making an argument—expressing an opinion, supporting it with strong reasons, and avoiding "fuzzy thinking."

What's Ahead

- Persuasive Thinking and Writing
- A Closer Look at the Persuasive Process
- Avoiding Fuzzy Thinking

Persuasive Thinking and Writing

When making an argument (or writing persuasively), you must connect your ideas in a clear, logical way. Your writing will always be persuasive if it . . .

- argues for a meaningful point of view (opinion);
- sounds reasonable and reliable from start to finish; and
- builds its argument, point by point, with convincing reasons.

Base your argument on facts and not on emotion or fuzzy thinking. (See pages 209–210.)

Becoming a Persuasive, Logical Thinker

Follow these steps, and you'll always be at your persuasive best.

- **Decide** on a controversial topic.
- **Gather** information on your topic.
- **Focus** on an opinion, a claim, or a main point that you can logically support.
- **Define** any unfamiliar terms.
- **Build** an argument based on convincing evidence.
- **Consider** any main objections to your opinion.
- **Counter** (or answer) objections. Admit that there may be some truth to objections, but also point out weaknesses. (See page 217.)
- **Restate** or reaffirm your main opinion.
- If necessary, **make** a call to action or urge the reader to accept your viewpoint.

Helpful Hint

You will probably not follow all of these steps each time you make an argument. Every situation is different and has its own special requirements.

A Closer Look at the Persuasive Process

The information that follows will help you develop strong arguments.

1. **Start with a worthy topic.**

A persuasive writing assignment is often based on a subject your class is studying. You will, however, need to choose a topic that is controversial (triggering differing opinions) and specific enough for an essay. The following chart shows the difference between weak and strong topics.

Weak Topics		Strong Topics	
Smoking cigarettes	There really is no controversy here. Smoking is a dangerous habit.	**Extending the school year**	This topic is clearly controversial; some people will agree with the idea, and others will not.
Bullying in school	No one would argue that bullying is a good thing, so again there's no controversy.	**Banning hunting in national parks**	Some would argue that animals should be protected, but others would say that overpopulation could result from a hunting ban.

2. **Know the difference between fact and opinion.**

An *opinion* is someone's view or belief. A good opinion is based on facts, but it is not a fact itself. *Facts* are statements that can be checked or proven to be true.

Opinion:
> Wild animals in Yellowstone National Park should be protected from hunting.

Fact:
> The reintroduction of wolves to Yellowstone provides a natural check on deer populations.

3. Write an opinion statement.

Follow this simple formula to help you write a strong opinion statement.

A specific topic		A specific opinion		A strong opinion statement
Wild animals in the park	**+**	should be protected from hunters	**=**	Wild animals in the park should be protected from hunters.

Helpful Hint

Opinions that include words that are strongly positive or negative—such as *all, best, every, never, none,* or *worst*—may be difficult to support. For example, an exaggerated opinion statement like "All wild animals are a nuisance in the park campgrounds" would be impossible to support.

4. Support your opinion.

Support or defend your opinion with clear, provable facts. Otherwise your reader won't accept your argument. Note the following supporting facts.

> **Provable fact:**
> Some species in the park, such as grizzly bears, have been endangered.
> (Official lists of endangered species could prove this.)
>
> **Not a provable fact:**
> Grizzly bears attack humans only when they are afraid.
> (This statement would be hard to prove.)

5. Organize your facts.

You can develop an argument in two ways. You can work *deductively,* stating your opinion in the opening part and then supporting it in the rest of your argument. (The persuasive essay on pages 212–213 is organized in this way.) Or you can work *inductively,* presenting convincing evidence that leads to your opinion.

Avoiding Fuzzy Thinking

Make sure that all ideas in a persuasive argument are well thought out. Poorly thought-out arguments are "fuzzy thinking"— logic that is weak, unclear, and unconvincing. Read the descriptions that follow to learn about different types of fuzzy thinking, and avoid these in your own writing.

■ Avoid statements that jump to a conclusion.

> Because wolves kill elk in Yellowstone Park, wolves must be eliminated.

This statement jumps to the conclusion that wolves should be eliminated. In fact, if wolves did not kill some elk, the elk could overpopulate the park and fall victim to starvation and disease.

■ Avoid statements that are supported with nothing more than the simple fact that most people agree with them.

> It is okay to feed black bears because most people don't think they are dangerous.

This type of statement suggests that if a group of people believe something, it must be true. In reality, black bears are wild animals; it is not safe to feed them.

■ Avoid statements that contain a weak or misleading comparison.

> A mountain lion, which weighs about 150 pounds, is no match for an elk, which weighs about 1,000 pounds.

This statement makes a misleading comparison. Although elk are much larger, mountain lions use their speed, strength, and stalking ability to overpower elk.

■ Avoid statements that exaggerate the facts or mislead the reader.

> If you meet a bear in the wild, the best thing to do is play dead.

This statement is misleading. Sometimes playing dead may actually work. If, however, you play dead in between a mother and her cubs, you may be in real trouble. Never use information that could mislead your reader.

■ **Avoid statements that appeal only to the reader's feelings and contain no factual information.**

> Baby bears are not dangerous because they are small and cute.

This statement appeals to our feelings about baby bears, rather than to actual facts. Even small bears can injure a person. Also, a mother bear that finds a human near her cubs may attack the person. The fact is, although small and cute, baby bears can be dangerous.

■ **Avoid statements that contain part of the truth, but not the whole truth. These statements are called half-truths.**

> At one time, people almost drove the coyote to extinction.

This statement is only partly true. In spite of people's efforts to drive coyotes to extinction, the animals have actually multiplied. While coyotes used to live only in some western states, they now are found in all parts of the country.

■ **Avoid statements that reduce a solution to two possible extremes: "America: Love it or leave it." "Put up or shut up." These statements eliminate every possibility in the middle.**

> Either grizzlies must be allowed to roam free in wilderness areas, or they will become extinct.

This statement doesn't allow for a logical discussion of the issue. Surely there are protection plans besides free roaming that could be considered.

"The whole of science is nothing more than a refinement of everyday thinking."

—— Albert Einstein

Persuasive Essays

Cesar Millan has made a life out of persuading dogs. Usually the pet owners have tried everything to break their dogs of biting or barking or straining at the leash or marking the recliner. Nothing works—until the "Dog Whisperer" shows up. His advice is simple: "Stay calm and assertive."

That's good advice for persuading people, too. When you write a persuasive essay, you want to sound knowledgeable, purposeful, and calm. This chapter will show you how to develop a persuasive essay that brings your topic to heel.

What's Ahead

- Persuasive Essay
- Quick Guide: Persuasive Writing
- Persuasive Topic Ideas
- Writing Guidelines
- Rubric for Persuasive Writing

Persuasive Essay

A persuasive essay provides an opinion and supports it with strong reasons. In the following persuasive essay, Dylan Elsen makes the case for clean energy.

Energy for the World

People are worried about energy. They seem to think that someday the lights of Broadway will go out and the freeways will turn into parking lots because we'll run out of fuel. Well, yes, fossil fuels will run out. The U.S. reached its peak oil production in 1971, Russia did in 1987, and Saudi Arabia will in 2014 (Wolf). But just because fossil fuels run out doesn't mean we have to run out of energy. The sun pours more energy on the earth in an hour than the whole world uses in a year. Restless winds and churning oceans and rolling rivers and even bubbling pools are all sources of energy. If we develop clean and renewable energy sources, we'll not only kick-start our economy but also save our planet.

The best aspect of new energy sources is that they are clean. Ever since cave dwellers discovered fire, humans have been burning things to cook their food and heat their homes. Eventually, they burned things to drive their machines, too. But whenever something is burned, it gives off carbon dioxide—a greenhouse gas that traps the sun's heat. The result is climate change, retreating glaciers, and rising oceans. A tenth of the world's population, 634 million people, live within 10 meters elevation from the current sea level ("The Risk"). If oceans rise, all these people will become refugees, and famines and wars will result. Using clean energy can slow or stop climate change.

The new energy sources are also renewable. The sun will not stop shining, the wind will not stop blowing, and the sea will not stop churning. Every place on earth has access to one or more of these types of energy. To be most efficient, energy will be produced where it is consumed—not shipped thousands of miles. That means local jobs and stronger economies. It also means fewer wars over resources.

Some people argue that the clean-energy technologies we have today cannot replace our current reliance on oil.

The writer addresses objections and answers them.

Photovoltaic cells, plates that convert light to electricity, are expensive to produce and don't work on cloudy days or at night. Electric cars do not have the range of gasoline vehicles and take a long time to recharge. Places with a lot of wind, such as Kansas and North Dakota, do not have large nearby cities to sell their electricity to.

Yes, these are real challenges, but challenges bring innovation. In 1961, John F. Kennedy challenged the U.S. to land a man on the moon by the end of the sixties ("Man on the Moon"). At the time, the country didn't have the technology to do so, but less than a decade later, it did. Similarly, in 2008, Al Gore confronted the U.S. with a bold new goal: "Today I challenge our nation to commit to producing 100 percent of our electricity from renewable energy and truly clean carbon-free sources within 10 years" (Gore). If we make clean energy our national goal, we can develop the new technologies we need and export them to the rest of the world.

Ending

The writer reviews the challenges and restates his opinion.

The world faces major challenges. Stores of fossil fuels are dwindling just as demand from China and India is surging. Fuel prices are spiking, which causes every other price to go up. Leaders turn fuel-hungry eyes on countries with large reserves, and armies of diplomats and soldiers go out to get them. Meanwhile, the seas rise. Climate change, wars, and economic meltdowns are symptoms of one problem, the world's addiction to fossil fuels. Clean energies can reduce all these problems and trigger economic development around the world.

Note: The works-cited page is not shown.

Patterns of Organization

Receptive Audience
Beginning
Most Important Reason
Less Important Reason
Objection and Answer
Ending

Resistant Audience
Beginning
Objection and Answer
Less Important Reason
Most Important Reason
Ending

Quick Guide ■ Persuasive Writing

To write persuasively, you need to convince your reader to agree with you or even to take action. That means you need to know a lot about your subject and about your reader. Only by thinking about the reader will you be able to appeal to the person's interests and desires.

Consider the Writing Situation

Ask yourself the following questions.

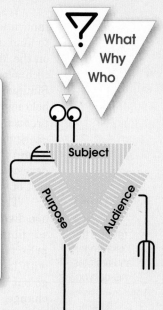

What
Why
Who

 Subject:
What subject do I have a strong opinion about?

 Purpose:
What reasons will help me persuade my reader?

 Audience:
How does my opinion match my reader's interests?

Link to the Traits

When prewriting, pay special attention to ideas, organization, and voice.

■ **Ideas:** Select a topic that you feel strongly about. State your opinion clearly and provide effective supporting reasons.

■ **Organization:** Organize the details in a persuasive order. If your audience is receptive, place your strongest reason up front. If your audience is resistant, start by answering objections.

■ **Voice:** Use a voice that shows you care about the topic— but avoid sounding too emotional. The most persuasive voice is calm but caring.

Persuasive Topic Ideas

The best persuasive writing begins with a topic you care about. Your job is to communicate your passion about the topic and convince your reader to care about it just as much. There are great topics all around you—at school, at home, in your community, and out in the world. Here are some persuasive topic ideas.

At School

Propose . . . starting school later, creating service learning, joining sports, joining theater, resolving conflicts, opting out of cliques, getting less homework, getting new computers, changing the school mascot, starting a new club

Promote . . . a concert, a fundraiser, a student band, a play, a sporting event, the school newspaper, school spirit, a new program or class, a favorite teacher, a new club, a candidate for student council, a new policy

At Home

Propose . . . rearranging the chores list, getting a new pet, rearranging a room, providing more privileges, setting up computer/TV rules, taking a family vacation, changing a holiday custom, negotiating a fairer bedtime, renovating a space

Defend . . . your right to privacy, your selection of clothes, your space, a friend who is not well liked, a family tradition, a favorite TV show, a favorite type of music, your weekend plans, how late you sleep

In the Community

Propose . . . building a skate park, beautifying the city, opening a teen center, saving a local theater, improving sidewalks, cleaning up a park, changing a curfew, starting a new organization

Promote . . . a charity event, a food bank, a car wash, an art exhibit, a museum, a local band, a community center, a building restoration, a community theater event, a haunted house, the Humane Society

In the World

Propose . . . ways to save the environment, ways to improve international relations, new technologies, better defenses, third-world debt relief, AIDS programs, help for disaster victims, better education, fairer trade

Promote . . . the Peace Corp, a branch of the military, a policy change, a candidate, a new law, an old custom, change in attitudes, international understanding, cultural exchange, family values, world music, open-mindedness

Writing Guidelines

Prewriting—Selecting a Topic

The first step in writing a persuasive essay is to find a topic you feel strongly about. Dylan came up with an idea by listing the best and worst things in his school, home, community—and the world. Then he chose a "best thing" he wanted to promote.

Best-Worst Chart

	School	Home	Community	World
Best	pep band	vacation	food bank	clean energy *
Worst	old gym	chores	crime	war

Forming an Opinion

After selecting a topic, you need to form your opinion about it. Your opinion can be a value claim (the goodness or badness of something), a policy claim (what should be done), or a truth claim (a hypothesis one hopes to prove). Dylan wrote each type of claim and then chose one to be his opinion statement (see asterisk).

Value claim: Our addiction to fossil fuels is causing many problems, problems that could be fixed by new energies.

Policy claim: The U.S. government should provide strong incentives for companies to develop alternative energies.

Truth claim: If we develop clean and renewable energy sources, we'll not only kick-start our economy but also save our planet.*

Helpful Hint

If you don't know enough about your topic, research it before forming your final opinion. Also be open to changing your mind as you research. The best opinions are *informed* opinions that are backed by accurate and complete information and facts.

Gathering Reasons

Once you have a strong opinion statement, you need to gather a variety of reasons to support it. Dylan gathered the following reasons.

Fact: The U.S. reached its peak oil production in 1971, Russia did in 1987, and Saudi Arabia will in 2014.

Statistic: A tenth of the world's population, 634 million people, live within 10 meters elevation from the current sea level.

Prediction: If oceans rise, all those people will become refugees, and famines and wars will result.

Anecdote: In 1961, John F. Kennedy challenged the U.S. to land a man on the moon by the end of the sixties. At the time, the country didn't have the technology to do so, but less than a decade later, it did.

Quotation: In 2008, Al Gore confronted the U.S. with a bold new goal: "Today I challenge our nation to commit to producing 100 percent of our electricity from renewable energy and truly clean carbon-free sources within 10 years."

Answering Objections

Next, you need to consider the opposing point of view. By mentioning an objection or two and then providing answers to the objections (countering them), you actually strengthen your argument. Dylan listed objections to his opinion and then wrote answers.

Objections

Current clean-energy technologies can't replace fossil fuels. Photovoltaic cells are expensive, and the sun doesn't always shine. Electric cars don't have a long range. Places with a lot of wind don't have nearby cities to sell their electricity to.

Answers

We can develop new technologies to answer these challenges. JFK proposed landing a man on the moon, and the technologies were created. Gore proposed 100 percent clean energy in 10 years. We could lead the development of new technologies and improve our economy.

Writing—Developing the First Draft

Now you are ready to write your persuasive essay. Each part of the essay has a different job to do.

Beginning ■ In the beginning, you need to get your reader's attention and lead up to your opinion statement. Here are some strategies for getting your reader's attention:

- Connect with the reader's concerns.
    People are worried about energy.

- Use a shocking statement.
    By 2014, oil production from Saudi Arabia—the largest oil producer in the world—will begin to decline.

- Begin with a strong quotation.
    "There are times in the history of our nation when our very way of life depends upon dispelling illusions and awakening to the challenge of a present danger," said Al Gore in 2008.

Middle ■ The middle part of your essay should present your reasons using order of importance. If your audience is receptive to your message, start with your strongest reason. If your audience is resistant, start by answering objections. Transition words and phrases can help you signal your organizational pattern. Here are some suggestions.

Transitions		
The main reason	In addition	Some people say
Most importantly	Furthermore	Opponents argue
By far the biggest reason	For that matter	Some challenges include

Ending ■ Develop a strong ending. Here are some strategies:

- Review your key reasons.
    Stores of fossil fuels are dwindling just as demand from China and India is surging.

- Sum up your argument.
    Climate change, wars, and economic meltdowns are symptoms of one problem, the world's addiction to fossil fuels.

- Revisit your opinion statement.
    Clean energies can reduce all these problems and trigger economic development around the world.

Revising and Editing—Improving the Writing

When you revise your persuasive essay, you add, cut, move, and rework ideas to make your writing stronger. Here's a quick checklist to guide your revising.

____ **Ideas** Is my opinion clear and supported by strong reasons?

____ **Organization** Do my reasons appear in the most persuasive order?

____ **Voice** Do I use a persuasive voice? (See below.)

____ **Word Choice** Do I use strong nouns and active verbs?

____ **Sentence Fluency** Do my sentences read smoothly?

____ **Conventions** Have I carefully checked punctuation, capitalization, spelling, and grammar?

A Closer Look at Revising: Persuasive Voice

Your best persuasive voice will connect to your topic and audience in the following ways:

1. **Knowledge of the topic** (Use a variety of details.)
2. **Concern about the topic** (Use a warm tone.)
3. **Respect for the reader** (Use appropriate language.)

If your voice is not persuasive, decide whether you need to show more knowledge, more concern, or more respect. Then revise your voice by following the advice listed in parentheses above.

A Closer Look at Editing: Punctuation

Commas are used to enclose an appositive—a word, phrase, or clause that follows a noun and renames, explains, or describes it.

> Photovoltaic cells, plates that convert light to electricity, are . . .
> └noun┘ └——————— appositive ———————┘
>
> A tenth of the world's population, 634 million people, live within . . .
> └noun┘   └——appositive——┘

If you can remove the appositive from the sentence without changing the meaning, use a comma before and after the appositive. If the appositive can't be removed, don't use commas.

Rubric for Persuasive Writing

Use this rubric to assess your persuasive writing.

Ideas

The writing . . .

— includes a clear, effective opinion statement.

— provides a variety of reasons to support the opinion statement.

— effectively answers objections.

Organization

— begins well by capturing the reader's interest and providing the opinion statement.

— effectively organizes the middle part.

— focuses on one main reason in each middle paragraph.

— ends well by reviewing the reasons and revisiting the opinion statement.

Voice

— shows that the writer cares about the topic.

— uses an appropriate emotional tone.

Word Choice

— uses precise nouns and active verbs.

Sentence Fluency

— uses a variety of sentence lengths and beginnings.

— flows smoothly from one sentence to another.

Conventions

— uses end punctuation and commas correctly.

— correctly capitalizes first words and proper nouns.

— avoids spelling errors.

— correctly uses words *(there, they're, their)*.

Other Forms of
Persuasive Writing

Can you remember the last time you went an entire day without having to deal with some sort of problem? Some problems are big and complicated, such as climate change. Other problems are small and easy to solve, such as feeling a little overheated.

In this chapter, you will learn how to write persuasively about the problems you encounter. You will also learn how to develop persuasive posters and brochures.

What's Ahead

- Problem-Solution Letter
- Writing Guidelines
- Persuasive Poster and Brochure
- Writing Guidelines
- Pet Peeve Essay
- Writing Guidelines

Problem-Solution Letter

Student Tyrell Cooper wrote the following problem-solution letter to his middle school principal after learning his school was considering canceling all field trips.

638 W. 43rd Street
Naperville, IL 60540
August 7, 2009

Mr. Edgar Martinez, Principal
Culver Middle School
4421 Wilson Drive
Naperville, IL 60530

Dear Principal Martinez:

Beginning
The beginning effectively leads up to the thesis statement (underlined).

I'll never forget the look on my brother's face after his seventh-grade field trip to the state capital. "What an incredible building!" he said, smiling from ear to ear. Ever since then, I have looked forward to visiting the capital. My excitement turned to disappointment this summer, though, when I read your letter stating that Culver Middle School is considering replacing field trips with virtual tours due to budget cuts and high gas prices. I don't want to see our school field trips canceled, and they will not have to be if students, teachers, and the community band together.

Middle
The first middle paragraph argues against cutting field trips, using various reasons.

Field trips are an important part of our education. Besides giving us a break from the daily grind of classroom work, field trips provide educational and sometimes life-changing experiences. A trip to an art museum could inspire a student to become an artist. In my brother's case, his field trip to the state capital sparked an interested in government. For some students, it's the first time they get to see what else life has to offer. These types of eye-opening experiences can't be duplicated in a classroom.

In your letter, you suggested replacing field trips with virtual tours. On the one hand, virtual tours give students

The second middle paragraph explains why one solution isn't the best.

an opportunity to see places from all over the world. On the other hand, I can watch those same tours at home or in the library. More importantly, the virtual experience does not have the same impact as reality. For example, compare a virtual tour of the Art Institute of Chicago to a field trip to the same place. What is more meaningful, seeing an awesome sculpture in person or seeing that same sculpture on a 14-inch computer screen? Seeing it in person, of course.

The last middle paragraph proposes the best solution.

A better solution is to organize a field-trip fund-raiser. I was thinking we could hold an all-school talent competition with the proceeds going toward funding field trips. Not only would this help raise money for our field trips, but it would also provide a great source of entertainment for everyone involved. Overall, the talent show would benefit our students, school, and community.

Ending
The ending counters a possible objection and gives a call to action.

People may think it's too much work to organize a successful fund-raiser such as a talent show, but all it takes is teamwork among students, teachers, parents, and community members. I hope this letter demonstrates how important field trips are to Culver students. It would be a shame to let them become a thing of the past.

Please consider my fund-raising idea as a solution to this problem.

Sincerely,

Tyrell Cooper

Tyrell Cooper

Pattern of Organization

Beginning	Middle	Ending
1. Grab the reader's attention.	3. Summarize the problem.	6. Answer an objection.
2. Introduce the problem.	4. Present possible solutions.	7. Give a call to action.
	5. Present best solution.	

Writing Guidelines

Prewriting—Selecting a Problem

When choosing a topic, consider problems in your home, school, or community. Once you have a topic in mind, identify a person or group who can help you solve the problem. Tyrell had a strong opinion about field trips and wanted to persuade his principal to take action to save them.

Gathering Details

Next, you will need to gather supporting information for your letter. You can do this by listing important questions (and answers) about your topic. Find out why the problem exists and why it should be solved. Here is the first part of Tyrell's list:

Details List

> **Why are field trips important?**
> - Spark students' interests in subjects
> - Provide a great visual learning tool
> - Give students a break from classroom work
> - Raise awareness of different cultures and lifestyles

You will also need to propose solutions to the problem. Tyrell completed a sentence starter to identify possible solutions.

Sentence Starter

> Field trips will be eliminated unless . . .
> the economy gets better.
> students pay with their own money.
> parents get involved.
> students start a fund-raiser.*
> our school wins the lottery.

> "Unless someone like you cares a whole awful lot, nothing is going to get better. It's not."
>
> Theodor Seuss Geisel, author of the Dr. Seuss books

Tyrell decided that a student fund-raiser would be the best possible solution to save his school's field trips.

Writing—Writing the First Draft

Beginning ■ Introduce the problem in an interesting way and then state the focus of your letter. Tyrell introduces his problem by sharing an experience. Here are three attention-grabbing strategies to consider:

- **Ask a question:** Would you rather see a famous sculpture in person or view it on a computer screen?
- **Quote someone:** "When you walk into that museum, your imagination explodes."
- **Share an experience:** I'll never forget the look on my brother's face after his seventh-grade field trip to the state capital.

Middle ■ In the first middle paragraphs, summarize the problem and offer possible solutions. Then present the best solution in the last middle paragraph. Tyrell's middle paragraphs follow this arrangement.

> **Helpful Hint**
>
> To make your writing voice sound convincing, use both mild helping verbs (like *could* and *may*) and strong ones (like *must* and *should*) with your persuasive verbs.

Ending ■ Answer any strong objection the reader might have and include a call to action. Tyrell's ending exhibits both these strategies:

- **Counterargument:** People may think it's too much work to organize a successful fund-raiser, but all it takes is a little teamwork.
- **Call to action:** Please consider my fund-raising idea as a solution to this problem.

Revising and Editing—Improving Your Writing

Use this checklist to help you revise and edit your letter.

____ **Ideas** Do I focus on a clear problem and solution?

____ **Organization** Does my letter have a clear beginning, middle, and ending?

____ **Voice** Does my voice sound polite, yet persuasive?

____ **Word Choice** Have I used specific nouns and persuasive verbs?

____ **Sentence Fluency** Do my sentences vary in length?

____ **Conventions** Is my writing free of errors?

Persuasive Poster and Brochure

Persuasive writing can combine with images in a poster or brochure, convincing people to attend an event. The poster and brochure below were created to work together, promoting a concert by a high school rock band.

Poster

A persuasive pitch calls the viewer to act.

An engaging image supports the pitch.

Answering the 5 W's helps the viewer act.

You've heard the rumors. . . .
Now hear the band!

The Cheetahs
Live in Concert
7:00 p.m., Saturday, May 5, Cooper Gym
$5 cover for **two hours of rock**

Brochure (front cover)

You've heard the rumors. . . .
Now hear the band!

The Cheetahs
Live in Concert
7:00 p.m., Saturday, May 5, Cooper Gym
$5 cover for **two hours of rock**

(interior spread)

The cheetahs . . . always prosper!
Who are the Cheetahs? They're a progressive rock power trio from right here in Burlington. On lead vocals, you'll find Karen Michaels. On guitars, you'll find Oscar Lohan. And on drums and sometimes bass, hear the sounds of Shriek Phillips.

(back cover)

What the critics are saying . . .

"The Cheetahs rocked Chocolate Fest, and now they'll rock Cooper Gym."
—Principal Armstrong

"When you hear Karen's vocals, Oscar's guitar riffs, and Shriek's crazy drums, you'll think you're at Alpine Valley."
—Mrs. Daily, music teacher

"Here's an up-and-coming high school band that's better than college groups and some of the stuff you hear on the radio."
—*Standard Press* review

"Don't walk. Don't run. Go cheetah-speed to hear this new group."
—Mrs. Michaels, band mother

Writing Guidelines

Prewriting

Selecting a Topic ■ Think of an event you want to promote in your school or community.

Gathering Details ■ Answer each of the 5 W's about the event—who, what, where, when, why.

Focusing Your Thoughts ■ Think about what your audience wants. Ask yourself how the event meets the audience's needs. Then write a persuasive pitch that connects to the audience's need:

> My audience wants . . . to have fun and be part of the "in" crowd.
> Persuasive pitch: You've heard the rumors. . . . Now hear the band!

Writing

Connecting Your Ideas ■ Create a poster or brochure that features your persuasive pitch. Add an image or two that will support your pitch. Then provide information to answer the 5 W's. Design your poster or brochure to effectively connect words and images.

Revising

Improving Your Writing ■ Make your poster or brochure better.

—— Does my persuasive pitch connect the event to the audience?
—— Do my images support my persuasive pitch?
—— Have I answered all 5 W's?
—— Have I encouraged the viewer/reader to act?
—— Is my poster/brochure eye-catching and well designed?

Editing and Proofreading

Checking for Conventions ■ Polish your poster or brochure.

—— Have I double-checked all facts (dates, times, locations, costs, names)?
—— Have I correctly capitalized first words and proper nouns?
—— Have I checked spelling and watched for easily confused words?

Pet Peeve Essay

In the following pet peeve essay, student writer Tessa Powell expresses her frustration about an unfortunate test-taking distraction. She uses an entertaining voice throughout the essay.

The Silence of the Sniffles

Beginning
The writer introduces her pet peeve by sharing a story.
She then leads to her thesis statement (underlined).

Miss Baker strode up and down the aisle placing a science test on each of our desks. I had studied for this monster for an entire week, and I felt confident that I could get an A. That is, until I heard it. "Ah-choo!" The boy next to me sneezed. I looked down at my test and tried to concentrate. But then the same boy started sniffling. These weren't ordinary sniffles, either. They were loud, growling sniffles. Twenty minutes later, he was still sniffling, and I was still working on the first part. When I'm trying to concentrate, nothing bugs me more than a classmate who constantly sniffles.

Middle
She uses humor to offer possible solutions.

Look, I understand how miserable it is to have a cold. Taking a super hard test while being congested is even worse. But is it that hard to walk up to the teacher's desk to grab a tissue? Better yet, can't the sniffler go to the bathroom and blow his nose? And if all else fails, can't he try breathing through his mouth? I heard that works just as well. He should just do something to spare the rest of the class from listening to his persistent sniffles.

Ending
The writer seizes upon a different approach to the problem.

It's foolish to assume anyone will follow my requests. For years, my test-taking abilities have suffered from others' loud sniffles, and I have done nothing to stop it. Maybe the best solution is to adapt to the situation, just like animals adapt to their environment. (You see? I told you I studied for my science test.) Somehow I need to muffle the sound of those annoying sniffles. Does anyone know where I can get some earplugs?

Writing Guidelines

Prewriting—Choosing a Topic

Picking a pet peeve topic is easy. You just need to think of something seemingly unimportant that *really* bugs you. Tessa used a cluster to find her topic.

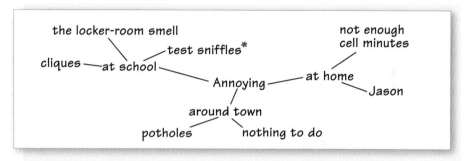

Gathering Details

Once you have a topic, consider specific experiences involving the pet peeve, why it upsets you, and how you can remedy the situation. Tessa gathered details by freewriting about the times when her pet peeve *really* upset her. (See page 34 for information about freewriting.)

Writing—Writing the First Draft

Beginning ■ Grab the reader's attention and reveal your true feelings about your pet peeve. Tessa introduces her pet peeve by sharing an experience.

Middle ■ Explain your pet peeve and offer some solutions. Tessa describes some ways in which people could get rid of their sniffles.

Ending ■ Present the best solution to your problem. Tessa admits her solutions probably won't work and offers a different approach to the problem.

Good Thinking

Pet peeve essays have an edge to them. One way to do this is to use sarcasm, or a mocking tone.

Revising and Editing Checklist ✓

When you revise, you make large-scale improvements by adding, moving, rearranging, and rewriting parts of your essay. When you edit, you make small-scale improvements by correcting any convention errors (punctuation, capitalization, spelling, and grammar). A checklist like the one that follows can help you revise and edit your pet peeve essay.

Pet Peeve Revising and Editing Checklist

Ideas
—— Does my essay focus on an identifiable pet peeve?
—— Do I include humorous or engaging details to explain the annoying problem?

Organization
—— Does my beginning grab the reader's attention and introduce the pet peeve?
—— Does the middle explain the pet peeve and offer solutions?
—— Does my ending leave the reader with a memorable idea?

Voice
—— Does my essay maintain an informal, entertaining voice?

Word Choice
—— Have I had fun with words? *(loud, growling sniffles)*

Sentence Fluency
—— Have I used different sentence lengths?

Conventions
—— Have I checked end punctuation and commas?
—— Have I correctly capitalized first words and proper nouns?
—— Have I checked spelling and easily confused words?

Editorials and Cartoons

In 1897, eight-year-old Virginia O'Hanlon heard her friends say Santa Claus didn't exist. She wasn't convinced, so she sent a letter to the editor of the *New York Sun* newspaper seeking the truth. The *Sun's* response remains one of the most read editorials in American history. Its message was this: "Yes, Virginia, there is a Santa Claus. He exists as certainly as love and generosity and devotion exist. Nobody sees Santa Claus, but that is no sign that there is no Santa Claus. The most real things in the world are those that neither children nor men can see."

Editorials are short persuasive essays of opinion found in newspapers. In most cases they respond to timely events and issues. In the course of history, editorials have influenced important decisions and helped shape public opinion. This chapter will show you how to write an editorial about the events happening around you.

What's Ahead

- Editorial
- Writing Guidelines
- Editorial Cartoons

Editorial

In the following editorial, Eduardo Balado presents his opinion that teenagers should be allowed to trick-or-treat on Halloween. His editorial was published in the opinion section in a local newspaper.

Teens Deserve a Treat, Too

Remember how much fun it was as a child to sort through handfuls of candy after trick-or-treating? This Halloween, Bridgewood teenagers won't have a chance to experience that feeling. The city is ordering an under-13 age limit for trick-or-treating. This decision is a mistake. Bridgewood should allow teenage trick-or-treating as a way to build community spirit.

The people who support a trick-or-treat age limit think teenagers are too greedy. Certainly, the goal of some teenagers is to get as much free candy as possible. But isn't stuffing bags with candy a trick-or-treating tradition for all ages, not just for teenagers?

Some people perceive teenagers as bullies who intimidate younger trick-or-treaters. The majority of teenagers simply are not this spooky. Instead of punishing a whole group based upon age, the city should ban the few bad apples.

Other citizens complain that teenagers shouldn't trick-or-treat because they don't bother to wear costumes. It's true that some teenagers go without costumes, but those who do dress up often wear the most creative costumes.

To make a teenager who is not in a costume "earn" a treat, a homeowner could ask the person to perform a simple talent. The trick-or-treater could tell a joke, do a cartwheel, or sing a song. In this way, teenagers and neighbors can have fun together instead of ignoring each other.

Ending
The ending leaves the reader with a strong final thought.

Or we could take the idea of teen trick-or-treating one step further and create a "Teen Trick-or-Treat for the Hungry" event. Teenagers who would want to dress up and experience trick-or-treating could collect canned goods in addition to getting candy on Halloween. The food would be donated to local charities or homeless shelters.

There are plenty of ways that teen trick-or-treating can be a positive experience for everyone. That's why the under-13 ban should be lifted. After all, Halloween brings out the kid in everyone. Don't make teenagers miss out on the fun.

Bridgewood Gazette

Opinion/Editorial

Teens Deserve a Treat, Too

Remember how much fun it was as a child to sort through handfuls of candy after trick-or-treating? This Halloween, Bridgewood teenagers won't have a chance to experience that feeling. The city is ordering an under-13 age limit for trick-or-treating. This decision is a mistake. Bridgewood should allow teenage trick-or-treating as a way to build community spirit.

The people who support a trick-or-treat age limit think teenagers are too greedy. Certainly, the goal of some teenagers is to get as much free candy as possible. But isn't stuffing bags with candy a trick-or-treating tradition for all ages, not just for teenagers?

Some people perceive teenagers as bullies who intimidate younger trick-or-treaters. The majority of teenagers simply are not this spooky. Instead of punishing a whole group based upon age, the city should ban the few bad apples.

Other citizens complain that teenagers shouldn't trick-or-treat because they don't bother to wear costumes. It's true that some teenagers go without costumes, but those who do dress up often wear the most creative costumes.

To make a teenager who is not in a costume "earn" a treat, a homeowner could ask the person to perform a simple talent. The trick-or-treater could tell a joke, do a cartwheel, or sing a song. In this way, teenagers and neighbors can have fun together instead of ignoring each other.

Or we could take the idea of teen trick-or-treating one step further and create a "Teen Trick-or-Treat for the Hungry" event. Teenagers who would want to dress up and experience trick-or-treating could collect canned goods in addition to getting candy on Halloween. The food would be donated to local charities or homeless shelters.

There are plenty of ways that teen trick-or-treating can be a positive experience for everyone. That's why the under-13 ban should be lifted. After all, Halloween brings out the kid in everyone. Don't make teenagers miss out on the fun.

Writing Guidelines

Prewriting—Selecting a Topic

An editorial without a strong opinion is like a song without a catchy chorus; it doesn't stick with the audience. Make sure you pick a topic you feel strongly about. It should be timely and of interest to your audience. Begin your topic search by finding out what's happening in your school and community.

If you can't think of a writing idea, try using sentence starters like Eduardo did for his trick-or-treat editorial.

Sentence Starters

At Bridgewood Middle School,
the biggest problem is . . . the library needs more computers.
the one change I would make is . . . getting better science equipment for experiments.

In the city of Bridgewood,
the biggest problem is . . . kids can't skateboard in the park.
one change I dislike is . . . that teenagers can't go trick-or-treating.

Gathering Details

Do plenty of research before you begin writing your editorial. You will need convincing support for your opinion in order to develop an effective editorial.

Eduardo interviewed friends and community members about teenage trick-or-treating. He created a quick list of the responses he received. Here is part of that list. (Eduardo put a star next to the response that he liked the most.)

Quick List

- Teenagers should not trick-or-treat because they are too old.
- Don't blame teenagers for carrying on such a fun tradition.
- Teenagers should have the courtesy to wear costumes.
- Teenage trick-or-treaters can build community spirit.*

Forming an Opinion Statement

Once you have researched your topic, you are ready to write an opinion statement. The opinion statement is a sentence that includes your opinion and the main reason for supporting it. Use the formula below to write an opinion statement for your editorial.

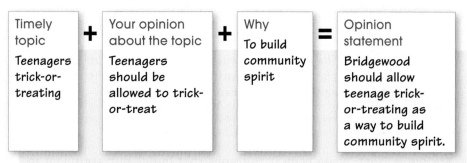

Timely topic	**+**	Your opinion about the topic	**+**	Why To build	**=**	Opinion statement
Teenagers trick-or-treating		Teenagers should be allowed to trick-or-treat		community spirit		Bridgewood should allow teenage trick-or-treating as a way to build community spirit.

Organizing Your Argument

The key to any good editorial is a convincing argument. To be convincing, you must address the opposing points of view and provide solid support for your own opinion. You can organize your argument in three different ways.

Opposition ⟶ Support ⟶ Solution

A common way to organize an argument is to begin by recognizing the other side's strongest point. Next, counter (reveal the weaknesses in) the opposing opinion and build support for your opinion. Finally, offer a solution that will solidify your argument.

Opposition 1 ⟶ Support 1 ⟶ Opposition 2 ⟶ Support 2 ⟶ Solution

When you must consider several strong opposing opinions, you may choose to address them one at a time. Organize the opposing points from most to least important. Also make a counterargument for each opposing point before moving on to the next. Eduardo uses this technique in his trick-or-treating editorial.

Support ⟶ Opposition ⟶ Solution

The third technique begins with your main points, addresses the opposition, and ends with a solution. This technique is usually used when the opposition has a weak argument.

Writing—Developing the First Draft

Beginning ■ Begin your editorial with a paragraph that grabs the reader's attention and includes your opinion statement. Notice how Eduardo starts his editorial with a thought-provoking question.

Eduardo's Beginning

> Remember how much fun it was as a child to sort through handfuls of candy after trick-or-treating? This Halloween, Bridgewood teenagers won't have a chance to experience that feeling. . . .

Middle ■ Next, write body paragraphs that build your argument in a logical way, address the opposing point of view, and offer a possible solution.

Helpful Hint

Your writing voice should sound confident but not arrogant. Be polite when addressing and countering the other side of the argument.

Ending ■ Close your editorial with a strong statement that will stick in the reader's mind.

Revising and Editing—Improving Your Writing

As you revise and edit your editorial, ask yourself if your work demonstrates the traits of effective writing.

____ **Ideas** Do I clearly state my opinion? Do I provide strong supporting reasons?

____ **Organization** Do I organize my arguments in an effective way?

____ **Voice** Is my voice polite and convincing?

____ **Word Choice** Do I use strong action verbs and specific nouns?

____ **Sentence Fluency** Do my sentences read smoothly?

____ **Conventions** Does my writing follow the rules of punctuation, capitalization, spelling, and grammar?

Editorial Cartoons

Cartoons are fun and entertaining, but they can also deliver a powerful message. Editorial cartoons use visual images and a few words to present an opinion. Most major newspapers have an editorial cartoonist on staff. Study how the following editorial cartoons respond to timely topics.

Sumay Bu's cartoon criticizes our TV-crazy culture.

Peter Boyle's cartoon comments on a problem in pro sports.

Chiara Lucinda's cartoon argues for a cleaner world.

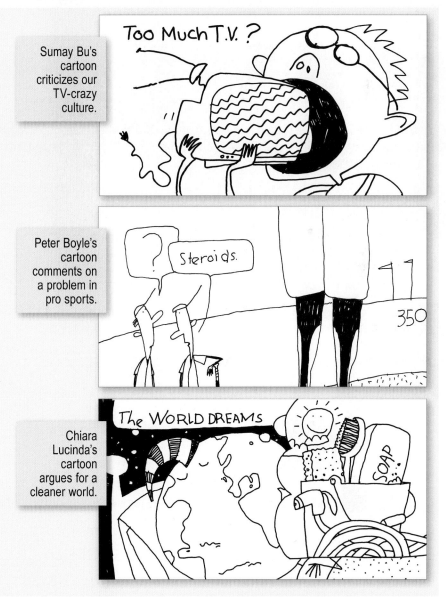

Writing About
Literature

Understanding
Literature

Literature is writing that is well crafted and packed with meaning. It often deals with events, emotions, and ideas that are common to all people. That's why you will find yourself nodding in agreement, laughing, and sometimes crying when you read a good book. And always, you will be left with something to think about. Here's a little secret: Good books usually hold more than one truth, which means that the message may be different from one reader to the next.

This chapter will prepare you for writing about literature. It names the different types of literature—each shares its message in a slightly different way. It also identifies the key parts or elements of literature— plot, characterization, theme, and so on. Lastly, this chapter includes ideas for writing literary analyses plus a list of common story patterns.

What's Ahead

- Types of Literature
- Elements of Literature
- Writing Topics
- Additional Starting Points for Writing
- Story Patterns

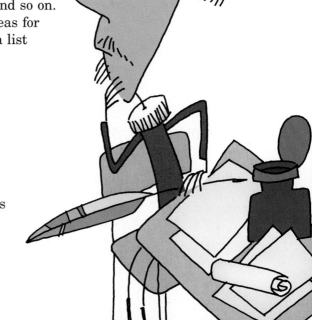

Types of Literature

These two pages identify many of the common types of literature.

Allegory	A story representing an idea or a truth about life
Autobiography	A writer's story of her or his own life
Biography	A writer's account of another person's life
Comedy	Writing that deals with life, often poking fun at people's mistakes
Drama	Writing that uses dialogue to share its message; meant to be performed in front of an audience
Epic	A long narrative poem telling of the deeds of a hero
Essay	Writing that expresses the writer's opinion or shares information
Fable	A brief story that teaches a lesson and often uses talking animals as the main characters
Fantasy	A story set in an imaginary world in which the characters usually have supernatural powers or abilities
Farce	Literature based on a humorous and improbable plot
Folktale	A story passed from one generation to another (The characters are usually all good or all bad and in the end are rewarded or punished as they deserve.)
Graphic Novel	A novel told through a combination of words and images
Historical Fiction	An imaginary story based on a real time and place in history
Memoir	Writing based on the writer's memory of a time, a place, or an incident

Myth	A story intended to explain some mystery of nature or cultural belief (The gods and goddesses have supernatural powers, but the human characters usually do not.)
Novel	A book-length, fictional prose story (Because of its length, a novel's plot can be complex and the characters can be many faceted.)
Novella	Literature that is longer than a short story, but shorter and less complex than a full-length novel
Parable	A short story that explains a belief or moral principle
Parody	Literature that intentionally uses comic effect to mock a literary work or style
Play	(See *drama*.)
Poetry	A literary work that uses concise language to express ideas or emotions (Examples: ballad, blank verse, free verse, elegy, limerick, sonnet)
Prose	Literature that uses the familiar spoken form of language, sentence after sentence
Realism	Writing that attempts to show life as it really is
Science Fiction	Writing based on real or imaginary scientific developments
Short Story	Literature that can usually be read in one sitting (It contains only a few characters and focuses on one problem.)
Tall Tale	A humorous, exaggerated story often based on the life of a real person (The main character usually accomplishes impossible things.)
Tragedy	Literature in which the hero is destroyed because of some tragic flaw in his or her character
Verse Novel	A novel told through the use of poetic form and language, featuring such techniques as rhyme, rhythm, metaphor, and symbolism

Elements of Literature

The next two pages describe important elements or parts of literature. This information will help you discuss and write about novels, poetry, essays, and other literary works.

Action Everything that happens in a story

Antagonist The person or force that works against the hero of the story (See *protagonist*.)

Character A person or an animal in a story

Characterization The methods a writer uses to develop a character

Here are three methods:

- Sharing the character's thoughts, actions, and dialogue
- Describing her or his appearance
- Revealing what others in the story think of this character

Conflict A problem or struggle between two forces in a story

Here are the five basic conflicts:

- **Person Against Person** A problem between characters
- **Person Against Self** A problem within a character's own mind
- **Person Against Society** A problem between a character and society, school, the law, or some tradition
- **Person Against Nature** A problem between a character and some element of nature—a blizzard, a hurricane, or so on
- **Person Against Destiny** A problem or struggle that appears to be well beyond a character's control

Dialogue The conversations between two or more characters

Foil A character who serves as a contrast or challenge to the main character

Mood The feeling or emotion a piece of literature creates in a reader

Moral The lesson a story teaches

Narrator The person or character who actually tells the story, giving background information and filling in details between portions of dialogue

Plot The action that makes up the story, following a plan called the plot line

Plot Line The planned action or series of events in a story (The basic parts of the plot line are the beginning, the rising action, the high point, and the ending.)

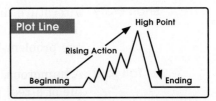

- **Beginning** The opening part of a story (Usually, the characters are introduced, the background is explained, and the setting is described in this part.)

- **Rising Action** The central part of the story during which a conflict is dealt with
- **High Point** The moment when the conflict is strongest and the main character must act upon it
- **Ending** The closing part of a story telling how the main character has changed

Point of View The angle from which a story is told (The angle depends upon the narrator, or person telling the story.)

- **First-Person Point of View** This means that one of the characters is telling the story: "Linda is my older sister, beautiful and popular."
- **Third-Person Point of View** In third person, someone from the outside of the story is telling it: "Linda is her older sister, beautiful and popular." There are three third-person points of view: *omniscient, limited omniscient,* and *camera view* (See the illustrations.)

Protagonist The main character or hero in a story

Setting The place and the time of a story

Theme The message that is directly or indirectly revealed in a story

Tone The writer's attitude toward his or her subject

Total Effect The impact that a story has on a reader

Third-Person Points of View

Omniscient point of view allows the narrator to share the thoughts and feelings of all the characters.

Limited omniscient point of view allows the narrator to share the thoughts and feelings of only one character.

Camera view (objective view) allows the storyteller to record the action only from his or her own point of view, unaware of the characters' thoughts or feelings.

Writing Topics

These ideas are arranged according to the four main elements of literature: *plot, characterization, setting,* and *theme.* You could write an effective literary analysis or book review by developing one or more of these ideas.

Plot   The action of the story

- How is suspense built into the story? (Consider the important events leading up to the high point.)
- The high point (the most important event) changes the story in an effective way . . . in a believable way . . . in an unbelievable way.
- The ending is surprising . . . predictable . . . unbelievable.
- Are there any twists or reversals in the plot? What do they add to the story?

Characterization   The people or animals in a story

- The main character changes from _____ to _____ by the end of the story.
- Certain forces or circumstances—people, setting, events, or ideas— make the main character or characters act as they do.
- _____ is the main character's outstanding personality trait.
- What if the main character had (or hadn't) . . .
- The main character acts or reacts to the conflict in a surprising, predictable, or unusual way.

Setting   The time and place of the story

- The setting helps make the story exciting or _____.
- The setting has an important effect on the main character.
- The setting (in a historical novel) offers important details about a certain time in history.
- The setting (in a science-fiction novel) creates a new and exciting world.

Theme   The author's statement or lesson about life

- Ambition . . . courage . . . jealousy . . . greed . . . happiness . . . peer pressure . . . is clearly a theme in (title of book).
- This book showed me what it is like to be . . .
- The moral "Don't judge a book by its cover," "Haste makes waste," "Hard work pays off," . . . is developed in (title of book).

Additional Starting Points for Writing

These questions may prompt your thinking for a literary analysis or another type of response to a novel. By changing the questions slightly, you can use this same list to react to plays, poems, and short stories.

■ Making Connections

1. What were your feelings after reading the opening chapter(s) of the book? After reading half of the book? After finishing the book?
2. Did the book make you laugh? Cry? Cringe? Smile? Explain.
3. What is the most important word in the book? The most important passage? The most important event? Explain.
4. Who else should read this book? Why?

■ Points of Interest

5. What are the best parts of this book? Why? The worst parts? Why?
6. Do you like the ending of the book? Why or why not?
7. What came as a surprise in the book? Why?
8. What parts of the book seem unbelievable? Why?
9. What makes you wonder in this book? What confuses you?

■ Character Study

10. In what ways are you like any of the characters? How so?
11. Do any of the characters remind you of a character in another piece of literature? Explain.
12. What would you and one of the characters talk about?
13. Which character would you like to be in this book? Why?
14. How does the main character act throughout the book? Explain. Do these actions change her or him in any way? How so?

■ Careful Reflections

15. Do you think the title fits the book? Why or why not?
16. What is the author saying about life and living?
17. How have you changed after reading this book? Explain.
18. How would you have liked the novel to end? Why?
19. What do you know now that you didn't know before?
20. What questions in this book would you like answered?

Story Patterns

Many of the short stories and novels that you read will follow one of the story patterns listed below. In a literary analysis, you could explain or reveal how a piece of literature follows one of these patterns.

■ The Discovery

In a *discovery* story, the main character follows a trail of clues to discover a secret. Mystery and suspense novels use this pattern.

A young man discovers a surprising box of receipts in his attic.

■ The Quest

In a *quest,* the main character goes on a journey into the unknown, overcomes a number of obstacles, and returns either victorious or wiser. Many ancient myths follow this pattern, but so do many modern stories.

A young woman sets out to find her long-lost father.

■ The Choice

The *choice* pattern shows the main character making a difficult decision. Suspense builds as the decision draws near.

A middle school student must decide between dating a popular boy or getting to know a boy who just moved to town.

■ The Rite of Passage

In the *rite of passage* pattern, a difficult experience changes the main character in a major and lasting way. These stories are also called "coming of age" stories.

A young soldier learns about courage while on the battlefield.

■ The Reversal

The *reversal* pattern is one in which the main character follows one course of action until something causes him or her to think or act in a different way.

A young woman lives for volleyball until her best friend comes down with a serious illness.

Literary Analysis

Developing a literary analysis helps you think critically about a piece of literature. In an analysis, you first identify an important feature to explore. For example, you could trace how the main character changes in a story, or you could discuss the importance of a particular symbol. Analyses usually deal with the main elements of literature—*plot, characterization, setting,* and *theme*. (See page 244.)

Base the ideas in your analysis on a close reading of the text. You will likely reread the text, or at least parts of it, more than once during the development of your writing. Your goal is to share something important that you have learned through your reading and analyzing. Present the results of your work in a carefully planned essay.

What's Ahead

- Literary Analysis
- Quick Guide: Literary Analysis
- Writing Guidelines
- Rubric for Writing About Literature

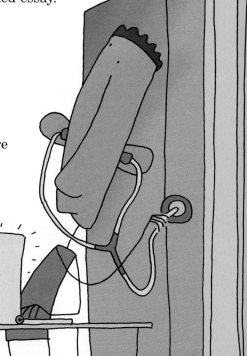

Literary Analysis

The short story "The War of the Wall" tells about a boy and his friend plotting to stop an artist from painting a mural on "their" wall. This analysis displays the writer's clear understanding of the story.

A Wall of Emotions

Beginning

The beginning introduces the story and states the thesis (underlined).

In Toni Cade Bambara's short story "The War of the Wall," a young boy fumes and stews as a lady comes into town to paint a mural. Her work dominates his every thought and feeling. <u>In a surprising turn at the end of the story, the boy learns that he shouldn't draw conclusions before learning all the facts.</u>

The story begins with the boy, who is the narrator of the story, and his friend Lou observing the painter lady at work. They're shocked that an outsider is doing anything to their wall. Older folks sit in its shade, and the boys pitch pennies against it. More importantly, Jimmy Lyon's name is chiseled high on the wall to honor him after he was killed in the Vietnam War. The boys tell the lady exactly what they think: "So we just flat out told the painter lady to quit messing with the wall" (328). But she just goes on about her work. This gets the narrator so steamed that he almost shakes the ladder she is on.

Middle

The middle paragraphs trace the development of the theme through the main character's actions.

When the boys return after school, the lady is chalking the wall into sections. She is so focused on her work that she doesn't take notice of the Morris twins holding a meal for her. Eventually, Side Pocket from the pool hall convinces the lady to come down from her ladder. She looks at the food, politely declines it, and climbs right back up the ladder. After watching this, the boy says, "Lou had to drag me away, I was so mad" (329). He couldn't believe that the lady could be so rude.

The boy then hopes that his mother and father will help him. Unfortunately, his father only wants to talk about going to the family farm. His mother does lose her patience with the lady that evening, but later feels bad about it because she knows that being an artist is hard. The boy says, "Me and Lou didn't want to hear that. Who did the lady think she was, coming into our neighborhood and taking over our wall?" (332). He realizes that the two of them will have to take care of things by themselves.

While at the farm, the boys decide to spray graffiti over the lady's work. So after school on Monday, they set out for the wall with some spray paint. Surprisingly, everybody except for the painter is crowded in front of the wall. The boy tries to describe what he sees: "Reds, greens, figures outlined in black. Swirls of purple and orange. Storms of blues and yellows. It was something" (333). It even had figures that resembled the boy and Lou.

The last things the boy sees leave him breathless. The lady had painted Jimmy Lyon's name in a rainbow and included an inscription saying that she dedicated the mural to her cousin Jimmy Lyon. This is where the story ends, so no one can know for sure what is going through the boy's mind. Undoubtedly, though, he must have felt ashamed about jumping to conclusions about the lady who gave the town such a treasure.

Direct quotations bring the main character to life.

Ending
The ending describes the last scene and revisits the theme.

This literary analysis is organized chronologically.

Patterns of Organization

Chronological Order

Beginning
First Part of the Story
Middle Part
Middle Part
Final Part
Ending

Order of Importance

Beginning
Least Important Point
Next Important Point
Most Important Point
Ending

Quick Guide ■ Literary Analysis

Your feelings about a book or a story serve as the perfect starting point for writing about it. You may have felt the main character's pain or shared in her or his joy. Then again, you may have thought that the ending was perfect or far too (yawn) predictable. When developing a literary analysis or a book review, you share feelings like these with the reader.

Consider the Writing Situation

To get started on a literary analysis or book review, think about the writing situation.

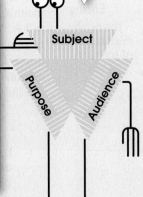

What
Why
Who

Subject

Purpose
Audience

 Subject:
What piece of literature do I feel strongly about?

 Purpose:
Am I writing to inform, persuade, entertain, or do some of each?

 Audience:
Will the reader be interested in this book or story?

Link to the Traits

Pay special attention to ideas, organization, and voice.

- **Ideas:** Write about a book that truly interests you. Focus your writing on one or two key elements and support your main points with examples from the text.

- **Organization:** Organize your writing in the most effective way—time order, order of importance, or logical order.

- **Voice:** Use a voice that shows your interest in the literature and that connects with the reader.

Writing Guidelines

Prewriting—Identifying Topic Ideas

To get started, use a chart to list two or three favorite stories. Then select one story to analyze.

Ideas Chart

Story and author	What the story is about	What the main character is like
"Thank You, Ma'm" by Langston Hughes	A boy tries to rob an old lady, but she drags him home.	Roger is a tough kid until he gets caught.
"Helen on Eighty-Sixth Street" by Wendi Kaufman	A girl tries to understand why her dad went away.	Vita is very smart.
∗ "The War of the Wall" by Toni Cade Bambara	A boy wants the outsider to leave "his" wall alone.	The boy seems very sure of himself.

Identifying an Element to Analyze

A literary analysis usually focuses on one of the main elements of fiction: plot, characterization, setting, or theme. (See page 244 for writing ideas.)

The literary analysis on pages 248–249 traces the story's theme.

Elements of Fiction

Plot: The action of the story; what happens first, next, last

Characterization: What the characters do, say, think, and so on

Setting: Where and when the story takes place

Theme: The message or lesson of a story; revealed either directly or indirectly

Prewriting—Focusing on Theme

The most challenging element to analyze may be theme, especially since it is seldom directly stated. Here are five ways to uncover the theme in a story.

Strategies for Identifying the Theme

1. Consider clues in the title.
   - "The War of the Wall"   - "There Will Come Soft Rains"

2. Follow the main character's words and actions.
   - In "The War of the Wall," the main character comes to many hasty conclusions about the outsider before he realizes his mistake.

3. Identify key figures of speech.
   - Authors often include a key metaphor, symbol, or other figure of speech to convey meaning. For example, Jimmy Lyon's name on the wall symbolizes the community.

4. Look for the author's statements about life.
   - "The very best thing in all this world that can befall a man is to be born lucky."
     —Mark Twain, "Luck"

5. Apply a common theme to the story.
   - Decide if the main character displays *courage, understanding, love, generosity,* or so on. Or determine if a lesson (moral) applies to your story.

Writing a Thesis Statement

Once you have a focus in mind, you are ready to write a thesis statement. This statement should identify the main point of your analysis. One way to do this is to connect the main character to the theme. Follow this simple formula to write your thesis statement.

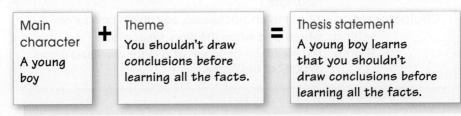

Main character		Theme		Thesis statement
A young boy	**+**	You shouldn't draw conclusions before learning all the facts.	**=**	A young boy learns that you shouldn't draw conclusions before learning all the facts.

Gathering Details

With a thesis in mind, you are ready to gather details for your analysis. Start by completing a character chart in which you trace the main character's thoughts, feelings, and actions throughout the story.

Character Chart

Story title: "The War of the Wall"

Theme: Don't draw conclusions before learning all the facts.

First stage: The main character's thoughts, feelings, and actions in the <u>beginning</u> of the story
- can't believe an outsider wants to change the wall
- tells the painter lady to leave the wall alone

Middle stage: The main character's thoughts, feelings, and actions in the <u>middle</u> part of the story
- thinks the lady is rude for not accepting a homemade meal
- asks his father for help
- hears his mother speaking up for the lady
- schemes with Lou on ways to reclaim the wall

Final stage: The main character's thoughts, feelings, and actions in the <u>last</u> part of the story
- plans on spray-painting over the lady's work
- looks in amazement at the completed mural
- realizes the mural honors a local boy killed in Vietnam

Helpful Hint

You can't analyze a piece of literature without talking about the main character and the plot. However, as you discuss these two elements, make sure that your essay doesn't turn into an extended plot summary.

Prewriting—Using Direct Quotations

During your planning, find a few quotations from the story to use in your analysis. Consider what each quotation reveals about your thesis. The student writer of the literary analysis on pages 248–249 gathered the following quotations.

Quotations

"So we just flat out told the painter lady to quit messing with the wall." (page 328)
- shows the main character lacks patience
- doesn't trust outsiders

"Lou had to drag me away, I was so mad." (page 329)
- anger intensifies
- thinks that the painter is rude

"Reds, greens, figures outlined in black. Swirls of purple and orange. Storms of blues and yellows. It was something." (page 333)
- looks in amazement at the mural
- left speechless by it

Organizing the Middle Paragraphs

In each middle paragraph, address a different stage in the development of your thesis. (See page 255.) This writer planned his middle paragraphs by writing a possible topic sentence for each one. (If necessary, you can change these sentences later on.)

Topic sentence 1 (first stage):
The story begins with the boy and his friend Lou observing the painter lady at work.

Topic sentence 2 (middle stage):
When the boys return after school, the lady is chalking the wall into sections.

Topic sentence 3 (middle stage):
The boy then hopes that his mother and father will help him.

Topic sentence 4 (final stage):
While at the farm, the boys decide to spray graffiti over the lady's work.

Writing—Developing the Beginning and Middle

Carefully develop each part of your essay following these guidelines.

Beginning ■ In the beginning paragraph, do three things:
- name the title and author of the story or book,
- give background information, and
- state your thesis.

> Background info
>
> Thesis
>
>   In Toni Cade Bambara's short story "The War of the Wall," a young boy fumes and stews as a lady comes into town to paint a mural. Her work dominates his every thought and feeling. <u>In a surprising turn at the end of the story, the boy learns that he shouldn't draw conclusions before learning all the facts.</u>

Middle ■ Support or develop the thesis in the middle paragraphs. Start each paragraph with one of your topic sentences (see page 254). Then work in supporting details. (See pages 253 and 256.)

> Topic sentence
>
> Specific details
>
> Quotation
>
>   <u>The story begins with the boy, who is the narrator of the story, and his friend Lou observing the painter lady at work.</u> They're shocked that an outsider is doing anything to their wall. Older folks sit in its shade, and the boys pitch pennies against it. More importantly, Jimmy Lyon's name is chiseled high on the wall to honor him after he was killed in the Vietnam War. The boys tell the lady exactly what they think: "So we just flat out told the painter lady to quit messing with the wall" (328). But she just goes on about her work. This gets the narrator so steamed that he almost shakes the ladder she is on.

Good Thinking

When good thinkers can't get started, they might (1) talk about the writing with a classmate, (2) illustrate important events and then write about each illustration, or (3) write a conversation between themselves and the main character.

Writing—Developing the Ending

Ending ■ The ending is your final chance to comment on and explore your thesis. Here are some suggestions for this final part of your essay:

- ■ Include a final idea.
- ■ Refer back to the thesis.
- ■ Use a revealing quotation from the story.
- ■ Tell how the main character has changed.
- ■ Include an important idea that keeps the reader thinking.

Final idea

Reference to thesis

> The last things the boy sees leave him breathless. The lady had painted Jimmy Lyon's name in a rainbow and included an inscription saying that she dedicated the mural to her cousin Jimmy Lyon. This is where the story ends, so no one can know for sure what is going through the boy's mind. Undoubtedly, though, he must feel ashamed about jumping to conclusions about the lady who gave the town such a treasure.

Adding Support in an Analysis

It's important to support or explain your thesis with details from the piece of literature. Here are some examples of support:

- ■ **Quotations** are word-for-word statements from a story or book. (See page 254.)
- ■ **Summaries** tell in a few sentences what the author says in a section of the story.
  While at the farm, the boys decide to spray graffiti over the lady's work. So after school on Monday, they set out for the wall with some spray paint.
- ■ **Sensory details** capture specific images from the story.
  Older folks sit in its shade, and the boys pitch pennies against it. More importantly, Jimmy Lyon's name is chiseled high on the wall to honor him after he was killed . . .
- ■ **Interpretations** give a specific view about part of the story.
  This is where the story ends, so no one can know for sure what is going through the boy's mind. Undoubtedly, . . .

Revising and Editing—Improving Your Writing

Once you finish your first draft, set it aside for a while, and then ask a trusted classmate or family member to read it. Ask the person what works well and what could work better. Then use the following checklist as your revising and editing guide.

____ **Ideas** Have I clearly stated and supported my thesis?

____ **Organization** Does my analysis have a clear beginning, middle, and ending?

____ **Voice** Does my voice sound knowledgeable?

____ **Word Choice** Have I used specific nouns and verbs?

____ **Sentence Fluency** Do my sentences read smoothly?

____ **Conventions** Is my writing free of errors?

A Closer Look at Revising: Completing Quotations

If you use quotations in your analysis, make sure that they flow logically from the preceding ideas and that you follow them with your own thoughts or with additional information.

In the writer's first draft, he concluded the third paragraph with a quotation. One of the changes he made was to add an idea to emphasize the quotation's importance in the development of the thesis.

> . . . She looks at the food, politely declines it, and climbs right back
>
> up the ladder. After watching this, the boy says, "Lou had to drag
>
  He couldn't believe that the lady could be so rude⊙
> me away, I was so mad" (329).∧

A Closer Look at Editing: Punctuating Quotations

To punctuate a quotation, put exact words from the story within quotation marks. To cite a quotation using MLA style, identify in parentheses the page on which it appears. (See page 328.)

> The boy says, "Me and Lou didn't want to hear that. Who did the lady think she was, coming into our neighborhood and taking over our wall?" (332).

Rubric for Writing About Literature

This rubric is a helpful checklist for assessing literary analyses and other responses to literature.

Ideas

The writing . . .

___ presents a clearly stated thesis that focuses on plot, characterization, setting, or theme.

___ includes specific details and quotations from the text to develop or support the thesis.

Organization

___ follows a specific pattern of organization: chronological, order of importance, or logical order.

___ contains an effective beginning, middle, and ending.

___ includes transitions as needed to connect ideas and paragraphs.

Voice

___ sounds believable and informed.

___ reflects the writer's clear understanding of the literature.

Word Choice

___ exhibits a careful choice of words.

___ explains unfamiliar terms.

Sentence Fluency

___ flows smoothly from one idea to the next.

Conventions

___ follows the standards for punctuation, capitalization, spelling, and grammar.

___ cites quotations correctly.

Other Forms of
Writing About
Literature

Many readers turn to their newspaper's entertainment section to read reviews of movies, books, and CD's. Reviews get people thinking and talking about current entertainment: "Hey, did you see what Novak had to say about . . . ?" They also help people decide if they should bother to see a current movie or read a new book in the first place. The best reviews are informative, persuasive, and entertaining.

Of course, a book review expresses a critic's opinion about the worth of a new book. But a good critic doesn't simply say that a book is good or bad. He or she includes specific details from the text, and, perhaps, references to similar books to support all opinions expressed. This chapter will help you (1) write effective book reviews of your own and (2) write a letter to an author.

What's Ahead

- Book Review
- Writing Guidelines
- Responding with a Letter

Book Review

In her review of Lois Lowry's *The Giver*, Natalie Jackson focuses on the main character's dilemma, or problem.

Beginning
The opening sets the scene and states the focus (underlined).

Middle
Specific examples from the novel support the focus.

Ending
The reviewer reflects on the book's value.

Better Safe Than Sorry?

Imagine a "safe" world with no muggings, stealing, or war. Would you like to live there? What if this place didn't let you make your own choices? Would you still be interested? In Lois Lowry's science-fiction novel *The Giver*, Jonas lives in such a place. He is quite satisfied with his life, until he meets the Giver, and then everything changes.

Jonas's world is an eerie place where the Elders control everything. When a boy wants to get married, the elders choose his wife. When a girl needs new clothes, the Elders give her a uniform. When a family needs food, the Elders choose the items. Worst of all, when someone turns 12, the Elders assign the person a job for life! Now that's spooky.

Jonas seems content, but, of course, this is the only world that he has known. Then, when he turns 12, the Elders make him the next Receiver of Memory. His job is to remember lessons from the past, when people made their own choices. The Giver is Jonas's teacher. He shows Jonas people in the past making bad choices that led to fighting and hate. But he also shows people making good choices that led to fun, family parties, and love.

Jonas has to choose between these two worlds, one safe and controlled, and the other one free but risky. The Giver also informs Jonas that the only "safe" people are those that the Elders think are useful. Useless people are usually killed. With all of this knowledge, Jonas is faced with his most important decision: How does he want to live, and for how long?

On one level, *The Giver* is a terrific page-turner. You won't be able to put the book down until you find out what happens to Jonas. On another level, the book gets you thinking about some heavy issues like governmental control, quality of life, and deciding your own fate. For both reasons, *The Giver* is a must-read.

Writing Guidelines

Prewriting—Choosing a Topic

Review a book that you have recently read, one that you have strong feelings about. But be sure that the book is appropriate for your audience.

Gathering Details

Use a basic collection sheet to plan your review. State the title and author at the top of the sheet; then list important ideas and examples from the book that you want to discuss.

Collection Sheet

<u>The Giver</u> by Lois Lowry

- The Elders in Jonas's world make all the decisions.
- When he turns 12, Jonas is chosen as the Receiver of Memory, and the Giver is his teacher.
- The Giver teachers Jonas about choices.
- Jonas has to choose between a safe or a risky world.

Writing—Writing the First Draft

Beginning ■ In the opening paragraph, grab the reader's interest, name the title and author of the book, and state your focus. Natalie uses questions to draw the reader into her review.

Middle ■ In the middle part, develop your focus. Natalie used her collection sheet to help her decide what to include.

Ending ■ In the closing paragraph, reflect on the book's value and discuss why the reader should (or shouldn't) read the book. Natalie discusses the book's value on two different levels.

Helpful Hint

Don't give away the whole story. Say just enough to get the reader's interest.

Revising **and** Editing—Improving the Writing

Remember that revising consists of adding, moving, reordering, and rewriting parts. Editing deals with checking the revised writing for correctness. The checklist that follows can help you revise and edit your book reviews.

_____ **Ideas** Have I included enough information to help a reader decide whether or not to read the book?

_____ **Organization** Does my review have a clear beginning, middle, and ending?

_____ **Voice** Do I sound informative, persuasive, and entertaining?

_____ **Word Choice** Have I used specific nouns and verbs?

_____ **Sentence Fluency** Does my writing flow smoothly from one idea to the next?

_____ **Conventions** Is my review free of errors?

A Closer Look at Revising: **Sentence Fluency**

After reviewing her first draft, Natalie felt that the sentences at the start of the fourth paragraph were too short and choppy. She combined them so that they read more smoothly.

> *one safe*
> Jonas has to choose between these two worlds, ~~One world is~~ and controlled, and the other one ~~safe and controlled. The other world is~~ free but risky. The Giver also informs Jonas that the only "safe" people are those that the Elders . . .

A Closer Look at Editing: **Using Commas in a Series**

While editing her revised writing, Natalie adds commas to separate three phrases in a series. (A series contains at least three items.)

> On another level, the book gets you thinking about some heavy issues like governmental control, quality of life, and deciding your own fate. . . .

Responding with a Letter

In the following letter to author J. K. Rowling, Devon Steel shares his appreciation for the Harry Potter series.

555 Broadway
New York, NY 10012
November 2, 2009

Dear J. K. Rowling,

    I've been an avid reader of the Harry Potter books for a number of years now. My favorite one is *Harry Potter and the Order of the Phoenix*. It has so much action and suspense that I needed to catch my breath after reading some chapters.

    One thing that you do so well is develop really intriguing characters. You always explain the hopes, dreams, and fears of the main characters like Harry, Ron, and Hermione, but you also tell about the lives of supporting characters like Luna Lovegood, Severus Snape, and Dobby, the house-elf.

    When you include supporting characters in a new scene, you say something about their appearance or you mention what they did in a previous chapter. I like this technique because it helps me remember how the characters fit into the story.

    I would like to know how you create all of these incredible individuals. I mean, there are hundreds of them in the series! When I try to write my own stories, I have a hard time developing just two or three characters. How do you do it? Do you have any tips for me?

    Thanks so much for creating Harry Potter. I'm sad the series is over, but it was one crazy adventure while it lasted. I hope you will have time to respond to my questions.

Sincerely,

Devon Steel

Devon Steel

Beginning
The writer introduces himself and his reason for writing.

Middle
The writer mentions what he likes and poses a question.

Ending
The writer thanks the author and asks for a reply.

Creative
Writing

Writing
Stories

In *One Thousand and One Arabian Nights*, a paranoid king decrees that his wife, a woman named Scheherazade, is to be beheaded in the morning. Scheherazade spends the night before her execution telling the king a fabulous story. Her tale is reaching the most exciting part when dawn breaks. The king wants so much to hear the amazing ending that he stays her execution until the next morning. That night, Scheherazade finishes the first story and starts another one, leading up to the most exciting part again when the sun rises. The king lets her live another day. And so, for 1,001 nights, Scheherazade tells stories that not only save her life but also rid the king of his paranoia.

This is the power of stories. Whether you are sitting by a campfire or are nestled in your favorite spot, stories entertain and enlighten. They help you make sense of your world. The model and guidelines in this chapter will help you write your own amazing tales.

What's Ahead

- How Stories Develop
- Short Story
- Writing Guidelines
- A Short-Story Sampler

How Stories Develop

Writing a story is like cooking food. First you gather the ingredients and then you prepare them according to a recipe. As you go along, you season your story with "spices," such as effective dialogue, colorful descriptions, and thoughtful explanations.

The Plot

The plot is the main ingredient in any story. It refers to all of the action—the events that move a story along from start to finish. A plot has five basic parts: *exposition, rising action, climax, falling action,* and *resolution*. The plot line that follows shows how these parts all work together.

Plot Line

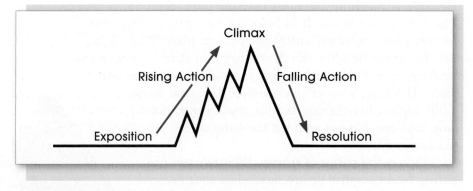

A Closer Look at the Parts . . .

■ Exposition

The exposition is the beginning part of a story in which the characters, setting, and conflict are usually introduced. There is at least one main character in all stories and, almost always, one or more supporting or secondary characters. The setting is where and when the story takes place, and the conflict is the main problem that fuels the action. Here is a summary of the exposition in one story.

> Callum is a shy seventh grader who receives a wristwatch for his birthday. Callum had wanted a digital watch, but this one is analog and needs to be wound. Worse yet, it doesn't keep accurate time. Frustrated, Callum tries to reset the watch, only to discover that by moving the hands backward and forward, he can travel through time.

Rising Action

In the rising action, the main character tries to solve his or her problem, getting involved in at least two or three important actions along the way. This builds suspense into the story.

First action: Callum and his watch travel backward in time to earlier that day, when Bruce Buckstead, the school bully, insulted him. This time, Callum has the perfect comeback ready, and the bully stalks away.

Second action: Callum returns to the present and begins using his watch whenever things don't go his way. If he trips, he goes back and corrects it. If he doesn't know the correct answer to a question, he finds out and then goes back in time and answers correctly.

Third action: Soon, Callum is considered the smartest, funniest, fastest, most amazing kid at his school. Bruce Buckstead becomes jealous and corners Callum in a hallway.

Climax

The climax is the most exciting or important part in a story. At this point, the main character comes face-to-face with his or her problem. (All of the action leads up to the climax.) This part is sometimes called the turning point.

Bruce tries to punch Callum, but Callum turns the watch back and dodges just in time. A crowd of kids gathers, watching Callum dodge punch after punch. But during one dodge, Callum's watch hits the wall and breaks. He's defenseless, and Bruce closes in.

Falling Action

In this part, the main character learns to deal with life "after the climax." Perhaps he or she makes a new discovery about life or comes to understand things a little better.

Bruce never touches Callum, though, because the other kids tell him to back off. They say they're done being bullied, and that if Bruce wants to get at Callum, he's got to go through all of them.

Resolution

The resolution brings a story to a natural, surprising, or thought-provoking conclusion. (The falling action and the resolution often are very closely related.)

Though Callum has lost his magic watch, he's gained a whole lot of new friends—and a lot more confidence.

Short Story

The following story by student writer Andrea Carpenter tells about a girl's first day at a new school and how she turns a disability into a special ability.

Exposition
The beginning introduces the characters and the conflict.

Dialogue shows the personality of the characters.

Rising Action
A series of actions develops the main conflict.

Dealing with Ceiling Fans

Felicity Silvers sat in the nurse's office of her new school, her fingers clinging tightly to the chair beneath her. She let her long black hair fall in a curtain across her face.

Nurse McCracken bustled in. "Welcome to Franklin Middle School, Felicity. I have to get a weight and height for all new students. Do you know how much you weigh?"

Felicity looked up with dread. "I weigh zero."

Nurse McCracken didn't smile. "No one weighs zero."

"I do," Felicity said. "That's the problem."

"Enough funny business, young lady," the nurse said, wagging her finger. "Please step up on the scale."

Felicity shrugged, knowing what would happen next. She peeled her fingers from the chair and slowly stood up. The moment her knees were straight, though, her feet left the floor, and she floated up into the air. "See?" Felicity said, flinging her hands out in exasperation.

Nurse McCracken gaped. "You get down from there, young lady! You can't just go floating around like that."

"I can't help it."

"Do you want to be suspended?"

"It looks like I already am."

Nurse McCracken's face turned white, and she pointed above Felicity. "Look out! The ceiling fan!"

"I know! I know!" Felicity replied. (People who weigh nothing get used to dealing with ceiling fans.) She reached up to the center hub and pushed off. The push sent her angling down toward the ground.

"That's better," Nurse McCracken began, but when Felicity's feet hit the floor, she pushed off again, flying out the door. "I've got to get to class."

"I need your weight and height!"

As Felicity floated away down the hall, she said, "You already know my weight, and I'd say I'm about nine feet high."

The writer provides background information.

That seemed to appease Nurse McCracken because she let Felicity drift away. Felicity couldn't really walk down the hallway. Instead, she had to sort of swim along or zigzag by bounding from wall to wall. Once, in her last school, she got caught in the hall during a passing period, and the other students bounced her like a beach ball. Felicity had tried wearing heavy boots or putting rocks in her pockets, but nothing worked. Whatever she wore turned weightless, too—like the Midas touch, but with gravity.

At last, Felicity reached the door to her first class. She clawed her way down the wall, grabbed the doorknob, and swung her feet to the floor. "Okay. Try to look normal." Felicity opened the door and stepped through, holding on to the door frame.

Thirty faces looked up from desks, and the teacher—Ms. Hornblow—stopped writing on the board and glanced her way. "You must be Felicity Silvers."

"Yes," said Felicity.

Ms. Hornblow gestured toward an empty desk at the back of the class. "Please, take a seat."

There was no way to get to the seat and keep her feet on the floor. Felicity drew a deep breath, looked Ms. Hornblow in the eye, and said, "There's something you need to know about me."

"Yes?"

"I can't walk."

Climax

Tension builds to crisis point.

Ms. Hornblow scowled. "Didn't you just walk through the door?"

Giggles from the class made Felicity's face flush, but she lifted her chin and said, "I can't walk. Not really. But I *can* fly." And with that, she launched herself over the heads of the class.

Some kids gasped. Others screamed. All watched in amazement as the new girl soared overhead.

One boy in back stood up and grabbed her hand, pulling her down. "Wow! You're like a superhero. Here, sit next to me."

Falling Action and Resolution

The final action leads to a surprising conclusion.

Felicity smiled, climbing into the seat. "Thanks."

"I always wanted to fly," the boy said. "I'm Matt."

"Felicity," she said. "And, yeah, I guess it *is* pretty cool." Maybe life at Franklin Middle School was going to work out after all.

Writing Guidelines

Prewriting—Creating a Character

Interesting characters make interesting stories. The desires of the characters shape the plot. By creating a character and understanding the person inside and out, you'll soon know what type of story you want to tell. Andrea created Felicity Silvers by filling out a character creator chart.

Character Creator Chart

Name: Felicity Silvers

Gender: Female   Age: 13

Height: 4'10"   Weight: 0

Hair: Black/Straight   Eyes: Brown

	1	2	3	4	5	6	7	8	9	10	
Weak		☆									Powerful
Slow								☆			Quick
Clumsy				☆							Dexterous
Dull							☆				Brilliant
Shy			☆								Outgoing
Insane								☆			Sane

The character wants . . . __to fit in with the other students at her new school.__

The character fears . . . __that people won't accept her because she weighs 0 pounds and floats through the air.__

The character plans to . . . __hide her problem from the people at her new school.__

Forming a Conflict

Once you have created a strong character, think about what challenge or problem the character would be likely to have. The main character's problem is the conflict, which comes in several forms. Andrea brainstormed different conflicts for her character.

Person vs. Person: Felicity's mother has "grounded" her, and Felicity has to find a way outside.

Person vs. Society: Felicity is arriving at school and is trying to fit in with people who don't float. *

Person vs. Nature: Felicity has to get to school on a windy day.

Person vs. Fate: Felicity realizes that she should use her weightlessness to become a superhero.

Person vs. Self: Felicity has a crush on a boy but fears rejection because she is weightless.

Creating a Plot

After choosing a conflict, imagine a set of events that demonstrate the conflict. Each event should challenge the main character, building toward a climax—the most exciting part. Andrea created the following plot.

Rising Action

Event 1: The nurse tries to get Felicity's weight.

Event 2: Felicity floats down the hall.

Event 3: Felicity has to reach the back of class.

Climax: She tells the class she can't walk, but then flies overhead.

Resolution: By being herself, Felicity makes a new friend and fits in.

Writing—Writing the First Draft

After completing the prewriting activities described on pages 270–271, begin writing your first draft.

Exposition ■ Grab your reader's attention by starting your story right in the middle of the action. As you develop this part, try to identify the main character, the setting, and the main problem. (See the beginning of the short story, page 268, for an example.)

Rising Action and Climax ■ Let your characters' conversations (dialogue) and actions move the story along as much as possible. (See "Writing Dialogue" below.)

Falling Action and Resolution ■ In most stories, the action quickly comes to a close after the climax. What happens in this part should show how the main character has been affected by the climax.

Helpful Hint

Readers don't need (or necessarily want) a nice, neat, "everybody lived happily ever after" ending. But give them something—even if it's nothing more than a natural, smooth close to the action.

Writing Dialogue

Refer to these guidelines when you develop dialogue in your short stories. (Also study the dialogue in the short story, pages 268–269.)

- Write the way people actually speak. (People often interrupt each other.)
- Focus on the speaker's beliefs or problem. (Generally, one speaker's beliefs clash with another's.)
- Keep the conversation moving along. (Characters don't have to say everything. Leave some things to the reader's imagination.)
- Present the dialogue so it is easy to read. (Indent every time someone new speaks and identify the speaker if it isn't clear who is talking. See pages 461–462 for help with punctuation.)

Revising and Editing—Improving Your Writing

Ask yourself the following questions when you review and revise your first draft.

- Do the characters' words and actions seem natural? (We wouldn't expect the neighborhood bully to talk like a college professor.)
- Is there a real or believable conflict that keeps the story going?
- Do all of the characters play an important role in the story? Are all of the conversations, explanations, and events important? (Make sure that your story moves along at a steady clip. You don't have to tell the reader everything.)
- Is the main character put to the test at the climax in the story? (The main character should undergo some change because of this event.)
- Does the story make sense and contain enough detail and background information? (Fill in any holes or gaps in the story line.)
- Does the narrator's voice engage the reader?
- Do the sentences read smoothly?
- Do all of the words "work" within the context of the story?
- Are punctuation, capitalization, spelling, and grammar correct?

Topping Off Your Writing

Here's how to top off your writing with a good title. Think of your title as fish bait: it should look juicy, it should dance slightly, and it should have a hook in it.

- To look juicy, a title must contain strong, colorful words. (*The Black Stallion, Brave New World*)

- To dance, it must have rhythm. (*The Old Man and the Sea,* not The Sea and the Old Man)

- And to hook your reader, it must grab the imagination. (*Never Cry Wolf,* not Life Among the Wolves)

List a number of possible titles; then select the one that provides the best bait for your reader.

A Short-Story Sampler

Here are brief descriptions of popular short-story types. Use these as starting points for your own stories.

■ Mystery

Think of a crime, a list of suspects, a criminal, a star detective, and you're ready to write your first whodunit. Pay close attention to the mysteries on TV to see how screenwriters develop their stories, or try reading books by Agatha Christie, Joan Lowery Nixon, Alane Ferguson, Tony Hillerman, and Sir Arthur Conan Doyle.

■ Fantasy

Add some fantastic elements to real-world situations and create a fantasy. Think of some of your favorite childhood stories for ideas. Many of these stories contain fantastic elements (animals that talk, bathtubs that become pirate ships, and so on.). Joan Aiken, Lloyd Alexander, and Alan Garner are fantasy writers you may enjoy reading.

■ Science Fiction

Imagine a world 100 years after a nuclear war. Who would be living? What would life be like? What would the people know about life as it was before the war? This is science fiction—when life as we know it is dramatically altered in some way. Read "By the Waters of Babylon" by Stephen Vincent Benét for a great story along these lines.

■ Myth

All of us have a fascination with myths. They are wonderful stories that attempt to explain some natural phenomenon. Create your own myth, explaining why we cry, why early summer is tornado season, or, perhaps, why diamonds are so valued. For inspiring stories, read ancient myths from cultures such as Greece, Egypt, Norway, or the indigenous people of North America.

■ Fable

Write a brief story that makes a point, teaches, or advises. There are two basic ways to do this: Start with a moral and develop a story that leads up to it, or develop a story and decide afterward what it teaches or advises. The ancient writer Aesop wrote many fables.

Writing
Plays

A play is basically a story brought to life. The words don't stay on the page, but instead come out of the mouths of actors. Descriptions turn into costumes and props and sets, and the play itself may be a little different every time it is performed —fresh, like a new creation.

This chapter will help you take a story you have written and turn it into a play, or it will help you generate a new play from scratch. Through dialogue and stage direction, you can bring any story to life.

What's Ahead

- Play
- Writing Guidelines

Play

Andrea Carpenter turned her story "Dealing with Ceiling Fans" (see pages 268–269) into a play. Part of the play follows.

Dealing with Ceiling Fans

The **cast of characters** introduces the people in the play.

Characters: **Felicity Silvers,** a student who weighs 0
Nurse McCracken, the school nurse
Ms. Hornblow, Felicity's first-hour teacher
Matt, Felicity's new friend

(Felicity sits clinging to a chair in the nurse's office as Nurse McCracken bustles in.)

Dialogue sets the scene and introduces the problem.

NURSE: Welcome to Franklin Middle School, Felicity. I have to get a weight and height for all new students. Do you know how much you weigh?
FELICITY: *(reluctantly)* I weigh zero.
NURSE: No one weighs zero.
FELICITY: I do. That's the problem.
NURSE: *(sternly)* Enough funny business, young lady. Please step up on the scale.

(Felicity slowly stands and begins to float.)

Stage directions (in parentheses) capture the action.

FELICITY: *(exasperated)* See?
NURSE: You get down from there, young lady! Do you want to be suspended?
FELICITY: It looks like I already am.
NURSE: Look out! The ceiling fan!
FELICITY: I know! I'm used to them!

(Felicity pushes off the center hub and drops toward floor.)

Special terms such as *offstage* help actors know what to do.

NURSE: That's better.
FELICITY: *(bounding off floor and offstage)* I've got to get to class.
NURSE: I need your weight and height!
FELICITY: *(offstage)* You already know my weight, and right now I'm about nine feet high! . . .

Writing Guidelines

Prewriting—Selecting a Topic and Gathering Details

Dramatize an existing story or create a new one. One student filled out the following plot chart to develop a new play.

Plot Chart

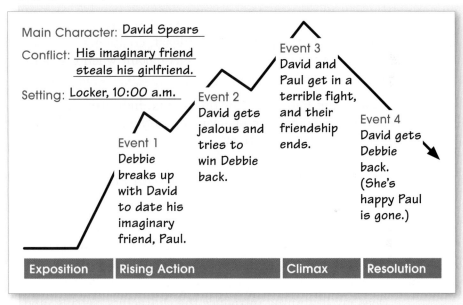

Main Character: David Spears

Conflict: His imaginary friend steals his girlfriend.

Setting: Locker, 10:00 a.m.

Event 1
Debbie breaks up with David to date his imaginary friend, Paul.

Event 2
David gets jealous and tries to win Debbie back.

Event 3
David and Paul get in a terrible fight, and their friendship ends.

Event 4
David gets Debbie back. (She's happy Paul is gone.)

| Exposition | Rising Action | Climax | Resolution |

A Closer Look at Stage Direction

You can use the following terms in your stage direction.

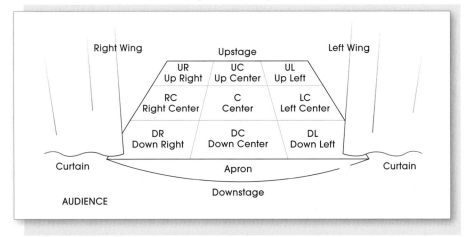

Right Wing Upstage Left Wing

UR Up Right	UC Up Center	UL Up Left
RC Right Center	C Center	LC Left Center
DR Down Right	DC Down Center	DL Down Left

Curtain Apron Curtain

Downstage

AUDIENCE

Writing—Developing Your Play

Beginning ■ Introduce your characters, establish the setting (time and place), and begin the conflict. Note how the play on page 276 does all of this by the time Felicity speaks her first line. Remember your tools:

- **Dialogue and action** reveal your characters' personalities and desires.
- **Costumes, props, and sets** help establish the setting.
- **Conflict** is a problem the character faces and must overcome.

Middle ■ Develop the conflict through a series of actions. Each action should intensify the problem or, at least, create greater risk for the character. Build the tension to a climactic point when the main character either succeeds or fails.

Ending ■ Show what happens after the climax, indicating how the main character has changed in one way or another. End with a surprising or thoughtful resolution.

Revising and Editing—Improving Your Play

Use the following checklist to revise and edit your play.

Ideas

____ Do I have interesting characters and a strong conflict?

____ Do I use dialogue and action to move the play along?

Organization

____ Does my beginning introduce the characters, setting, and conflict?

____ Does my middle build the conflict toward the climax?

____ Does my ending show how the character has changed?

Voice

____ Does my dialogue fit the characters' personalities?

Word Choice

____ Does my stage direction use the appropriate terms?

Sentence Fluency

____ Does my dialogue sound natural and conversational?

Conventions

____ Does my play follow the proper format? (See page 276.)

____ Have I checked my capitalization, punctuation, and spelling?

____ Does my grammar reflect the way people actually talk?

Writing
Poetry

Of all forms of creative writing, none is more loved, or more hated, than poetry. Some people love the unique way in which poetry allows them to share their thoughts and feelings. Others enjoy reading and listening to the rhymes, rhythms, and images of poetry. As for those who dislike poetry? Well, they probably haven't given it a good try lately— at least not as it is described in this chapter.

Actually, you've probably had more experience with poetry than you think. As an infant, you were rocked to sleep with cradle rhymes like "Rock-a-bye baby, in the treetop." Later, you chanted jump-rope jingles like "Hank and Frieda / sittin' in a tree / K-I-S-S-I-N-G." Today, you certainly have favorite song lyrics and advertising jingles. All of these examples are poetry of a sort.

What's Ahead

- What Is Poetry?
- Reading and Appreciating Poetry
- Writing Guidelines
- Traditional Techniques of Poetry
- Traditional Forms of Poetry
- Other Forms of Poetry

Poet Tree

What Is Poetry?

The poet Marianne Moore defines poetry as "imaginary gardens with real toads in them." This definition may seem strange, but that's why it suits poetry so well. Other writing may be serious and factual, but good poetry is always creative and, at times, a bit playful. An effective poem takes us away to an "imaginary garden," yet it often springs from a real experience—one of the many "toads" hopping in and out of our daily lives.

What makes poetry different from prose (the regular writing you do)? Here are some of the differences that make poetry so special.

■ Poetry looks different from prose.

Poems are written in lines and stanzas (groups of lines), leaving a fair amount of white space on the page. Here is a four-line stanza from a poem about a visit to the beach:

> My little sister took her stand
> on the pavement, off the sand,
> staring out toward the ocean,
> wide-eyed at the waves' commotion.
> —Fredrick Silguero

■ Poetry sounds different.

Poets pay special attention to the sounds in their writing. Here are some of the techniques that make poems pleasing to the ear.

- **Repeat words:** I see water, I see sky, and I see sun.
- **Rhyme words:** Ever go away? . . . Happy every day.
- **Repeat vowel sounds:** Lonely old bones.
- **Repeat consonant sounds:** Sparkling silver stars.
- **Use words that sound like what they mean:** Eggs crack. Splat!

■ Poetry speaks to the heart.

Poetry asks you to feel something (that's the heart part), not just think about it. You can tell how the poet feels about being alone in the following example:

> On a lonely day
> a book of poems can be
> like a new friend
> saying
> "I once was lonely too."
> —Arielle Homburg

■ Poetry speaks to the senses.

Poets create word pictures that build an image in your mind. Notice how the following examples appeal to different senses.

> From up here, everything is angles.
> Brown fields and pale green fields square off.
> Straight gray roads intersect, paralleled by fences.
> Even the sun behind the clouds spreads
> two bright rays like the legs of a compass.
> —Scott Galvis

> The clack and scratch
> of chalk on a blackboard
> sounds confident,
> not like the squeak and squish
> of a marker on whiteboard.
> —Julee Jue

> Stiff old gym socks
> soften up
> when feet start to sweat.
> —Doug Rosener

Reading and Appreciating Poetry

If you know the rules and the strategies, watching a baseball game can be almost as much fun as playing baseball yourself. Real fans of the sport not only enjoy the game as it unfolds, but they also love to talk about the experience afterward.

The same is true of poetry. Once you know something about the rules and conventions, reading poetry can be extremely enjoyable. Of course, writing a poem or two of your own increases your appreciation, as does talking about favorite poems with other "fans." The following suggestions will help you get the most out of the poems you read.

Apply Your Knowledge

As you read a poem, apply what you know about poetry in general.

- Ask yourself what pictures come to mind. What do you see and hear? How does the poem make you feel?
- Pay attention to the poem's structure. How does it look on the page? Does the poem have a unique shape?
- Pay attention to the words and the sounds in the poem. Is rhyme or repetition used? What other creative uses of language do you notice?
- Does the poem follow a definite pattern of rhythm, or does it seem to flow more naturally?

Read Carefully

Use these tips as a general guide to reading poetry.

- Read the poem slowly and carefully. Enjoy each and every word.
- Read the poem several times. With each reading, you will notice new things about the poem, and you will enjoy it more.
- Read the poem aloud. Notice the way its words and phrases flow.
- Try to catch the general meaning of the poem during your first reading. Knowing the general meaning will help you understand the poem's more difficult parts.
- Share the poem with your friends and discuss it afterward. Their insights will help you enjoy the poem even more.

Poems

Read and enjoy the following two student poems. (Remember to follow the tips and strategies listed on the previous page.)

Sidewalk Crack

What images do you see as you read this poem?

There's a crack in the sidewalk
in front of our house
where a tree root grows
and it keeps getting bigger.

When I was little
it was just a bump
for the left rear tire
of my red tricycle
as I rode down the block,
then again on the right
as I rode back.

What rhythm do you hear in the lines of this poem?

Nowadays I use it
as a skateboard ramp.
It's just a few inches
but I can pretend
I'm an X Games champ.

My mom says we need
to get that root out
but I've seen flat sidewalks
and they're no fun.

—Moises Leacock

Precious

How does reading this poem affect your understanding of the title?

When my little dog lies in the sun,
the light glows golden on his fur.
And sometimes when he turns his head
his eye becomes a gem of amber.

—Daniela Michalec

Writing Guidelines

Writing poetry is a lot of fun. It allows you to use language in special ways. It also lets you share an experience or a feeling in ways that will stir your reader's emotions.

Writing poetry is also work. Good poets write and rewrite their poems many times to get the best effect from the fewest words. The guidelines that follow will help you write a free-verse poem, a poem that does not require regular rhythm or rhyme.

Prewriting—Choosing a Topic

Choose a topic you really care about.

- **Remember an important time or event in your life:** a special trip, the first day at a new school, a special gathering you attended.
- **Look at the world around you:** the sparkle of summer sun on a pond, a stuffed animal, loose litter cluttering a yard.
- **Describe something you like or dislike:** a tasty food, a favorite sweater, a case of the flu, a muggy day.
- **Think of a favorite person:** a grandparent, a historical figure, a sports hero, your best friend.

Gathering Details

Begin collecting ideas about your subject. Student writer Lauren Moran decided to write about a grassy lawn. Here is her initial cluster of ideas.

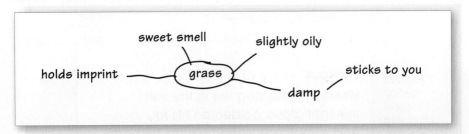

After you have collected enough details, look for a powerful idea or image (mental picture) to use as the main focus of your poem.

Writing—Writing the First Draft

Don't worry about writing the perfect poem in your first draft; just write freely until you've said all that you need to say about your subject. And don't overlook the senses—the sights, sounds, and tastes related to the topic.

One of the nice things about writing a free-verse poem is that it can take any form. Often the form will develop naturally as you write—perhaps a simple list of phrases will do the job. As long as it makes sense to you and the reader, your poem can look any way you like. Lauren Moran wrote her first draft in list form.

> GRASS POEM
> the damp grass sweet scented
> oily clippings clinging to our hair
> and clothes as we stood up
> leaving our own imprints on the lawn
>   —Lauren Moran

Revising—Improving Your Writing

After you complete your first draft, carefully review your poem. Also make sure to have at least one other person read and react to it. Use the following checklist as your reviewing guide:

_____ **Ideas** Are my ideas complete? Do they convey the meaning and feeling I want to convey?

_____ **Organization** Do the line breaks work well? Does the form add to the poem's effect?

_____ **Voice** Does my voice fit the topic, the meaning, and the feeling of the poem?

_____ **Word Choice** Have I carefully selected each word for sound and meaning?

_____ **Sentence Fluency** Does my poem flow as I intend?

Editing—Checking for Style and Accuracy

Check your revised poem for punctuation, capitalization, spelling, and grammar errors. Ask someone else to check your work for errors as well. Then write a correct final copy of your poem. Proofread this copy before sharing it.

Helpful Hint

In a free-verse poem, you do not have to capitalize the first word in each line. The choice is yours. Use end punctuation marks or other punctuation as you would in regular prose. Or don't use punctuation at all if you don't feel it is necessary. (See the poem below.)

Free-Verse Poem

Lauren Moran decided to write the final version of her poem in the shape of a blade of grass. (Or is it a sickle?) Notice that she changed some of the words and images she used in her first draft.

Grass Poem

the
damp
grass
sweet
scented
clippings
clinging to
our hair &
clothes as
we rose
leaving
imprints
on the
lawn

—Lauren Moran

Publishing

Poems can be shared in many creative ways. For example, poetry and art complement each other extremely well. Poetry can also be performed. All you need is a bit of preparation and a willing audience.

Poetry and Art

- **Poster:** Present your poem, together with an illustration or a drawing, on a piece of poster board.
- **Bookmark:** Write your poem on a colorful piece of paper cut to bookmark size and shape. Decorate the bookmark in any way you wish.
- **Greeting Card:** Create a greeting card. Write your poem on the front and add a personal message inside. Or write your poem inside and illustrate the front of the card.

Poetry and Drama

- **Oral Reading:** Reciting poetry aloud is an effective way to share its rhythm. Consider using background music for your performance. Be sure to practice your delivery until it is smooth and dramatic before you read to your audience.
- **Perform a Poem:** It can be fun to perform a poem with different people reciting different sections. To get started, script the poem to show who should read the different lines. A script for Scott Galvis's poem about angles (page 281) is provided below.

Script

Three voices are needed. The poem is color-coded to indicate voice 1, voice 2, and voice 3.

> From up here, everything is angles.
> Brown fields and pale green fields square off.
> Straight gray roads intersect, paralleled by fences.
> Even the sun behind the clouds spreads
> two bright rays like the legs of a compass.

Traditional Techniques of Poetry

Most traditional poems follow exact patterns of rhyme and rhythm. Consider this famous traditional poem by Leigh Hunt:

Rondeau

Jenny kissed me when we met,	(a)
Jumping from the chair she sat in;	(b)
Time, you thief, who love to get	(a)
Sweets into your list, put that in:	(b)
Say I'm weary, say I'm sad,	(c)
Say that health and wealth have missed me,	(d)
Say I'm growing old, but add,	(c)
Jenny kissed me.	(d)

Rhyme and Meter

In most traditional poetry, the rhyme is organized in patterns called **rhyme schemes**. (See the letters in parentheses above.)

Meter is the rhythm, or pattern of accented (´) and unaccented (˘) syllables, in the lines of a poem. In the poem above, every other syllable is accented. (Jénnў kíssed me whén wĕ mét.) This pattern of accented and unaccented syllables creates the poem's meter. (See *foot* and *verse* on page 289 for more information on meter.)

Other Poetry Techniques

Alliteration ■ The repeating of beginning consonant sounds.
    creamy and crunchy

Assonance ■ The repetition of vowel sounds, as in the following lines from "The Hayloft" by Robert Lewis Stevenson.
    Till the shining scythes went far and wide
    And cut it down to dry.

Consonance ■ The repetition of consonant sounds anywhere within words, not just at the beginning.

> The sailor sings of ropes and things
> In ships upon the seas.

End Rhyme ■ The rhyming of words at the ends of lines, as in the following familiar lines.

> My country, 'tis of thee,
> Sweet land of liberty . . .

Foot ■ One unit of meter. There are five basic feet:
Iambic: An unaccented syllable followed by an accented one (rĕ péat)
Trochaic: An accented syllable followed by an unaccented (old ĕr)
Anapestic: Two unaccented syllables before one accented (ĭn tĕr rúpt)
Dactylic: An accented syllable followed by two unaccented (ó pĕn lў)
Spondaic: Two accented syllables (heárt breák)

Internal Rhyme ■ The rhyming of words within one line of poetry.

> Jack Sprat could eat no fat (or) Peter Peter pumpkin eater.

Onomatopoeia ■ The use of a word whose sound makes you think of its meaning, as in *buzz, gunk, gushy, swish, zigzag, zing,* or *zip.*

Quatrain ■ A four-line stanza. Common rhyme schemes in quatrains are *aabb, aaba,* and *abab.*

Repetition ■ The repeating of a word or phrase to add rhythm or to focus on an idea, as in Edgar Allan Poe's "The Raven."

> While I nodded, nearly napping, suddenly there came a tapping,
> as of someone gently rapping, rapping at my chamber door—

Stanza ■ A division in a poem named for the number of lines it contains. Below are the most common stanzas.

Couplet	two-line stanza	*Sestet*	six-line stanza
Triplet	three-line stanza	*Septet*	seven-line stanza
Quatrain	four-line stanza	*Octave*	eight-line stanza

Verse ■ A name for a line of poetry written in meter. Verse is named according to the number of "feet" per line. Here are eight types:

Monometer	one foot	*Pentameter*	five feet
Dimeter	two feet	*Hexameter*	six feet
Trimeter	three feet	*Heptameter*	seven feet
Tetrameter	four feet	*Octometer*	eight feet

Traditional Forms of Poetry

Poetry has been around for centuries, beginning with bards and messengers who used poems to pass along news, songs, and stories. Today, we find poetry in songs, on greeting cards, in reading anthologies, and so on. Here are some traditional forms of poetry.

Ballad ■ A ballad is a poem that tells a story. Ballads are usually written in four-line stanzas called quatrains. Often, the first and third lines have four accented syllables; the second and fourth have three. (See "Quatrain" on page 289 for possible rhyme schemes.) Here is a quatrain from "The Enchanted Shirt" by John Hay.

> The King was sick. His cheek was red
> And his eye was clear and bright;
> He ate and drank with a kingly zest,
> And peacefully snored at night.

Blank Verse ■ Blank verse is unrhymed poetry with meter. The lines in blank verse are 10 syllables in length. Every other syllable, beginning with the second syllable, is accented. (*Note:* Not every line will fit this description exactly.) Consider these first three lines from "Andrea Del Sarto" by Robert Browning.

> But do not let us quarrel any more,
> No, my Lucrezia; bear with me for once:
> Sit down and all shall happen as you wish.

Cinquain ■ Cinquain poems are five lines in length. There are syllable and word cinquain poems.

Syllable Cinquain

Line 1: Title	2 syllables
Line 2: Description of title	4 syllables
Line 3: Action about the title	6 syllables
Line 4: Feeling about the title	8 syllables
Line 5: Synonym for title	2 syllables

Word Cinquain

Line 1: Title	1 word
Line 2: Description of title	2 words
Line 3: Action about the title	3 words
Line 4: Feeling about the title	4 words
Line 5: Synonym for title	1 word

Couplet ■ A couplet is two lines of verse that usually rhyme and state one complete idea. (See *stanza* on page 289.)

Elegy ■ An elegy is a poem that states a poet's sadness about the death of an important person. In "O Captain, My Captain," Walt Whitman writes about the death of Abraham Lincoln.

Epic ■ An epic is a long story poem that describes the adventures of a hero. "The Odyssey" by Homer is a famous epic about the Greek hero Odysseus.

Free Verse ■ Free verse is poetry that does not require meter (regular rhythm) or a rhyme scheme.

Haiku ■ Haiku is a type of Japanese poetry that presents a picture of nature. A haiku poem is three lines in length. The first line is five syllables; the second, seven; and the third, five.

> Like a bad landscape
> with neither depth nor feeling;
> the world through one eye
> —Derek Lam

Limerick ■ A limerick is a humorous verse of five lines. Lines one, two, and five rhyme, as do lines three and four. Lines one, two, and five have three stressed syllables; lines three and four have two.

> There once was a panda named Lu,   (a)
> Who always ate crunchy bamboo.   (a)
> He ate all day long,   (b)
> Till he looked like King Kong.   (b)
> Now the zoo doesn't know what to do.   (a)
> —Sarah Diot

Lyric ■ A lyric is a short poem that expresses personal feeling.

> **My Heart Leaps Up When I Behold** (first 5 lines)
>
> My heart leaps up when I behold
> A rainbow in the sky;
> So was it when my life began;
> So is it now I am a man;
> So be it when I shall grow old.
> —William Wordsworth

Ode ■ An ode is a long lyric that is deep in feeling and rich in poetic devices. "Ode to a Grecian Urn" is a famous ode by John Keats.

Sonnet ■ A sonnet is a 14-line poem that states a poet's personal feelings. The Shakespearean sonnet follows the *abab/cdcd/efef/ gg* rhyme scheme and an iambic pentameter format. (See *foot* and *verse* on page 289.)

Other Forms of Poetry

Don't be afraid to try something new the next time you sit down to write a poem. The forms of poetry that follow will help you get started.

Alphabet Poetry ■ A form of poetry that states a creative or humorous idea using part of the alphabet.

We	Animals,
X-ray	Best to
Young	Catch
Zoo	Disease.

　　　　—Zachariah Surrency

Clerihew Poetry ■ A form of humorous or light verse created by Edmund Clerihew Bentley. A clerihew poem consists of two rhyming couplets. The name of some well-known person creates one of the rhymes.

Edmund Clerihew Bentley
Brooded intently
On many a foible
He thus made enjoyable.
　　　　—Colin Burke

Concrete Poetry ■ A form of poetry in which the shape or design helps express the meaning or feeling of the poem.

pEAKs VALLEYS LIFE!

Contrast Couplet ■ A couplet in which the first line includes two words that are opposites. The second line makes a comment about the first.

Some hours are too short, and some are too long.
I wonder who made the clocks all wrong.
　　　　—L. Winfred Smith

Definition Poetry ■ Poetry that defines a word or an idea creatively.

Temptation—
the modern Pied Piper,
calling, willing, drawing
the soul resisting,
the brain relenting.
　　　　—Kristin Mueller

List Poetry ■ A form of poetry that lists words or phrases.

> **Rooms**
> There are rooms to start up in
> Rooms to start out in
> Rooms to start over in
> Rooms to lie in
> Rooms to lie about in
> Rooms to lay away in . . .
> —Ray Griffith

Name Poetry ■ A form of poetry in which the letters of a name are used to begin each line in the poem.

> Amazing
> Silly
> Happy
> Loud
> Even though she's only two, she can still say "I love
> You!"
> —Roman Leykin

Phrase Poetry ■ A form of poetry that describes an idea with a list of phrases instead of complete sentences.

> foggy mist of rain
> dark cement and shiny pavement
> hiss of tires
> silver puddles
> one wet sock
> —Stacie Foiles

Terse Verse ■ A form of humorous verse made up of two words that rhyme, have the same number of syllables, and describe the title.

Clock Poem	**Wilted Flower**	**Tardy Visitor**
Time	Floppy	Late
Rhyme	Poppy	Date

—Katheryn Smith

Title-down Poetry ■ A form of poetry in which the letters that spell the subject of the poem are used to begin each line.

> Cuddled in my
> Arms, purring as I
> Tickle its fur.

> Flits around my head.
> Lands on my nose. Makes me
> Yell!

—Candace Smith

Research Writing

Using
Information

As a child, you probably asked your parents questions like "Why is the sky blue?" "Where does the wind come from?" That's research—looking for answers.

As a student, you may be asked to write a research report, and the idea is the same. You will ask questions about a topic and find answers.

Knowing where and how to look for answers is a key research skill, as is judging the quality of what you find and understanding how to fit that information into your writing.

In this chapter, you will learn about **primary** and **secondary sources**, and how to evaluate each. You will also learn how to **credit** sources so that your reader can find them (and so that you avoid **plagiarism**).

What's Ahead

- Primary vs. Secondary Sources
- Evaluating Sources
- Crediting Sources

Primary vs. Secondary Sources

Primary sources are original sources. They give you firsthand information and can involve observing or participating in an activity, interviewing someone who knows about your topic, or reading historical documents or diaries. (See page 297.)

Secondary sources, on the other hand, are not original sources. They provide information that has been gathered by another person, which makes them at least once removed from the original. Secondary sources often analyze, interpret, or evaluate in some way. Most magazines, newspapers, encyclopedias, and nonfiction books are considered secondary sources of information.

Helpful Hint

A *primary source* of information can be traced no further than its author. A *secondary source* can be traced beyond its author to at least one or more other individuals. Both are valid sources for your research.

Primary Sources	Secondary Sources
A Interview with a sports trainer	A Article that quotes a sports trainer
B Visit to a training room	B Encyclopedia entry about sports training
C Work with a sports trainer	C Television special about sports training

Types of Primary Sources

Because primary sources offer you firsthand information, they may get you closer to the truth about a topic. This page discusses five types of primary sources.

Observation and participation ▪ Carefully observing people, events, and places is a common primary source, as is actually participating in an event. For example, if you were doing a report on iguanas, going to a zoo to observe the animals would be a primary source.

Surveys and forms ▪ A survey or questionnaire can be a helpful primary source of information. For example, you could use a survey to gather neighborhood opinions about street traffic. This sort of research can be done by phone, in person, by e-mail or another online form, or through the mail.

Interviews ▪ In an interview, you talk directly with someone who has expert knowledge or experience concerning your topic. You can interview someone in person, by phone, by e-mail or online chat, or by mail. (See page 200.)

Presentations ▪ Going to lectures, visiting museum displays, and attending exhibits can provide you with firsthand information about many different topics. Remember to listen or observe closely and think about what you are seeing and hearing.

Diaries, journals, and letters ▪ A diary, journal, or collection of letters from an expert or a celebrity offers you that person's thoughts. These sources can provide fascinating details for your research. Look for these writings in autobiographies, in biographies, and at historical museums.

Evaluating Sources

You may have heard the tale of the blind men and the elephant. Each touched a different part of the animal and described it in those terms. One grabbed the tail and said, "It's like a snake." One grabbed a leg and said, "It's like a tree." Another touched its side and said, "No, it's like a wall." And so on.

The point, of course, is that the truth is often larger and more complex than any one person might believe. For that reason, it is important to consider different sources in your research and to evaluate the perspective and trustworthiness of each one. Ask yourself these questions:

Is the source primary or secondary?

Firsthand information from a primary source is often more trustworthy than secondhand accounts, simply because there are fewer people between you and the facts. A secondary source may give you biased information, including certain details and excluding others.

Is the source an expert?

An expert is someone regarded as an authority on a certain subject. (Note, however, that an expert on one topic is not necessarily an expert on others.) If you aren't sure about someone's expertise on a subject, ask your teacher, a parent or guardian, or your librarian for advice.

Is the source highly regarded?

A news source like the *Chicago Tribune* is more highly respected than a supermarket tabloid. Again, if you aren't sure about the credentials of a source, ask an adult.

Is the information accurate and reliable?

The best way to judge this is to compare two or more highly regarded sources. If they are in agreement about the details of your topic, the information is probably correct. If they disagree, you'll need to do more research to uncover the facts.

Is the information complete?

Often, a source will tell you only one side of the story. This may be especially true on the Web, where information may be posted by individuals or groups who want to sway you to their way of thinking, without concern for balance or fairness. If an author tells you only facts that support his or her opinion, something important is probably missing. Look further.

Is the information current?

Generally, you will want the very latest information on a subject, especially when it comes to science, technology, and current events. Look for articles and books with a recent copyright date. (See page 314 for copyright information.) And always check the date of Web postings. If no date is posted, don't assume that the information is recent.

Is the source biased?

A "bias" means literally a tilt toward one side. Biased sources—politicians, TV infomercials, and many Web sites—have something to gain by using facts, "loaded words," and emotional appeals to put themselves in the best light. Obviously, you'll want to avoid using biased sources. (See page 307 to learn more about emotive words.)

Good Thinking

When doing research, good thinkers don't just choose sources that support their own knowledge of a topic or opinion about it. They also seek out sources that add to or even disagree with their position. Learning about opposing viewpoints can broaden and deepen their grasp of a subject, helping them to better know their own position.

Crediting Sources

Crediting your sources helps you to avoid **plagiarism**, which means presenting someone else's words or ideas as your own. (See pages 319–322.) Never plagiarize.

Crediting your sources also lends authority to your writing. It says, "Here are the people who stand behind my details." Not crediting your sources is like telling the reader, "This information is true because I said so." Nobody wants to hear that.

Finally, in our information-rich world, time is precious. Always reveal your sources of information so that the reader can easily find and read more about your topic.

When to Credit Sources

The basic rule for deciding when to credit a source is to ask yourself, "Is this information *common knowledge*?" Common knowledge can be found in a general dictionary or encyclopedia and does not need to be credited (but don't copy it word for word).

However, facts that cannot be found in a general dictionary or encyclopedia must be credited to the source in which you found them.

How to Credit Sources

- Within the text of an *informal report,* mention the specific source of each quotation, fact, or summary of information that you use. At the end of the report, provide a list of these sources in a bibliography or works-cited page (see pages 330–332).
- Within the text of a *formal research paper,* such as the MLA-style report on pages 333–337, you must not only mention the source of any borrowed information but also provide a page number. Besides the "in-text citations," a works-cited page is required at the report's end. (See the MLA report chapter on pages 323–337 for more details.)
- In an *electronic document,* such as a Web page, a blog post, or an e-mail, you can *hyperlink* directly from your information to its source online. (See page 328.) You may also include a bibliography or works-cited page, which can also be hyperlinked to online sources.

Note: Always ask your teacher what the documentation requirements are for your current writing assignment.

Using the
Internet

The text you are reading is two things: (1) a set of characters physically printed in ink on paper and (2) the words and thoughts those characters generate in your mind.

Similarly, the Internet is two things: (1) a physical network of computers and (2) a cyberspace of hyperlinked text, audio, video, and animated graphics.

In other words, the Net is merely the latest in a set of tools—spoken language, writing, drawing, printing, audio recordings, telephone, video recordings, and so on—that humans have invented for capturing and sharing their thoughts. What makes the Net so powerful is the way it combines all of those previous technologies into one supertool and connects people all around the globe.

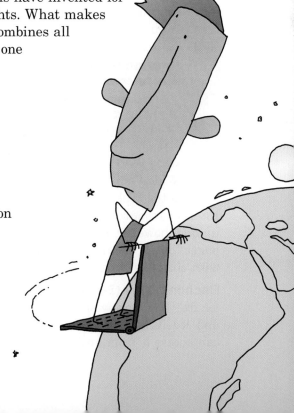

What's Ahead

- A Guide to the Internet
- Researching on the Net
- Evaluating Online Information
- Saving What You Find
- Quick Guide: Surfing Tips

A Guide to the Internet

The Internet may have started small—as a way to share files between remote computers. But it didn't stay "small" for long. Soon e-mail was added. Next came bulletin boards, Usenet newsgroups, and list servers. Then the World Wide Web was invented. Weblogs followed. Search engines sprang up. Chat rooms and instant messaging were developed. Music, movies, and interactive games became available, and on and on.

The most important parts of the Net are listed below and diagrammed on the next page.

Personal Computer (PC) ■ A personal computer serves as your usual access point to the Internet. As smartphones and other such portable devices gain more computing power, they are offering access to some services on the Net, as well.

Local Area Network (LAN) ■ While the Internet is a global network, many schools, businesses, and homes have a small network of computers to share files locally. Some LAN's are also connected to the Internet.

Internet Service Provider (ISP) ■ An Internet service provider connects a PC or LAN to other computers on the Internet. Your ISP may also provide e-mail service and supply space where you can create Web pages of your own.

Good Thinking

Good thinkers ask their Internet providers for help when they have a question. They phrase their requests—via e-mail—clearly and politely.

World Wide Web ■ Some people mistake the World Wide Web for the Internet itself. That's because the Web provides access to so many Internet resources. What makes the Web unique, however, is its use of "hyperlinked pages." Each document on the Web is a page with clickable links to other pages.

It is the hyperlinks that make the Web so easy to explore.

Electronic Mail (E-mail) ■ Web-based e-mail accounts are available for free from many sites, including the major search sites. E-mail sent and received in this way is stored on a remote computer so that you can access it from any Internet-connected PC.

The Net at a Glance

An Internet service provider (ISP) allows you to conduct research and communicate online. The ISP gives you access, via a personal computer or LAN, to the World Wide Web, e-mail, and other services. (See the diagram below.)

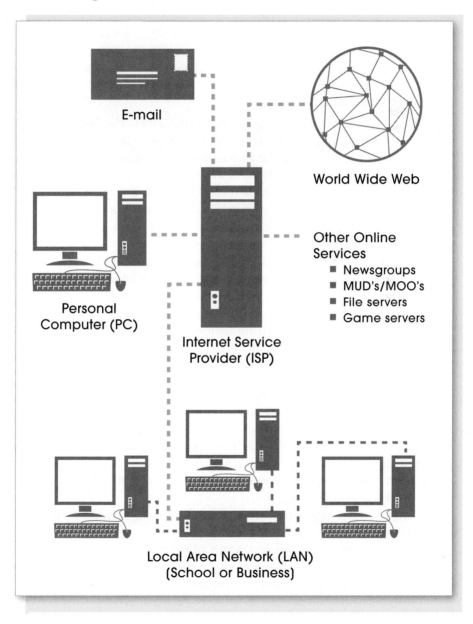

Researching on the Net

For many of you, research means opening a search page, typing in a few keywords, and clicking on some of the results. But trying to learn about a topic that way is like studying fish by waterskiing across a lake. You're just skimming the surface.

Using Search Sites

Knowing how search sites work can help you use them.

How Search Sites Work

1. All day, every day, robot programs "crawl" the Web, following hyperlinks from page to page. The robots scan each page, looking for important words and phrases, and report them back to search sites.
2. Search sites store words and phrases in a database.
3. They compare similar words and phrases and use a mathematical algorithm to rank which pages are most significant.
4. You visit the search site and enter keywords.
5. The search site returns a list of pages related to your terms, in the order it believes is most helpful.
6. You scan the results, reading titles and descriptions, hoping to find something useful.

There are many chances for error during online searches: A page designer may not use the best terms; a robot may not find a link to a page; a search engine's algorithm may rank a page below thousands of others; and your choice of search terms may be ineffective. Here are some tips to make your searching productive:

- **Be patient.** Good research can mean sifting lots of "sand" before finding treasure.
- **Try different keywords.** If one search phrase doesn't work, try a different one. And check your spelling.
- **Check more than the first page of results.** What you need may be on the second or third page, or even later.
- **Learn advanced keyword strategies.** Refer to the next page for a list of ways to conduct an effective word search.

Word-Searching Guide

Search sites are becoming better and better at predicting the best results for your searches, but the key still lies in how you phrase things. The same words used in different orders or different combinations often return different results.

■ If you type in one word, the search program will look for all pages that include that word.

> **Try it!** Type homework; then start your search program.

■ If you type in more than one word, the search program will look for all pages that contain any of those words.

> **Try it!** Type in homework help; then start your search program.

■ If you type a phrase in quotation marks, most search programs will look for all pages that contain exactly that phrase.

> **Try it!** Type "homework help"; then start your search program.

■ Most search programs allow you to use Boolean words (such as *and*, *or*, and *not*) or symbols (such as "+" for *and* and "-" for *not*) to help control your search.

> **Try it!** Type homework and help; then start your search program.

■ Search programs often have even more advanced options for fine-tuning your results. Check for a link to advanced search options on your favorite search site.

Helpful Hint

It can be useful (1) to try different groups and orders of words in your search and (2) to compare the results of different search sites. Visit www.thewritesource.com/research.htm for a list of recommended search sites.

Other Online Resources

Directories

In a directory, listings are organized by subject headings, subheadings, and so on. Instead of searching by keywords, you choose a broad subject heading and then "drill down" through subheadings until you find the information you need.

Metasearch Sites

Metasearch sites run your keywords through several search engines and then compare the results. To find a metasearch engine, type "metasearch" into your favorite search site.

Online Libraries

The Internet Public Library (ipl.org) and the Library of Congress (www.loc.gov) provide a wide range of online texts and research tools. Project Gutenberg (www.gutenberg.org) also hosts a steadily growing number of classic books (text and audio).

Government and School Sites

National and state governments maintain many useful research sites. NASA, for instance, has an amazing site for science research, at www.nasa.gov.

Publication Databases

Your public or school library may subscribe to a service such as EBSCO, which provides a searchable database of newspaper, magazine, and journal articles.

E-mail, Chat, Texting, Message Boards, and Wikis

Sometimes the best way to get started with your topic research is to ask other people about it. E-mail, online chat, or text messaging can serve this purpose well. You can also post your question to a message board, or check a wiki—which is an online encyclopedia to which anyone can contribute.

Evaluating Online Information

Always check your information for timeliness and balance.

Timeliness

Online information can be more up to date than print publications, but always check the date on any Web page you hope to use. If the date is old, or if no date is displayed, the information may no longer be accurate.

Remember: Not everything online is current.

Balance

Much of what is published online has a commercial purpose or a bias. Watch for the ways in which a page tries to shape your thinking:

Color and Layout ■ Web designers study the effects of color on people. For example, blue tends to evoke trust, black a sense of mystery, and white a businesslike manner.

Photos and Illustrations ■ In politics, one site may choose a photo that makes a candidate look inspiring, while another site chooses a photo that makes the same candidate look frustrated or mean.

Emotive Words ■ "Extraordinary" and "foolhardy" are examples of words that can color your opinion about the facts: *He made an extraordinary attempt to stop the car. He made a foolhardy attempt to stop the car.* The fact is he tried to stop the car, but your feelings about it are being manipulated.

Saving What You Find

Here are a few ways to save online information:
- **Bookmark it:** If you're on your home computer, you can bookmark the page or save it to your "favorites."
- **Make a printout:** A print copy can be very handy. Just be sure that it includes the Internet address of the page.
- **Save an electronic copy:** You can save the whole page or just block-and-copy the parts you'll need. Just remember to also save the page address. Many people carry a USB "thumb drive" for saving files.
- **E-mail a copy or the link:** If you're not at your own computer, e-mail yourself the Internet address.

Quick Guide ■ Surfing Tips

Here are some tips for surfing the Internet. ("Surfing" means riding Internet links from page to page in search of information.)

■ **Stay focused:** When you're doing research, be careful not to get distracted by unrelated information. Make sure to stay focused on your specific task. Otherwise, you may find yourself wasting a lot of time and have little, if anything, to show for your efforts.

■ **Check your facts:** The Internet is sometimes called a global town square because anyone can speak out. Some people are not always careful with their facts and opinions, so don't believe everything that is posted. (See pages 298–299.)

■ **Preserve your privacy:** You wouldn't stand in New York's Times Square with a bullhorn, shouting out your family's address, telephone number, and credit card numbers. Nor should you reveal personal details on the Internet. Always check with your parents or guardians or a teacher before posting anything on the Net.

■ **Protect yourself:** If you find an Internet site offensive, go somewhere else. Just about any newsgroup can get barraged by offensive messages (spammed).

■ **Use netiquette:** Netiquette means being considerate of others when you are online. Follow these practices:

- ■ **Scout the territory:** When using a site, read its instructions. Check for a FAQ ("frequently asked questions") list before requesting help.
- ■ **Post clear messages:** Don't assume your readers will understand; *make sure* they understand.
- ■ **Don't SHOUT:** Use caps only when necessary—for titles, emphasis, and other special uses.

Helpful Hint

When you finish using a public computer, always remember to log out of your personal account (if, in fact, you used it). Otherwise, the next person at the computer can use your account!

Conducting
Library Research

When it comes to research, you might consider going to the library a bit old-fashioned. After all, the Internet is so quick and easy to use, and it provides a wealth of information. This makes the Internet a good place to start your research. The library, on the other hand, serves as a better place to continue it.

A visit to a library provides you with thousands of books and other reliable materials on almost any topic. And now that the library catalog is searchable on computers, you no longer have to thumb through "old-fashioned" card catalogs to find the materials you need. The library also offers trained professionals to help you with your research in the library and on the Internet.

What's Ahead

- Searching for Information
- Using the Catalog
- Finding Books
- Using Reference Books
- Understanding the Parts of Books

Searching for Information

Begin searching for what you need by exploring your library's computer catalog. This catalog lists all the books and materials held in that particular library.

Using the Catalog

There are three ways to approach your catalog search—by title, by author, or by subject.

1. **Title entries** If you already know the title of the book you wish to access, simply type it in the search box: *Hatchet, Voyage of the Dawn Treader, Bodies from the Ash: Life and Death in Ancient Pompeii.*
2. **Author entries** If you know the author of the book you are looking for or are searching for multiple books by one author, type the person's name in the search box.
3. **Subject entries** If you are searching for several books on the same topic, type the subject or a keyword, which is a word related to the subject: *Pompeii, Beijing Olympics, Lebron James.*

Computer Catalog Entry

Author:	Bausum, Ann
Title:	Freedom Riders John Lewis and Jim Zwerg on the Front Lines of the Civil Rights Movement
Published:	National Geographic, 2005 80 pp.
Subjects:	Civil Rights Biographies

STATUS:	CALL NUMBER:
Not checked out	378.30973

LOCATION:
General collection

Finding Books

Nonfiction Books ■ Many of the books you will use for classroom reports and research papers will be nonfiction, or true, books. These books are assigned call numbers that tell where to find the books on the library shelves. Most libraries organize nonfiction books by the Dewey decimal system, which has 10 subject categories.

The Ten Classes of the Dewey Decimal System

000	General Topics	**500**	Pure Science
100	Philosophy	**600**	Technology
200	Religion	**700**	The Arts and Recreation
300	The Social Sciences	**800**	Literature and Rhetoric
400	Language	**900**	Geography and History

Using Call Numbers ■ A call number often has a decimal in it, followed by the first letters of an author's name, such as 932.2 HOF.

- **Call numbers containing decimals**
  The call number 932.167 is actually smaller than 932.2. This is true because 932.2 is really 932.200 without the two zeros. A book with the call number 932.167 will be on the shelf before one with 932.2.

- **Call numbers containing letters**
  A book with the call number 932.2 will be on the shelf before one with 932.2F.

Biographies ■ Biographies and autobiographies are assigned the call number 921 and arranged according to the last name of the subject of the book. A book about John Glenn would have the number 921GLENN on its spine and be shelved accordingly.

Fiction Books ■ Fiction books are shelved by the first three letters of the author's last name. If you know the name of the author, you can go directly to the fiction shelves and find books by that author.

Using Reference Books

Reference books are kept in a special section in a library. Here you will find encyclopedias, atlases, almanacs, indexes, dictionaries, thesauruses, and so on.

Encyclopedias

An encyclopedia is a set of books, a CD, or a Web site with articles on almost every topic imaginable.

- It is a good starting point for gathering information.
- Articles are arranged alphabetically by topic.
- Related topics are listed at the end of most articles.
- Different encyclopedias include different information.
- An index lists all the places in the encyclopedia where you will find more information about a topic. (See the example below.) The index is usually in the back of the last volume of a printed set.

Encyclopedia Index

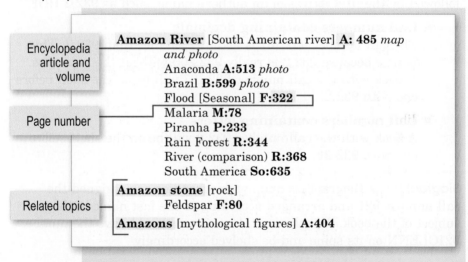

Encyclopedia article and volume

Page number

Related topics

Amazon River [South American river] **A: 485** *map and photo*
    Anaconda **A:513** *photo*
    Brazil **B:599** *photo*
    Flood [Seasonal] **F:322**
    Malaria **M:78**
    Piranha **P:233**
    Rain Forest **R:344**
    River (comparison) **R:368**
    South America **So:635**
Amazon stone [rock]
    Feldspar **F:80**
Amazons [mythological figures] **A:404**

Atlases

An atlas is a collection of maps.

- Some atlases include maps and facts about the whole world; others cover only certain states, countries, or regions.
- Atlases to consider: *Atlas of the World, National Geographic Atlas of the World, Concise Atlas of World History*

Almanacs

An almanac is an annual publication containing lists, charts, and tables of information about different topics.

- General almanacs contain facts and figures about many topics.
- Special-interest almanacs cover a single subject, such as movies or basketball.
- Look in the most recent editions for the latest facts.
- Almanacs to look for:

  The World Almanac and Book of Facts: Contains facts and figures about history, politics, business, sports, and entertainment.

  Old Farmers Almanac: Includes information about weather forecasts, ocean patterns, astronomy, and farming. Also predicts future trends in fashion, food, and technology.

  Time Almanac: Features world statistics and countries, astronomy and space, calendar and holidays, health and nutrition, the Internet and Web-site guides, and more.

Periodical Indexes

- Ask the librarian if your library has a print or electronic version of the *Readers' Guide to Periodical Literature,* a reference guide to recent articles in magazines and scholarly journals. This index is arranged alphabetically by subject.
- Also ask the librarian what Internet-based databases the library subscribes to. These online subscription services allow you to search for and read periodicals on the Internet.

Other Helpful Reference Books

- ***The World Factbook:*** Published by the Central Intelligence Agency (CIA), this almanac-style reference book gives in-depth information about the culture, economy, and makeup of countries around the world.
- ***Bartlett's Familiar Quotations:*** Contains 20,000 quotations arranged in chronological order from ancient times to the present.
- ***Merriam-Webster's Geographical Dictionary:*** Includes information on more than 48,000 mountains, lakes, towns, and countries in alphabetical order.
- ***Who's Who in America:*** Features biographical information on more than 100,000 of the United States' most influential people, both past and present.

Understanding the Parts of Books

If the book you have searched for and located in the library is a nonfiction or reference book, you need to know how to use that book efficiently. It is especially important, for instance, to make full use of the index and special glossaries and tables when using nonfiction books. Here is a list of book parts and tips to help you use the nonfiction books you find in the library.

- The **title page** is usually the first printed page in a book. It tells (1) the book's title, (2) the author's name, (3) the publisher's name, and (4) the place of publication.
- The **copyright page** follows the title page and gives the year the copyright was issued. When you are looking for up-to-date facts, be sure you use a book with a recent copyright date.
- A **preface**, a **foreword**, or an **introduction** sometimes follows the copyright page. This part usually tells something about the book and why it was written. It may also include an **acknowledgement**, or thank-you, to people who helped make the book possible.
- The **table of contents** gives the names and page numbers of chapters and sections in the book. Looking through this part will tell you the general topics covered in the book.
- The **body** of the book is the main part of the text.
- An **appendix** may follow the body. It contains information that supplements the main text—sometimes maps, charts, tables, copies of letters, official documents, or other special information.
- Some books also contain a **glossary** (minidictionary) of special terms that are used throughout the book. Whenever you don't understand a term, look it up in the glossary.
- A **bibliography** is a list of other books and articles about the same subject or sources the author used in research.
- Finally, you will find the **index**. This is an alphabetical listing of all of the important topics covered in the book and page numbers where you can find them.

Helpful Hint

The index is probably the most useful part of a reference book. By scanning the index, you can tell whether the book contains the information you need for your research.

Summarizing, Paraphrasing, and **Quoting**

"What happened?" asks your parent, pointing at the ruined front wheel of your bike. "Well, it's a long story," you reply. But your parent wants the short version: "Summarize!"

Summarizing is taking a lot of information and boiling it down to its essence. In life, you may summarize to appease an angry parent. In research, you summarize to tell the reader only what matters.

Summarizing is a key research strategy, along with paraphrasing (putting other people's ideas in your own words) and quoting (letting other people's exact words speak). This chapter will help you decide which strategy to use and how to use it.

A·a·a·a

What's Ahead

- Article and Summary
- Writing Guidelines
- Paraphrasing and Quoting

Article and Summary

A summary captures the main point of a reading and provides the most important supporting details. Read the science article and the student summary that follows it.

Life on a Giant Magnet
By Bill Taylor

Our planet has the perfect combination of factors to support life—liquid water, a relatively stable climate, abundant oxygen, and a molten mantle. Molten mantle? Yes. Aside from producing volcanoes and earthquakes, our molten mantle also produces the strong magnetic field that protects our earth from the deadly solar wind.

The rocks and metals in the molten mantle of the earth are in constant motion. The convection currents of the metals turn the earth into a giant magnet, which creates a protective field all around our planet. To visualize this field, place a bar magnet in iron filings, and the filings will form a series of rings like the layers of an onion.

Geologists discovered, though, that the North Pole hasn't always had the north polarity of this great magnet. In fact, the earth's polarity has flipped multiple times in the past. Changes in the currents in the mantle can change the polarity of the great magnet we live on.

Some scientists are suggesting that the earth's polarity is getting ready to flip. Large pockets of northern polarization are appearing in the southern hemisphere. If the polarity flips, it is likely that the earth will endure a period of weakened magnetic fields—which means more ultraviolet radiation, more sunburns, and skin cancer. But this flip would also make the famous auroras visible everywhere around the world!

Student Summary

The **topic sentence** names the article and author and provides the main point.

Supporting sentences explain the topic sentence.

The **closing sentence** returns to the main point.

A Magnetic World

In "Life on a Giant Magnet," Bill Taylor points out that the molten mantle of the earth makes it a giant magnet. Metals and rock flow beneath the crust, creating a magnetic field around the earth. This field protects our planet from the deadly solar wind, but the field has changed a number of times in history. Some scientists think the polarity of the earth is about to flip, so that the South Pole would have a north polarity and vice versa. If this happens, the planet will have a weaker magnetic field, allowing more ultraviolet radiation and skin cancer, but also allowing everyone to see the auroras. Life has survived many other polarity shifts on this giant magnet called Earth.

Writing Guidelines

Prewriting—Planning Your Writing

Read through the selection once to get an overall understanding of it. Then reread the selection and write down the main point. Read one final time and note the most important supporting details.

Main Point: Earth is a giant magnet.

Detail 1: The molten mantle causes it.
Detail 2: The magnetic field protects the earth.
Detail 3: The field might be about to flip.
Detail 4: A flip would cause more skin cancer and auroras.

Writing—Creating the Summary

Create a **topic sentence** that names the original source and expresses the main point in an interesting way. Then write a sentence or two for each important detail. Finish by writing a **closing sentence** that restates the main point.

Revising and Editing—Improving Your Writing

Use the following checklist to improve your summary.

Ideas
____ Do I identify the source and main point?
____ Do I include only the most important details?

Organization
____ Do I have an effective topic sentence and closing sentence?

Voice
____ Does my voice fit the subject and purpose?

Word Choice
____ Have I correctly used terms from the original selection?

Sentence Fluency
____ Do my sentences read naturally?

Conventions
____ Have I checked my punctuation, capitalization, spelling, and grammar?

Paraphrasing and Quoting

Paraphrasing is expressing someone else's ideas in your own words. Quoting is providing the exact words of someone else. Either way, you need to credit your sources.

Paraphrasing

When you paraphrase, you restate the ideas in a source using your own words. Follow these steps:

1. **Read the part you want to paraphrase.** Understand it as a whole.
2. **Paraphrase sections, not sentences.** Put the main *idea* of the section in your own words, writing your own sentences to show your understanding.
3. **Check for fairness.** Make sure your paraphrase reflects the writer's original intention.
4. **Cite your sources.** (See the "Helpful Hint" below.)

Quoting

Quote only passages that express an idea especially well, and then make sure you quote the *exact* words of the person. Follow these tips:

1. **Set off quotations.** Use quotation marks correctly.
2. **Check the original.** Make sure you have quoted exactly.
3. **Keep quotations short.** Don't allow them to overwhelm your own ideas.
4. **Introduce quotations and/or follow them with comments.** Don't just let a quotation hang there.
5. **Cite your sources.** (See the "Helpful Hint" below.)

Helpful Hint

You cite sources to give credit to other thinkers. You also cite sources so the reader will know where you found your information. Here are three ways to cite sources:

- Name the source and writer in the text.
  In "Life on a Giant Magnet," Bill Taylor points out that the molten mantle of the earth makes it a giant magnet.
- Use MLA parenthetical references and a works-cited page. (See pages 328 and 330–332.)
  The molten mantle of the earth makes it a giant magnet (Taylor).
- If your work and your source are both online, provide a hyperlink.
  The molten mantle of the earth makes it a giant magnet.

Avoiding
Plagiarism

"Want to hear a joke I just came up with?" you ask a friend. After you tell it, your friend cracks up but then turns to someone else and says, "Want to hear a joke I just came up with?" What kind of a friend is that, taking credit for your joke? That's plagiarism!

Now imagine your friend giving you credit. "Want to hear a joke that _____ came up with?" That's different. It's almost an honor. It shows that your friend likes your joke well enough to share it *and* give you credit for it.

Avoiding plagiarism in your writing is just as important. All you have to do is give credit to the sources of the ideas that you use. This chapter will show you how.

What's Ahead

- Original Article
- Examples of Plagiarism
- Avoiding Plagiarism

Original Article

The article below talks about some of the effects of aging on the human body. After reading it, note the examples of plagiarism on the next page.

"Old Age Isn't for Sissies"
Frank Bell

The famous actress Bette Davis once said, "Old age isn't for sissies." But what effects does aging have on human beings? The slow march of time takes its toll on our skin, our hair, and the very shape of our bodies.

Old and young (photo by Mandy Godbehear)

Aging and Skin

Over time, muscles grow weaker, and the skin over the muscles begins to sag. It also loses elasticity, so that once-tight skin becomes loose or wrinkled. These factors, combined with a gradual thinning of skin, make for the changes we so often see in aging faces: bags under the eyes, wrinkles beside the eyes and mouth, dangling and double chins, and a translucent quality that makes skin look mottled. Sun damage accelerates these processes.

Aging and Hair

Hair is colored by a pigment called *melanin*, which is produced by the hair follicles. As follicles age, they produce less melanin, and hair slowly loses its color. Black hair may go to salt-and-pepper, to gray, then to silver, and finally white. Meanwhile, especially in men, the long-term effects of the hormone *testosterone* cause hair to recede from the head—and to crop up in unwanted places such as the ears and back.

Aging and the Body

Aging reduces muscle mass and increases fat storage. As a result, our shoulders get narrower and our waistlines get rounder. Time also ravages the skeletal system, reducing calcium content, especially in women. In fact, it is not uncommon for people over the age of 40 to lose a centimeter of height every 10 years.

Examples of Plagiarism

Below are four common types of plagiarism, often committed by accident. The plagiarized parts are shown in **red**.

■ Using Copy-and-Paste Without Credit

> Changes in the face show what is going on underneath the skin. Over time, muscles grow weaker, and the skin over the muscles begins to sag. Wrinkles and bags can result.

■ Using Images Without Credit

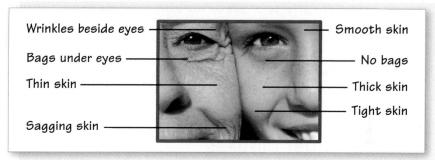

Wrinkles beside eyes — Smooth skin

Bags under eyes — No bags

Thin skin — Thick skin

— Tight skin

Sagging skin

■ Paraphrasing Without Credit

> Melanin, produced by the hair follicles, is a pigment that colors hair. Hair slowly loses its color when follicles age and produce less melanin. White hair may come from black hair that has gone through stages—from salt-and-pepper to gray to silver to white.

■ Forgetting Quotation Marks

> The changes in the body might be the most extreme. Frank Bell writes that it is not uncommon for people over the age of 40 to lose a centimeter of height every 10 years. In that way, while young people grow up, older people grow down.

Avoiding Plagiarism

Avoiding plagiarism is important. Follow these tips.

- **Keep track of sources.** Write down the names of books or articles and the names of their authors. If you use Internet sources, either print out a page with the URL or write down the URL and name of the Web page.

- **Cite sources.** As you write your first draft, note where ideas come from. You can do so by using MLA parenthetical citations and a works-cited page (see pages 328, 330–332). Another way is to mention the source and author in the text:

> In his article " 'Old Age Isn't for Sissies,' " Frank Bell tells about the effects of age on our skin, hair, and bodies.

- **Remember why.** The reason for citing sources is to give credit where it is due and to help other people find the same sources of information.

Avoiding Other Misuses

Here are a few other forms of source abuse to avoid.

- **Using sources inaccurately:** Always preserve the author's original meaning. Don't twist her or his words.

- **Overusing source material:** Don't let others' ideas drown out your own. Your own thoughts, with assists from other sources, should dominate your report.

- **"Plunking" source material.** Don't simply drop in a quotation without introducing it or following it with a comment. Smoothly engage quotations, paraphrases, and summaries with your own writing.

- **Using only one source.** Avoid relying too much on one source. Instead, combine information from a number of reliable sources.

Writing
Research Papers

When you write a research paper, you must do two things: (1) learn as much as you can about a specific topic by reading, observing, reflecting, asking questions, and so on, and (2) share this information in a clear, organized paper.

A research paper may include information gathered from books, magazines, newspapers, interviews, videos, or the Internet. All ideas borrowed from these sources must be credited to the original writer or speaker. Most research papers are at least three pages in length and may include a title page, an outline, the actual essay, and a works-cited page or a bibliography.

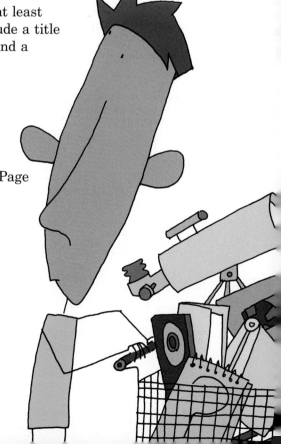

What's Ahead

- Writing Guidelines
- Adding an MLA Works-Cited Page
- Adding a Title Page
- Works-Cited Entries
- MLA Research Paper

Writing Guidelines

Prewriting—Choosing a Topic

Your teacher will probably provide you with a *general* subject, and it will be up to you to find a *specific* topic for your paper. *Remember:* You'll find it much easier to write a paper about a topic that truly interests you.

Let's say you've been assigned a research paper in science class. Your teacher has asked you to write about a modern-day scientific breakthrough.

You begin your search by checking the Internet or the library for recent developments in space exploration and in medicine. Whatever topic you choose, you must be able to find enough information about it to write a research paper or report.

Topic Web

Completing a web or cluster is one way to search for a topic. Begin by writing the general subject in the center. Then cluster related ideas around it.

Topic Web

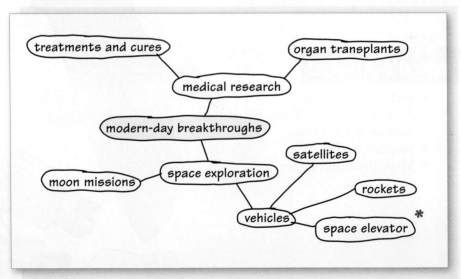

Gathering Your Information

Once you have selected a topic, you need to begin gathering information about it. Find plenty of books, magazines, Web articles, and other sources on the topic. Evaluate the reliability of these sources (see pages 298–299), and then take notes on the important facts and details you find. (See pages 397–402 for additional help.)

Ask questions. ■ To organize your reading and note taking, write questions about your topic that you would like to answer. Put each question at the top of a separate note card. (See the examples below.) Any time you find a fact that answers one of your questions, write it down on the appropriate card. Be sure to note the source.

5 W and H Questions

1. **What** is a space elevator?
2. **Who** came up with the idea?
3. **When** will it be built?
4. **Where** is it being developed?
5. **What** problems are involved?
6. **Why** do we need one?
7. **How** will it affect our lives?

Note Cards

④
Where is it being developed?

⑥
Why do we need a space elevator?
- Safer than rockets
- Cheaper than rockets
- Better for the environment
- Build a moon base
- Tourism in space

Source: <u>What's Going On Up There?</u> video

Prewriting—Organizing Your Information

Select a main point. ■ Once you have finished your reading and note taking, review the information you have gathered. As you do this, identify a specific part, feature, or feeling about the topic to be the focus of your report. The focus of the research paper on pages 333–337 is the story behind the development of the space elevator.

Arrange your cards. ■ Keeping the focus of your paper in mind, put your note cards in the best possible order.

Outlining Your Information

Write a rough outline. ■ Finally, prepare an outline for the body of your paper. Begin by listing the headings (questions) written on the top of your note cards in the same order that you have just arranged them. Leave enough space between the headings to include supporting facts and details. If you are not required to include a formal outline with your report, this quick outline may be all you need.

Rewrite your outline. ■ If you are required to do a formal outline, rework your rough outline into a clear sentence outline. Reword the questions into main ideas and number them with Roman numerals: I., II., III., IV., and so on. Include supporting details under each main idea and order them with capital letters A., B., C., and so on. (See page 111 for more information.)

Elevator to the Stars

Questions turned into main ideas

Supporting details

I. This strange idea has been discussed for over a century.
    A. In 1895, Konstantin Tsiolkovski suggested a tower to orbit.
    B. Other scientists and engineers debated possibilities for 90 years.
    C. In 1975, Jerome Pearson suggested hanging a cable from orbit.

II. Carbon nanotubes make Pearson's idea possible.
    A. Carbon nanotubes were discovered in 1991.
    B. They are 400 times stronger than steel.
    C. Once we can mass-produce them, we can build the cable.

Considering Your Audience

At some point during your planning, you should see how well your topic matches up to the reader. Ask yourself the following questions.

Questions to Consider

- **Who is my reader?** (You're probably writing for your teacher and classmates.)
- **What does the reader need to know?** (Your reader needs to know facts and details that can explain the main points of your writing.)
- **What does the reader want to learn?** (Your reader wants to learn something new and interesting.)

Writing—Writing the First Draft

Write an opening paragraph. ▪ In the first few sentences, get the reader's attention; then write a sentence that states the topic or thesis of your paper. This sentence serves as the controlling idea for the research paper.

The writer of the research paper on page 333 identifies the topic of her report in the opening.

> **Controlling idea:** Businesses and universities are tackling different parts of the same project: to build an elevator to space.

(If you're expected to write a thesis statement, see page 110 for help.)

Develop the middle paragraphs. ▪ Follow your outline when writing the body of your research paper. Each main point (I., II., and so on) serves as the topic sentence of a paragraph, and the details (A., B., and so on) become the supporting sentences. Also feel free to add new ideas as they come to mind.

Create an ending paragraph. ▪ Use one or more of the following ideas to form an effective closing:

- ▪ Summarize your main points.
- ▪ Restate your thesis.
- ▪ Reflect on the topic.
- ▪ Make a final strong statement.

Writing—Giving Credit for Information

Giving credit to your sources isn't just about being honest. It's also about supporting your ideas and helping the reader find more information about your subject. Plagiarism—which means not crediting a source—cheats you, your source, and your reader. Here are three common ways to give credit. (See also pages 319–322.)

Hyperlink ■ In an electronic document, such as a Web page or a multimedia report, you can directly link your text to the source. Some people add a sentence to do this. For example, "Click here to learn more about NASA's space elevator program." However, it is better to fit the link naturally into your text: "NASA's space elevator program hosts annual competitions."

Bibliography ■ In some instances, a bibliography may be all the documentation your teacher requires. In that case, at the end of your report, simply include an alphabetical list of sources you consulted during your research.

MLA Style ■ In an MLA-style report (see pages 333–337), a works-cited page lists all sources used in the paper. Within the essay, the source of each borrowed quotation, paraphrase, or fact must be identified. In the example below, facts in the first two sentences are credited to the author Ohlson, while those in the third sentence are credited to Lewis.

Currently, NASA sponsors yearly competitions for experimental climbers powered by a ground-based laser. Photoelectric cells on these machines convert the laser light into electrical power (Ohlson). However, because carbon nanotubes are a very good conductor of electricity, engineers in Japan hope to make a ribbon that can itself conduct power to the cars (Lewis).

Sometimes, to make it clear where borrowed information begins and ends, you will need to work the source into the sentence itself and cite the page numbers at the end, as in this example:

To build the first space elevator, Bradley and Ragan say that scientists plan to wind a ribbon of the fiber 20 centimeters wide and 63,000 miles long onto a spool the size of a semitruck. . . . [S]mall climbing machines will travel up this first elevator, each adding more ribbon to its width (46–54).

Revising—Improving Your Writing

Use the expository or persuasive rubric (page 184 or 220) as a general guide when reviewing and revising your research paper. Also keep the following points in mind.

- **Making Changes** . . . Review your first draft to be sure it says what you want it to say. As necessary, add, rearrange, or cut ideas so that (1) your beginning paragraph gains the reader's attention and identifies your topic or thesis, (2) each middle paragraph develops a main point about the topic, and (3) your closing paragraph keeps the reader thinking about the topic.

- **Getting Help** . . . Have at least one other person (writing peer, teacher, family member) review your first draft. Share any concerns you have about your writing and ask if the reviewer is confused by anything or has any questions.

- **Documenting Your Sources** . . . Be sure to give credit in your paper for ideas and direct quotations that you have borrowed from your sources. In addition, prepare a works-cited or bibliography page, listing all of the sources you have cited in your paper. (See pages 330–332 and 337 for help.)

Editing—Checking for Accuracy

Use the following checklist to help you edit your research paper. Also refer to the rubrics on pages 184 and 220.

Conventions Checklist

- _____ Have I used proper end punctuation for my sentences?
- _____ Have I capitalized first words of sentences and proper nouns?
- _____ Have I used the correct forms of verbs *(give, gave, given)*?
- _____ Do my subjects and verbs agree *(Smith doesn't,* not *Smith don't)*?
- _____ Have I correctly punctuated direct quotations? (See pages 461–462.)
- _____ Does my final copy follow the correct format assigned by my teacher?

Adding an MLA Works-Cited Page

A works-cited page lists in alphabetical order the books and materials you refer to in your report. Follow your teacher's guidelines and those in this section. Double-space the information you include in your works-cited page, indenting the second line of each entry 1/2 inch (5 typed spaces). Underline titles and other words that would be italicized in print. (See page 463.)

- **Books**—A typical entry for a book
  Author (last name first). <u>Title of the book</u>. City where
      book is published: Publisher, copyright date.

- **Magazines**—A typical entry for a magazine
  Author (last name first). "Title of the article." <u>Title of the
      magazine</u> day month year: page numbers.

- **Internet**—A typical entry for a Web page
  Author (last name first). "Post title." <u>Site title</u>.
      Post date or last update. Host site.
      Date accessed <Electronic address>.

Helpful Hint

Information that can be found in a general dictionary or encyclopedia is considered common knowledge and does not require documentation. However, this doesn't mean that you can copy the information word for word.

Adding a Title Page

Center the following information on a separate sheet of paper to prepare your title page, if it is required. (Follow your teacher's guidelines.)

- title of your report
- your name
- your teacher's name
- the name of the course
- the date

Works-Cited Entries

Print Sources

One Author
Meldrum, Christina. Madapple. New York: Knopf, 2008.

Two or Three Authors
Edwards, Bradley C., and Philip Ragan. Leaving the Planet by Space Elevator. Seattle: Lulu.com, 2006.

More Than Three Authors
Fawcett, Bill, et al. Liftport—The Space Elevator: Opening Space to Everyone. Decatur, GA: Meisha Merlin, 2006.

Single Work from an Anthology
Baum, L. Frank. "The Capture of Father Time." The Norton Anthology of Children's Literature. Ed. Jack Zipes. New York: Norton, 2005. 571–576.

One Volume of a Multivolume Work
Bauer, Susan Wise. The Story of the World: History for the Classical Child. Vol. 3. Charles City, VA: Peace Hill, 2004.

Signed Article in a Magazine
Flight, Georgia. "The 62,000-Mile Elevator Ride." Business 2.0 Magazine 1 Mar. 2006: 12–13.

Unsigned Article in a Magazine
"Classic Tours." National Geographic Traveler May/June 2008: 108–109.

Signed Newspaper Article
Veragon, Dan. "Census of All Sea Life Tallies Up Surprises." USA Today 10 Nov. 2008: D5.

Unsigned Editorial or Story
"My name is URL." Toronto Star 10 Aug. 2008: E2.

Government Publication
United States. Federal Citizen Information Center. Catch the Spirit: A Student's Guide to Community Service. Pueblo, CO: GPO, 2007.

Signed Pamphlet
Grayson, George W. Mexico's Struggle with 'Drugs and Thugs'. New York: Foreign Policy Associates, Inc., 2008.

Electronic Sources

Filmstrip, Slide Program, DVD, Videocassette

Galvin, Maryanne. What's Going On Up There? DVD. MG
Productions, 2007.

Television or Radio Program

"Alien from Earth." Nova. PBS. MPTV, Milwaukee, WI.
11 Nov. 2008.

Online Article

Shelef, Ben. "Where's My Space Elevator?" Discovery Space
20 Oct. 2008. Discovery Communications, LLC. 26 Oct.
2009 <http://dsc.discovery.com/space/my-take/
space-elevator-ben-shelef.html>.

Online Book

Irving, Washington. The Adventures of Captain Bonneville.
Project Gutenberg. 18 Feb. 2006. 15 Sept. 2009 < http://
www.gutenberg.org/files/1372/1372.txt>.

E-mail

Faraday, Ralph. E-mail to the author. 25 Nov. 2009.

Web Site

NASA Quest. Ed. Linda Conrad. June 2007. NASA. 26 Oct.
2009 <http://quest.nasa.gov>.

Reference Book on CD-ROM

"Quantrill's Raiders." Civil War Encyclopedia. CD-ROM.
Bridgewater, WV: CounterTop Software, 2001.

MLA Research Paper

Student writer Roselle Gower wrote the following research paper about a very old idea that is becoming a new possibility.

Roselle Gower
Mr. Clos
Science 8
October 1, 2009

Elevator to the Stars

Beginning
The beginning grabs the reader's attention, introduces the topic, and provides a controlling idea (underlined).

A new space race is on! Unlike the first space race, which was a twentieth-century struggle between two global superpowers, this one is a friendly competition between businesses and universities all around the world. In many cases, they are each tackling different parts of the same project: to build an elevator to space.

The idea of a space elevator may seem unbelievable at first. Even Arthur C. Clarke, who described it in his 1979 novel *The Foundations of Paradise*, said that the first space elevator will be built "about 10 years after everyone stops laughing" (Shelef). However, the idea has been discussed among scientists for more than 100 years.

Middle
The first middle paragraphs provide background information.

Early Dreaming

It was first proposed in 1895 by a Russian scholar named Konstantin Tsiolkovski. After seeing the Eiffel Tower at the World's Fair in Paris, he imagined a tower reaching all the way to orbit (Edwards and Ragan 22).

Gower 2

Other scientists and engineers debated the possibilities for the next 90 years, trying to figure out how to accomplish it. Then, in 1975, Jerome Pearson suggested creating an orbital station and hanging a cable from there all the way to the ground (23).

Pearson's idea remained in the realm of science fiction for years because no material existed to make a cable strong enough to bear its own weight over the great distance from ground to orbit. Then, in 1991, a Japanese researcher discovered carbon nanotubes, and that changed everything (David). Carbon nanotubes are 400 times stronger than steel. Woven together into a fiber, they are less strong, but a hair-thin strand can still hold the weight of an automobile (Ohlson). Once we can mass-produce these fibers, the space elevator becomes a possibility.

Middle
The writer indicates sources in the text, and uses parenthetical citations to refer to the works-cited page.

Present-Day Planning

To build the first space elevator, Bradley and Ragan say that scientists plan to wind a ribbon of the fiber 20 centimeters wide and 63,000 miles long onto a spool the size of a semitruck. A rocket will carry that spool into geosynchronous earth orbit (GEO), about 30,000 miles up, where it will begin unwinding the ribbon toward the ground while the spool itself travels farther upward. The bottom end will then be attached to an ocean platform, while the empty spool remains at the top as a counterweight. Next,

The discussion shifts to modern plans for the elevator.

Gower 3

small climbing machines will travel up this first elevator, each adding more ribbon to its width (46–54). The final result will be a ribbon three feet wide and as thick as a sheet of plastic wrap, though 180 times as strong as steel (Flight 13). Because the far end of the ribbon circles the earth at the same speed as the planet turns, the ribbon will stretch straight up into the sky.

Once this ribbon is finished, climbing cars the size of a jumbo jet will use it, carrying cargo and even people into space (12). Unlike rockets, these climbers won't need rapid acceleration to escape Earth's gravity. Instead, they will smoothly speed up to about 120 miles per hour, taking a seven-day trip to reach GEO, where an enormous space station will be built (Edwards and Ragan 56). Because GEO is at zero gravity, this space station can be expanded to any size without straining the elevator ribbon (65–66).

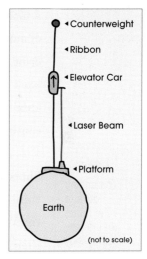

◄ Counterweight

◄ Ribbon

◄ Elevator Car

◄ Laser Beam

◄ Platform

Earth

(not to scale)

Unlike rockets, which have to carry their own fuel, the climbers will be powered from the ground. Currently, NASA sponsors yearly competitions for experimental climbers powered by a ground-based laser. Photoelectric cells on these machines convert the laser light into electrical power

Hand-drawn illustrations help the reader understand the text.

Transition words and phrases connect ideas.

(Ohlson). However, because carbon nanotubes are a very good conductor of electricity, engineers in Japan hope to make a ribbon that can itself conduct power to the cars (Lewis).

Future Space Travel

The completed space elevator will make travel into space much safer and cheaper than by rocket. From there, a moon base can be built for the same cost as a single flight of our current space shuttle. More satellites can be put into orbit, including big solar-power satellites to beam energy back to Earth. Tourists will be able to travel to the zero-G space station just as people today take jet flights from one continent to another (Galvin).

All of this is likely to happen much sooner than you think. Consider that in 1903 the Wright brothers made their first successful airplane flight, and by 1918 airplanes were delivering U.S. mail ("Airplane"). As Edwards and Ragan point out, "In 1957, no rocket had entered space, yet 12 years later men were walking on the moon!" (41). Given the work now being done to develop the space elevator, we may be the first generation of space tourists!

NASA artist's image of a climber on the space elevator.

Ending
The ending looks to the future of the new technology and provides a strong final thought.

Gower 5

Works Cited

The works-cited page includes a variety of sources.

"Airplane Timeline." Greatest Engineering Achievements of the 20th Century. 2008. National Academy of Engineering. 28 Oct. 2009 <http://www.greatachievements.org/?id=3728>.

Only works actually cited in the paper are listed.

David, Leonard. "Going Up? Private Group Begins Work on Space Elevator." Space.com. 19 Aug. 2002. 27 Oct. 2009 <http://www.space.com/businesstechnology/technology/elevator_update_020819.html>.

Edwards, Bradley C., and Philip Ragan. Leaving the Planet by Space Elevator. Seattle: Lulu.com, 2006.

Entries are alphabetical by author or by title if no author is given.

Flight, Georgia. "The 62,000-Mile Elevator Ride." Business 2.0 Magazine. 1 Mar. 2006: 12-13.

Galvin, Maryanne. What's Going On Up There? DVD. MG Productions, 2007.

All entries are double-spaced, with a hanging indent.

Lewis, Leo. "Ground floor, Earth. Going up! First floor, astronomy and space suits. Thank you for riding the elevator to the stars." The Times 22 Sept. 2008, Overseas news: 32.

Ohlson, Kristin. "Space Odyssey." Entrepreneur June 2007: 36.

URL's are broken only after a slash.

Shelef, Ben. "Where's My Space Elevator?" Discovery Space 20 Oct. 2008. Discovery Communications, LLC. 26 Oct. 2009 <http://dsc.discovery.com/space/my-take/space-elevator-ben-shelef.html>.

Workplace
Writing

Writing in the
Workplace

You already know that novelists and journalists write for a living. But did you know that writing is important in just about every work area, including public safety, science, and government? Firefighters, for instance, write incident reports, business letters, and e-mail messages. Scientists write lab reports and scholarly articles. Politicians draft new legislation, write proposals, and correspond with their constituents.

In today's workplace, individuals must be able to write clearly and concisely to do their jobs well. This chapter lists some common forms of workplace writing that you can use in school or on the job. Also included is a rubric for workplace writing.

What's Ahead

- Types of Workplace Writing
- Workplace Writing in School
- Rubric for Workplace Writing

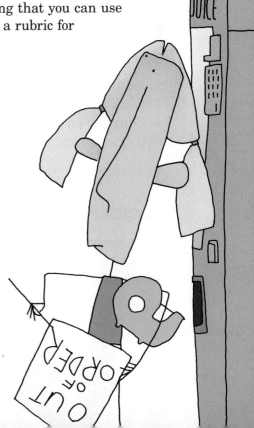

Types of Workplace Writing

There are many forms of workplace writing. Listed below are a few of the most common types.

Letters

Letters of Application

Thank-You Letters

Letters of Complaint

Bad-News Letters

Letters of Request

Informative Letters

Letters Promoting Something

E-Mail Messages

Brief Reminders

Information Exchanges

Recommendations

Announcements

Thank-You Notes

Problem-Solution E-Mail

Reports

Sales Reports

Minutes of Meetings

Accident or Injury Reports

Job Completion Summaries

Proposals for New Products

Progress Reports

Research Reports

Case Studies

Special Forms

News Releases

Product Brochures

Newsletters

Advertisements

Manuals

Blogs

Workplace Writing in School

Writing letters, e-mails, and proposals can help you improve your communication skills, which, in turn, will help you become a better student. Here are some of the ways you can use workplace writing in school:

Letters

You might write . . .

- a **thank-you letter** expressing your appreciation for the help a professional gave you for a school project.
- a **letter of complaint** to a school official stating your concern about a new or existing situation.

> Writing a thoughtful letter shows that you really care.

E-Mail Messages

You might write . . .

- an **e-mail message** to your teacher updating your progress (or lack of it) on an important assignment.
- an **e-mail message** to the principal reminding him or her about the next student-council meeting.

Reports

You might write . . .

- a **summary report** of a field trip or a visit to a specific workplace.
- a **proposal** for a science project or research paper.

Special Forms

You might write . . .

- a **news release** about an upcoming school activity.
- a **pamphlet or brochure** telling new students about a particular club or organization.

Rubric for Workplace Writing

Use this rubric as a guide when you assess your workplace writing.

Ideas

The writing . . .

—— has a clear, central message.
—— provides details that support the central message.

Organization

—— begins by capturing the reader's interest and introducing the message.
—— develops the message in the middle paragraphs.
—— ends by reviewing the message or making a call to action.

Voice

—— sounds knowledgeable and informed.
—— speaks in a voice appropriate to the audience.

Word Choice

—— uses precise nouns and active verbs.

Sentence Fluency

—— uses a variety of sentence lengths and beginnings.
—— flows smoothly from one sentence to another.

Conventions

—— uses end punctuation and commas correctly.
—— correctly capitalizes first words and proper nouns.
—— avoids spelling errors.
—— correctly uses words *(there, they're, their)*.
—— follows the correct format for the type of message.

Business
Letters

Even in this era of e-mail messages and fax sheets, people in the workplace still write traditional business letters. They use this form of communication for many reasons—sharing ideas, promoting products, asking for help. An effective business letter gets the reader's attention, and it gets things done, which is what business is all about.

Business letters can help you get things done, too—both in and out of school. Letters can connect you with experts, organizations, and companies that can give you information, help you solve problems, and much more. This chapter covers everything you need to know about writing business letters, from understanding the basic parts to sending the finished product.

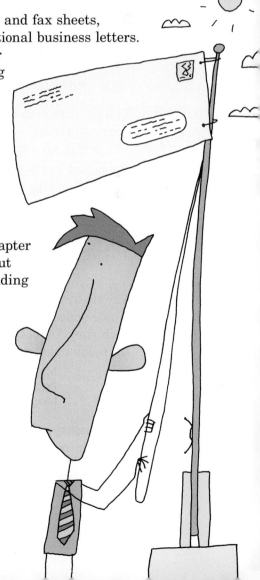

What's Ahead

- Parts of a Basic Business Letter
- Writing Guidelines
- Using Clear, Fair Language
- Sending Your Letter
- Business-Letter Sampler

Parts of a Basic Business Letter

A business letter is made up of six basic parts: the **heading**, **inside address**, **salutation**, **body**, **closing**, and **signature**.

1 The heading gives the writer's complete address, plus the date the letter was written.

2 The inside address gives the name, title, and address of the person or organization you are writing to.
- If the person has a title, make sure to include it. If the title is short, write it on the same line as the name, separated by a comma. If the title is long, write it on the next line.
- If you are writing to an organization or a business, but not to a specific person, begin the inside address with the name of the organization or business.

3 The salutation is the greeting. Always insert a colon after your salutation.
- Use *Mr., Mrs.,* or *Ms.* plus the person's last name. Do not guess at *Miss* or *Mrs.*
- If you don't know the name of the person who will read your letter, use a salutation like one of these:

> Dear Store Owner: (the person's title)
> Dear Sir or Madam:
> Dear American Red Cross:
> Attention: Customer Service

4 The body is the main part of the letter. It should have single-spaced paragraphs with double spacing between each one. (Do not indent paragraphs.) If the letter is longer than one page, make a heading on the second page.

> Ms. Bednarik (reader's name)
> Page 2
> March 10, 2009 (date)

5 The closing ends the letter politely. Use *Sincerely, Yours sincerely,* or *Yours truly* followed by a comma.

6 The signature, including the writer's handwritten and typed name, make the letter official.

Basic Business Letter

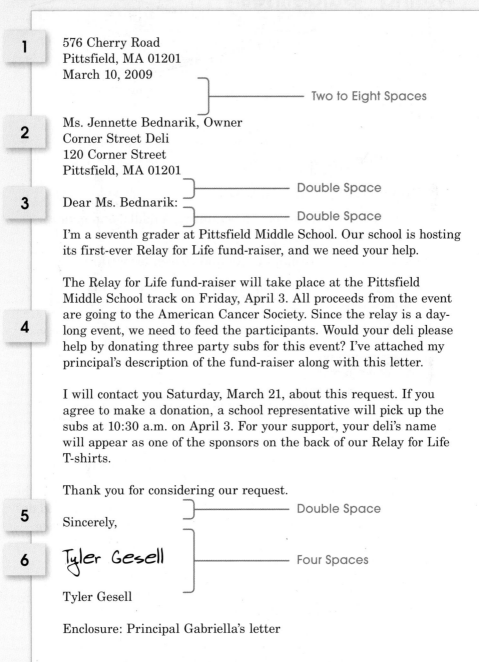

1

576 Cherry Road
Pittsfield, MA 01201
March 10, 2009

———— Two to Eight Spaces

2

Ms. Jennette Bednarik, Owner
Corner Street Deli
120 Corner Street
Pittsfield, MA 01201

———— Double Space

3

Dear Ms. Bednarik:

———— Double Space

I'm a seventh grader at Pittsfield Middle School. Our school is hosting its first-ever Relay for Life fund-raiser, and we need your help.

4

The Relay for Life fund-raiser will take place at the Pittsfield Middle School track on Friday, April 3. All proceeds from the event are going to the American Cancer Society. Since the relay is a day-long event, we need to feed the participants. Would your deli please help by donating three party subs for this event? I've attached my principal's description of the fund-raiser along with this letter.

I will contact you Saturday, March 21, about this request. If you agree to make a donation, a school representative will pick up the subs at 10:30 a.m. on April 3. For your support, your deli's name will appear as one of the sponsors on the back of our Relay for Life T-shirts.

Thank you for considering our request.

5

Sincerely,

———— Double Space

6

Tyler Gesell

———— Four Spaces

Tyler Gesell

Enclosure: Principal Gabriella's letter

Writing Guidelines

Prewriting—Choosing a Topic

- Think about your goal or purpose. In one sentence, write your reason for writing—what you want your reader to know or do.
- Gather your information. List the details you will need to include in your letter. Then think about the best way to present them.

Writing—Writing the First Draft

Always think in terms of the beginning, middle, and ending when you write your letter.

Beginning ▪ Introduce your subject and reason for writing.

Middle ▪ Present all of the important facts and details in short, clearly stated paragraphs.

Ending ▪ Explain what action you would like your reader to take.

Helpful Hint

State all of your ideas positively and politely. Your reader will more likely respond favorably to your letter if it has a positive tone.

Revising and Editing—Improving Your Writing

____ **Ideas** Does my letter have one clear focus? Do I support the focus with details? Do I state what I want the reader to do?

____ **Organization** Does my opening get the reader's attention and state my reason for writing? Is the middle well organized? Do I end the letter well?

____ **Voice** Does my voice sound reasonable and respectful?

____ **Word Choice** Have I used clear, fair language?

____ **Sentence Fluency** Does my letter read smoothly and clearly?

____ **Conventions** Have I carefully checked punctuation, capitalization, spelling, and grammar?

____ **Presentation** Have I followed the letter format? Have I correctly addressed and stamped my envelope?

Using Clear, Fair Language

When you write, make every effort to treat both genders fairly. Be especially careful of using male-only words.

- Use equal language for both genders:
  > The men and the women worked together on the committee.
  > Dwight and Jenna
  > Mr. Ian Thompson, Mrs. Shirley Thompson

  Don't give special treatment to one of the genders:
  > The men and the ladies worked together on the committee.
  > Dwight and Miss Johnson
  > Mr. Ian Thompson, Mrs. Ian Thompson

- Use *he or she,* or make the antecedent and its pronoun plural:
  > A politician leads a public life when he or she runs for office.
  > Politicians lead public lives when they run for office.

- Address a position:
  > Dear Personnel Officer:
  > Dear Members of the Big Bird Fan Club:

  Don't use gender-specific references in the salutation of a business letter when you don't know the person's name:
  > Dear Sir: Dear Gentlemen:

- Use gender-free words or titles:

Yes	No
chair	chairman
salesperson	salesman
mail carrier	mailman
police officer	policeman
flight attendant	stewardess
doctor	lady doctor
nurse	male nurse
housekeeper	maid

Sending Your Letter

Addressing the Envelope

Place the return address in the upper left corner, the destination address in the center, and the correct postage at the upper right.

```
TYLER GESELL
576 CHERRY ROAD
PITTSFIELD MA 01201                              postage


              MS JENNETTE BEDNARIK
              CORNER STREET DELI
              120 CORNER STREET
              PITTSFIELD MA 01201
```

Acceptable Envelope Forms

There are two acceptable forms for addressing the envelope. You can use upper- and lowercase letters as well as punctuation, or as the postal service recommends, you can use all caps and no punctuation.

Traditional Form	New Form
Mr. James Evans	MR JAMES EVANS
512 N. Adams Ave.	512 N ADAMS AVE
Seattle, WA 98102-3421	SEATTLE WA 98102-3421

U.S. Postal Service Guidelines

1. Capitalize everything and leave out ALL punctuation.
2. Use the list of common abbreviations found in the National ZIP Code Directory. (See page 349.) Use numerals rather than words for numbered streets and avenues (9TH AVE NE, 3RD ST SW).
3. If you know the ZIP + 4 code, use it. You can get this information by phoning the postal service.

Folding the Letter

1. Fold the bottom third of the letter up, and crease.
2. Fold the top third of the letter down, and crease.
3. Insert the letter (with the open end at the top) into the envelope.

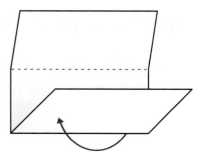

State Abbreviations

	Traditional	Postal		Traditional	Postal		Traditional	Postal
Alabama	Ala.	AL	Louisiana	La.	LA	Oklahoma	Okla.	OK
Alaska	Alaska	AK	Maine	Maine	ME	Oregon	Ore.	OR
Arizona	Ariz.	AZ	Maryland	Md.	MD	Pennsylvania	Pa.	PA
Arkansas	Ark.	AR	Massachusetts	Mass.	MA	Puerto Rico	P.R.	PR
California	Calif.	CA	Michigan	Mich.	MI	Rhode Island	R.I.	RI
Colorado	Colo.	CO	Minnesota	Minn.	MN	South		
Connecticut	Conn.	CT	Mississippi	Miss.	MS	Carolina	S.C.	SC
Delaware	Del.	DE	Missouri	Mo.	MO	South Dakota	S.D.	SD
District			Montana	Mont.	MT	Tennessee	Tenn.	TN
of Columbia	D.C.	DC	Nebraska	Neb.	NE	Texas	Tex.	TX
Florida	Fla.	FL	Nevada	Nev.	NV	Utah	Utah	UT
Georgia	Ga.	GA	New			Vermont	Vt.	VT
Guam	Guam	GU	Hampshire	N.H.	NH	Virginia	Va.	VA
Hawaii	Hawaii	HI	New Jersey	N.J.	NJ	Virgin Islands	V.I.	VI
Idaho	Idaho	ID	New Mexico	N.M.	NM	Washington	Wash.	WA
Illinois	Ill.	IL	New York	N.Y.	NY	West Virginia	W.Va.	WV
Indiana	Ind.	IN	North			Wisconsin	Wis.	WI
Iowa	Iowa	IA	Carolina	N.C.	NC	Wyoming	Wyo.	WY
Kansas	Kan.	KS	North Dakota	N.D.	ND			
Kentucky	Ky.	KY	Ohio	Ohio	OH			

Address Abbreviations

	Traditional	Postal		Traditional	Postal		Traditional	Postal
Avenue	Ave.	AVE	Lake	L.	LK	Road	Rd.	RD
Boulevard	Blvd.	BLVD	Lane	Ln.	LN	Rural	R.	R
Court	Ct.	CT	North	N.	N	South	S.	S
Drive	Dr.	DR	Park	Pk.	PK	Square	Sq.	SQ
East	E.	E	Parkway	Pky.	PKY	Street	St.	ST
Expressway	Expy.	EXPY	Place	Pl.	PL	Terrace	Ter.	TER
Heights	Hts.	HTS	Plaza	Plaza	PLZ	Turnpike	Tpke.	TPKE
Highway	Hwy.	HWY	Ridge	Rdg.	RDG	Village	Vil.	VLG
Hospital	Hosp.	HOSP	River	R.	RV	West	W.	W

Business-Letter Sampler

On the following pages, you will find three different types of business letters. Turn here for help when you need to make a request, state a problem, or apply for something.

Request Letter

2778 E. Washington Avenue
Albuquerque, NM 87101
February 3, 2009

Mr. Eduardo Santora
Albuquerque Humane Society
404 Mesa Drive
Albuquerque, NM 87101

Beginning
State your purpose.

Dear Mr. Santora:

I'm writing to set up an interview with a representative from the Albuquerque Humane Society.

Middle
Explain your need.

For my eighth-grade school research project, I need to gather information about animal rescue in this area. I'm curious to understand the local Humane Society's involvement with this issue. I was wondering if you, or someone else from the Humane Society, would be available to answer a few of my questions regarding animal rescue.

Ending
Help the reader fulfill the request.

Could we plan on meeting Tuesday, February 10, around 4:00 p.m., for the interview? On Monday, February 9, I will call to confirm this time or work out a time and date more convenient for you.

Thank you.

Sincerely,

Emma Leslie

Emma Leslie

Letter Stating a Problem

3434 North Boulevard
Minneapolis, MN 55400
July 22, 2009

Southside Shoes
5667 68th Street
Flushing Meadows, NY 11365

Attention: Customer Service Department

Beginning
Identify the
problem.

On July 15, 2009, I purchased your company's
"Sporty Sandals" at a local shoe store for $15.99. I love the
way they feel on my feet, especially the extra comfort layer
on the soles. However, after wearing the sandals for one
week, the comfort layer has nearly peeled completely off
my right sandal.

Middle
Supply the
necessary
details.

I can understand how normal wear and tear could lead to
this problem, but it shouldn't happen after just one week.
It appears the sandal was not properly put together.

Identify the
best solution.

I brought the sandals back to the store where I purchased
them but was unable to obtain a refund. I'm sending you
both sandals with a copy of my receipt. If the sandals were
not properly made, I would like a refund or a new pair.

Ending
Provide
your contact
information.

If you have questions, please call me at 317-686-2185 after
3:30 p.m. I look forward to hearing from you.

Sincerely,

Alvaro Tevez

Alvaro Tevez

Enclosure: sandals and receipt

Application Letter

4293 Kessler Street
Columbia, MO 65203
November 19, 2009

Mrs. Tillie Shaw
3458 Charles Lane
Columbia, MO 65203

Dear Mrs. Shaw:

Beginning
Identify the
position.

My math teacher, Mrs. Conley, mentioned that you are looking for a new babysitter for your 5-year-old son and 3-year-old daughter. I am an experienced babysitter and would love the opportunity to work for you.

Middle
Discuss your
qualifications.

For the past two summers, I have been a babysitter for my neighbor's two young children. I also volunteer at a day-care center in town. I would be available for babysitting services after school and on weekends. Attached to this letter is the contact information for the neighbor that I worked for.

Ending
Ask for an
interview.

I would be happy to meet you in person at your convenience. You can contact me any weekday after 3:30 p.m. at 529-8899. Thank you for considering my application.

Sincerely,

Latesha Harris

Latesha Harris

Enclosure: reference

Special Forms of
Workplace Writing

Workplace writing is practical writing. E-mail messages, minutes, proposals, and lab reports—all these forms of workplace writing are used by millions of workers. They also play an important role in a full-time job you know a lot about—being a student. Learning how to use these forms will help you become a better communicator, record-keeper, and planner now and for years to come.

This chapter contains guidelines and samples for e-mail messages, minutes, proposals, and lab reports. You will find these forms of writing especially useful now as you plan and carry out classroom assignments and projects.

What's Ahead

- E-Mail
- Minutes
- Proposal
- Lab Report

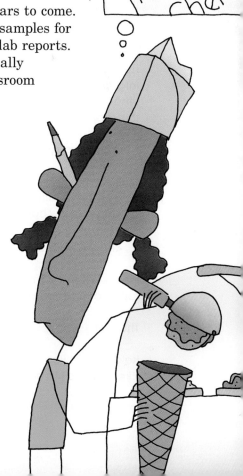

E-Mail

E-mail has largely taken the place of the friendly letter as a quick way to stay in touch with friends and family. It also helps students and teachers exchange information. Student Keigan Eastwood wrote the following e-mail about an upcoming project.

E-Mail Message

Send   Cancel   Save   Attach

To: nwhitmore@ips-jefferson.edu

Subject: Topic for Cultural Research Project

Hi, Ms. Whitmore:

I've done some research on modern Egyptian culture for my project, but I was wondering if I could change my topic to the culture of modern Georgia (the country, not the state). While I was researching Egypt, I stumbled upon some pretty cool information about Georgia. This information got me curious about Georgian culture, and I thought the country would make an interesting topic for this project.

Here are two good Web sites I found about Georgian culture:

1. Georgia: Culture
   <http://www.cac-biodiversity.org/geo/geo_culture.htm>
2. Culture of Georgia
   <http://www.everyculture.com/Ge-It/Georgia.html>

Please let me know if it is okay for me to change my topic, or if I should stick with my original choice.

Thanks!

Keigan Eastwood
<keastwood14@hotmail.com>

Writing Guidelines

E-mail is an incredible medium that allows you to communicate quickly and easily. Sometimes, though, the ease of e-mail does more harm than good when the sender fails to take care in her or his writing. Poorly written e-mails can be confusing and reflect negatively on the sender, so be sure to take extra care when you send them to your teachers, administrators, officials, and so on.

Prewriting—Choosing a Topic

- Be clear about the purpose for your message.
- Then gather all the details you need to include.

Writing—Writing the First Draft

Beginning ■ Complete the e-mail's header as directed by your program. Then type a subject line that tells your reader the topic at a glance. At the beginning of your message, greet the reader and state your reason for writing.

Middle ■ Provide all the details that the reader needs, carefully organized and clearly stated.

Ending ■ If follow-up action is needed, spell it out. If not, politely end the message.

Revising and Editing—Improving Your Writing

Check your e-mail before sending it. Although an e-mail can be informal, it shouldn't be messy, wordy, or full of careless errors.

_____ Is my message **accurate**—from the reader's e-mail address to each fact or detail I've provided?

_____ Is my message **complete**—providing all the information needed so that I don't have to send another message?

_____ Is my message **clear**—written in short, double-spaced paragraphs with numbers, lists, and headings?

_____ Is my e-mail **correct**—have I checked for spelling, punctuation, and other errors?

Minutes

Minutes track the official business of a meeting. The following minutes record a student council meeting.

Minutes

Beginning
Identify the group and its members.

Middle
Number each topic with the year (09) and item number. Item numbers start over with a new year.

Ending
List future business.

Minutes

Marshall Middle School Student Council Meeting
Thursday, Nov. 5, 2009: Room 218

Present: Val Bulmer, president; Rolando Latorre, vice president; Neomi Sheplar, Caitlin McDonald, Shaun Macivor, class reps; Mr. Walsh, faculty rep.

09.147   Val called the meeting to order. The agenda was approved.

Old Business

09.148   The secretary read the minutes of the October 30 meeting. They were accepted without change.

New Business

09.149   Shaun proposed that the school should join in the "Holiday Giving Project" (December 1–7). These were his reasons:

1. The event would make students more aware of the less fortunate.
2. The money raised would help buy presents for struggling families during the holiday season.

The motion to sponsor this event passed. Details will be discussed in two weeks.

Next Meeting

09.150   The lunch-hour policy will be discussed.

09.151   The next meeting will be on Nov. 12 at 3:30 p.m. (Room 218).

Submitted by Caitlin McDonald, secretary

Writing Guidelines

Minutes summarize a meeting—what was discussed, what was decided upon, and what action will be taken. The guidelines below will help you take good notes and write clear meeting minutes.

Prewriting—Choosing a Topic

- Come to the meeting prepared with the proper materials— paper, pen, or even a laptop.
- Review the previous minutes and the meeting's agenda.
- Take notes of key points, speaker's names, and important decisions.

Writing—Writing the First Draft

Beginning ■ List details identifying the meeting—the group's name; the meeting's purpose, location, and time; and the names of those present. (Also name those people who are absent.)

Middle ■ Identify all issues discussed, any decisions made (sometimes called *motions*), and any follow-up actions needed (including names and deadlines).

Ending ■ Give details about the next meeting.

Revising and Editing—Improving Your Writing

Use the following checklist to improve your minutes.

____ Are all of the details accurate—names, dates, item numbers, wording of decisions?

____ Is my tone neutral? Have I left out feelings and judgments?

____ Have I checked the spellings of all of the names in the minutes?

____ Have I checked all my punctuation carefully?

Helpful Hint

With minutes, timing is important. Draft the minutes *right after* the meeting, and distribute copies to all of the group members *within a day or two*.

Proposal

A proposal suggests a change or outlines a project. In the proposal below, student Ted Hillestad details a castle construction project.

Proposal

Proposal

Date: January 13, 2009
To: Mrs. Michelle Parker
From: Ted Hillestad
Subject: Castle Construction for History Project

Project Description: For my history project on medieval life, I plan to build a scale model (2' x 2' x 2') of an English castle and write an essay to go with it.

Materials Needed:
1. Books on medieval life and on castles
2. 3' x 3' plywood board (for base)
3. Clay (for walls)
4. Toilet-paper rolls (for frame of towers)
5. Toothpicks and glue (for ladders, gates)
6. Popsicle sticks and string (for drawbridge)
7. Cloth (for banners and tapestries)

Deadlines and Procedure:
1. Jan. 27   Research medieval castles
2. Feb. 4   Design my model on paper as a blueprint
3. Feb. 17   Plan and write first draft of paper
4. Feb. 23   Complete paper and present project to class

Outcome: My project will help the class understand how a castle was built and how it was used.

Is this project acceptable for this assignment? I would appreciate any suggestions.

Beginning
Introduce your project's precise topic.

Middle
Explain in detail the materials needed to complete the project.

Present your project schedule.

Ending
Focus on results and ask for approval.

Writing Guidelines

Is there a project you want to do in one of your classes? Do you see a problem that needs fixing in your school or community? Then present it in a proposal—a detailed plan for doing a project, solving a problem, or meeting a need.

Prewriting—Choosing a Topic

- Study the problem, project, subject, or need. Define it, know its parts, and explore its background.
- Research your solution or idea. Will it work? Why or how?
- Think about your reader. How can you convince him or her of your idea's value?

Writing—Writing the First Draft

Beginning ■ Briefly introduce the problem, need, or idea that you're addressing. Then describe what you propose to do.

Middle ■ Provide convincing details supporting your proposal. Why is the problem, need, or idea important? Is your project workable? Why is your solution the best one? Include these details:

1. Equipment, material, and other resources needed
2. Steps to take and a schedule for completing them
3. Results expected

Ending ■ Focus on the benefits of the project and ask for its approval.

Revising and Editing—Improving Your Writing

Use the following checklist to improve your proposal.

___ Is my proposal detailed, specific, and accurate?
___ Have I organized my points in an effective way? Will my reader say, *This will work!*
___ Do I show that I care about the project?
___ Have I used headings, lists, and white space?
___ Have I checked punctuation, capitalization, spelling, and grammar?

Lab Report

Lab reports outline the results of experiments, focusing on the application of the scientific method. By describing the purpose, variables, hypothesis, experiment, observations, and conclusion, the report provides complete information for the reader. The following report outlines an experiment about growing mold.

Lab Report

A Moldy Problem

Beginning
State your purpose, variables, and hypothesis.

Purpose: Find out what conditions will make mold grow fastest on bread.

Variables: Temperature and moisture

Hypothesis: Mold will grow fastest on bread that is kept warm and moist.

Middle
Explain the details of the experiment and your observations.

Experiment: Three slices of freshly baked white bread were put into separate sandwich bags and labeled A, B, and C. A small amount (2 T.) of water was placed in Bag A, and the bag was placed inside a warm, dark cabinet. Bags B and C got no water. Bag B was placed in the refrigerator and Bag C was placed inside a cool, dark cabinet. The bags were checked daily for one week, and any changes were observed.

Observations: Nothing happened until the fifth day. The bread in the refrigerator appeared fresh. The bread in the cool, dark cabinet had no mold. The moist bread in the warm cabinet was starting to grow spots of greenish-gray mold on the crust.

Ending
Report your conclusion.

Conclusion: The hypothesis that mold will grow fastest on bread that is kept warm and moist was correct. However, it was expected that the mold would appear sooner than it did.

Writing Guidelines

When scientists conduct experiments, they document their findings in lab reports. You may be asked to write lab reports in your science classroom. If so, the following guidelines will help.

Prewriting—Choosing a Topic

- Choose a science topic related to a subject you are studying and that interests you. (Your science teacher may assign you a specific topic.)
- Research your topic and plan your experiment by reading relevant articles and jotting down details. Then decide what your experiment will be.

Writing—Writing the First Draft

A basic lab report has six parts: **(1)** purpose, **(2)** variables, **(3)** hypothesis, **(4)** experiment, **(5)** observations, and **(6)** conclusion. Each part should be labeled and addressed in a separate paragraph.

Beginning ■ Begin by briefly explaining the purpose of your experiment. Next, state which variables you will test. Finally, write a hypothesis, telling what you think you will find out from your experiment.

Middle ■ Explain the experiment and record your observations. Organize the details in time order (what happened first, second, next, and so on).

Ending ■ Lastly, write your conclusion. It should tell whether or not your hypothesis was correct.

Revising and Editing—Improving Your Writing

____ Do I clearly state the purpose, variables, hypothesis, and conclusion?
____ Do I include all of the necessary details of the experiment?
____ Are my observations clear and thorough?
____ Have I used headings and lists?
____ Have I checked my punctuation, capitalization, spelling, and grammar?

The Tools of
Learning

Study-Reading
Skills

In the past, people got most of their information from books—information that had been carefully written, selected, revised, edited, and finally published. That's a lot of refinement. Now, people (and that includes you) get a lot of information from Web sites, and these are not *always* carefully written or refined. That means you need to know how to sort through information on the Web to find what is reliable, balanced, and useful.

This chapter will help you safely navigate your study-reading of both online information and printed books and articles. You will also learn about common patterns of nonfiction, such as description and comparison/contrast.

What's Ahead

- Reading on the Internet
- Study-Reading Strategies
- Patterns of Nonfiction
- Study-Reading Review

Reading on the Internet

Reading on the Internet requires you to read at different speeds, for different purposes. Here are some of the types of reading you need to do.

■ Scanning

When you first conduct a search, scan the results page, looking for Web sites that may have the information you need. Read the heading and the first few lines of each suggested site to make sure it matches your **subject** and **purpose**. For example, this search for "Amazon rainforest" produced three top sites—one informational, one persuasive, and one commercial.

■ Evaluating

Once you select a site, quickly evaluate it to make sure it matches your needs. Ask yourself the following:

_____ Does the site look professional?

_____ Is the site free of obvious errors?

_____ Has the site been recently updated?

_____ Does the text seem fair and balanced?

_____ Do the images seem fair and balanced?

_____ Is the source clear?

Helpful Hint

Education (.edu), organization (.org), and government (.gov) sites are often more reliable than commercial (.com) sites.

Skimming

After you establish the reliability of a site, skim the contents, focusing on

- headings,
- images,
- links, and
- first and last sentences.

Skimming helps you preview the site. The cues above help you understand what information is available and how it is organized.

Study-Reading

Now you're ready to read the material with more care. For specific study-reading strategies, see pages (366–367).

Interacting

Many Web pages provide information in interactive forms, including videos, podcasts, surveys, contests, scavenger hunts, puzzles, games, and so on. For example, by mousing over a graphic, you may find additional information. So be sure to explore the interactive elements.

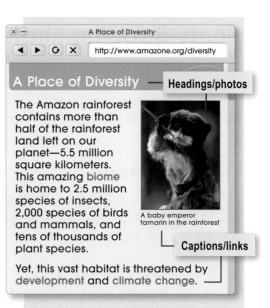

A Place of Diversity

http://www.amazone.org/diversity

A Place of Diversity — Headings/photos

The Amazon rainforest contains more than half of the rainforest land left on our planet—5.5 million square kilometers. This amazing biome is home to 2.5 million species of insects, 2,000 species of birds and mammals, and tens of thousands of plant species.

A baby emperor tamarin in the rainforest

Captions/links

Yet, this vast habitat is threatened by development and climate change.

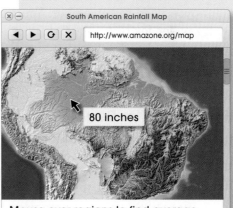

South American Rainfall Map

http://www.amazone.org/map

80 inches

Mouse over regions to find average yearly rainfall.

Study-Reading Strategies

Learning to be a good reader saves you time, adds to your understanding, and may result in better grades. When you are doing a reading assignment related to social studies, science, or another content subject, try using either the "Think and Read" or the "KWL" strategy.

Think and Read

Reading is thinking prompted by printed writing. Under each of the headings below, choose one or more of the suggestions to help you become a more thoughtful reader.

■ Think **Before** Reading

- Ask yourself what you already know about the topic.
- Skim over the text. (See "Skimming," page 365.)

■ Pause During Reading

- Write out questions, definitions, and important facts or ideas you need to remember. You can use sticky tabs or notebook paper for this.
- Reread difficult parts aloud. Then continue reading.
- To discover the definition of a word you don't know, use context clues, a dictionary, a glossary, or ask someone.

■ Reflect After Reading

- Tell yourself (or someone else) what you learned.
- List the points you want to remember.
- Write a summary of your reading.
- Determine which pattern of nonfiction the text follows. (See pages 368–379.) Create your own graphic organizer and take notes on the piece.

Helpful Hint

Turn to "Taking Reading Notes" on page 401 for more tips on reading to learn.

KWL

KWL is an effective study-reading strategy to use when you already know something about the topic. KWL stands for what I "Know," what I "Want" to know, and what I "Learned."

How to Use a KWL Chart

1. Write the topic of your reading at the top of a sheet of paper. Then divide the sheet into three columns and label them *K*, *W*, and *L*.
2. List what you already know in the K column.
3. Fill in the W column with questions you want to explore.
4. When you finish reading, fill in the L column with information you learned or still hope to learn.

The Milky Way

K	W	L
(What do I know?)	(What do I want to know?)	(What I learned or still hope to learn.)
It's a galaxy.	What's a galaxy?	A galaxy is a family of stars.
It's very big.	How big is the Milky Way?	The Milky Way is more than 100,000 light years across.
Our sun is a part of it.	Are there other suns in the Milky Way?	There are other suns, which may have planets orbiting them. (Have astronomers discovered any yet?)

Patterns of Nonfiction

Knowing the common patterns of nonfiction makes it easier to understand your assigned reading. Six of these patterns are reviewed in this chapter: *description, main idea/supporting details, comparison/ contrast, chronological order, cause and effect,* and *process.*

Description

This page from a Web site about earth science **describes** a geologic event called *subduction.* The page uses metaphors, relationships, and definitions to describe the event.

Study-Reading

As you read, notice important information you will want to record.

Previewing

ESExtravaganza.org

http://www.ESExtravaganza.org/tellme/subduction

ESExtravaganza

Home   Plate Tectonics   Rock Cycle   Rock ID   Fossils

Subduction: When Plates Collide

The ancients used to say we lived on the back of a giant turtle, floating on an endless ocean. In a sense, they were right. After all, we do live on a hard shell of rock that is floating on top of a sea of magma.

That's right. The continents literally float. The rock that makes up the continents is less dense than the rock in the mantle—and it's a good thing, or we'd sink to the core of the world.

Now, the crust of the earth isn't one solid piece, but rather is made up of curved stone plates that are jostling against each other. The movement of these plates is called plate tectonics. But what is moving the plates? Currents in the magma, that's what. Some currents rise up between plates, pushing them apart. These areas are called divergent boundaries, because the plates are spreading apart by centimeters each year. In other places, the currents sink away between the plates, drawing them together. These areas are called convergent boundaries. Imagine two inflatable rafts colliding. If they hit hard enough, one raft will slip under the other one—what in geological terms is a subduction zone.

As the plates grind past each other, earthquakes result. But this is just the beginning. The plate that is being thrust 100 kilometers down into the earth begins to melt, and all those light materials that make it up start bubbling to the surface again. The molten material surfaces in the form of volcanic eruptions.

Have you ever noticed that the places that have a lot of earthquakes often have a lot of volcanoes? That's because subduction zones create both phenomena.

This illustration shows how a volcano forms from layers that break through sedimentary strata.

Now, the crust of the earth isn't one solid piece, but rather is made up of curved stone plates that are jostling against each other. The movement of these plates is called **plate tectonics**. But what is moving the plates? Currents in the magma, that's what. Some currents rise up between plates, pushing them apart. These areas are called **divergent boundaries**, because the plates are spreading apart by centimeters each year. In other places, the currents sink away between the plates, drawing them together. These areas are called **convergent boundaries**. Imagine two inflatable rafts colliding. If they hit hard enough, one raft will slip under the other one—what in geological terms is a **subduction zone**.

Web ■ Use a web to help you organize the important information you noticed that follows a **description** pattern.

Note Taking

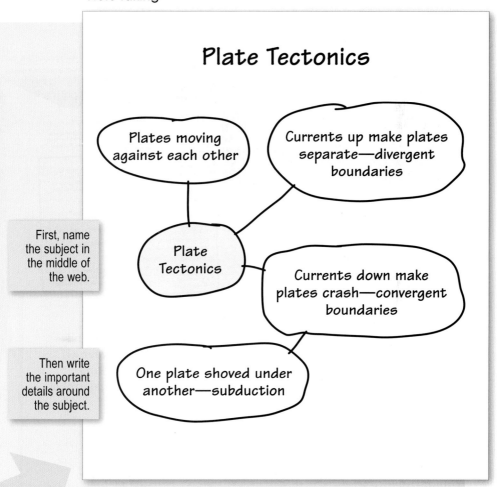

Plate Tectonics

Plates moving against each other

Currents up make plates separate—divergent boundaries

Plate Tectonics

Currents down make plates crash—convergent boundaries

One plate shoved under another—subduction

First, name the subject in the middle of the web.

Then write the important details around the subject.

Main Idea/Supporting Details

This information from a Web site about tae kwon do follows the **main idea/supporting details** pattern. The heading at the top of the page introduces the subject, the first couple of sentences share the main idea, and the rest of the page gives details that support this idea.

Previewing

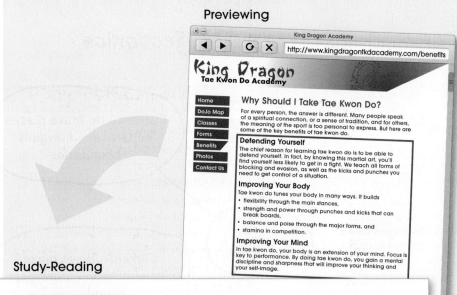

Study-Reading

Defending Yourself

The chief reason for learning tae kwon do is to be able to defend yourself. In fact, by knowing this martial art, you'll find yourself less likely to get in a fight. We teach all forms of blocking and evasion, as well as the kicks and punches you need to get control of a situation.

Improving Your Body

Tae kwon do tunes your body in many ways. It builds

- flexibility through the main stances,
- strength and power through punches and kicks that can break boards,
- balance and poise through the major forms, and
- stamina in competition.

Improving Your Mind

In tae kwon do, your body is an extension of your mind. Focus is key to performance. By doing tae kwon do, you gain a mental discipline and sharpness that will improve your thinking and your self-image.

Table Organizer ■ When a selection follows the **main idea/supporting details** pattern, use a table organizer to help you sort out the important details.

Note Taking

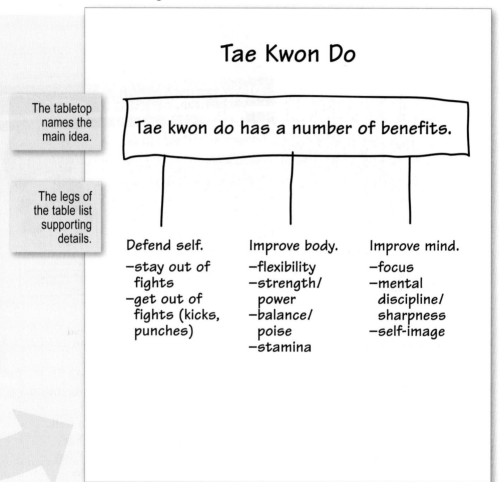

The tabletop names the main idea.

The legs of the table list supporting details.

Tae Kwon Do

Tae kwon do has a number of benefits.

Defend self.
—stay out of fights
—get out of fights (kicks, punches)

Improve body.
—flexibility
—strength/ power
—balance/ poise
—stamina

Improve mind.
—focus
—mental discipline/ sharpness
—self-image

Comparison/Contrast

Comparison/contrast is another important pattern of nonfiction. The information below, from an astronomy Web site, compares Venus and Earth. The first paragraph in the excerpt describes similarities between the planets. The second paragraph focuses on the differences.

Previewing

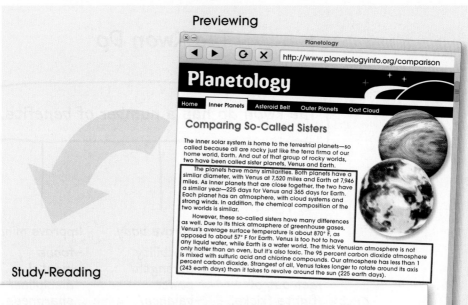

Study-Reading

The planets have many similarities. Both planets have a similar diameter, with Venus at 7,520 miles and Earth at 7,946 miles. As inner planets that are close together, the two have a similar year—225 days for Venus and 365 days for Earth. Each planet has an atmosphere, with cloud systems and strong winds. In addition, the chemical composition of the two worlds is similar.

However, these so-called sisters have many differences as well. Due to its thick atmosphere of greenhouse gases, Venus's average surface temperature is about 870° F, as opposed to about 57° F for Earth. Venus is too hot to have any liquid water, while Earth is a water world. The thick Venusian atmosphere is not only hotter than an oven, but it's also toxic. The 95 percent carbon dioxide atmosphere is mixed with sulfuric acid and chlorine compounds. Our atmosphere has less than 1 percent carbon dioxide. Strangest of all, Venus takes longer to rotate around its axis (243 earth days) than it takes to revolve around the sun (225 earth days).

Venn Diagram ■ A Venn diagram is an effective way to organize important information that **compares** two subjects.

Note Taking

Venus vs. Earth

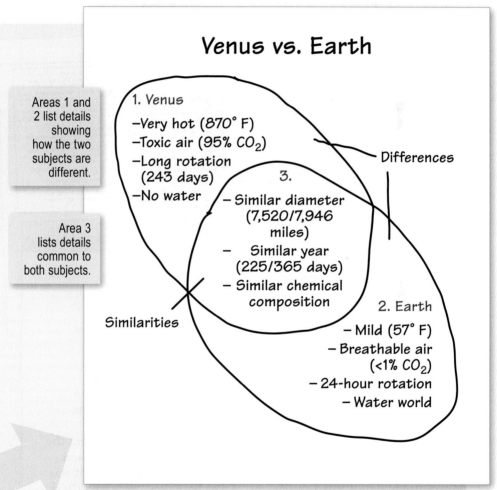

Areas 1 and 2 list details showing how the two subjects are different.

Area 3 lists details common to both subjects.

1. Venus

−Very hot (870° F)
−Toxic air (95% CO_2)
−Long rotation (243 days)
−No water

Differences

3.
− Similar diameter (7,520/7,946 miles)
− Similar year (225/365 days)
− Similar chemical composition

Similarities

2. Earth
− Mild (57° F)
− Breathable air (<1% CO_2)
− 24-hour rotation
− Water world

Chronological Order

This article taken from a history textbook follows the **chronological** (time order) pattern of organization. The article gives the basic facts about the Lewis and Clark expedition that opened up the western part of the United States.

Previewing

221

Lewis and Clark Expedition

In January of 1803, President Thomas Jefferson asked Congress for $2,500 to pay for an expedition to the Louisiana Territory. Congress quickly agreed to the request. Jefferson appointed his secretary, Meriwether Lewis, to recruit the other members of the expedition and to plan the trip.

On May 14, 1804, the expedition, led by Mr. Lewis and William Clark, left St. Louis, Missouri, on its journey up the Missouri River. Their destination was the Pacific Ocean, but to reach it they would have to travel through a wilderness that no white person had ever seen and that appeared on no map.

The Corps of Discovery, as the expedition was called, spent the winter of 1804-1805 at a village

they built near today's Bismarck, North Dakota. They called the village Fort Mandan, because it was near a Mandan tribal settlement. It was here that Lewis and Clark met Sacagawea, the Shoshone teenager who would be an invaluable interpreter for them on the rest of the journey.

On November 7, 1805—a year and a half after leaving St. Louis—the expedition reached its goal. Clark wrote in his journal: "Great joy in camp. We are in view of the ocean, this great Pacific Ocean which we [have] been so long anxious to see."

Nearly a year later, on September 23, 1806, the explorers returned to St. Louis, where they were welcomed as heroes.

Study-Reading

In January of 1803, President Thomas Jefferson asked Congress for $2,500 to pay for an expedition to the Louisiana Territory. Congress quickly agreed to the request. Jefferson appointed his secretary, Meriwether Lewis, to recruit the other members of the expedition and to plan the trip.

On May 14, 1804, the expedition, led by Mr. Lewis and William Clark, left St. Louis, Missouri, on its journey up the Missouri River. Their destination was the Pacific Ocean, but to reach it they would have to travel through a wilderness that no white person had ever seen and that appeared on no map.

The Corps of Discovery, as the expedition was called, spent the winter of 1804–1805 at a village they built near today's Bismarck, North Dakota. They called the village Fort Mandan, because it was near a Mandan tribal settlement. It was here that Lewis and Clark met Sacagawea, the Shoshone teenager who would be an invaluable interpreter for them on the rest of the journey.

On November 7, 1805—a year and a half after leaving St. Louis—the expedition reached its goal. Clark wrote in his journal: "Great joy in camp. We are in view of the ocean, this great Pacific Ocean which we [have] been so long anxious to see."

Nearly a year later, on September 23, 1806, the explorers returned to St. Louis, where they were welcomed as heroes.

Time Line ■ A time line is an efficient way to show the **chronological order** of events.

Note Taking

Lewis and Clark Expedition

January 1803	Jefferson asked Congress for funds for an expedition to explore the Louisiana Territory.
May 14, 1804	Lewis and Clark headed up the Missouri River from St. Louis—then west toward the Pacific Ocean.
Winter, 1804–1805	Lewis and Clark expedition spent the winter in North Dakota at Fort Mandan. There they met Sacagawea, a Native American interpreter.
November 7, 1805	Expedition reached the Pacific Ocean.
September 23, 1806	Expedition returned to St. Louis.

Cause and Effect

This information from a magazine article about Easter Island follows the **cause and effect** pattern. It discusses a change in the food chain that may explain why the ancient Easter Islanders deserted their home.

Previewing

Easter Island:
A Small Island with a Puzzling Past

Easter Island has been part of Chile since 1888, and its 2,000 inhabitants are Chilean citizens. Yet the tiny island lies 2,200 miles west of mainland Chile in the South Pacific. Strong trade winds blow constantly across the isolated, 46-square-mile island. It is covered with grasslands and fields cultivated by Polynesian farmers who grow maize, sweet potatoes, pineapples, melons, bananas, figs, and other crops. The islanders also raise sheep and export their wool.

History: Blanks in the Record Book

Created by ancient volcanic eruptions, Easter Island is a unique and puzzling place. The island got its name on Easter Day in 1722, when it was sighted by Dutch navigator Jakob Roggeveen, the first European to visit.

The history of Easter Island before Europeans visited it is uncertain because the people who lived there left no written records that we can decipher. Some scientists think that Easter Island was inhabited in ancient times and then deserted for a period of time. No one knows what happened to the people who lived there. One theory is that the ancient islanders lived on a diet of birds, rats, and other small animals. They cut down the island's trees for cooking fires and to build canoes. When all the trees had been cut down, the birds had no place to nest, and left the island. Other animals that had lived on the birds and their eggs were left without food, and died out. That meant the people of Easter Island also had no food, and left the island. The next settlers on Easter Island were probably farmers who did not depend on wild animals for food.

Workers would pull the
that it was laying on
several men would
dragging the statue
ey reached the statue's
orkers would build a
ke a little hill, in front
They would pull the
mp and let it drop over
mp onto its platform.

tion Marks

the statues, past
e island built an
val-shaped stone
s with rooms
eir bases probably
1600's.

yphs are the final
he history of the
an unknown
carved into the
se writings may
Easter Island's
t for now, they too,

ysterious statues
of Easter Island
storic monument.

Study-Reading

The history of Easter Island before Europeans visited it is uncertain because the people who lived there left no written records that we can decipher. Some scientists think that Easter Island was inhabited in ancient times and then deserted for a period of time. No one knows what happened to the people who lived there. One theory is that the ancient islanders lived on a diet of birds, rats, and other small animals. They cut down the island's trees for cooking fires and to build canoes. When all the trees had been cut down, the birds had no place to nest and left the island. Other animals that had lived on the birds and their eggs were left without food and died out. That meant the people of Easter Island also had no food and left the island. The next settlers on Easter Island were probably farmers who did not depend on wild animals for food.

Cause-Effect Organizer ■ Use a cause-effect organizer to keep track of important information that shows **causes and effects**.

Note Taking

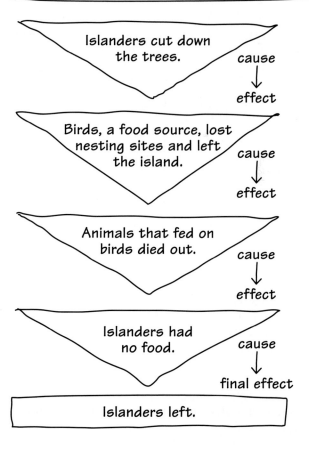

A Theory About Ancient Easter Islanders

Assumption:

Some scientists think the island was inhabited and then deserted.

Islanders cut down the trees. *cause*
↓
effect

Birds, a food source, lost nesting sites and left the island. *cause*
↓
effect

Animals that fed on birds died out. *cause*
↓
effect

Islanders had no food. *cause*
↓
final effect

Islanders left.

Process

The text in this later part of the Easter Island article (page 376) follows a **process** pattern. It describes how some scientists think the large statues of Easter Island were built over time.

Previewing

Easter Island:
A Puzzling Past

The Biggest Mystery of All

The biggest mystery of Easter Island is a puzzle carved in stone: Hundreds of huge stone statues of human heads and torsos, carved centuries ago out of the island's gray volcanic rock. The statues are 10 to 40 feet tall and weigh up to 85 tons. No one knows for sure exactly when the statues were made, why they were made, or how their creators moved them long distances from inland quarries to the giant stone platforms along the coast where they still stand, seeming to stare out to sea.

Scientists think that the earliest stone platforms were built in about 700 C.E., but that the first statues weren't added to the platforms until the 1100s. The largest statues probably were built around 1300. Scientists theorize that the statues were carved inside volcanoes, where there were massive walls of stone. The carvers would complete the front and sides of a statue while it was still part of the wall. Then they would chip away at its back to separate it from the rock wall. Once the statue was finished, workers would use rope to tie a large, flat, V-shaped stone to the front of the statue. This stone would

act like a sled. Workers would pull the statue down so that it was lying on the "sled." Then several people would pull the ropes, dragging the statue along. When they reached the statue's platform, the workers would build a ramp, shaped like a little hill, in front of the platform. They would pull the statue up the ramp and let it drop over the top of the ramp onto its platform.

Still More Question Marks

In addition to the statues, past inhabitants of the island built an entire village of oval-shaped stone houses thought to date from around 1500. Stone towers with rooms hollowed out of their bases probably were built in the 1600s.

Ancient hieroglyphs are the final question mark in the history of the island. Messages in an unknown script can be found carved into the island's rocks. These writings may hold the answers to Easter Island's many mysteries, but for now, they too, are a riddle.

Because of its mysterious statues and hieroglyphs, all of Easter Island has been made a historic monument.

Ranks in the Record Book

...d by ancient volcanic ...Easter Island is a unique ...ng place. The island got its ...aster Day in 1722, when it ...l by Dutch navigator Jakob ...he first European to visit.

...ory of Easter Island before ...visited it is uncertain, ...people who lived there ...en records that we can ...me scientists think that ...d was inhabited in ancient ...en deserted for a period ...ne knows what happened ...who lived there. One ...the ancient islanders ...of birds, rats, and other ...s. They cut down the ...for cooking fires and to ...When all the trees had ...the birds had no place ...ft the island. Other ...ad lived on the birds ...were left without food, ...hat meant the people ...d also had no food, and ...The next settlers on ...ere probably farmers ...end on wild animals

Study-Reading

Scientists think that the earliest stone platforms were built in about 700 C.E., but that the first statues weren't added to the platforms until the 1100s. The largest statues probably were built around 1300. Scientists theorize that the statues were carved inside volcanoes, where there were massive walls of stone. The carvers would complete the front and sides of a statue while it was still part of the wall. Then they would chip away at its back to separate it from the rock wall. Once the statue was finished, workers would use rope to tie a large, flat, V-shaped stone to the front of the statue. This stone would act like a sled. Workers would pull the statue down so that it was lying on the "sled." Then several people would pull the ropes, dragging the statue along. When they reached the statue's platform, the workers would build a ramp, shaped like a little hill, in front of the platform. They would pull the statue up the ramp and let it drop over the top of the ramp onto its platform.

Process List ■ Important information that follows the **process** pattern can be arranged in a list or a circle.

Note Taking

Easter Island's Statues: A Theory

1. First, stone platforms were built.

   ↓

2. Statues were carved out of walls inside volcanoes.

   ↓

3. Workers tied a V-shaped stone "sled" to front of statue.

   ↓

4. Workers pulled statue down and dragged it, on sled, to the platform.

   ↓

5. Workers built a hill-shaped ramp in front of the platform.

   ↓

6. Finally, workers pulled the statue up the ramp and let it drop onto its platform.

This list shows the steps, or stages, in the order that they appear in the reading.

Study-Reading Review

Here is a quick set of guidelines for Internet and text reading.

1. **Search:** Search online or in a library catalog using keywords about the subject, author, or title.

2. **Scan:** Quickly check the results of your search, reading the heading and first few lines to find a source that fits the subject and purpose of your investigation.

3. **Evaluate:** After selecting a source, quickly review it to see if it meets your needs and is reliable. Ask the following questions:
   - Where does the information come from?
   - Is it up to date?
   - Is the information presented clearly?
   - Is it fair and balanced?
   - What is the author's purpose?

4. **Skim:** Quickly skim the headings, links, images, captions, and first and last sentences of a paragraph or Web page to get the overall sense of the material it contains.

5. **Study-Read:** Carefully read the whole article or section, using the "Think and Read" or "KWL" strategy (see pages 366–367). Take notes. If it is helpful, use a graphic organizer to plot out the main points of the piece (see pages 368–379).

6. **Interact:** Try interactive features and follow links to see where they lead.

Helpful Hint

Books and articles usually have a clear beginning, middle, and ending. The Internet does not. Instead of reading in a straight line, you wander through material. The key is to explore, read at different levels, and connect the ideas you are learning.

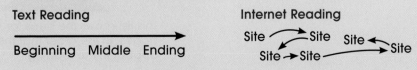

Text Reading

Beginning Middle Ending

Internet Reading

Site → Site Site ← Site Site → Site → Site

Reading
Charts

Our world is increasingly visual. When driving down any street in any city, a person is bombarded with visual information—everything from road signs to traffic lights to advertisements. And the Internet delivers even more visual information to sort through. That's why visual literacy has become such an important skill.

Charts provide a great deal of information visually—and in a compact space. Learning to read and understand the different types of charts will help you access information on the Internet and in the world around you. This chapter will help you sort it all out.

What's Ahead

- Understanding Graphs
- Understanding Tables
- Understanding Diagrams

Understanding Graphs

Graphs are pictures of information, not pictures of things. The information in graphs is often called *data*. The most common kinds of graphs are *line graphs, pie graphs,* and *bar graphs.*

Line Graph

A line graph shows how things change over time. It starts with an L-shaped grid. The horizontal line of the grid stands for *passing time* (seconds, minutes, years, or even centuries). The vertical line of the grid shows the *subject* of the graph. The subject of the graph below is the change in global temperature.

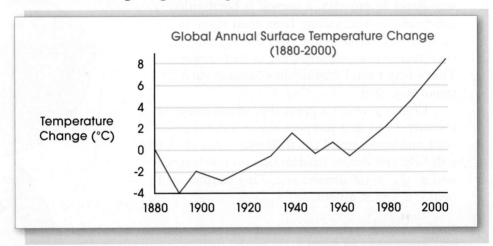

Pie Graph

A pie graph shows proportions and how each proportion, or part, relates to the other parts and to the whole "pie." In this pie graph, you can see what percentage of first-language English speakers come from particular regions of the world.

If percentages are used, they should add up to 100%; if numbers are used, the graphs may add up to some other total.

Bar Graph

A bar graph uses bars (sometimes called *columns*) to show how different things compare to one another at the same time. The horizontal line shows what is being compared. The vertical line shows what the comparison is about.

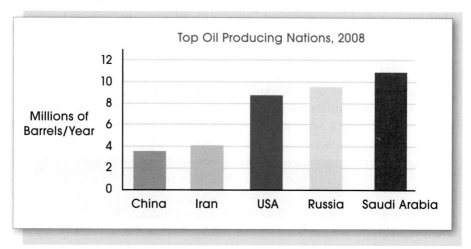

Top Oil Producing Nations, 2008

Stacked Bar Graph

A stacked bar graph gives more detailed information than a regular bar graph. Besides comparing the bars, it compares parts within the bars themselves.

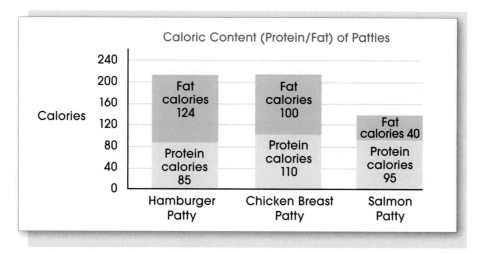

Caloric Content (Protein/Fat) of Patties

Understanding Tables

Tables organize words and numbers so that it's easy to see how they relate to one another. Each table has *rows* (going across) and *columns* (going down). Rows contain one kind of information, while columns contain another kind of information. *Comparison tables, distance tables,* and *conversion tables* are three common types, although you can build your own table to meet a special need.

Comparison Table

The table below is a comparison table that makes it easy to see the bloom color of different plants. The rows show kinds of plants; the columns show colors. (A • means that a plant has flowers of that color.)

Plant	Bloom Colors				
	yellow-orange	pink-red	blue-purple	white	multi
Aster		•	•	•	
Begonia		•		•	
Dianthus		•	•	•	•
Gazania	•	•		•	•

Distance Table

Another common kind of table is a distance or mileage table. To read a distance table, find your starting point in the row and your destination in the column (or the other way around). Then find the distance between the two locations where the row and column meet.

	Mileage Table		
	Los Angeles	Seattle	Baltimore
Los Angeles	0	1,141	2,681
New York	2,787	2,912	197
Tampa	2,591	3,096	997
Chicago	1,989	2,043	697
Houston	1,581	2,498	1,420

Conversion Table

Another very useful table is a conversion table. This is a table that converts (changes) information from one form to another. The table below converts degrees Fahrenheit to degrees Celsius. (The formula is to subtract 32 from Fahrenheit and multiply by .56 to find Celsius.)

Degrees Fahrenheit	Degrees Celsius
0	-17.9
32	0
40	4.5
50	10.1
60	15.7
70	21.3
80	26.9
90	32.5
100	38.1

Custom-Made Tables

Tables are a good way to record all kinds of information. Imagine that you need to gather facts about several different countries and then compare some of the information. You could make a custom-made table like the one below.

Comparing Countries			
	Canada	Mexico	U.S.
Size (Sq. Miles)	3.85 million	759,000	3.6 million
Type of Government	Parliamentary	Republic	Republic
Voting Age	18	18	18
Literacy	99%	87%	98%

Understanding Diagrams

A diagram is a drawing that shows how something is put together, how its parts relate to one another, or how it works. The two most common types of diagrams are the *picture diagram* and the *line diagram*.

Picture Diagram

A picture diagram is just that—a labeled picture or drawing of the subject being discussed. Some parts of the subject may be left out of the diagram to emphasize the parts the writer wants to show. For example, this picture diagram of a cell shows only the largest, most important parts.

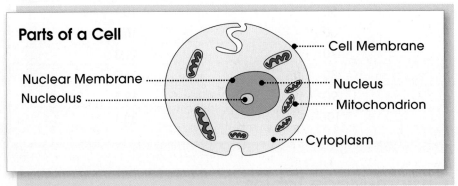

Parts of a Cell

Nuclear Membrane
Nucleolus

Cell Membrane
Nucleus
Mitochondrion
Cytoplasm

Line Diagram

Another type of diagram is a line diagram. A line diagram uses lines, symbols, and words to show the relationship between ideas. The problem-solving diagram below is a common kind of line diagram that helps you understand how to solve a scientific problem. *Note:* When a diagram shows a process, it usually shows the steps from top to bottom (as in the example below) or from left to right.

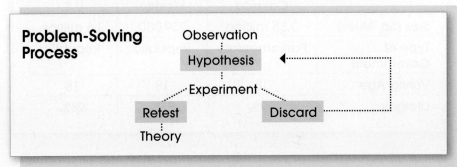

Problem-Solving Process

Observation
Hypothesis
Experiment
Retest   Discard
Theory

Improving Your
Vocabulary

Your vocabulary is all the words you know and use. Building your vocabulary will improve your ability to understand what you read and hear, and to write and communicate more effectively.

One of the best ways to improve your vocabulary is to read. Books, magazines, newspapers, and the Internet are filled with all kinds of new words and ideas. When you come across an unfamiliar word, find out its meaning, and then begin to use the word in your daily work. This is a sure way to increase your vocabulary.

What's Ahead

- Using Context
- Referring to a Thesaurus
- Checking a Dictionary
- Keeping a Personal Dictionary

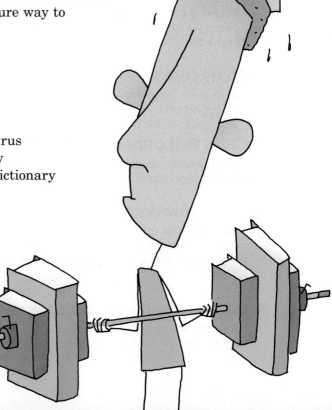

Using Context

When you come across a word you don't know, you can often figure out its meaning from the other words in the sentence or sentences around it. The other words form a familiar context, or setting, for the unfamiliar word. Looking closely at these surrounding words will give you hints, or clues, about the meaning of the new word. Seven common types of context clues are listed below with examples. (Unfamiliar words are shown in red, context cues in blue.)

Types of Context Clues

■ **Clues from synonyms:**

Sara had an **ominous** feeling when she woke up, but she felt less **anxious** when she saw she was in her own room.

■ **Clues from antonyms:**

Boniface **had always been quite heavy, but** he looked **gaunt** when he returned from the hospital.

■ **Clues contained in comparisons and contrasts:**

Riding a mountain bike in a **remote** area is my idea of a great day. I wonder why some people like to ride motorcycles on **busy six-lane highways.**

■ **Clues contained in a definition or description:**

Manatees, large aquatic mammals (sometimes called sea cows), can be found in the warm coastal waters of Florida.

■ **Clues that appear in a series:**

The campers spotted **sparrows, chickadees, cardinals,** and **indigo buntings** on Saturday morning.

■ **Clues provided by the tone and setting:**

Mom lined us up in the living room—combing our hair, straightening our ties, flicking lint off our suits. "But, Mom, it's just Dad," I complained. She shook her head gravely. "He's not just Dad. He's Lieutenant Charles, back from Iraq. This is an **auspicious** day."

■ **Clues derived from cause and effect:**

The amount of traffic at 6th and Main doubled last year, so crossing lights were placed at that corner to **avert** an accident.

Referring to a Thesaurus

A thesaurus is a reference book that gives synonyms and antonyms for words. A thesaurus helps you in two ways:

1. It helps you find just the right word for your writing.
2. It keeps you from using the same words again and again.

If a thesaurus is organized alphabetically, look up the word as you would in a regular dictionary. If you have a traditional thesaurus, look for your word in the book's index.

Finding the Best Word

A thesaurus would be helpful if you needed one effective word to mean *laugh suddenly* in the following sentence.

> Whenever science fiction writer Isaac Asimov mentioned a space elevator to his physicist friends, they laughed suddenly.

Thesaurus Entry

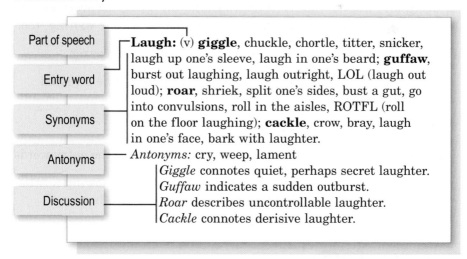

After reading the list of synonyms, you decide on *guffawed* because it fits best.

> Whenever science fiction writer Isaac Asimov mentioned a space elevator to his physicist friends, they guffawed.

Checking a Dictionary

The dictionary is, of course, your most reliable source for learning the meanings of new words. The dictionary also offers the following aids and information:

Guide words are words located at the top of every page. They list the first and last entry words on a page, and they help you know which words fall in alphabetical order between the entry words.

Entry words are the bold words that are defined on the dictionary page. Entry words are listed in alphabetical order.

Parts of speech labels tell you the different ways a word can be used. For example, the word *grief* is used only as a noun. On the other hand, the word *griddle* can be used as a noun *(The griddle was ready for the pancakes)* or as a verb *(I'll griddle the pancakes)*.

Syllable divisions show where you can divide a word into syllables. Some dictionaries use heavy black dots to divide the syllables. Other dictionaries put extra space between syllables.

Spelling and **capital letters** (if appropriate) are given for every entry word. If an entry is capitalized, capitalize it in your writing, too.

Illustrations are often provided to make the definition clearer.

Accent marks show which syllable or syllables should be stressed when you say a word.

Pronunciations are phonetic respellings of a word.

Pronunciation key gives symbols to help you pronounce the entry words.

Etymology gives the history of a word [in brackets]. Knowing a little about its history can make a word easier to remember.

Helpful Hint

Remember: A word often has more than one meaning, so read them all. This will give you the best chance of using the word correctly.

Dictionary Page

Guide words — **carbon dioxide | carburetor** 150

Entry word

carbon dioxide *n.* A colorless or odorless gas that does not burn, composed of carbon and oxygen in the proportion CO_2 and present in the atmosphere or formed when any fuel containing carbon is burned. It is ex- haled from an animal's lungs during respiration and is used by plants in photosynthesis. Carbon dioxide is used in refrigeration, in fire extinguishers, and in carbonated drinks.

Part of speech

carbonic acid *n.* A weak acid having the formula H_2CO_3. It exists only in solution and decomposes readily into carbon dioxide and water.

Syllable division

car·bon·if·er·ous (kär′bə-nĭf′ər-əs) *adj.* Producing or containing carbon or coal.

Spelling and capitalization

Carboniferous *n.* The geologic time comprising the Mississippian (or Lower Carboniferous) and Pennsylvanian (or Upper Carboniferous) Periods of the Paleozoic Era, from about 360 to 286 million years ago. During the Carboniferous, widespread swamps formed in which plant remains accumulated and later hardened into coal. See table at **geologic time.—Carboniferous** *adj.*

Spelling of verb forms

car·bon·ize (kär′bə-nīz′) *tr. v.* **car·bon·ized, car·bon·iz·ing, car·bon·iz·es 1.** To change an organic compound into carbon by heating. **2.** To treat, coat, or combine with carbon.—**car′bon·i·za′tion** (kär′be-nĭ-zā′shən) *n.*

carbon monoxide *n.* A colorless, odorless gas that is extremely poisonous and has the formula CO. Carbon monoxide is formed when carbon or a compound that contains carbon burns incompletely. It is present in the exhaust gases of automobile engines.

Illustration

air
air filter
choke valve
gas
gas and air mixture
float
venturi
throttle valve
float chamber

carburetor
cross section of a carburetor

carbon paper *n.* A paper coated on one side with a dark coloring matter, placed between two sheets of blank paper so that the bottom sheet will receive a copy of what is typed or written on the top sheet.

Accent marks

carbon tet·ra·chlor·ide (tĕt′rə-klôr′īd′) *n.* A colorless poisonous liquid that is composed of carbon and chlorine, has the formula CCl_4, and does not burn although it vaporizes easily. It is used in fire extinguishers and as a dry-cleaning fluid.

Pronunciation

Car·bo·run·dum (kär′bə-rŭn′dəm) A trademark for an abrasive made of silicon carbide, used to cut, grind, and polish.

ă	pat	ôr	core
ā	pay	oi	boy
âr	care	ou	out
ä	father	ŏŏ	took
ĕ	pet	ōŏr	lure
ē	be	ōō	boot
ĭ	pit	ŭ	cut
ī	bite	ûr	urge
îr	pier	th	thin
ŏ	pot	*th*	this
ō	toe	zh	vision
ô	paw	ə	about

Pronunciation key

car·bun·cle (kär′bŭng′kəl) *n.* **1.** A painful inflammation in the tissue under the skin that is somewhat like a boil but releases pus from several openings. **2.** A deep-red garnet.

car·bu·re·tor (kär′bə-rā′tər *or* kär′byə-rā′tər) *n.* A device in a gasoline engine that vaporizes the gasoline with air to form an explosive mixture. [First written down in 1866 in English, from *carburet*, carbide, from Latin *carbō*, carbon.]

Etymology

Keeping a Personal Dictionary

You can improve your vocabulary by keeping a personal dictionary. Put each new word in a notebook, in a section of your journal, or on a note card. You may also find it helpful to group your words according to topic. Include the following items for each entry:

- pronunciation
- a definition
- a sentence using the word
- synonyms and antonyms for the word

<u>Social Studies</u>

ratify (răt′ ə fī)
To approve

Will Congress ratify
the new tax law?

Synonyms: approve,
support, confirm

<u>Literature</u>

furtive (fûr′-tĭv)
Done in a sneaky or sly manner

Huck gave Tom a furtive look.

Synonyms: secret, sly, sneaky

<u>Music</u>

libretto (lĭ-brĕt′-ō)
The text of an opera or a musical

We found the libretto for <u>Joseph and
the Amazing Technicolor Dreamcoat</u> on
the Internet.

Keeping a
Learning Log

Let's say that you've just learned two new math concepts, and you want to make sure that you understand them. You could work a few related math problems and see how that goes. Or you could write about the concepts in a learning log. A learning log is a journal for your school work. It is a place where you can explore your thoughts, feelings, and questions about your class work.

Writing in a learning log will help you (1) connect new information to what you already know, (2) identify ideas that you're not clear about, and (3) serve as a study sheet for tests. This chapter will help you start your own learning log and also includes two sample entries—one for science and the other for math.

What's Ahead

- Keeping a Learning Log
- Science Log
- Math Log

Keeping a Learning Log

A learning log is a place to write down your thoughts, feelings, and questions about subjects you are studying. In this way, learning-log notes are different from lecture and reading notes. Here are some tips:

Keep a learning log for any subject, but especially for one that is hard for you. This will help you learn the subject better.

Use graphic organizers and drawings. (See page 395.)

Write freely. Don't worry about getting every word correct.

Write about any of the following ideas:

- the most important thing you learned from a reading assignment or lecture
- questions you have plus your plan for finding answers
- your thoughts about a group project
- what you learned from an experiment
- a list of key words that come to mind after a lesson
- your feelings about something you learned
- your feelings about how you are doing in the subject

Writing-to-Learn Activities

Here are more ideas for writing in a learning log.

- **First Thoughts:** List your first impressions about something you are studying or reading.
- **Nutshelling:** Try writing down in one sentence the importance of something you are studying or reading.
- **Stop 'n' Write:** Stop studying or reading whatever you have in front of you and start writing about it. This will keep you on task.
- **Admit Slips/Exit Slips:** Submit brief writings to your teacher before or after class. Write about an idea related to the class that confuses you, interests you, upsets you, and so on. Ask your teacher to react to your comments.
- **Synergizing:** Generate ideas with a classmate. Take turns writing statements (or questions and answers). This is especially effective when reviewing.

Science Log

Learning logs work in any class and for any subject. Learning logs work best if you think and write freely, personalizing the information. The entry below is a reaction to a lecture on flies and mosquitoes.

Feb. 5   Flies

Key words: Diptera
halteres
viruses, bacteria, protozoans
malaria

I thought flies and mosquitoes were a pain just because they bite. But it turns out that you can get more than an itchy bump from a mosquito. It can carry germs that cause serious diseases such as malaria. (Fortunately, mosquitoes in the United States do not carry malaria.) Doctors think that, in all of history, more people have died of malaria than any other disease. And it still kills many people today, especially in Africa. Malaria was also one of the reasons why the Roman Empire fell. That means that mosquitoes have had a pretty big effect on history.

History-making pest!

Math Log

Students in Mr. Manzo's algebra class keep learning logs to help them think through math concepts. Each day they write down a question about a concept discussed in class and answer it later in their learning logs. Below are two of Paul Scholl's entries.

Mon., Sept. 14

Question: Why should I "show my work" in algebra class?

Answer: I know why Mr. Manzo wants me to show my work. That way he knows that I did the problem myself, and he can see how I did it. If I get stuck, my writing helps him understand how to help me. Most times, showing work makes sense.

But sometimes it doesn't. Sometimes I can figure a problem in my head. Then what? Why can't I just write the answer? Why do I have to write all the stuff about how I got the answer?

Thurs., Sept. 17

Question: What are two meanings of the minus sign?

Answer: One meaning of the minus sign is "subtraction." Another meaning is "negative number."

For example, the minus sign in the left side of the equation below means "subtract 3." But the minus sign in the right side means "negative 3."

$$7 - 3 = 7 + (-3)$$

Note
Taking

When you're in school, your main job is to learn. You learn by listening to your teachers, reading, talking about ideas, reflecting, and completing assignments. You can become an even better learner by developing good note-taking skills.

Taking notes will help you (1) pay attention, (2) understand new material, and (3) remember what you learn. Your notes will also prove invaluable when you study for tests. This chapter serves as a guide to effective note taking.

What's Ahead

- Setting Up Your Notes
- Taking Classroom Notes
- Taking Reading Notes
- Reviewing Your Notes

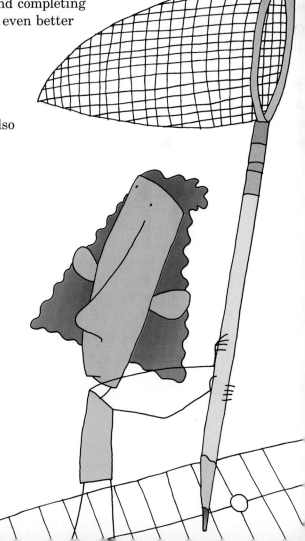

Setting Up Your Notes

Use a notebook or a three-ring binder for your notes. A three-ring binder allows you to add and remove pages as needed. Use the following format when your class notes are very different from your reading notes. Write on only two-thirds of each page, leaving room for review notes (see page 402).

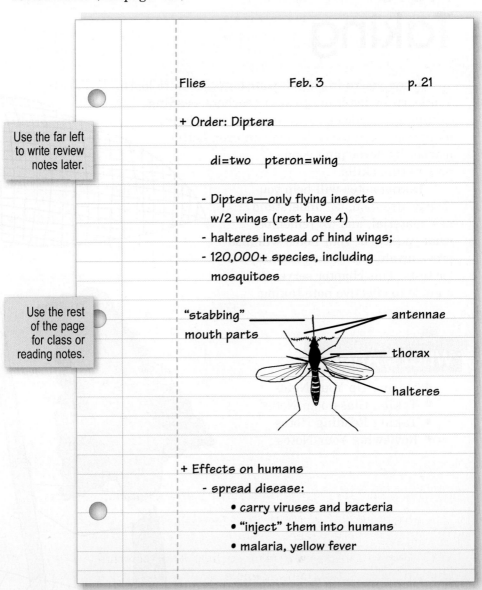

Use the far left to write review notes later.

Use the rest of the page for class or reading notes.

Flies   Feb. 3   p. 21

+ Order: Diptera

    di=two   pteron=wing

    - Diptera—only flying insects
      w/2 wings (rest have 4)
    - halteres instead of hind wings;
    - 120,000+ species, including
      mosquitoes

"stabbing" _____   antennae
mouth parts
                                         thorax

                                         halteres

+ Effects on humans
    - spread disease:
        • carry viruses and bacteria
        • "inject" them into humans
        • malaria, yellow fever

Three-Column Notes

Use the following note-taking format if your classroom lectures or discussions closely follow your textbook reading assignments.

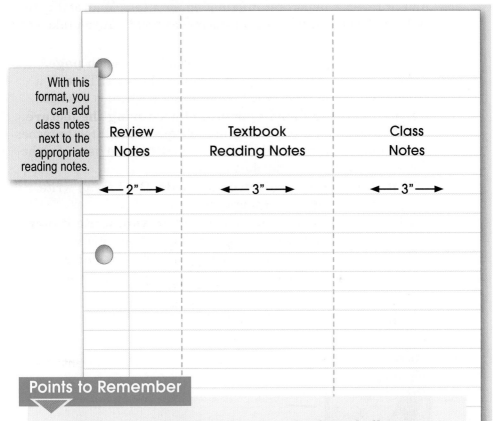

With this format, you can add class notes next to the appropriate reading notes.

Review Notes ←2"→

Textbook Reading Notes ←3"→

Class Notes ←3"→

Points to Remember

- **Organize your notes** using plus signs, hyphens, bullets, or numbers. For example, you could use a plus sign to identify a key point and hyphens to indicate subpoints or details.

  + _____
  - _____
  - _____

- **Use <u>underlining</u> or ALL CAPS to highlight information.**

- **Leave as much white space as possible.** This makes your notes easier to read.

- **Reserve the last few lines on each page** for personal reflections, summaries, and so on.

Taking Classroom Notes

The following tips will help you take notes during a lecture or a talk that your teacher may present when she or he introduces a new unit or reviews important information for a test. Your ability to remember and understand a lecture increases greatly if you take good notes.

- **Write the topic and the date at the top of each page.** You may also want to number each page of notes. Then, if a page gets out of order, you'll know exactly where it belongs.
- **Listen carefully for important clues during the lecture.** Your teacher may say, "I'm going to explain the three branches of the federal government." This clue tells you to listen for the names of the three branches.
- **Write your notes in your own words.** Don't try to write down everything the teacher says.
- **When you hear a word that is new to you, write it down.** Don't worry about spelling. Just make your best guess.
- **Draw pictures to help you remember things better.**
- **Listen for key words such as *first, second, last, most important,* and so on.**
- **Copy what the teacher writes on the board or overhead projector.**

Some students create their own shorthand for notes—using "+" for *and*, "p" for *pages*, "ch" for *chapter*, and so on.

Helpful Hint

The real secret to taking good notes is listening. Don't get so busy writing that you forget to listen. If you listen carefully, you will hear details that you can add to your notes later.

Taking Reading Notes

Taking notes while you read is easier than taking notes while you listen to a lecture. As you read, you can stop anytime to write a note or to look up additional information. Here are some tips for taking reading notes:

1. **Preview the assignment.** Read the title, introduction, section headings or subtitles, and summary. Look at any pictures, charts, and maps. This information will tell you what the reading is about.

2. **Skim through the whole assignment once** before you take any notes. Also, if there are questions that go with the reading, look them over before you begin.

3. **Take notes** as you read the material again—this time reading more slowly and thoroughly.

   - **Write down only the important information and ideas.**

   - **Try to write your notes in your own words.** Don't just copy from the book.

   - **You may write down each heading or subtopic,** recording the most important facts under each heading. (Pay close attention to words in **boldface** or *italics*.)

   - **Remember to take notes about important pictures, charts, or maps.** You may also make drawings of your own.

   - **Use graphic organizers.** (See pages 366–379.)

   - **Make a list of new words.** Also write down the page number where you found each word. Look up each word in a glossary or dictionary. Choose the meaning that best fits the way the word is used and write it in your notes.

   - **Summarize difficult or important material** out loud before taking notes on it.

   - **Write down any questions you have for your teacher.**

Helpful Hint

Turn to "Study-Reading Skills," beginning on page 363, for more ways to take notes while you read.

Reviewing Your Notes

Look over your reading and lecture notes each day.

- **Circle the words and phrases that you don't understand** and look them up in a dictionary or the glossary of your textbook. Then write each word (spelled correctly) and its meaning in the margin of your notes. (See the example in blue below.)

- **Write any questions you may have in the margins of your notes.** Talk over your questions with a classmate or your teacher. Then write down what you've learned.

- **Use a highlighter to mark important parts of your notes.**

- **Rewrite your notes if they are sloppy or if you want to reorganize them.**

- **Review your notes again before the next class.**

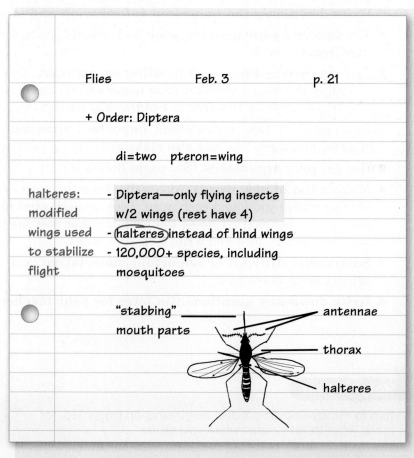

Social
Networking

When you hang out with friends, what do you do? If you're like most middle schoolers, your answer sounds something like this: "We talk, mostly. Joke around. Play games. Goof off. Take videos and photos of ourselves goofing off. Maybe go to a store. You know—hang out."

Social networking allows you to do the same sorts of activities with friends, even when you aren't *with* your friends. Social networking sites help you set up an online profile and then "hang out" with your friends. The difference is that all your hanging out happens with words and pictures. You need to select those words and pictures carefully so that your friends will see you as you want to be seen. This chapter can help.

What's Ahead

- Profile Page
- Setting Up Your Profile Page
- Connecting with Friends
- Interacting Online
- Avoiding Dangers

Profile Page

Social networking sites are based upon profiles—pages that describe each person and provide a location for uploading photos, videos, links, and other digital media. The profile page is basically your digital stand-in. Instead of seeing your face, friends see a picture that represents you. Instead of hearing your voice, they read what you have written about yourself. Here is Raul Ortega's profile page.

Profile Page

A photo shows who you are.

A profile provides information about you.

A friends list helps you connect with friends.

In Touch

http://www.intouch.com/home.php

In Touch

Home | Profile | Friends | In Box

Raul Ortega

Wall | Info | Photos

Basic Information

Networks:
Milwaukee, WI

Birthday:
July 22, 1996

Personal Information

Activities:
track, theater, guitar

Interests:
salsa music, video games, baseball, girls

Favorite Music:
Babasonicos, Belanova, Cultura Profética Gondwana, Locos por Juana, Los Cafres, Manu Chao, Molotov, Siete

Favorite TV Shows:
CSI, Doctor Who, MythBusters

Favorite Movies:
The Dark Knight, Shrek series, Spider-Man series

Favorite Books:
A Long Way Gone, Mister Pip, Tamar, American Shaolin

Favorite Quotations:
"Outside of a dog, a book is a man's best friend. Inside of a dog, it's too dark to read."
—Groucho Marx

Information

Networks:
Milwaukee, WI

Birthday:
July 22, 1996

Friends:

Jarrod   Lynne

Lupita   Pete

Setting Up Your Profile Page

Before setting up a profile on a social networking site, get the permission of your parent or guardian. Then go to a social networking site and create a username and password. The site will prompt you to enter information about yourself. Follow these tips as you set up your profile.

- **Present yourself in the best light.** Imagine you are walking into a room filled with friends *and* strangers. How do you want to come across? Confident? Friendly? Fun? The words and images you provide will represent you to friends and others, so build your profile carefully.

- **Consider your profile a work-in-progress.** You can change your profile at any time, so experiment. See what works and what doesn't and make adjustments as you go.

- **Think about search terms.** Most networking sites use your profile to help other people find you—and to help advertisers target you. For example, if you indicate what school you go to, other people from your school will likely ask to become an online "friend." If you indicate a favorite band, don't be surprised to see an ad pop up for the band's new album or latest concert tour.

- **Think about privacy.** Remember that a networking site is basically a form of publication. What you post will be seen by many people—including your parents and the parents of friends. Don't post secrets.

- **Listen to your gut.** If you feel uncomfortable about providing some information, leave it out. If posting a photo of yourself bothers you, post a cartoon character, a former president, or some other picture. Don't post photos or information that would embarrass you, your family, or your friends.

Helpful Hint

Remember that other people must ask to become your friends, and you must accept them before they can view any part of your profile. You have control over your circle of friends.

Connecting with Friends

Once you have a profile set up, you can search for friends on the same social networking site. You can also search for the name of your school or town to see if you can find other possible friends. When you find someone you want to connect with, you can request that the person become a friend. If the person accepts, you will be able to view each other's pages, send messages to each other, and interact with games and other features. This page shows Raul's interactions.

Interactions

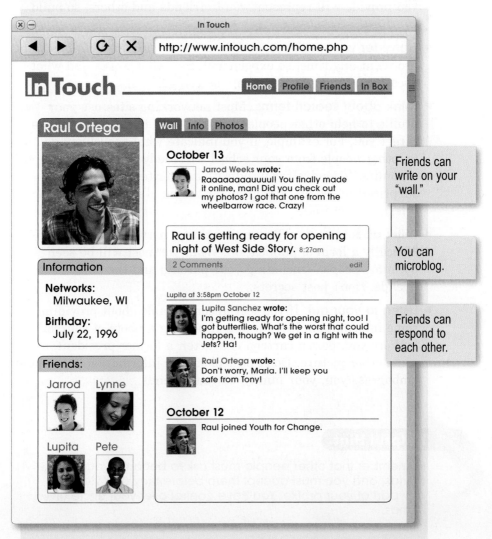

In Touch

http://www.intouch.com/home.php

In Touch — Home Profile Friends In Box

Raul Ortega

Wall Info Photos

Information

Networks:
Milwaukee, WI

Birthday:
July 22, 1996

Friends:
Jarrod Lynne
Lupita Pete

October 13

Jarrod Weeks **wrote:**
Raaaaaaaauuuul! You finally made it online, man! Did you check out my photos? I got that one from the wheelbarrow race. Crazy!

Raul is getting ready for opening night of West Side Story. 8:27am
2 Comments   edit

Lupita at 3:58pm October 12

Lupita Sanchez **wrote:**
I'm getting ready for opening night, too! I got butterflies. What's the worst that could happen, though? We get in a fight with the Jets? Ha!

Raul Ortega **wrote:**
Don't worry, Maria. I'll keep you safe from Tony!

October 12

Raul joined Youth for Change.

Friends can write on your "wall."

You can microblog.

Friends can respond to each other.

Interacting Online

Social networking sites provide many opportunities to interact with friends online. You can share ideas with them, join groups with them, and just have fun. Here are a few of the typical offerings.

■ Sharing

- **Writing on "the wall":** When you have something you would like to say publicly to a friend, write on the person's wall. Other people who visit the person's home page will be able to read what you say. It's like saying something out loud at a party.
- **Sending a message:** When you want to say something privately to a friend, send a message. This is like pulling the person aside and whispering a secret.
- **Microblogging:** By writing down what you are doing at any given time, you can keep friends up to date with your life. It's as if all your friends are around you, and you are aware of the little things they are doing.
- **Sharing videos or photos:** You can share videos or photos that you have uploaded, or pass along links to Web pages you want friends to check out.

■ Joining

- **Joining groups and clubs:** You and your friends can join groups and clubs that connect you to other people to support a good cause or enjoy similar interests.
- **Nominating friends:** You can also nominate your friends for various awards, such as "Friend of the Year" or "Guy with the Best Hair."

■ Having Fun

- **Playing games:** Numerous add-on pieces of software allow you to play games online. You might take superhero names and personas and battle supervillains, or you might become a zombie and try to turn other people into zombies.

Networking helps you build friendships.

Avoiding Dangers

By following these precautions, you can safely enjoy social networking online.

■ Get your parent's permission first.

Let your parent or guardian know you want to start networking, and recognize that your parent or guardian may start networking, too. It may feel weird to add your mom as a "friend," but it's a way for you to stay connected and for her to see that you are staying out of trouble.

■ Protect your privacy.

Decide what you are (and are not) willing to tell the world about yourself, and then hold the line. Do not give out information, such as your social security number or address, that would let someone steal your identity.

■ Connect with people you trust.

Though some people have thousands of "friends," the purpose of social networking is not to have a huge number of friends, but to have good friends. Befriend the same sort of people online that you know and trust offline. Then use the same discretion in dealing with them.

■ Don't bully, and don't tolerate bullying.

Avoid starting fights with anyone online. Don't trash-talk others, and if they start trash-talking you, send them a message politely asking them to stop. If they don't, remove them from your friends list and talk to your parent or teacher.

■ If worse comes to worst, start over.

If you can't stop someone from harassing you, cancel your personal network account and, if you wish, start a new one. Think about what went wrong last time and how you can avoid the same problems again.

■ Keep perspective.

You know who your real friends are, whether they're sitting across the room from you or chatting online with you. All the rest are just pictures in your "friends" column.

Preparing a
Speech

No doubt, you enjoy talking to your friends as often as you can. It's just as certain, though, that you do not enjoy giving a speech in front of your classmates. For one thing, a speech is such a formal activity—you have to have all of your thoughts and ideas worked out ahead of time. For another thing, everyone is just sitting there, waiting for you to say something brilliant or funny or . . .

So, don't think of it as a speech. Imagine instead that you're making a sandwich for a friend. You start by gathering yummy ingredients—a topic that will truly interest the person, with plenty of juicy details. Then you put the ingredients together in the right order. That's right—a fresh beginning and ending, with great ideas sandwiched in between. Practice to make sure you've included just the right flavors. Finally, you'll be ready to deliver your speech—or, shall we say, your food for thought.

What's Ahead

- Writing Guidelines
- Creating a Multimedia Presentation

Writing Guidelines

Prewriting—Planning Your Speech

To get started, you need to understand the purpose of your speech, select a specific topic, and collect interesting details.

Understanding Your Purpose

There are three main purposes for formal speaking: *to inform, to persuade,* and *to demonstrate.*

- **Informing:** If your purpose is to inform, you are preparing an *informative* speech. (Collect plenty of details.)
- **Persuading:** If your purpose is to argue for or against something, you are preparing a *persuasive* speech. (Develop a convincing and logical argument. See pages 205–210.)
- **Demonstrating:** If your purpose is to show how to do something or to show how something works, you are preparing a *demonstration* speech. (Put together a clear explanation.)

Selecting a Specific Topic

A good speech starts with a good topic—one that you think will interest your audience. Here are some important points to consider:

- **Know your topic:** Either know your topic well or be able to learn about it in a short time.
- **Choose the right topic:** Check that your topic meets the requirements (and purpose) of the assignment.
- **Choose a specific topic:** Pick a topic that is specific enough to cover in the time allowed for your speech.

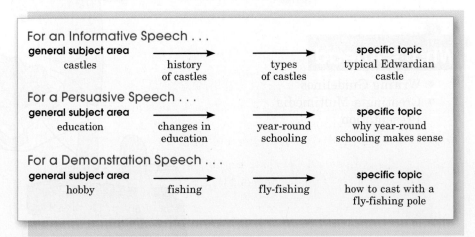

For an Informative Speech . . .

general subject area			specific topic
castles	history of castles	types of castles	typical Edwardian castle

For a Persuasive Speech . . .

general subject area			specific topic
education	changes in education	year-round schooling	why year-round schooling makes sense

For a Demonstration Speech . . .

general subject area			specific topic
hobby	fishing	fly-fishing	how to cast with a fly-fishing pole

Collecting Interesting Details

Listed below are different sources of information for your research. Always consult as many sources as time permits.

- **Tap your memory:** If your speech is based on an experience, write down the facts, details, and feelings as you remember them.
- **Talk with people:** Discuss your subject with a variety of people who may be able to provide details from their own experiences.
- **Get firsthand experience:** Experiencing (or trying out) your subject is especially important for demonstration speeches.
- **Search the library:** Make sure to check different library resources, including books, magazines, pamphlets, videos, and so on.
- **Explore the Internet:** Check out appropriate Web sites and newsgroups for information.

> Imagine questions your audience might have. Be sure to have the information to answer each one.

Points to Remember

- **Gather more facts and details than you need.** You can decide which ones to use as you write your speech.

- **Take good notes and write down all of the sources of your information.** You can write each main point or fact on a separate note card. This will help you later on when you are ready to write your speech. (See pages 414–415.)

- **Look for photographs, maps, models, artifacts, charts, and so on.** Showing such items can make any speech more interesting and helpful, especially a demonstration speech.

- **Create your own graphics or charts if you can't find ones that meet your needs. (See pages 381–386.)**

Writing—Developing Your Speech

As you write your speech, remember that your ideas will be heard, not read; so let your personality come through.

> I would like to tell you about a typical Edwardian castle built in Wales in the late 1200s. We'll call it Lord Aaron's Castle.

In addition, use specific words that help listeners picture in their minds what you are saying.

> Slabs of gray stone are chiseled into blocks and cemented with mortar to build a mighty tower. This is the heart of the castle.

Creating an Attention-Getting Beginning

The beginning of your speech must get your listeners' attention and, of course, tell what your speech is about. Here are five ways to begin:

- Ask a question.
- Give a surprising fact.
- Tell an interesting or a surprising story.
- Ask listeners to imagine something.
- Repeat a famous quotation.

In the speech shown on page 415, student Aaron Stalzer uses two of these starting methods. First, he asks listeners to imagine something; then he identifies his subject in a closing question.

> Imagine that you are an engineer at the time of King Edward I of England and the king hires you to build a castle that will keep the French out. The king will give you 1,500 workers to build your castle, but you have to design it. How will you make the castle strong and safe?

Writing a Convincing Middle Part

Once you decide how to begin, turn your attention to the body of your speech. If you used note cards to gather details, move them around until you get everything in the best order. (See page 414 for help.)

As you write, turn each fact or detail into an interesting, smooth-reading sentence. Explain or describe each part of your topic clearly so that your audience can follow along easily and enjoy what you say.

You may decide not to use all of your note cards; or, after you review your notes, you may choose to do additional research.

Preparing a Strong Ending

Your ending should be just as interesting as the beginning. Here are different ways to end a speech:

- Tell one last interesting fact or story.
  (This is a good way to end an informative speech.)
- Explain why the topic is important.
  (This is a good way to end a persuasive speech.)
- Sum up the most important ideas in your speech.
  (This is a good way to end a demonstration speech.)
- Share a final idea that will keep the topic in your listeners' thoughts.

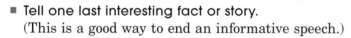

Aaron ended his speech with an interesting story about castles.

If you're wondering about the dungeon, here is an interesting story: At the time of King Edward I, "donjon" was another name for the tower. It was also called a "keep" because it was used to keep people and treasure safe from invaders. Later, when people didn't live in castles anymore, someone had the idea to use the towers, or donjons, as prisons. That's where the word "dungeon" comes from.

Note Cards

One way to present a speech is to use note cards. Aaron wrote out the full beginning and ending parts on cards. The other cards contained only main ideas. (Not all cards are shown below.)

BEGINNING   ①

Imagine that you are an engineer at the time of King Edward I of England and the king hires you to build a castle that will keep the French out. The king will give you 1,500 workers to build your castle, but you have to design it. How will you make the castle strong and safe?

③

— gray stones chiseled into blocks and cemented with mortar into a tower

④

— around the moat is a large, grassy courtyard with a wall, gardens, stables, and farm animals

ENDING   ⑥

If you're wondering about the dungeon, here is an interesting story: At the time of King Edward I, "donjon" was another name for the tower. It was also called a "keep" because it was used to keep people and treasure safe from invaders. Later, when people didn't live in castles anymore, someone had the idea to use the towers, or donjons, as prisons. That's where the word "dungeon" comes from.

Speech

When you want to deliver a speech word for word, you can write it out as a complete manuscript. Here is Aaron's speech word for word.

Beginning
The writer draws the listener in and names the subject (underlined).

Lord Aaron's Castle

Imagine that you are an engineer at the time of King Edward I of England and the king hires you to build a castle that will keep the French out. The king will give you 1,500 workers to build your castle, but you have to design it. How will you make the castle strong and safe?

Based on the latest building techniques of the time, you've created the following design. We'll call it Lord Aaron's Castle, and it will be located in Wales.

The castle rises from the top of a hill, so its defenders can easily see enemies approaching. Slabs of gray stone are chiseled into bricks and cemented with mortar to build a mighty tower, the heart of the castle. The tower is surrounded by a 10-foot-deep moat that can be crossed only when a heavy wooden drawbridge is lowered. When it is raised, enemies have no way to get across.

Middle
Each middle paragraph covers a main point.

Around the moat is a large, grassy courtyard with a well (so the defenders will have water if the enemy lays siege to the castle), gardens, horse stables, and farm animals. Surrounding the courtyard is a 10-foot-high stone wall with only one gate. This gate is on a different side of the tower than the drawbridge. So if enemies do get through the gate, they must still work to get into the tower. As they walk or ride around the courtyard toward the drawbridge, defending soldiers can shoot arrows down at them.

The tower is divided into four levels or stories. Lord Aaron's wife will have her room on the top floor. Below that will be the lord's quarters, and below that the dining rooms and servants' quarters, and then the treasure rooms.

Ending
The writer closes with an interesting story.

If you're wondering about the dungeon, here is an interesting story: At the time of King Edward I, "donjon" was another name for the tower. It was also called a "keep" because it was used to keep people and treasure safe from invaders. Later, when people didn't live in castles anymore, someone had the idea to use the towers, or donjons, as prisons. That's where the word "dungeon" comes from.

Revising and Editing—Refining Your Speech

Making a Final Copy

- Type in your speech on a computer or neatly write it out.
- If you type it in, make sure to use a type font that is easy to read.
- Double- or triple-space and use wide margins.
- Never run a sentence from one page to another.
- Never use abbreviations unless you plan to say them as they are written. For example, don't write "A.M." when you intend to say "morning."
- Number each page to keep things in order.

Practicing Your Speech

- Start practicing your speech at least two days ahead of time.
- Practice by yourself at first. If possible, record yourself.
- Then get friends or family members to listen to your speech. (Ask for honest, constructive advice.)
- Practice until you know your speech inside and out.

Giving Your Speech

- Stand straight and tall.
- Speak loudly and clearly.
- Take your time, and use your voice to add color and interest to your speech.
- Look up as often as you can. (You don't have to make direct eye contact if that makes you nervous. Just scan the audience as you look up.)
- Use your hands in a planned way. At the very least, hold your note cards or written speech. But don't tap your fingers on the speaker's stand or make any nervous movements with your hands.
- Keep your feet firmly on the floor. Don't sway from side to side.
- Show interest in your topic all the way through your speech, and wait a few seconds after you are done before you sit down.

Creating a Multimedia Presentation

In addition to using visual aids with your speech, you can also create a multimedia presentation using a slide show of images and words. You might even record your voice and include it with the slide show to create an interactive report or digital story. Follow these tips when creating a multimedia presentation.

- **Create a title slide** that identifies your presentation and helps your reader understand what it is about.

- **Combine words and images** to make your ideas clear.

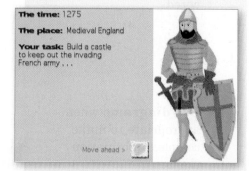

- **Focus on one main point** per slide so that your audience does not get overwhelmed.

- **Use readable fonts** so that even people in the back of the room (or people with small computer monitors) can see what you have written.

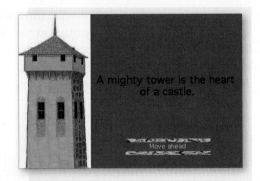

A mighty tower is the heart of a castle.

Move ahead

- **Pace your words and images** so the audience has enough time to see each slide, but not enough time to become bored.

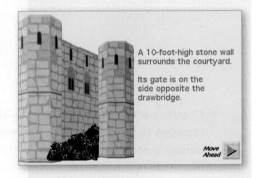

A 10-foot-high stone wall surrounds the courtyard.

Its gate is on the side opposite the drawbridge.

Move Ahead

- **Use diagrams** when appropriate to make complex information clear.

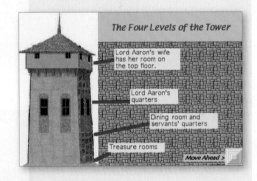

The Four Levels of the Tower

Lord Aaron's wife has her room on the top floor.

Lord Aaron's quarters

Dining room and servants' quarters

Treasure rooms

Move Ahead >

Helpful Hint

To view this multimedia presentation—and also an interactive report—visit http://www.thewritesource.com/ws2000.html.

Viewing
Skills

Do you spend more time watching TV, or surfing the Internet? Only a few years ago, viewing was a fairly passive activity. Now, whether you are viewing online or on TV, you are probably more actively involved. With video sites, online streaming, cable television, and digital video recorders, you have many more choices to make about what you view.

As a result, viewing these days is much more demanding. There are many insightful and creative options to sort through, and then you have to interpret the sites and programs you do choose to watch. This chapter can help you improve your viewing skills.

What's Ahead

- Viewing on the Internet
- Watching the News
- Watching Documentaries
- Watching Commercials

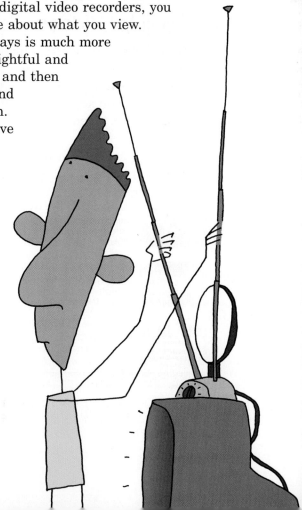

Viewing on the Internet

The Internet has many video-sharing sites, with millions of uploaded videos. There are a number of reasons to visit these sites.

- **Current events:** Find current news stories and reactions, including straight reports and satires.
- **Research:** Experience important moments in history, such as Martin Luther King, Jr.'s, "I have a dream" speech.
- **World viewpoints:** Learn about the culture and viewpoints of people from other countries.
- **Instruction:** Find how-to instructions, such as how to play a popular song on the guitar.
- **Popular culture:** Enjoy current and classic entertainers.
- **Amateur entertainment:** View many inspiring videos created by people just like you.

Searching for Videos

Looking for online videos is like any other Internet search—simply enter keywords into the search bar of the video site. After results appear, check the information to decide if you want to view that video. Below, the keyword "Hurricane" produced two news reports and a music video.

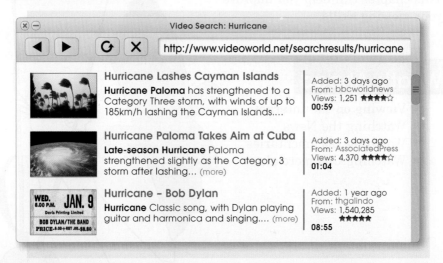

Evaluating Videos

When you find a video you are interested in, click on it to watch it. Afterward, if you are a member of the video-sharing site, you can rate the video and leave comments.

- **Rating videos:** Rating the video (often by giving it from one to five stars) helps other viewers decide if they want to watch it.
- **Leaving comments:** Responding to the video or to another person's comments gives you the opportunity to "talk with" other viewers and share ideas.

Sharing Videos

After you view a video, the site may suggest similar videos. Consider the picture, heading, ratings, and other information before deciding to watch other videos.

If you find a video you really like, the site often allows you to mark it in a number of ways:

- **Favorites:** Keep a list of favorite videos to easily find them again.
- **Playlists:** Keep a list of videos you enjoy viewing together, one after another.
- **Share:** Share videos by posting them to your page on a social networking site. (See 407.)

Watching the News

Whether on TV or on a video-sharing site, you can tune in to the news to find out what is happening in your city or beyond. In either case, you need to watch and listen carefully and then judge whether a news story is complete, correct, and unbiased.

Watch for Completeness

A good news story is complete. It answers the 5 W's (*who? what? where? when?* and *why?*). Here is the beginning of a news story. Notice how all 5 W's are answered in the first sentence.

> The <u>people of Cuba</u> are <u>bracing tonight for Hurricane Paloma,</u>
>   Who   What
> <u>which should make landfall</u> on <u>Cuba</u> <u>midday Saturday</u>. President
>   Why   Where   When
> Raul Castro has issued evacuation orders to a country still reeling
>
> from Hurricanes Ike and Gustav earlier in the season. . . .

When viewing a news story, always listen carefully for its context. The story above went on to describe the active Atlantic hurricane season, which even postponed the Republican National Convention due to a Gulf Coast hurricane on a path similar to the devastating Hurricane Katrina. The context of background information gives the listener a better understanding of the meaning and importance of a story.

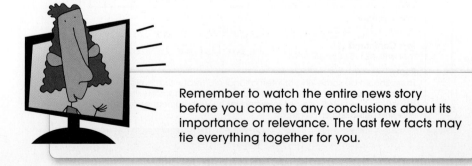

Remember to watch the entire news story before you come to any conclusions about its importance or relevance. The last few facts may tie everything together for you.

Watch for Correctness

A good news story must be correct. If reporters are unsure of all the facts, they must carefully word their stories to indicate this. Compare the following two news clips, for example. The first gives information that was available just after the event. The second gives information that only became available later in the day.

First report ■ A high-speed train derailed in Germany today, and early reports are that as many as 30 people may have been killed.

Second report ■ The death toll now stands at 100 in the derailment of a German train. Rescuers continue to search the wreckage.

Helpful Hint

Remember that early reports about a news event often are not complete or correct. Keep checking until all the facts are in.

Watch for Point of View

No two people ever tell the same story exactly the same way. This is also true of news reporters. When you watch a TV news story, you are getting the news team's point of view. They have made decisions that shape what you see and hear. Here are two ways that this is done:

1. News teams decide which facts to tell and which pictures to show. A story about a high-crime area may show houses with broken windows and littered yards, but may neglect to show any of the well-kept homes in the same neighborhood.

2. News teams decide which people to interview. Telling both sides of a story is important, but the individuals chosen to speak for each side will affect your opinion. For example, interviewing a popular police chief who supports a new law, and a gang leader who is against it, would have a definite persuasive effect.

Helpful Hint

Notice the facts, pictures, and people included in a news story. Think about what may have been left out. Consider how these choices may affect your opinion about a situation.

Watching Documentaries

Documentaries are programs that tell about one subject in depth. Their main purpose is to inform, although many are entertaining as well. If you are an active, thoughtful viewer, you can learn a lot from a good documentary. Here are some tips:

Before you watch . . .

- Find out what the program is about.
- Make a list of your questions after thinking about what you already know about the subject and what you'd like to learn. Leave room between questions for notes.
- Make sure you understand any questions your teacher may have given you to answer.

While you watch . . .

- Take a few brief notes. Spend most of your time watching; just write down key words that will help you compose complete answers later.
- Watch for completeness, correctness, and point of view.
- Jot down any additional questions you think of.

After you watch . . .

- Write complete answers to your questions while the program is fresh in your mind.
- Talk with someone else who watched the program. Individuals notice and remember different things. Ask each other, "What did you find most interesting? What was the name of that red bird? Did you understand the part about . . . ?" and so on.
- Write or talk about your feelings about the program. Did anything make you laugh, upset you, or confuse you? Exploring your feelings will help you remember more about the subject.
- Write a summary to help you remember the main points and ideas in the program. (See the next page.)

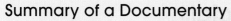

Summary of a Documentary

What follows is a summary based on one student's understanding of a documentary about the Nile River. It was written after the student talked about the program and reviewed her notes.

Nile: River of Gods

Main Idea

This video showed why civilization first appeared on the banks of the Nile River in Africa. The Nile provided everything needed to build the wealthy, advanced Egyptian society.

Important Details

Most importantly, the Nile provided rich soil and water for farming. Every year, the river would flood. Afterward, a layer of mud was left behind. It contained all the nutrients needed to grow crops such as barley, millet, rice, wheat, and flax. The Nile also provided irrigation water for the crops. This combination of good soil, water, and lots of sun meant that Egyptians could grow more food than they needed.

The Nile River also provided transportation, giving the people a way to trade their extra grain for other goods and materials needed to build cities and develop the Egyptian culture. The Nile's mud was also used to make bricks and pottery.

Interesting Final Fact

The Nile River has been called the "river of gods" because the ancient Egyptians found inspiration for their gods from the animals that lived in and around it. The lion, buffalo, falcon, crocodile, hippo, and ibis are just some of the animals that became gods to the people. The ibis became the god of knowledge because these birds always seemed to know when the river would flood, arriving just beforehand.

Watching Commercials

News programs and documentaries have the same main purpose: to inform you. But commercials have a completely different purpose: primarily to persuade you to buy something. People who create TV commercials have several tried-and-true techniques for making people want to buy products. Here are a few of their favorite selling methods.

■ Slice of Life

A slice-of-life commercial looks like it was filmed with someone's home video camera. It seems to show a bunch of real people having a great time drinking Brand X cola or wearing Brand X athletic shoes. These commercials can be convincing, but the people in them are actors. Each scene is carefully staged and rehearsed. It's very possible that the actors holding cans of Brand X cola have never even tasted it!

■ Famous Faces

A famous-face commercial shows a celebrity using Brand X. This selling method is effective because many people want to be like their favorite celebrities. The idea is to make people think that if they buy Brand X cola, they will be more like the beautiful movie star or the superstar athlete who is in the commercial.

■ Just the Facts

A just-the-facts commercial uses facts and figures to sell a product. For example, it may say, "Nine out of ten teenagers say Brand X is the best cola." But the commercial may not tell you anything about the survey that produced these results. Since you can't be sure the survey is trustworthy, it's difficult to believe the commercial.

■ Problem-Solution

A problem-solution commercial shows someone with a problem, and then shows the product solving the problem. For example, a new kid moves to town. His problem is that he doesn't know anybody or have any friends. Then he has an idea: He buys a few cans of Brand X cola and offers them to the guys playing basketball in the park. The guys love Brand X cola, so they decide the new guy is cool. Brand X solved his problem. Of course, this only happens in the world of TV commercials!

Group
Skills

Collaborate means "to work together." You have probably collaborated on many school projects in the past, and will certainly collaborate on many more in the future. But, as you know, working in small groups or on teams can be difficult—not everything always goes smoothly.

The following skills will help you work and learn better in groups: **listening**, **observing**, **cooperating**, **clarifying**, **responding**, and **resolving conflicts,**. These skills are often called "people skills" because they help people work together successfully in groups, on teams, and within families. They are also known as "team skills" or "group skills."

Whatever name they go by, the ability to use these skills is very important for success in a variety of situations.

What's Ahead

- Listening
- Observing, Cooperating, Clarifying
- Responding
- Resolving Conflicts
- Collaborating Online

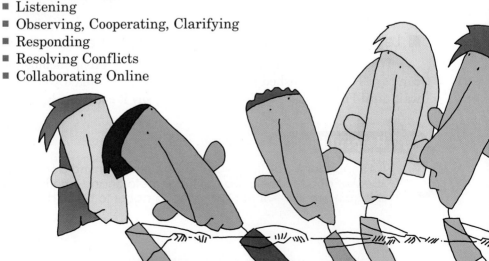

Listening

Good listening requires practice. People tend to listen in spurts. A spurt may last from a few seconds to a few minutes, but no one can listen with complete attention for very long. This is why it's important to know how to listen effectively when you work in a group.

■ Listen actively.

To be a good listener, you must be an active listener. This means you should let the speaker know you are listening. You can make eye contact, nod your head, and remain attentive. You can also let the speaker know you have listened by asking a good question, by summarizing, or by offering a compliment or comment.

■ Listen accurately.

Hearing is not the same as listening. Hearing involves your ears; listening involves your ears and your mind. You need to think about what you hear. Listen with pen in hand. Jot down a word, phrase, or question to help you remember what you've heard and what you may want to ask or add. Then, when the speaker stops, offer your ideas.

■ Know when—and how—to interrupt.

If you are a good listener, sooner or later you will have a comment, a question, or an important fact to add. Even so, interrupting someone who is speaking is not usually a good idea.

But sometimes it is necessary to interrupt a group member who has wandered off the topic. When that happens, you can say, "Excuse me, but I think we should get back to the main point of our discussion."

■ Learn how to respond when you are interrupted.

When you are interrupted for any reason by a group member, you can say, "I wasn't finished making my point yet" or "Could you please wait until I'm finished?" Whatever you say, say it courteously.

Helpful Hint

It's important for all listeners to keep an open mind about the speaker and the topic. Do not judge beforehand whether you are going to like—or not like—what is about to be said.

Observing

Being observant is an important group skill. People "say" as much with their actions and tone of voice as with their words.

■ Watch body language.

At times you can "see" what a person is saying or feeling. Such *body language* includes facial expressions, hand gestures, and body positions.

■ Offer words of encouragement.

When you encourage someone, you show your appreciation of that person's ideas. All of us are more likely to participate in groups if we feel that what we say will be accepted.

Cooperating

■ Offer compliments.

We too often forget to compliment or thank others when we work in groups. Simply say, "I really like your suggestion," or "That's a great idea."

■ Never use put-downs.

Put-downs must be avoided in group work. They not only disrupt the group but destroy members' self-confidence as well.

> Cooperating means "working together"—using common sense and common courtesy to reach a common goal.
>
> — Dave Kemper

Clarifying

Clarifying means "making something clear, easy for others to understand."

■ Offer to explain or clarify.

If what you say is long or complex, end by asking, "Are there any questions?"

■ Request help or clarification when needed.

Summarize what you heard and end with a question: "Is that about it, or did I miss something?"

Responding

When you work in a group, nearly everything you say and do is a response to what someone else has said or done. First, you hear others' statements or observe their behavior. Second, you take a moment to think about the ways you could respond. Third, you choose your response.

■ Think before responding.

Someone may make a statement: "Maroon 5 is a dumb group." Before you knew about group skills, you might respond by saying, "Yeah, well I think you're dumb." If you respond in this way, the other person has dragged you into a dead-end argument instead of a discussion.

But you can choose how you will respond. You can avoid an argument by saying, "Everyone is entitled to his or her own opinion." You can look for details by asking, "Why do you feel they're dumb?" Or you can seek clarification by asking, "What do you mean by 'dumb'?" After trying to answer the questions, the speaker may change his or her position—or you may change yours.

■ Learn how to disagree.

Never say, "I disagree with you." Say instead, "I disagree. I think Maroon 5 is a great group." This is disagreeing with the idea, not the speaker. You can continue by listing your reasons for disagreeing. Then you can discuss these points with the speaker.

Communicating with Respect

Whenever you work with a group, you must be respectful and courteous.

1. Respect yourself by
   - believing that your own thoughts and feelings have value,
   - taking responsibility for what you say, and
   - accepting that others may disagree with you.
2. Respect others by
   - encouraging everyone to participate,
   - listening openly to what they have to say, and
   - using compliments whenever you can.

Resolving Conflicts

Whenever you are dealing with people, conflicts may come up. People disagree, and that's okay. To manage conflicts, think about the situation.

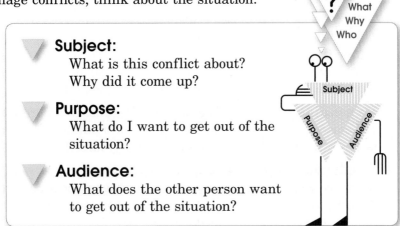

Subject:
What is this conflict about?
Why did it come up?

Purpose:
What do I want to get out of the situation?

Audience:
What does the other person want to get out of the situation?

Strategies for Conflict Resolution

There are four ways to resolve conflict: assert, cooperate, defer, or compromise.

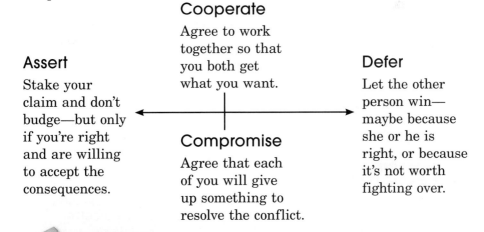

Cooperate
Agree to work together so that you both get what you want.

Assert
Stake your claim and don't budge—but only if you're right and are willing to accept the consequences.

Defer
Let the other person win— maybe because she or he is right, or because it's not worth fighting over.

Compromise
Agree that each of you will give up something to resolve the conflict.

Helpful Hint

You can also agree to disagree. Instead of resolving the conflict, both sides decide that they must stick with their positions.

Collaborating Online

Wikis, chat rooms, classroom blogs, and social networking sites allow you to collaborate with others online. Follow these tips for online collaboration:

Tips for Online Collaboration

- **Know the rules.** Follow the rules of whatever collaborative space you are visiting. Remember that classroom collaborative spaces are extensions of the classroom, with all the rules that apply.

- **Be genuine.** Don't use fake names or log-ins. Don't pretend to be someone you are not. The whole point of online collaboration is to work with others, so you need to be yourself.

- **Weigh your words.** Choose words that represent you well. Since readers cannot see your body language or hear the tone of your voice, your words need to do all the communicating for you.

- **Act as you would in public.** Know that whatever you post will be viewed by many people, so conduct yourself as if many people are watching—because they are.

- **Show respect.** Be polite, encouraging, and complimentary. Avoid put-downs and negativity. Do not alter another person's posts unless you know that you are supposed to.

- **Be smart about conflicts.** Conflicts happen online just as they happen in face-to-face communication. Use the strategies you learned on page 431 to resolve those conflicts, and involve your teacher or parent if things get out of hand.

- **Avoid dangers.** Don't give out private information. Don't bully and don't tolerate bullying. If you become uncomfortable with what's happening online, involve your teacher and parent.

Helpful Hint

When you collaborate online, you create a digital projection of your personality. Take special care. People will perceive who you are based on

- the words you use,
- the pictures and videos you post,
- the links you connect to,
- the groups you join, and
- the ideas you express.

Taking
Tests

Taking a test is a little bit like giving a speech: no matter how well prepared you are, you always feel a little nervous about it. And that's okay. A little nervousness can help you stay mentally alert. For the most part, however, you want to remain cool, calm, and focused. To do so, keep up with all your class work and study effectively. Then there will be no surprises the next time you sit down to take a test.

To do well on a test, start with an effective test-taking plan. Your plan should include organizing the test material, reviewing it, remembering it, and finally, employing what you have learned on the test. You also need a clear understanding of objective tests and essay tests.

What's Ahead

- Preparing for a Test
- Taking a Test
- Taking Objective Tests
- Taking Essay Tests

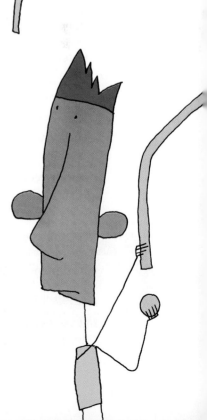

Preparing for a Test

■ **Ask Questions**
- What material will be covered on the test?
- What kind of questions will be on the test?

■ **Review the Material**
- Start reviewing a few days before the test.
- Review all the material. Then focus on the difficult parts.
- Divide your study time into two or three sessions if there is a lot to cover.

■ **Study Your Notes**
- Reread the material. Then put it in your own words.
- Make lists, flash cards, or rhymes to help you remember.
- Use graphic organizers to organize your thoughts.
- Picture the material in your mind (or draw pictures).
- Explain the material to someone else.

Taking a Test

1. **Listen carefully to directions.** Be sure you know the amount of time you have, how to fill in your answers, and so on.

2. **Ask for help.** If there is anything unclear or confusing about the test, ask your teacher to explain.

3. **Look over the whole test quickly.** First answer the questions you are sure of; then answer the other questions.

4. **When you finish, use any extra time you have to check your test.** Make sure you answered all of the questions.

Helpful Hint

If you want to remember a list of words, make up a silly sentence. Here's a sentence to help you remember the planets listed in order of distance from the sun.

My very elegant moose just sips unsweetened nectar.
(Mercury, Venus, Earth, Mars, Jupiter, Saturn, Uranus, Neptune)

Taking Objective Tests

There are four common kinds of objective tests. (Objective means "based on facts.") Here are some tips to help you do well on each kind.

True/False Test

A true/false test is a list of sentences or statements. You decide if each statement is true or false.

- **Read the whole statement carefully.** If any part of the statement is false, the answer is false.

> _false_   Tom Sawyer, Becky Thatcher, and David Copperfield are characters in the novel _The Adventures of Tom Sawyer_.

- **Be careful when you see words such as** _always, all, never,_ **and** _no._ Very few things are _always_ true or _never_ true.
- **Watch for words that mean "not."** These words include _no, not, nothing, don't, doesn't, didn't, isn't, wasn't,_ and _weren't._

> _true_   Tom isn't happy when his aunt makes him paint the fence.

Matching Test

A matching test has two lists. You match a word in one list to a word or phrase in another list.

- **Read both lists before you begin answering.**
- **Read the directions carefully.** If an answer can be used only once, check it off after using it. This makes it easy to see which answers you have left.

> **1.** ____ Sid   **A.** was lost in the cave with Tom
> **2.** ____ Huck   **B.** never took part in Tom's schemes
> **3.** ____ Becky   **C.** was Tom's best friend

Multiple-Choice Test

A multiple-choice test gives several answers for each question. You decide which answer is correct, and then you mark it.

- **On most multiple-choice tests, you most often mark only one answer for each question or statement.** However, watch for directions that may tell you to mark all answers that are correct or to mark the best answer.

> Which of the following people are Tom's friends?
> - **A.** Huck Finn
> - **B.** Becky Thatcher
> - **C.** Willie Mufferson
> - **D.** Both A and B

- **Read the question carefully.** One word can change the meaning of the whole question.

> Tom's adventures take him to every imaginable scary place except
> - **A.** a graveyard
> - **B.** a cave
> - **C.** a pirate ship
> - **D.** a haunted house

- **Read all of the answers before you mark the one you think is correct.**

Fill-in-the-Blanks Test

On a fill-in-the-blanks test, you fill in the missing words.

- **Each blank usually stands for one word.** If there are three blanks in a row, you need to write in three words.

> Tom finds twelve thousand dollars' worth of _____ _____ _____ in the cave.

- **If the word just before the blank is "an," the answer probably begins with a, e, i, o, or u.**

> Tom has an _____ named Polly and a _____ named Sid.

Taking Essay Tests

In an essay test, you write a short essay that answers a specific question. This kind of test involves several steps—reading the question, thinking about what you know, planning your answer, and, finally, writing your answer. It's a big job, so take it one step at a time.

Understand the Question

Read the question carefully—at least two times. As you read, look for the *key word* or words that tell you exactly what to do. Here are some key words you will often find in essay questions.

Compare means "tell how these things are alike."

Contrast means "tell how these things are different." Some essay questions ask you to compare *and* contrast.

Define means "tell what a word or subject means, what its function or role is, what group or category it belongs to, and how it is different from other members of the group."

Describe means "tell how something looks, sounds, or feels." In some cases, you may even describe how something smells and tastes.

Evaluate means "give your opinion." You may share both good points and bad points about a topic. It is very important to tell why you have this opinion and to give facts and details that support it.

Explain means "tell how something happens or how it works." You should give reasons, causes, or step-by-step details.

Identify means "answer *who? what? when? where?* and *why?* about a subject."

List means "include a specific number of examples, reasons, or causes."

Outline means "organize your answer into main points and specific examples." Sometimes you may be asked to prepare an actual outline.

Prove means "present facts and details that show something is true."

Review means "give an overall picture of the main points about a subject."

Summarize means "tell the important points in a shortened form."

Plan Your Answer

Find the key word in the question and underline it. Copy the word onto your paper and write what it means. Begin writing down facts and details indicated by the key word. You may use a graphic organizer or just make a list.

Science Test—Chapter 18

Question: <u>Describe</u> the sun. Give as many details as you can.

<u>Describe:</u> Tell how it looks, sounds, or feels.

THE SUN
* size, age
  • yellow dwarf
  • medium size
  • 4.6 billion years old
  • over a million kilometers in diameter
  • more than 99% of mass in solar system
  • creates strong gravitational pull
* structure and gases
  • 4 layers: photosphere, convection zone, radiation zone, core
  • core temperature: more than 15,000,000 degrees centigrade
  • hydrogen changed to helium = energy

Helpful Hint

It's not necessary to write down everything you know about the subject. Instead, think carefully about the question and write down only the information you need to answer it.

Write a One-Paragraph Answer

If the question is not too complicated, you may answer it in one paragraph, using all of your main points and supporting details. Remember to arrange the information in the best possible way.

Science Test—Chapter 18

Question: Describe the sun. Give as many details as you can.

Science Test — Chapter 18

The sun is a yellow dwarf star that scientists think is about 4.6 billion years old. It is over 1 million kilometers in diameter and contains more than 99 percent of the mass in the whole solar system. Because of its huge mass, the sun has a strong gravitational pull. The sun is made up of gases and has four layers. The surface is called the photosphere. The next layer is the convection zone, then the radiation zone, and at the center is the core. The core temperature is more than 15 million degrees centigrade. At the core, hydrogen is turned into helium by a process called nuclear fusion. This process creates many forms of energy, including heat and light. Without the heat and light of the sun, we could not exist on planet Earth.

Write a Multiparagraph Answer

Sometimes, with a more complicated question, you will need to write a multiparagraph answer. For example, the question below asks students to describe two different things. Notice that the answer addresses the first part of the question in one paragraph and covers the second part of the question in another.

Science Test—Chapter 18

Question: Describe the sun and its effects on the planets in our solar system.

The sun is a yellow dwarf star that scientists think is about 4.6 billion years old. Even though the sun is only a medium-size star, it is 1,392,000 kilometers in diameter. The sun is made up of four layers of gases. The surface is called the photosphere. The next layer is the convection zone, then comes the radiation zone, and at the center is the core. At the core, which is more than 15 million degrees centigrade, hydrogen is turned into helium by a process called nuclear fusion. This process creates many forms of energy, including heat and light.

The sun has many powerful effects on the planets in our solar system. Because of its huge mass, the sun has a strong gravitational pull. This is what keeps the planets orbiting around the sun. The sun's light and heat travel through space to the planets, making nearby planets such as Mercury and Venus very hot, while leaving faraway planets such as Uranus and Neptune extremely cold.

To sum up, without the sun and its gravitational pull, our solar system would not exist. Without the heat and light from the sun, <u>we</u> would not exist.

Responding to a
Prompt

Some people just seem to excel when the pressure is on. A star baseball player will often make a key play when the game is on the line. A skilled politician will almost always give thoughtful, articulate answers when questioned about important issues. Surprisingly, their actions appear natural and effortless, and there's a reason for that—they spend endless hours preparing for pressure-packed moments.

A big-time baseball player fields hundreds of fly balls, day after day. An influential politician studies the issues thoroughly so no question will stump him or her. In the same way, you can prepare yourself to respond to a prompt in a timed writing. Then you, too, can excel during "crunch time." This chapter will show you how.

What's Ahead

- Prompt and Response
- Writing Guidelines
- Responding to Prompts Review

Prompt and Response

Many state and school writing tests ask you to respond to a prompt in a timed writing. An expository prompt, such as the one that follows, asks you to explain something. Study the prompt and student response on these two pages.

Expository Prompt

Everyone has heard the phrase "close friend," but each of us has different ideas about what makes one. In an essay, define "close friend" and include examples to explain your main points about the concept.

Response

Beginning

The beginning paragraph introduces the topic and states the thesis. (underlined).

When you're really little, you don't worry about friends. You just hang out at home, being cared for by your family. Even in preschool and kindergarten, you don't really have friends. You're still too attached to home. But at some point, maybe during first or second grade, you want friends to play with. Then, before you know it, one or two of these friends take on special importance and become close friends. A close friend is someone who connects with you on a very personal level.

A close friend shares your interests. If you enjoy computer games or like to play soccer, your close friend will, too. Justin Kacinski is my closest friend, and we both love to play baseball and to watch dumb comedy movies. We even have the same taste in music, fringe rock. Without these common interests, Justin and I obviously wouldn't want to hang out together.

Middle

Each middle paragraph covers one main point.

A close friend is someone you enjoy being with. There's a comfort level that you both feel. You laugh at the same jokes and wear the same types of clothes. You almost know what each other is thinking. When Justin and I are together, something always gets us laughing, almost uncontrollably. We go on weekend trips with each other's family and even make meals together. On weekends and in the summer, the first thing that I do is find out what Justin is up to.

Specific examples and explanations are included.

Most importantly, a close friend is also someone who helps you through tough times. When you need advice, support, or assistance, a close friend will be there. Before one of our baseball games, I had to mow our lawn and trim the bushes. I didn't think I could get everything done in time, so, just like that, Justin took care of the trimming. A few days ago, Justin's girlfriend broke up with him. Once I heard about it, I called him right away to make sure that he was doing okay. I wanted to be there for support.

Ending
The ending adds one last idea and refers to the thesis.

The true test of our friendship will come next year. Justin will be going to the Catholic high school, and I will be going to the public high school. Will we still be close friends? Or will we drift away from each other because of our new schools? If we are true friends, we'll find ways to keep the special connection going. No one said keeping a close friendship will always be easy.

Patterns of Organization

Order of Importance

- Beginning
- Least important point
- Next important point
- Most important point
- Ending

Extended Definition

- Beginning
- Personal definition
- Negative definition (What it is not)
- Synonyms and antonyms
- Examples and comparisons
- Ending

Writing Guidelines

Prewriting—Analyzing a Prompt

A **prompt** is a set of directions that tells you what to write. It's important to analyze a prompt carefully to make sure that you understand every part of it. That is the only way to make sure that your response will fit the requirements of the timed writing.

Using the STRAP Questions

When you analyze a prompt, use the following STRAP questions as a guide.

Subject:	What topic should I write about?
Type:	What form of writing should I create?
Role:	What position (student, son or daughter, friend) should I assume?
Audience:	Who is the intended reader?
Purpose:	What is the goal of my writing?

The Process in Action

Here is an analysis of the expository prompt on page 442.

Some prompts do not answer every question.

Expository Prompt

Everyone has heard the phrase "close friend," but each of us has different ideas about what makes one. In an essay, define "close friend" and include examples to explain your main points about the concept.

Subject:	close friends
Type:	expository essay
Role:	friend/student
Audience:	not stated, but will address classmates and teacher
Purpose:	to define and explain

Planning Your Response

Once you have answered the STRAP questions, quickly plan your response. First write a thesis statement. Follow this formula if you have trouble writing your thesis:

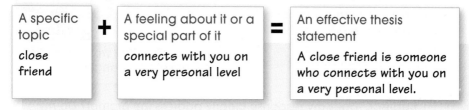

A specific topic	+	A feeling about it or a special part of it	=	An effective thesis statement
close friend		connects with you on a very personal level		A close friend is someone who connects with you on a very personal level.

Then list the main points that you want to cover in your response. These points should support or explain your thesis. Here is a quick list of the main points covered in the sample response.

Quick List

- Someone who shares your interests
- Someone who you enjoy being with
- Someone who helps you through tough times

Writing—Writing Your Response

Stick to your plan as much as possible, but add any new ideas that come to mind if they add strong support for your thesis.

Beginning ■ Begin with a few general comments that introduce your topic. Make these comments as interesting as possible. Then state your thesis.

Middle ■ Develop the middle paragraphs, following your quick list or other planning guide. Be sure to add specific examples to support your main ideas.

Ending ■ Bring your response to a close by trying one or more of the following: (1) summarize your main points, (2) add one final idea, or (3) refer to your thesis.

Revising—Improving Your Writing

Most writing tests allow you to revise your response. Begin by reading it through once for clarity and completeness. Then check it using the STRAP questions as a guide.

> *Remember:* You won't have time to make big changes.

<u>S</u>ubject: Does my response clearly address the prompt? Do my main points support the thesis?

<u>T</u>ype: Have I followed the correct form (essay, letter, article)?

<u>R</u>ole: Have I taken the position indicated in the prompt?

<u>A</u>udience: Does my response speak to the intended audience?

<u>P</u>urpose: Does my prompt accomplish its goal (to explain, to persuade)?

Editing—Checking Your Response

Check your response for punctuation, capitalization, spelling, and grammar. Make corrections as neatly as possible.

____ Have I used end punctuation after every sentence?
____ Have I capitalized all proper nouns and first words of sentences?
____ Have I checked my spelling?
____ Do my subjects and verbs agree?
____ Have I used the right word *(their, there, they're)*?

Helpful Hint

Always allow time for planning and for revising and editing. For example, with 45 minutes to respond to a prompt, use 5 to 10 minutes to analyze the prompt and plan your response, 30 to 35 minutes for your writing, and the last 5 minutes for revising and editing.

Responding to Prompts Review

Use the following tips as a guide for responding to prompts.

■ **Before you write . . .**

Analyze the prompt.

- Use the STRAP questions as a guide.
- Remember that expository prompts ask you to explain or to inform; persuasive prompts ask you to persuade or defend an opinion.

Plan your time wisely.

- Use the first 5 minutes for planning and the last 5 minutes for revising and editing. Focus on the actual writing for the rest of the time.

■ **As you write . . .**

Stick to your initial planning as much as possible.

- You don't have time for much rethinking or refocusing.

Get the reader's attention in the beginning.

- Open with a few general comments about the topic.
- Then state your thesis.

Be selective in the middle paragraphs.

- Start each paragraph with a main point about the topic.
- Support the main points with explanations and examples.

End in a meaningful way.

- State a final important idea.
- Restate the thesis.

■ **After you write . . .**

Check for completeness and clarity.

- Use the STRAP questions as a revising guide.

Check for conventions.

- Correct any punctuation, capitalization, spelling, or grammar errors.

Proofreader's Guide

Marking **Punctuation**

Period

A **period** is used to end a sentence. It is also used after initials, after abbreviations, and as a decimal point.

449.1 At the End of Sentences
A period is used to end a sentence that makes a statement, a request, or a mild command.

Homes in the future will have many high-tech features. (statement)

Check your video doorbell to see who stopped by while you were gone. (request)

Don't worry. (command)

Your household robot (yes, you'll probably own one) will not reveal your whereabouts unless programmed to do so. (statement)

Note: It is not necessary to place a period after a statement within parentheses that is part of another sentence.

449.2 After an Initial
A period should be placed after an initial.

J. R. R. Tolkien (author)   **E. Benjamin Nelson** (politician)

449.3 After Abbreviations
A period is placed after each part of an abbreviation—unless the abbreviation is an acronym. An acronym is a word formed from the first (or first few) letters of words in a set phrase. (See 471.5.)

Abbreviations: Mr. Mrs. Ms. Dr. B.C.E. C.E.

Acronyms: AIDS NASA FEMA

Note: When an abbreviation is the last word in a sentence, use only one period at the end of the sentence.

Fossil fuels must eventually be replaced by renewable energy sources such as hydropower, wind, solar, geothermal, etc.

449.4 As a Decimal
Use a period as a decimal point and to separate dollars and cents.

For $4.99 on Tuesdays, I can rent three DVD's. But is it a bargain to spend 33.3 percent of my allowance on DVD's?

Question Mark

A **question mark** is used after an interrogative sentence and to show doubt about the correctness of a fact or figure.

450.1 | **Direct Question**
A question mark is used at the end of a direct question (an interrogative sentence).

> Have you ever heard of a sunken galleon code-named the *Black Swan* by those who discovered it?

450.2 | **Indirect Question**
No question mark is used after an indirect question.

> Mr. Dehnke asked if anyone was interested in doing a report on the ship and its treasure.

> He also asked if we knew the significance of the name *Black Swan*.

450.3 | **To Show Doubt**
The question mark is placed within parentheses to show that the writer isn't sure a fact or figure is correct.

> The treasure, worth $500 million (?), has become the object of several court battles.

Exclamation Point

An **exclamation point** may be placed after a word, a phrase, or a sentence to show emotion. (The exclamation point should not be overused.)

450.4 | **To Express Strong Feeling**
The exclamation point is used to show excitement or strong feeling.

> Yeah! Wow! Oh my!

> Surprise! You've won the million-dollar sweepstakes!

Caution: Never use multiple exclamation points; such punctuation is unnecessary.

> Unnecessary: I'm rich!!!

> Correct: I'm rich!

Ellipsis

An **ellipsis** (three periods) is used to show a pause in dialogue or to show that words or sentences have been left out. (Leave one space before, between, and after the periods.)

451.1 **To Show a Pause**

An ellipsis is used to show a pause in dialogue.

> "My report," said Reggie, "is on . . . um . . . cars of the future. One Web site that I . . . um . . . found online said that cars would someday run on sunshine. Is this . . . um . . . a plot to keep teenage drivers home at night?"

451.2 **To Show Omitted Words**

An ellipsis can be used to show that one or more words have been left out of a quotation. Read this excerpt from a report:

> The Arctic ice cap is shrinking fast. Scientists agree that this is happening because of climate change. Heat-trapping gases, called greenhouse gases, are emitted into the atmosphere and raise the temperatures at the North Pole.

Here's how to quote the report, leaving some words out.

> "The Arctic ice cap is shrinking . . . because of climate change. Heat-trapping gases . . . raise the temperatures at the North Pole."

451.3 **At the End of a Sentence**

If the words left out are at the end of a sentence, use a period followed by an ellipsis.

> "The Arctic ice cap is shrinking fast. . . . Heat trapping gases . . . raise the temperatures at the North Pole."

Comma

Commas are used to indicate a pause or a change in thought. Commas keep words and ideas from running together, making writing easier to read. No other punctuation mark is more important to understand than the comma.

452.1 **Between Items in a Series**

Commas are used between words, phrases, or clauses in a series. (A series contains at least three items.)

> Spanish, French, and German are the languages most often taught in schools today, but Chinese, English, and Hindi are the languages spoken by the most people in the world. (words)

> Being comfortable with technology, working well with others, and knowing another language and culture are important skills for today's workers. (phrases)

452.2 **To Keep Numbers Clear**

Commas are used to separate the digits in a number in order to distinguish hundreds, thousands, millions, and so on.

> In 2007, 660,477 immigrants became U.S. citizens. The greatest number of these people came from Mexico (122,258), India (46,871), and the Philippines (38,830).

Note: Commas are not used in years. It is also acceptable to use a combination of numerals and words for large numbers in the millions and billions. (See page 472 for more information.)

452.3 **In Dates and Addresses**

Commas are used to distinguish items in an address and items in a date.

> Rev. Martin Luther King, Jr., was born on January 15, 1929, in his father's house at 501 Auburn Avenue, Atlanta, Georgia.

> On August 28, 1963, he gave his famous "I Have a Dream" speech. Rev. Martin Luther King, Jr., was assassinated on April 4, 1968.

> The King Center, founded on the principle of nonviolent social change, is located at 449 Auburn Avenue NE, Atlanta, Georgia 30312.

Note: There is no comma between the state and the ZIP code.

453.1 **To Set off Dialogue**
Commas are used to set off the exact words of the speaker from the rest of the sentence.

> "And with this new TTS software," said the salesman, "you can just sit back and relax while your computer reads your e-mail to you."

Note: When you are reporting or summarizing what someone said, do not use a comma (or quotation marks), as in the example below. The words *if* and *that* often signal dialogue that is being reported rather than quoted.

> The salesman said that with this new TTS software, I can just sit back and relax while my computer reads my e-mail to me.

453.2 **To Set Off Interruptions**
Commas are used to set off a word, phrase, or clause that interrupts the main thought of a sentence. Such expressions can be identified with the following tests:

1. You can omit them without changing the meaning of the sentence.
2. You can place them nearly anywhere in the sentence without changing its meaning.

> New Technology changes how we live. Many people, *for example*, check the time on their cell phones. *As a result*, they don't need their wristwatches anymore.

453.3 **To Set Off Interjections**
A comma is used to separate an interjection or a weak exclamation from the rest of the sentence.

> *Really*, I haven't worn my watch for months!

> *Sure*, but you'll want the new watch-style computer they're developing. *Man*, a flick of the wrist and you've got the time and you're online.

453.4 **In Direct Address**
Commas are used to separate a noun of direct address from the rest of the sentence. (A noun of direct address is the noun that names the person spoken to in the sentence.)

> *Jana*, are you watching videos on YouTube instead of doing your homework?

> No, *Mom*, I'm doing research for my report on independent filmmakers.

Comma . . .

454.1 **To Enclose Information**
Commas are used to enclose a title or initials and names that follow a person's last name.

> Alan Bernstein, *PH.D.,* is the first executive director of the Global HIV Vaccine Enterprise. Anthony Fauci, *M.D.,* is a member of the coordinating committee. Bhan, *M. K.,* and Trias, *Octavi Q.,* are also committee members.

454.2 **Between Two Independent Clauses**
A comma may be used between two independent clauses that are joined by coordinate conjunctions such as *and, but, or, nor, for, so,* and *yet.*

> Many businesses are selling their products on the Internet, *and* online shopping has become popular with millions of people.

> **Avoid Comma Splices** A comma splice results when two independent clauses are "spliced" together with only a comma—and no conjunction. (See page 84.)

454.3 **To Separate Clauses and Phrases**
A comma should separate an adverb clause or a long modifying phrase from the independent clause that follows it.

> *Because we have busy schedules,* shopping online is very convenient. (adverb clause)

> *According to health officials,* that convenience may be encouraging too much sitting. (long modifying phrase)

> *Many times* the better choice would be to get ourselves to a store and walk around *while we shop.* (Commas are often omitted after short introductory phrases, and when the adverb clause follows the independent clause.)

454.4 **To Set Off Appositives**
An appositive is a word or phrase that identifies or renames a noun or pronoun. (Do not use commas with restrictive appositives, which are necessary to the meaning of the sentence.)

> COBOL, *a programming language based on English words and phrases,* was developed by Grace Hopper, *a U.S. Navy admiral.* (The two appositive phrases are set off with commas.)

> The programming language *COBOL* made computers far more user friendly. (The restrictive appositive, *COBOL,* is not set off because it's needed to make the sentence clear.)

455.1 **To Separate Adjectives**

Commas are used to separate two or more adjectives that equally modify the same noun.

> Many *intelligent, well-educated* scientists think that one of Jupiter's 16 moons shows signs of life.

Intelligent and *well-educated* are separated by a comma because they modify *scientists* equally.

Note: **No** comma is used between the last adjective (*well-educated*) and the noun (*scientists*).

> A Nasa mission to send a space probe to this *cold Jovian* moon lost its funding in 2007.

Cold and *Jovian* do not modify *moon* equally; therefore, no comma separates the two.

Use these tests to help you decide if adjectives modify equally:
1. **Switch the order** of the adjectives; if the sentence is clear, the adjectives modify equally.
2. **Put the word *and*** between the adjectives; if the sentence reads well, use a comma when *and* is taken out.

455.2 **To Set Off Phrases**

Commas are used to separate an explanatory phrase from the rest of the sentence.

> English, *the language computers speak worldwide*, is also the most widely used language in science and medicine.

455.3 **To Set Off Nonrestrictive Phrases and Clauses**

Commas are used to punctuate **nonrestrictive** phrases and clauses (those phrases or clauses that are not necessary to the basic meaning of the sentence).

> Glaciers, *which begin as layer upon layer of snow,* are rivers of ice. The Bering Glacier, *North America's largest,* is in Alaska. This glacier has been thinning and retreating, *which means it weighs less.*

The clause *which begin . . . snow,* the phrase *North America's largest,* and the clause *which means . . . less* are **nonrestrictive** (not required); they include additional information. If they were left out, the meaning of the sentence would remain clear.

> The fault line *that lies under the lighter Bering Glacier* is now less compressed and less stable. That means more earthquakes.

The clause *that lies . . . Glacier* is **restrictive** (required); it is needed to complete the meaning of the sentence and, therefore, is not set off with commas.

Semicolon

A **semicolon** is a cross between a period and a comma. As such, it sometimes serves as a stopping point, and other times, as a pause.

456.1 **To Join Two Independent Clauses**

A semicolon is used to join two independent clauses that are not connected with a coordinate conjunction. (Independent clauses can stand alone as separate sentences.)

I'll admit it; I'm a bit of gear-headed gadget freak.

> See 498 for an explanation and
> examples of independent clauses.

456.2 **To Set Off Two Independent Clauses**

Use a semicolon to separate independent clauses if they are long, or if they already contain commas.

My uncle has given me several gadgety gifts for my birthdays—everything from an automatic potato peeler to a robotic scorpion; but I'm saving my money for the very latest, have-to-have-it robot dinosaur!

456.3 **With Conjunctive Adverbs**

A semicolon is also used to join two independent clauses when the clauses are connected only by a conjunctive adverb (*also, as a result, for example, however, therefore, instead*).

It's a baby Camarasaurus that chortles and snorts just like the "real thing"; however, I'm a little worried about my protective little Chihuahua getting along with Cammy.

456.4 **To Separate Groups That Contain Commas**

A semicolon is used to distinguish groups of items within a list.

The three R's have been used to mean different things—reading, 'riting (writing), and 'rithmetic (arithmetic); relief, recovery, and reform; reduce, reuse, and recycle; to name just a few.

We can remember lists with the help of acronyms—HOMES for (Lakes) Huron, Ontario, Michigan, Erie, and Superior; ROY G. BIV for (rainbow colors) red, orange, yellow, green, blue, indigo, and violet; and SPRAP for (freedoms) speech, press, religion, assembly, and petition.

Colon

A **colon** may be used to introduce a letter, a list, or an important point. Colons are also used between the numbers in time.

457.1 **After a Salutation**
A colon may be used after the salutation of a business letter.

Dear Mr. Gore:

457.2 **As a Formal Introduction**
A colon may be used to formally introduce a sentence, a question, or a quotation.

Here's how one scientist explained the importance of protecting the environment: "It's like pulling bricks from a wall; everything will seem fine until the wall suddenly collapses."

457.3 **For Emphasis**
A colon is used to emphasize a word or phrase.

Because of pollution, loss of habitat, and a strange fungal disease, one group of animals is dying off worldwide: amphibians.

457.4 **Between Numerals Indicating Time**
A colon is used between the parts of a number that indicates time.

My older brother takes a college class, called Biodiversity, from 1:50 p.m. to 3:00 p.m. every Monday, Wednesday, and Friday.

457.5 **To Introduce a List**
A colon is used to introduce a list.

Here are several reasons to stop using foam containers: they quickly fill our landfills and take 500 years to dissolve, they give off close to 90 harmful gases if incinerated, and they are made from nonrenewable oil or natural gas.

Note: When introducing a list, place the colon after summary words—*the following, these things*—or after words that describe the subject of the list.

Incorrect: **To conserve water you should: install a low-flow showerhead, turn the water off while brushing your teeth, and fix drippy faucets.**

Correct: **To conserve water do the following three things: install a low-flow showerhead, turn the water off while brushing your teeth, and fix drippy faucets.**

Dash

The **dash** can be used to show a sudden break in thought, to set off added information, to show that someone's words are being interrupted, and to emphasize an idea.

458.1 To Indicate a Sudden Break

A dash can be used to show a sudden break in a sentence.

> There is one thing—actually several—that my parents dislike about cell phones: being "connected" *all* the time, looking out for drivers who are talking on the phone, and getting "surprise" charges on the phone bill.

458.2 To Set Off Added Information

A dash can be used to add explanatory information to a sentence.

> Interest in clean energy systems—including solar, wind, geothermal, and others—is creating new jobs.

> A degree in renewable energy—something previously unheard of—is offered at a number of technical institutes and colleges around the country.

458.3 To Show Interrupted Speech and for Emphasis

Dashes are used to show interruptions in someone's speech.

> Why, hello—yes, I understand—no, I remember—oh—of course, I won't—I'll—sure, right away.

A dash is also used to emphasize the idea that follows it.

> I know only one thing for sure about my aunt—she's always in a hurry.

Parentheses

Parentheses are used around words that add information to a sentence or help make an idea clearer.

458.4 To Add Information

Use parentheses when adding or clarifying information.

> Colombia (a country in South America) has established a rain forest reserve (Orito Ingi-Ande). This reserve will conserve medicinal plants (those that contain healing compounds for treating diseases).

Hyphen

The **hyphen** is used to divide words at the end of a line, to join the words in compound numbers from twenty-one to ninety-nine, and to form compound words. It is also used to join numbers that indicate the life span of an individual, the scores of a game, and so on.

459.1 | **To Divide a Word**
The hyphen is used to divide a word when you run out of room at the end of a line. Divide words only between syllables. Here are some additional guidelines:

- Never divide a one-syllable word: *raised, through.*
- Avoid dividing a word of five letters or less: *paper, study.*
- Never divide a one-letter syllable from the rest of the word: *omit-ted,* not *o-mitted.*
- Never divide abbreviations or contractions.
- Never divide the last word in more than two lines in a row or the last word in a paragraph.
- When a vowel is a syllable by itself, divide the word after the vowel: *epi-sode,* not *ep-isode.*

459.2 | **In Compound Words**
The hyphen is used to make some compound words.

e-commerce	eco-conscious
toll-free number	retro-rocket
three-story building	all-star

459.3 | **To Avoid Confusion or Awkward Spelling**
Use a hyphen with prefixes or suffixes to avoid confusion or awkward spelling.

Re-cover (not *recover*) the display tables with clean shelf paper.

It has a bell-like (not *belllike*) shape.

459.4 | **Between Numbers in a Fraction**
A hyphen is used between the numbers in a fraction, but not between the numerator and denominator when one or both are already hyphenated.

four-tenths

five-sixteenths

seven thirty-seconds (7/32)

Hyphen . . .

460.1 **To Create New Words**
A hyphen is used to form new words beginning with the prefixes *self, ex, all, great,* and so on. A hyphen is also used with suffixes such as *elect* and *free*.

> Easy access to health information on the Internet has given rise to a lot of self-diagnosing.

> Despite high-tech health care, we have not created a germ-free world. Some superbugs no longer respond to all-purpose antibiotics.

460.2 **To Join Letters and Words**
A hyphen is used to join a capital letter to a noun or participle.

U-turn	T-bar lift
X-ray therapy	PG-rated movie

460.3 **To Form an Adjective**
Use the hyphen to join two or more words that work together to form a single-thought adjective before a noun.

> voice-recognition software
> in-the-park home run
> microwave-safe cookware

Note: When words forming the adjective come after the noun, do not hyphenate them.

> These dishes are microwave safe.

Caution: When the first of the words ends in *ly*, do not use a hyphen; also, do not use a hyphen when a number or letter is the final part of a one-thought adjective.

newly designed computer	freshly painted room
grade A milk	type B personality

SCHOOL DAZE

Well, this is a none-too-long essay, but my summer vacation was none too long, either.

Quotation Marks

Quotation marks are used to set off the exact words of a speaker, to show what a writer has "borrowed" from another book or magazine, to set off the titles of certain publications, and to show that certain words are used in a special way.

461.1 | **To Set Off Direct Quotations**
Quotation marks are placed before and after direct quotations.

Futurist Don Reynolds says, "Today's students will go through an average of four careers in one life span."

461.2 | **For Quoting a Quotation**
Single quotation marks are used to punctuate a quotation within a quotation.

"When Mr. Kurt said, 'Read this book by tomorrow,' I was stunned," said Sung Kim.

461.3 | **For Long Quotations**
If more than one paragraph is quoted, quotation marks are placed before each paragraph and at the end of the last paragraph.

In research papers or reports, quotations that are more than four lines on a page are usually set off from the rest of the paper by indenting 10 spaces from the left.

Note: Long quotations that are set off require no quotation marks either before or after the quoted material, unless quotation marks appear in the original copy.

Quotation Marks . . .

462.1 · **Placement of Punctuation**

Periods and commas are always placed inside quotation marks.

> **"Let's go," said Angelo.**
> **Angelo said, "Let's go."**

An exclamation point or a question mark is placed **inside** the quotation marks when it punctuates the quotation; it is placed **outside** when it punctuates the main sentence.

> **Ari asked, "How much do skydiving lessons cost?"**
>
> **Did I hear Angelo say, "I love skydiving"?**

Semicolons or colons are placed **outside** quotation marks.

> **Ari memorized the poem "Sky"; he also recites the poem "Come to the Edge."**

462.2 · **For Special Words**

Quotation marks also may be used (1) to set apart a word that is being discussed, (2) to indicate that a word is slang, or (3) to point out that a word or phrase is being used in a special way.

> **1. Ari's vocabulary suddenly contains words like "drop zone" and "aerodynamics."**
>
> **2. He's sure that diving out of a plane with a parachute is "all good."**
>
> **3. Ari's parents wish he would "dive" into some other hobby.**

462.3 · **To Punctuate Titles**

Quotation marks are used to punctuate titles of songs, poems, short stories, lectures, episodes of radio or television programs, chapters of books, and articles found in magazines, newspapers, or encyclopedias.

> **"Change the World"** (song)
>
> **"The Raven"** (poem)
>
> **"The Pearls of Parlay"** (short story)
>
> **"A House Is Not a Home "**
> (a television episode)
>
> **"We'll Never Conquer Space"**
> (a chapter in a book)
>
> **"Teen Rescues Stranded Dolphin"**
> (newspaper article)

Other Titles
For help punctuating titles not listed above, turn to 463.1.

Note: When you punctuate a title, capitalize the first word, last word, and every word in between except for articles, short prepositions, and coordinating conjunctions.

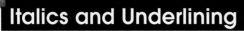

Italics and Underlining

Italics is slightly slanted type. In this sentence, the word *happiness* is typed in italics. In handwritten material, each word or letter that should be in italics is underlined.

463.1 **In Titles**

Underline (or *italicize*) the titles of books, plays, book-length poems, magazines, radio and television programs, movies, videos, CD's, the names of aircraft and ships, and newspapers.

Woods, Ponds, & Fields (book)   *The Young and the Hopeless* (CD)

EarthFocus (magazine)   U.S.S. *Enterprise* (carrier ship)

Everwood (TV program)   *Endeavour* (space shuttle)

The Dark Knight (movie)   *Boston Globe* (newspaper)

Note: Titles are put in italics (underlining) or quotation marks to set them off when you refer to them in your writing. The titles are not punctuated in these ways on the works themselves. Therefore, do not use underlining or quotation marks for your titles at the tops of your papers.

463.2 **For Foreign Words**

Underline (or *italicize*) foreign words that are not commonly used in everyday English. Also underline scientific names.

My little brother, terror that he is, often exclaims, "*Veni, vidi, vici!*"

Scientists are worried about the survival of *Ursus maritimus*, the large creamy-white bear of the North.

463.3 **For Special Uses**

Underline (or *italicize*) any number, letter, or word that is being discussed or used in a special way. (Sometimes quotation marks are used for this same purpose. See 462.2.)

On the map, the letters *A*, *J*, and *Z* appeared in various sequences, ending with the word *tesoro*.

463.4 **Handwritten**

When writing by hand, underline words that should be italicized.

In <u>Tuck Everlasting</u>, the author explores the idea of living forever.

463.5 **Printed**

When using a computer, put words in italics.

In *Tuck Everlasting*, the author explores the idea of living forever.

Apostrophe

An **apostrophe** is used to show possession, to form plurals, or to show that one or more letters have been left out of a word.

464.1

In Contractions
An apostrophe is used to show that one or more letters have been left out of a word to form a contraction.

don't (do not; *o* is left out)

she'd (she would; *woul* is left out)

it's (it is; *i* is left out)

464.2

In Place of Omitted Letters or Numbers
An apostrophe is used to show that one or more digits have been left out of a number, or that one or more letters have been left out of a word to show its special pronunciation.

class of '08 (*20* is left out)

y'all (the letters *ou* are left out)

Note: Letters and numbers are usually not omitted in formal writing. They are, however, often left out in dialogue because dialogue needs to sound natural.

464.3

To Form Plurals
An apostrophe and *s* are used to form the plural of a letter, a sign, a number, or a word discussed as a word.

A's   +'s   8's   *to*'s

Don't use too many *and*'s in your writing.

464.4

To Express Time or Amount
An apostrophe is used with an adjective that indicates time or amount.

Today's students have many online classes available to them.

Three years' study time earned my sister her bachelor's degree.

464.5

To Form Possessives in Compound Nouns
The possessive of a compound noun is formed by placing the possessive ending after the last word.

her sister-in-law's doo-wop music (singular)

her sisters-in-law's tastes in music (plural)

the secretary of state's schedule (singular)

the secretaries of state's schedules (plural)

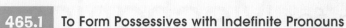

465.1 **To Form Possessives with Indefinite Pronouns**
The possessive of an indefinite pronoun is formed by adding an apostrophe and *s*.

everyone's   anyone's   somebody's

Note: For two-word pronouns, add an apostrophe and *s* to the second word.

somebody else's

465.2 **To Form Singular Possessives**
To form the possessive of a singular noun, add an apostrophe and *s*.

Al Gore's belief is that our country's electricity can be produced exclusively with renewable energy sources by 2018.

Note: You may add just an apostrophe to a singular noun ending with an *s* or a *z* sound.

Texas' wind farms (or) Texas's wind farms

Alexis' electric bill (or) Alexis's electric bill

Note: You usually add an apostrophe and *s* to singular **one-syllable** nouns that end with an *s* or a *z* sound.

boss's birthday   Chris's report

465.3 **To Form Plural Possessives**
The possessive form of plural nouns ending in *s* is usually made by adding just an apostrophe. For plural nouns not ending in *s*, an apostrophe and *s* must be added.

students' homework   children's toys

Remember! The word immediately before the apostrophe is the owner.

bus's new seat belts (*bus* is the owner)

buses' new seat belts (*buses* are the owners)

465.4 **To Show Shared Possession**
When possession is shared by more than one noun, add an apostrophe and *s* to the last noun in the series.

Ray, Liz, and Mark's robot project
(All three work on the same project.)

Ray's, Liz's, and Mark's robot projects
(Each has her or his own project.)

Editing for **Mechanics**

Capitalization

466.1 **Proper Nouns, Adjectives**
Capitalize all proper nouns and all proper adjectives. A proper noun is the name of a particular person, place, thing, or idea. A proper adjective is an adjective formed from a proper noun.

Common Noun	country, president, continent
Proper Noun	Canada, Andrew Jackson, Asia
Proper Adjective	Canadian, Jacksonian, Asian

466.2 **Names of People**
Capitalize the names of people and also the initials or abbreviations that stand for those names.

Michelle Obama, J. R. R. Tolkien, Martin Luther King, Jr., Sandra Cisneros, Johnny Depp

466.3 **Historical Events**
Capitalize the names of historical events, documents, and periods of time.

the Iraq War, the Bill of Rights, the Magna Carta, the Middle Ages, the Stone Age

466.4 **Abbreviations**
Capitalize abbreviations of titles and organizations.

M.D., Ph.D., B.A., Dr., CIW (Certified Internet Webmaster), FBI, NJHS (National Junior Honor Society)

466.5 **Organizations**
Capitalize the name of an organization, an association, or a team and its members.

Big Brothers Big Sisters, the Red Cross, Natural Resources Defense Council, the Miami Dolphins, Republicans, the Democratic Party

466.6 **Names of Subjects**
Capitalize the name of a specific course, but not the name of a general subject. (**Exception:** The names of languages are proper nouns and are always capitalized—*French, Hindi, German, Chinese.*)

Mr. Zach is teaching a ceramics course called Cookin' with Clay.

467.1 First Words

Capitalize the first word of every sentence and the first word in a direct quotation. Do not capitalize the first word in an indirect quotation.

In many families, pets are treated like people, according to an article in the *Kansas City Star.* (sentence)

Marty Becker, coauthor of *Chicken Soup for the Pet Lover's Soul,* says that pets have moved out of kennels and basements and into living rooms and bedrooms. (indirect quotation)

Becker reports, "Seven out of ten people let their pets sleep on the bed." (direct quotation)

"I get my 15 minutes of fame," he says, "every time I come home."
(Notice that *every* is not capitalized because the word does not begin a new sentence.)

"It's like being treated like a rock star," says Becker. "I have to tell you that feels pretty good."
(*I* is always capitalized, but in this case, it also begins a new sentence.)

467.2 Capitalize Geographic Names

Planets and heavenly bodies	**Earth, Jupiter, Milky Way**
Continents	**Europe, Asia, South America, Australia, Africa**
Countries	**Mexico, Haiti, Greece, Chile, United Arab Emirates**
States	**New Mexico, Alabama, Wyoming, Delaware, Iowa**
Provinces	**Alberta, British Columbia, Quebec, Ontario**
Counties	**Sioux County, Kandiyohi County, Wade County**
Cities	**Montreal, Baton Rouge, Albuquerque, Portland**
Bodies of water	**Delaware Bay, Chickamunga Lake, Indian Ocean, Gulf of Mexico, Skunk Creek**
Landforms	**Appalachian Mountains, Bitterroot Range, Death Valley**
Public areas	**Tiananmen Square, Sequoia National Forest, Constitution Gardens, Eiffel Tower, Statue of Liberty, Black Mountain Open Space Park, Vietnam Veterans Memorial**
Roads and highways	**New Jersey Turnpike, Interstate 80, Central Avenue, Chisholm Trail, Mutt's Road**
Buildings	**Pentagon, Globe Theatre, Notre Dame Cathedral**

Capitalization . . .

468.1 **Particular Sections of the Country**
Capitalize words that indicate particular sections of the country; words that simply indicate a direction are not capitalized.

the West, the East Coast, the Deep South, the Midwest, the Far North

northern region, eastern shore, moving south, traveling west

Also capitalize proper adjectives formed from names of specific sections of a country. Such adjectives usually describe the section's culture or experience.

Southern hospitality
Northern winters
Midwestern accent

468.2 **Names of Languages, Races, Nationalities, Religions**
Capitalize the names of languages, races, nationalities, and religions, as well as the proper adjectives formed from them.

Arab	**Islam**
Burmese	**African** art
Spanish	**Irish** linen
Judaism	**Mexican** food

468.3 **Words Used as Names**
Capitalize words such as *mother, father, aunt,* and *uncle* when these words are used as names.

First Uncle Marius started to sit in his chair. (*Uncle* is part of the name "Uncle Marius.")

But Uncle stopped in midair. (*Uncle* is used as a name.)

My aunt was calling him. (The word *aunt* describes this person but is not used as a name.)

Then my dad and mom walked in. (The words *dad* and *mom* are not used as names in this sentence.)

"Hi, Mom. Is this a family meeting?" I asked. (*Mom* is used as a name.)

Note: Words such as *aunt, mom, dad, grandma,* and so on, are not capitalized if they come after a possessive pronoun (*my, his, our*).

468.4 **Days, Months, Holidays**
Capitalize the names of days of the week, months of the year, and special holidays.

Friday, Saturday   July, August   Independence Day, Earth Day

Note: Do not capitalize the names of seasons.

winter, spring, summer, fall (autumn)

469.1 **Official Names**

Capitalize the names of businesses and the official names of their products. (These are called *trade names*.) Do not, however, capitalize a general descriptive word like *toothpaste* when it follows the trade name.

The Gap, Radio Shack, Microsoft,

Levi's, Rollerblades, Kodak digital camera, Crest toothpaste

469.2 **Titles Used with Names**

Capitalize titles used with names of persons and abbreviations standing for those titles.

President Hu Jintao	**Dr. Irina Zelinsky**
Governor Jennifer Granholm	**Rev. James Offutt**
Senator Joe Lieberman	

469.3 **Titles**

Capitalize the first word of a title, the last word, and every word in between except articles (*a, an, the*), short prepositions, and coordinate conjunctions. Follow this rule for titles of books, newspapers, magazines, poems, plays, songs, articles, movies, works of art, pictures, stories, and essays.

Who Put That Hair in My Toothbrush? (book)
Miami Herald (newspaper)
Sports Illustrated (magazine)
"Before the World Intruded" (poem)
Someone to Watch over Me (play)
Little Miss Sunshine (movie)
"Bridge over Troubled Water" (song)
Poplars on the Epte (work of art)

Capitalize	Do Not Capitalize
American	un-American
January, February	winter, spring
the Ohio River	the Missouri and Ohio rivers
The South is quite conservative.	Turn south at the stop sign.
Duluth Central High School	a Duluth high school
Governor Sarah Palin	Sarah Palin, our governor
President Shimon Peres	Shimon Peres, Israel's president
Ford Mustang GT	a Ford automobile
Planet Earth rotates.	The earth has a molten core.
I'm taking History 101.	I'm taking history.

Plurals

470.1 | **Nouns Ending in a Consonant**
The plurals of most nouns are formed by adding *s* to the singular.

> cheerleader — cheerleaders   wheel — wheels

The plural form of nouns ending in *ch, sh, s, z,* and *x* is made by adding *es* to the singular.

> lunch — lunches   dish — dishes   fox — foxes
> mess — messes   buzz — buzzes

470.2 | **Nouns Ending in *o***
The plurals of nouns ending in *o* with a vowel just before the *o* are formed by adding *s.*

> radio — radios   studio — studios   rodeo — rodeos

The plurals of most nouns ending in *o* with a consonant letter just before the *o* are formed by adding *es.*

> echo — echoes   hero — heroes   tomato — tomatoes

Exception: Musical terms always form plurals by adding *s.*

> alto — altos   solo — solos   piano — pianos

470.3 | **Nouns Ending in *ful***
The plurals of nouns that end with *ful* are formed by adding an *s* at the end of the word.

> three platefuls   four cupfuls

470.4 | **Nouns Ending in *f* or *fe***
The plurals of nouns that end in *f* or *fe* are formed in one of two ways: If the final *f* sound is still heard in the plural form of the word, simply add *s;* if the final sound is a *v* sound, change the *f* to *ve* and add *s.*

> roof —roofs   chief — chiefs (plural ends with *f* sound)
> wife — wives   loaf — loaves (plural ends with *v* sound)

470.5 | **Nouns Ending in *y***
The plurals of common nouns that end in *y* with a consonant letter just before the *y* are formed by changing the *y* to *i* and adding *es.*

> fly — flies   jalopy — jalopies

The plurals of common nouns that end in *y* with a vowel before the *y* are formed by adding only *s.*

> donkey — donkeys   monkey — monkeys

The plurals of proper nouns ending in *y* are formed by adding *s.*

> There are three Circuit Citys in our metro area.

471.1 **Compound Nouns**
The plurals of some compound nouns are formed by adding *s* or *es* to the main word in the compound.

brothers-in-law   **maids of honor**   **secretaries of state**

471.2 **Irregular Spelling**
Some words (including many foreign words) form a plural by taking on an irregular spelling; others are now acceptable with the commonly used *s* or *es* ending.

child .... **children**   **goose** .... **geese**

cactus .... **cacti or cactuses**

471.3 **Adding an** *'s*
The plurals of symbols, letters, numbers, and words discussed as words are formed by adding an apostrophe and an *s*.

#'s, &'s, $'s, +'s, ='s

p's and q's, DVD's, rpm's, PH.D.'s

3's, 8's, Grandma lived into her 90's.

Manny used a lot of *cool's* **and** *dude's* **in his report.**

Abbreviations

> For information on forming plural possessives, see 465.3.

471.4 **Abbreviations**
An abbreviation is the shortened form of a word or phrase. The following abbreviations are always acceptable in any kind of writing:

Mr., Mrs., Ms., Dr., a.m., p.m. (A.M., P.M.), B.C.E. (before the common era), C.E. (common era), B.A., M.A., Ph.D., M.D.

Caution: Do not abbreviate the names of states, countries, months, days, or units of measure in formal writing. Also, do not use signs or symbols (%, &) in place of words.

471.5 **Acronyms and Initialisms**
Most abbreviations are followed by a period. Acronyms and initialisms are exceptions. An acronym is a word formed from the first (or first few) letters of words in a phrase. An initialism is the same but cannot be pronounced as a word.

URL — uniform resource locator   **NASA — National Aeronautics and Space Administration**

WHO — World Health Organization

PBS — Public Broadcasting System   **MADD — Mothers Against Drunk Driving**

HDTV — high-definition television

Numbers

472.1 | **Numbers Under 10**
Numbers from one to nine are usually written as words; all numbers 10 and over are usually written as numerals.

two   seven   nine
10   25   106

472.2 | **Very Large Numbers**
You may use a combination of numerals and words for very large numbers.

1.3 million   17 billion

You may spell out large numbers that can be written as two words.

two thousand; but 2001

472.3 | **Sentence Beginnings**
Use words, not numerals, to begin a sentence.

Eleven out of twenty-four students said they spent two or more hours on the Internet each day.

472.4 | **Numerals Only**
Use numerals to express money, decimals, percentages, chapters, pages, time, telephone numbers, dates, identification numbers, ZIP codes, addresses, and statistics.

$2.39	26.2	serial no. 1721AX
July 6, 1942	8 percent	44 B.C.E.
chapter 7	79 C.E.	pages 287–289
a vote of 23 to 4	4:30 P.M.	34 mph
2125 Cairn Road	1-800-555-1212	

472.5 | **Comparing Numbers**
If you are comparing two or more numbers in a sentence, write all of them either as numerals or as words.

Students from 9 to 14 years old are invited.
Students from nine to fourteen years old are invited.

472.6 | **Numbers in Compound Modifiers**
Numbers that come before a compound modifier that includes a numeral should be written as words.

We need twelve 10-foot lengths to finish the floor.
Within the last year, Jing-Ho wrote twenty-five 12-page reports.

Improving **Spelling**

Spelling

473.1 *i* before *e*
Write *i* before *e* except after *c* or when sounded like *a* as in *neighbor* and *weigh*.

> **belief, relieved, grieve, achieve, chief, perceive, conceit, receive, receipt, eight, freight, weight, reign**

Exceptions to the rule: *counterfeit, either, financier, foreign, height, heir, leisure, neither, seize, sheik, species, their, weird*

473.2 Silent *e*
If a word ends with a silent *e*, drop the *e* before adding a suffix that begins with a vowel.

> **state** .... **stating** .... **statement**
> **game** .... **gaming** .... **gamelike**

Note: You do not drop the *e* when the suffix begins with a consonant. Exceptions include *truly, argument,* and *ninth*.

473.3 Words Ending in *y*
When *y* is the last letter in a word and the *y* comes just after a consonant, change the *y* to *i* before adding any suffix except those beginning with *i*.

> **fry** .... **fries** .... **frying**   **hurry** .... **hurried** ...... **hurrying**
> **lady** .... **ladies**   **beauty** .... **beautiful**

When forming the plural of a word that ends with a *y* that comes just after a vowel, add *s*.

> **toy** .... **toys**   **play** .... **plays**   **monkey** .... **monkeys**

473.4 Consonant Ending
When a one-syllable word ends in a consonant *(bat)* preceded by one vowel *(bat)*, double the final consonant before adding a suffix that begins with a vowel *(batting)*.

> **sum** .... **summary**   **god** .... **goddess**

When a multisyllable word ends in a consonant *(control)* preceded by one vowel *(control)*, the accent is on the last syllable *(control)*, and the suffix begins with a vowel *(ing)*—the same rule holds true: double the final consonant *(controlling)*.

> **prefer** .... **preferred**   **begin** .... **beginning**

Yellow Pages Guide to Improved Spelling

Be patient. Learning to become a good speller takes time.

Check your spelling by using a dictionary or list of commonly misspelled words (like the list that follows).

Learn the correct pronunciation of each word you are trying to spell. Knowing the correct pronunciation of a word will help you remember how it's spelled.

Look up the meaning of each word as you are checking the dictionary for pronunciation. (Knowing how to spell a word is of little use if you don't know what it means.)

Practice spelling the word before you close the dictionary. Look away from the page and try to see the word in your mind's eye. Write the word on a piece of paper. Check the spelling in the dictionary and repeat the process until you are able to spell the word correctly.

Keep a list of the words that you tend to misspell.

Write often. As noted educator Frank Smith said, "There is little point in learning to spell if you have little intention of writing."

Commonly Misspelled Words

A

ab-bre-vi-ate
a-board
a-bout
a-bove
ab-sence
ab-sent
ab-so-lute (-ly)
a-bun-dance
ac-cel-er-ate
ac-ci-dent
ac-ci-den-tal (-ly)
ac-com-pa-ny
ac-com-plice
ac-com-plish
ac-cord-ing

ac-count
ac-cu-rate
ac-cus-tom (ed)
ache
a-chieve (-ment)
a-cre
a-cross
ac-tu-al
a-dapt
ad-di-tion (-al)
ad-dress
ad-e-quate
ad-just (-ment)
ad-mire
ad-ven-ture
ad-ver-tise (-ment)
ad-ver-tis-ing
a-fraid

af-ter
af-ter-noon
af-ter-ward
a-gain
a-gainst
a-gree-a-ble
a-gree (-ment)
ah
aid
airy
aisle
a-larm
al-co-hol
a-like
a-live
al-ley
al-low-ance
all right

al-most
al-ready
al-though
al-to-geth-er
a-lu-mi-num
al-ways
am-a-teur
am-bu-lance
a-mend-ment
a-mong
a-mount
an-a-lyze
an-cient
an-gel
an-ger
an-gle
an-gry
an-i-mal

an-ni-ver-sa-ry
an-nounce
an-noy-ance
an-nu-al
a-non-y-mous
an-oth-er
an-swer
ant-arc-tic
an-tic-i-pate
anx-i-ety
anx-ious
any-body
any-how
any-one
any-thing
any-way
any-where
a-part-ment
a-piece
a-pol-o-gize
ap-par-ent (-ly)
ap-peal
ap-pear-ance
ap-pe-tite
ap-pli-ance
ap-pli-ca-tion
ap-point-ment
ap-pre-ci-ate
ap-proach
ap-pro-pri-ate
ap-prov-al
ap-prox-i-mate
ar-chi-tect
arc-tic
aren't
ar-gu-ment
a-rith-me-tic
a-round
a-rouse
ar-range (-ment)
ar-riv-al
ar-ti-cle

ar-ti-fi-cial
a-sleep
as-sas-sin
as-sign (-ment)
as-sis-tance
as-so-ci-ate
as-so-ci-a-tion
as-sume
ath-lete
ath-let-ic
at-tach
at-tack (ed)
at-tempt
at-ten-dance
at-ten-tion
at-ti-tude
at-tor-ney
at-trac-tive
au-di-ence
Au-gust
au-thor
au-thor-i-ty
au-to-mo-bile
au-tumn
a-vail-a-ble
av-e-nue
av-er-age
aw-ful (-ly)
awk-ward

bag-gage
bak-ing
bal-ance
bal-loon
bal-lot
ba-nan-a
ban-dage
bank-rupt
bar-ber
bar-gain

bar-rel
base-ment
ba-sis
bas-ket
bat-te-ry
beau-ti-ful
beau-ty
be-cause
be-come
be-com-ing
be-fore
be-gan
beg-gar
be-gin-ning
be-have
be-hav-ior
be-ing
be-lief
be-lieve
be-long
be-neath
ben-e-fit (-ed)
be-tween
bi-cy-cle
bis-cuit
black-board
blan-ket
bliz-zard
both-er
bot-tle
bot-tom
bough
bought
bounce
bound-a-ry
break-fast
breast
breath (n.)
breathe (v.)
breeze
bridge
brief

bright
bril-liant
broth-er
brought
bruise
bub-ble
buck-et
buck-le
bud-get
build-ing
bul-le-tin
buoy-ant
bu-reau
bur-glar
bury
busi-ness
busy
but-ton

cab-bage
caf-e-te-ria
cal-en-dar
cam-paign
ca-nal
can-cel (ed)
can-di-date
can-dle
can-is-ter
can-non
can-not
ca-noe
can't
can-yon
ca-pac-i-ty
cap-tain
car-bu-re-tor
card-board
ca-reer

care-ful
care-less
car-pen-ter
car-riage
car-rot
cash-ier
cas-se-role
cas-u-al-ty
cat-a-log
ca-tas-tro-phe
catch-er
cat-er-pil-lar
cat-sup
ceil-ing
cel-e-bra-tion
cem-e-ter-y
cen-sus
cen-tu-ry
cer-tain (-ly)
cer-tif-i-cate
chal-lenge
cham-pi-on
change-a-ble
char-ac-ter (-is-tic)
chief
chil-dren
chim-ney
choc-o-late
choice
cho-rus
cir-cum-stance
cit-i-zen
civ-i-li-za-tion
class-mates
class-room
cli-mate
climb
clos-et
cloth-ing
coach
co-coa
co-coon

cof-fee
col-lar
col-lege
colo-nel
col-or
co-los-sal
col-umn
com-e-dy
com-ing
com-mer-cial
com-mis-sion
com-mit
com-mit-ment
com-mit-ted
com-mit-tee
com-mu-ni-cate
com-mu-ni-ty
com-pan-y
com-par-i-son
com-pe-ti-tion
com-pet-i-tive (-ly)
com-plain
com-plete (-ly)
com-plex-ion
com-pro-mise
con-ceive
con-cern-ing
con-cert
con-ces-sion
con-crete
con-demn
con-di-tion
con-duc-tor
con-fer-ence
con-fi-dence
con-grat-u-late
con-nect
con-science
con-scious
con-ser-va-tive
con-sti-tu-tion
con-tin-ue

con-tin-u-ous
con-trol
con-tro-ver-sy
con-ve-nience
con-vince
cool-ly
co-op-er-ate
cor-po-ra-tion
cor-re-spond
cough
couldn't
coun-ter
coun-ter-feit
coun-try
coun-ty
cour-age
cou-ra-geous
court
cour-te-ous
cour-te-sy
cous-in
cov-er-age
co-zy
crack-er
crank-y
crawl
cred-i-tor
cried
crit-i-cize
cru-el
crumb
crum-ble
cup-board
cu-ri-os-i-ty
cu-ri-ous
cur-rent
cus-tom
cus-tom-er
cyl-in-der

D

dai-ly
dair-y
dam-age
dan-ger (-ous)
daugh-ter
dealt
de-ceive
de-cided
de-ci-sion
dec-la-ra-tion
dec-o-rate
de-fense
def-i-nite (-ly)
def-i-ni-tion
de-li-cious
de-pen-dent
de-pot
de-scribe
de-scrip-tion
de-sert
de-serve
de-sign
de-sir-a-ble
de-spair
des-sert
de-te-ri-o-rate
de-ter-mine
de-vel-op (-ment)
de-vice
de-vise
di-a-mond
di-a-phragm
di-a-ry
dic-tio-nar-y
dif-fer-ence
dif-fer-ent
dif-fi-cul-ty
din-ing
di-plo-ma
di-rec-tor

dis-agree-a-ble
dis-ap-pear
dis-ap-point
dis-ap-prove
dis-as-trous
dis-ci-pline
dis-cov-er
dis-cuss
dis-cus-sion
dis-ease
dis-sat-is-fied
dis-tin-guish
dis-trib-ute
di-vide
di-vine
di-vis-i-ble
di-vi-sion
doc-tor
doesn't
dol-lar
dor-mi-to-ry
doubt
dough
du-al
du-pli-cate

 E

ea-ger (-ly)
e-con-o-my
edge
e-di-tion
ef-fi-cien-cy
eight
eighth
ei-ther
e-lab-o-rate
e-lec-tric-i-ty
el-e-phant
el-i-gi-ble
el-lipse
em-bar-rass

e-mer-gen-cy
em-pha-size
em-ploy-ee
em-ploy-ment
en-close
en-cour-age
en-gi-neer
e-nor-mous
e-nough
en-ter-tain
en-thu-si-as-tic
en-tire-ly
en-trance
en-vel-op (v.)
en-ve-lope (n.)
en-vi-ron-ment
e-quip-ment
e-quipped
e-quiv-a-lent
es-cape
es-pe-cial-ly
es-sen-tial
es-tab-lish
ev-ery
ev-i-dence
ex-ag-ger-ate
ex-ceed
ex-cel-lent
ex-cept
ex-cep-tion-al (-ly)
ex-cite
ex-er-cise
ex-haust (-ed)
ex-hi-bi-tion
ex-is-tence
ex-pect
ex-pen-sive
ex-pe-ri-ence
ex-plain
ex-pla-na-tion
ex-pres-sion
ex-ten-sion

ex-tinct
ex-traor-di-nar-y
ex-treme (-ly)

 F

fa-cil-i-ties
fa-mil-iar
fam-i-ly
fa-mous
fas-ci-nate
fash-ion
fa-tigue (d)
fau-cet
fa-vor-ite
fea-ture
Feb-ru-ar-y
fed-er-al
fer-tile
field
fierce
fi-ery
fif-ty
fi-nal-ly
fi-nan-cial (-ly)
fo-li-age
for-ci-ble
for-eign
for-feit
for-mal (-ly)
for-mer (-ly)
forth
for-tu-nate
for-ty
for-ward
foun-tain
fourth
frag-ile
freight
friend (-ly)
fright-en
ful-fill

fun-da-men-tal
fur-ther
fur-ther-more

 G

gad-get
gauge
gen-er-al-ly
gen-er-ous
ge-nius
gen-tle
gen-u-ine
ge-og-ra-phy
ghet-to
ghost
gnaw
gov-ern-ment
gov-er-nor
grad-u-a-tion
gram-mar
grate-ful
grease
grief
gro-cery
grudge
grue-some
guar-an-tee
guard
guard-i-an
guess
guid-ance
guide
guilt-y
gym-na-si-um

H

ham-mer
hand-ker-chief
han-dle (d)
hand-some
hap-haz-ard
hap-pen
hap-pi-ness
ha-rass
hast-i-ly
hav-ing
haz-ard-ous
head-ache
height
hem-or-rhage
hes-i-tate
his-to-ry
hoarse
hol-i-day
hon-or
hop-ing
hop-ping
hor-ri-ble
hos-pi-tal
hu-mor-ous
hur-ried-ly
hy-drau-lic
hy-giene
hymn

I

i-ci-cle
i-den-ti-cal
il-leg-i-ble
il-lit-er-ate
il-lus-trate
im-ag-i-nar-y
im-ag-i-na-tive
im-ag-ine
im-i-ta-tion
im-me-di-ate (-ly)
im-mense
im-mi-grant
im-mor-tal
im-pa-tient
im-por-tance
im-pos-si-ble
im-prove-ment
in-con-ve-nience
in-cred-i-ble
in-def-i-nite-ly
in-de-pen-dence
in-de-pen-dent
in-di-vid-u-al
in-dus-tri-al
in-fe-ri-or
in-fi-nite
in-flam-ma-ble
in-flu-en-tial
ini-tial
ini-ti-a-tion
in-no-cence
in-no-cent
in-stal-la-tion
in-stance
in-stead
in-sur-ance
in-tel-li-gence
in-ten-tion
in-ter-est-ed
in-ter-est-ing
in-ter-fere
in-ter-pret
in-ter-rupt
in-ter-view
in-ves-ti-gate
in-vi-ta-tion
ir-ri-gate
is-land
is-sue

J

jeal-ous (-y)
jew-el-ry
jour-nal
jour-ney
judg-ment
juic-y

K

kitch-en
knew
knife
knives
knock
knowl-edge
knuck-les

L

la-bel
lab-o-ra-to-ry
la-dies
lan-guage
laugh
laun-dry
law-yer
league
lec-ture
le-gal
leg-i-ble
leg-is-la-ture
lei-sure
length
li-a-ble
li-brar-y
li-cense
lieu-ten-ant
light-ning
lik-a-ble

like-ly
li-quid
lis-ten
lit-er-a-ture
liv-ing
loaves
lone-li-ness
loose
lose
los-er
los-ing
lov-a-ble
love-ly

M

ma-chin-er-y
mag-a-zine
mag-nif-i-cent
main-tain
ma-jor-i-ty
mak-ing
man-u-al
man-u-fac-ture
mar-riage
ma-te-ri-al
math-e-mat-ics
max-i-mum
may-or
meant
mea-sure
med-i-cine
me-di-um
mes-sage
mile-age
min-i-a-ture
min-i-mum
min-ute
mir-ror

mis-cel-la-neous
mis-chie-vous
mis-er-a-ble
mis-sile
mis-spell
mois-ture
mol-e-cule
mo-not-o-nous
mon-u-ment
mort-gage
moun-tain
mus-cle
mu-si-cian
mys-te-ri-ous

N

na-ive
nat-u-ral (-ly)
nec-es-sar-y
ne-go-ti-ate
neigh-bor (-hood)
nei-ther
nick-el
niece
nine-teen
nine-teenth
nine-ty
nois-y
no-tice-a-ble
nu-cle-ar
nui-sance

O

o-be-di-ence
o-bey
ob-sta-cle
oc-ca-sion
oc-ca-sion-al (-ly)
oc-cur

oc-curred
of-fense
of-fi-cial
of-ten
o-mis-sion
o-mit-ted
op-er-ate
o-pin-ion
op-po-nent
op-por-tu-ni-ty
op-po-site
or-di-nar-i-ly
o-rig-i-nal
out-ra-geous

P

pack-age
paid
pam-phlet
par-a-dise
par-a-graph
par-al-lel
par-a-lyze
pa-ren-the-ses
par-tial
par-tic-i-pant
par-tic-i-pate
par-tic-u-lar (-ly)
pas-ture
pa-tience
pe-cu-liar
peo-ple
per-haps
per-ma-nent
per-pen-dic-u-lar
per-sis-tent
per-son-al (-ly)
per-son-nel
per-spi-ra-tion
per-suade
phase

phy-si-cian
piece
pitch-er
planned
pla-teau
play-wright
pleas-ant
plea-sure
pneu-mo-nia
pol-i-ti-cian
pos-sess
pos-si-ble
prac-ti-cal (-ly)
prai-rie
pre-cede
pre-cious
pre-cise (-ly)
pre-ci-sion
pref-er-a-ble
pre-ferred
prej-u-dice
prep-a-ra-tion
pres-ence
pre-vi-ous
prim-i-tive
prin-ci-pal
prin-ci-ple
pris-on-er
priv-i-lege
prob-a-bly
pro-ce-dure
pro-ceed
pro-fes-sor
prom-i-nent
pro-nounce
pro-nun-ci-a-tion
pro-tein
psy-chol-o-gy
pump-kin
pure

Q

quar-ter
ques-tion-naire
qui-et
quite
quo-tient

R

raise
re-al-ize
re-al-ly
re-ceipt
re-ceive
re-ceived
rec-i-pe
rec-og-nize
rec-om-mend
reign
re-lieve
re-li-gious
re-mem-ber
rep-e-ti-tion
rep-re-sen-ta-tive
res-er-voir
re-sis-tance
re-spect-ful-ly
re-spon-si-bil-i-ty
res-tau-rant
re-view
rhyme
rhythm
ri-dic-u-lous
route

S

safe-ty
sal-ad
sal-a-ry
sand-wich
sat-is-fac-to-ry
Sat-ur-day
scene
sce-ner-y
sched-ule
sci-ence
scis-sors
scream
screen
sea-son
sec-re-tar-y
seize
sen-si-ble
sen-tence
sep-a-rate
sev-er-al
sher-iff
shin-ing
sim-i-lar
since
sin-cere (-ly)
ski-ing
sleigh
sol-dier
sou-ve-nir
spa-ghet-ti
spe-cif-ic
sphere
sprin-kle
squeeze
squir-rel
stat-ue
stat-ure
stat-ute
stom-ach

stopped
straight
strength
stretched
study-ing
sub-tle
suc-ceed
suc-cess
suf-fi-cient
sum-ma-rize
sup-ple-ment
sup-pose
sure-ly
sur-prise
syl-la-ble
sym-pa-thy
symp-tom

T

tar-iff
tech-nique
tem-per-a-ture
tem-po-rar-y
ter-ri-ble
ter-ri-to-ry
thank-ful
the-ater
their
there
there-fore
thief
thor-ough (-ly)
though
through-out
tired
to-bac-co
to-geth-er
to-mor-row
tongue
touch

tour-na-ment
to-ward
trag-e-dy
trea-sur-er
tried
tries
tru-ly
Tues-day
typ-i-cal

U

un-con-scious
un-for-tu-nate (-ly)
u-nique
uni-ver-si-ty
un-nec-es-sary
un-til
us-a-ble
use-ful
us-ing
usu-al (-ly)
u-ten-sil

V

va-ca-tion
vac-u-um
val-u-a-ble
va-ri-e-ty
var-i-ous
veg-e-ta-ble
ve-hi-cle
very
vi-cin-i-ty
view
vil-lain
vi-o-lence
vis-i-ble
vis-i-tor
voice

vol-ume
vol-un-tary
vol-un-teer

W

wan-der
weath-er
Wednes-day
weigh
weird
wel-come
wel-fare
whale
where
wheth-er
which
whole
whol-ly
whose
width
wom-en
worth-while
wreck-age
writ-ing
writ-ten

Y

yel-low
yes-ter-day
yield

Using the **Right Word**

481.1	**a, an** *A* is used before words that begin with a consonant sound; *an* is used before words that begin with a vowel sound. *a* heap, *a* historian, *a* cat, *an* idol, *an* elephant, *an* honor
481.2	**accept, except** The verb *accept* means "to receive"; the preposition *except* means "other than." Azad graciously *accepted* the trophy. (verb) All the team members *except* Zach were there. (preposition)
481.3	**affect, effect** *Affect* is always a verb; it means "to influence." *Effect* can be a verb, but it is most often used as a noun that means "the result." How does climate change *affect* us? What are the *effects* of climate change?
481.4	**allowed, aloud** The verb *allowed* means "permitted" or "let happen"; *aloud* is an adverb that means "in a normal voice." We weren't *allowed* to read *aloud* in study hall.
481.5	**allusion, illusion** An *allusion* is a brief reference or mention of a famous person, place, thing, or idea. An *illusion* is a false impression or idea. Mrs. Dexter made an *allusion* to the Flat Earth Society. She believes the 1969 moon landing was a staged *illusion*.
481.6	**a lot** *A lot* is not one word, but two; it is a general descriptive phrase (meaning "plenty") that should be avoided in formal writing.
481.7	**already, all ready** *Already* is an adverb that tells when. *All ready* is a phrase meaning "completely ready." Aunt Zoe is *all ready* to purchase a car that runs on vegetable oil. She's *already* planning how to spend the gas money she will save.

482.1 **altogether, all together**
Altogether is an adverb meaning "completely." *All together* is used to describe people or things that are gathered in one place at one time.

The snow finally stopped *altogether*.

Dad was happy to have his children *all together* for Friday night supper.

482.2 **among, between**
Among is used when speaking of more than two persons or things. *Between* is used when speaking of only two.

The three friends talked *among* themselves as they tried to choose *between* seeing The Incredible Hulk or Kung Fu Panda.

482.3 **amount, number**
The noun *number* is used for persons or things you can actually count. The noun *amount* is used for things you cannot count but can measure according to their whole effect.

In most classes, the *number* of A's and B's received is directly proportional to the *amount* of effort put forth.

482.4 **annual, biannual, semiannual, biennial, perennial**
An *annual* event happens once every year.

A *biannual* (or *semiannual*) event happens twice a year.

A *biennial* event happens every two years.

A *perennial* event happens year after year.

SCHOOL DAZE

John, I've got the projects **all together**. Now which one is yours?

I'm not **altogether** sure. See if there's one with a missing piece.

483.1 | **ant, aunt**
Aunt is a relative. *Ant* is an insect.

My favorite *aunt* is an entomologist, a scientist who studies *ants* and other insects.

483.2 | **ascent, assent**
Ascent is the act of rising or moving upward; *assent* is agreement.

The *ascent* of Everest looked treacherous.

Two climbers *assented* to remain behind.

483.3 | **bare, bear**
The adjective *bare* means "naked." A *bear* is a large animal with shaggy hair.

The old *bear* rug was warm beneath our *bare* feet.

The verb *bear* means "to put up with" or "to carry."

Angelo could not *bear* another evening of reality TV.

483.4 | **base, bass**
Base is the foundation or the lower part of something, and *bass* (pronounced the same way) is a deep sound or tone.

At the *base* of the cliff, we heard our instructor's calm *bass* voice.

Bass (rhyming with *mass*) is a fish.

We came back to camp with a mess of *bass* and walleyes to clean.

483.5 | **beat, beet**
The verb *beat* means "to strike or to defeat"; a *beet* is a root vegetable.

Emil *beat* the eggs while Jackie chopped up *beet* greens.

483.6 | **berth, birth**
Berth is a space or compartment. *Birth* means "bearing young."

From our *berth* on the train, we saw prairie life. A buffalo had given *birth* to an albino calf.

483.7 | **beside, besides**
Beside means "by the side of." *Besides* means "in addition to."

Besides a flashlight, Kedar keeps a cell phone *beside* his bed.

483.8 | **billed, build**
Billed means either "to be given a bill" or "to have a beak." The verb *build* means "to construct."

Long-*billed* hummingbirds drink nectar and *build* tiny nests.

484.1 board, bored

Board can mean "a piece of wood" or "a group that runs an organization." *Bored* means "weary or tired of something."

We installed a pine-*board* floor.

The *board* members were *bored* by the long speech.

484.2 brake, break

A *brake* is a device used to stop a vehicle. *Break* means "to split, crack, or destroy."

I hope my *brakes* never *break*.

484.3 bring, take

Use *bring* when the action is moving toward the speaker; use *take* when the action is moving away from the speaker.

Take this monitor to the shop and *bring* me one that works.

484.4 by, buy, bye

By is a preposition meaning "near or past." *Buy* is a verb meaning "to purchase."

The friends waited *by* the store but did not *buy* anything.

A *bye* is an automatic advancement to the next tournament round.

Our soccer team received a *bye* because of our winning record.

Bye is also short for "good-bye."

484.5 can, may

Can means "able to" while *may* means "permitted to."

"*Can* I eat this cake?" means "Do you think I'm able to eat it?"

"*May* I eat this cake?" means "Do I have your permission to eat it?"

484.6 cannon, canon

A *cannon* is a big gun; a *canon* is a rule or law.

484.7 canvas, canvass

Canvas is a heavy cloth; *canvass* means "to go out and ask people for votes or opinions."

484.8 capital, capitol

Capital can be a noun referring to a city or to money, or it can be an adjective meaning "excellent or important." *Capitol* refers to a building.

The *capital* of Wisconsin is Madison. Its *capitol* is an impressive domed building.

Refurbishing the old theater is a *capital* (excellent) idea. Do we have *capital* (money) for the project?

485.1 cell, sell
Cell means "a small room" or "a small unit of life that makes up all plants and animals." *Sell* is a verb meaning "to give up for a price."

485.2 cent, sent, scent
Cent is a coin; *sent* is the past tense of the verb "send"; *scent* is an odor or a smell.

The *scent* of fresh flowers *sent* Alex into a sneezing fit.

In June 2008, one U.S. *cent* was worth eleven Mexican centavos.

485.3 chord, cord
A *chord* is the sound of three or more musical tones played at the same time. A *cord* is a string or rope.

The band struck a *chord* just as the mayor pulled the *cord* to unveil the new downtown mural.

485.4 chose, choose
Chose (chōz) is the past tense of the verb *choose* (chooz).

Selena *chose* to discontinue her landline plan and will *choose* a new cell-phone plan instead.

485.5 coarse, course
Coarse means "rough or crude." *Course* means "a path or direction taken" or "a class or series of studies."

The *coarse* terrain was littered with boulders.

Our geography *course* has a unit about natural resources.

485.6 complement, compliment
Complement means "to complete or go with." A *compliment* is an expression of admiration or praise.

To say that the flavors in this meal *complement* each other is a *compliment* to the chef.

485.7 counsel, council
When used as a noun, *counsel* means "advice"; when used as a verb, *counsel* means "to advise." *Council* refers to a group that advises.

The student *council* wants our school to "go green," but they need *counsel* about how to get started.

485.8 creak, creek
A *creak* is a squeaking sound; a *creek* is a stream.

Grandma used lard to silence the awful *creak* in the door hinge.

Oak *Creek* rose to flood stage after the spring rains.

486.1 **cymbal, symbol**
A *cymbal* is a plate-like metal instrument. A *symbol* is one thing that represents another thing or idea.

Trumpets blared, *cymbals* clashed, and the colorful flag, a *symbol* of our country, waved above us.

486.2 **dear, deer**
Dear means "loved or valued" and is also used as an interjection. *Deer* are woodland animals.

"Oh, *dear*. They're serving venison (*deer* meat) tonight," whispered my vegan friend.

486.3 **desert, dessert**
A *desert* is a barren wilderness. *Dessert* is a food served at the end of a meal.

On our *desert* hike, we ate tunas (prickly pear fruit) for *dessert*.

(The verb *desert* means "to abandon"; the noun *desert,* pronounced like the verb, means "a deserved reward or punishment.")

486.4 **die, dye**
Die (dying) means "to stop living." *Dye* (dyeing) is used to change the color of something.

486.5 **faint, feign, feint**
Faint means "to be feeble, without strength." *Feign* is a verb that means "to pretend or make up." *Feint* is a noun that means "pretending in order to divert attention."

Tobias felt *faint* in the dentist chair but *feigned* being brave.
The bird's injury was a *feint* to keep us from finding her nest.

486.6 **farther, further**
The adjective *farther* is used for a physical distance, and the adjective *further* is used to mean "additional."

Nests on the *farther* shore were abandoned. *Further* research would reveal why.

486.7 **fewer, less**
Fewer refers to the number of units; *less* refers to bulk quantity.

Less rain means we will harvest *fewer* ears of corn.

486.8 **fir, fur**
Fir refers to a type of evergreen tree; *fur* is animal hair.

486.9 **flair, flare**
Flair means "a natural talent"; *flare* means "to light up quickly or burst out."

487.1 for, fore, four

For is a preposition; it is also a conjunction meaning "because." *Fore* means "in front," and *four* is the number.

A new idea *for* saving the planet has come to the *fore*—sustainable living.

The *four* hikers needed a compass, *for* they were confused.

487.2 good, well

Good is an adjective; *well* is nearly always an adverb.

Damita looked *good* in the trials and ran *well* in the afternoon meet. (The adjective *good* modifies *Damita;* and the adverb *well* modifies *ran.*)

When used in writing about health, *well* is an adjective.

Yesterday she wasn't feeling *well.*

487.3 hare, hair

Hair is the growth covering the heads and bodies of animals and human beings; *hare* refers to a rabbit-like animal.

Would the snowshoe *hare,* if kept inside for the winter, still develop white *hair,* or fur, for the season?

487.4 heal, heel

Heal means "to mend or restore to health." *Heel* is the back part of a human foot.

The arrow pierced Achilles' *heel,* and the wound would not *heal.*

487.5 hear, here

You *hear* with your ears. *Here* is the opposite of *there* and means "nearby."

487.6 heard, herd

Heard is the past tense of the verb "hear"; *herd* is a group of animals.

The dog *heard* the shepherd's whistle and moved to flank the *herd.*

SCHOOL DAZE

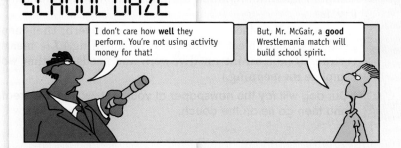

I don't care how **well** they perform. You're not using activity money for that!

But, Mr. McGair, a **good** Wrestlemania match will build school spirit.

488.1 heir, air

Heir is a person who inherits something; *air* is the gas we breathe.

Will the next generation be *heir* to terminally polluted *air*?

488.2 hole, whole

A *hole* is a cavity or hollow place. *Whole* means "entire or complete."

The *hole* in the ozone layer is a serious problem requiring the attention of the *whole* world.

488.3 immigrate, emigrate

Immigrate means "to come into a new country or area." *Emigrate* means "to go out of one country to live in another."

Hser, a Burmese refugee, will *emigrate* from Thailand in 2008. He and his family hope to *immigrate* to the United States.

488.4 imply, infer

Imply means "to suggest indirectly"; *infer* means "to draw a conclusion from facts."

The salesman did *imply* that the cream really moisturizes the skin. Having tried it, I *infer* that he exaggerated.

488.5 it's, its

It's is the contraction of "it is." *Its* is the possessive form of "it."

It's an interesting idea—a robot repairing *its* own malfunction.

488.6 knew, new

Knew is the past tense of the verb "know." *New* means "recent or modern."

Melony *knew* she could not afford *new* shoes.

488.7 know, no

Know means "to understand." *No* means "the opposite of yes."

I *know* that going "carbon neutral" may help; but, *no*, I don't think it's the complete solution to climate change.

488.8 lay, lie

Lay means "to place." (*Lay* is a transitive verb; that means it needs a direct object to complete its meaning.) *Lie* means "to recline." (*Lie* is an intransitive verb and needs no other word to complete its meaning.)

Our dog will *lay* the newspaper at your feet, wait for her treat, and then go *lie* on the couch.

489.1 **lead, led**
Lead (lēd) is a verb meaning "to guide." The past tense of the verb is *led*. *Lead* (lĕd) is also a noun referring to the metal.
Mr. Thielen has *led* the campaign to get *lead* out of the school's drinking water.

489.2 **learn, teach**
Learn means "to get information"; *teach* means "to give information."
What I *learn* today, I will *teach* tomorrow.

489.3 **leave, let**
Leave means "to allow something to remain behind." *Let* means "to permit."
The principal *let* the students *leave* school early.

489.4 **like, as**
Like is a preposition meaning "similar to"; *as* is a conjunction meaning "to the same degree" or "while." *Like* usually introduces a phrase; *as* usually introduces a clause.
As the music played, the children marched *like* good soldiers.

489.5 **loose, lose, loss**
Loose (lüs) means "free or untied"; *lose* (lüz) means "to misplace or fail to win"; *loss* means "something lost."
***Loose*-fitting clothes are comfy.**
Last week's *loss* was awful; now it looks like we will *lose* again.

489.6 **made, maid**
Made is the past tense of "make," which means "to create." A *maid* is a female servant; it also describes an unmarried girl.
The *maid* asked if our beds needed to be *made*.

489.7 **mail, male**
Mail refers to letters or packages handled by the postal service. *Male* refers to the masculine gender.

489.8 **main, mane**
Main is an adjective that means "principal or most important." *Mane* is a noun and refers to the long hair growing on the head or neck of an animal like a horse or a lion.

489.9 **meat, meet**
Meat is food or flesh; *meet* means "to come upon or encounter."
The committee will *meet* today.
***Meat* is an excellent source of protein.**

490.1 | metal, meddle, medal, mettle
Metal is an element like iron or gold. *Meddle* means "to interfere or take interest in." *Medal* is an award. *Mettle*, a noun, refers to quality of character.

Isaac Newton did *meddle* in alchemy, a medieval science that tried to turn base *metals* into gold.

The soldier's bravery proved her *mettle* and earned her the Congressional *Medal* of Honor.

490.2 | miner, minor
A *miner* digs in the ground for valuable ore. A *minor* is a person who is not legally an adult. A *minor* problem is one of no great importance.

Selling alcohol to *minors* is a major offense, not a *minor* one.

490.3 | moral, morale
Moral relates to what is right or wrong. *Morale* refers to a person's attitude or mental condition.

It is often unpopular to make the *moral* choice.

The town's *morale* was low in the aftermath of the storm.

490.4 | morning, mourning
Morning refers to the first part of the day before noon; *mourning* means "showing sorrow."

Don't waste time *mourning* lost opportunities. Instead, get up each *morning* and look for new ones.

490.5 | oar, or, ore
An *oar* is a paddle used in rowing or steering a boat. *Or* is a conjunction indicating choice. *Ore* refers to a mineral made up of several different kinds of material, as in iron ore.

490.6 | pain, pane
Pain is the feeling of being hurt. *Pane* is a section or part of something, as in a framed section of glass in a window or door.

490.7 | pair, pare, pear
A *pair* is a couple (two); *pare* is a verb meaning "to peel"; *pear* is the fruit.

491.1 past, passed

Passed is always a verb. *Past* can be used as a noun, as an adjective, or as a preposition.

I *passed* the science test! (verb)

The *past* is interesting to historians. (noun) Studying *past* events may help to solve present problems. (adjective)

491.2 peace, piece

Peace means "harmony or freedom from war." *Piece* is a part or fragment of something.

Peace gave way to the children arguing over a *piece* of cake.

491.3 personal, personnel

Personal means "private." *Personnel* are people working at a job.

491.4 plain, plane

Plain means "an area of land that is flat or level"; it also means "clearly seen or clearly understood" or "not fancy."

The *plain* truth is that we ought to preserve our nation's *plains*.

The adjective *plane* means "flat, level, and even," the noun means "a tool for smoothing wood," and the verb means "to make smooth."

Wally will *plane* the rough pine floor and then paint it.

491.5 pore, pour, poor

A *pore* is a tiny opening. *Pour* means "to cause a constant flow or stream." *Poor* means "needy."

We saw many *poor* children.

Pour the milk, Maggie.

Plants transpire and humans perspire though their *pores*.

491.6 principal, principle

As an adjective, *principal* means "primary." As a noun, it can mean "a school administrator" or "a sum of money." *Principle* means "idea or doctrine."

On weeknights my *principal* activity is studying.

Our *principal* values the students' opinions.

The amount of money borrowed is called the *principal* of the loan.

Principles of honesty and hard work will help you graduate.

491.7 quiet, quit, quite

Quiet is the opposite of "noisy." *Quit* means "to stop." *Quite* means "completely or entirely."

The assembly grew *quiet* as the speaker urged, "Don't *quit* now. We're *quite* close to solving this problem."

492.1 raise, rays, raze

Raise is a verb meaning "to lift or elevate." *Rays* are thin lines or beams, as in rays of sunlight. *Raze* is a verb that means "to tear down completely."

To *raise* the bar means "to reach for a higher standard."

A laser focuses *rays* of electromagnetic radiation.

We'd rather renovate the old theater than *raze* it.

492.2 red, read

Red is a color; *read* (rĕd) is the past tense of the verb *read* (rēd), which means "to understand written words and symbols."

492.3 right, write, rite

Right means "correct or proper"; it also means "anything to which a person has a legal claim," as in the right to vote. *Write* means "to record in print." *Rite* is a ritual or ceremonial act.

Don't argue. Mom is always *right*.

Authors sometimes *write* about *rites* of passage.

492.4 scene, seen

Scene can mean "the location of a happening," "a part of a movie," or "a sight or spectacle." *Seen* is a form of the verb "see."

Luke has *seen* the movie and described some hilarious *scenes*.

492.5 seam, seem

Seam is a line formed by connecting two pieces of material. *Seem* means "to appear to exist."

Margarete *seems* tired, and no wonder, after sewing *seam* after *seam* all day.

492.6 sew, so, sow

Sew is a verb meaning "to stitch"; *so* is a conjunction meaning "in order that." The verb *sow* means "to plant."

Hannah likes to *sew* her own clothes *so* she can express herself.

492.7 sight, cite, site

Sight means "the ability to see" or "something that is seen." *Cite* means "to quote or refer to." A *site* is a location or position, as in "job site."

492.8 sit, set

Sit means "to put the body in a seated position." *Set* means "to place."

Just *sit* down, Dad. I'll *set* the table.

493.1 **sole, soul**
Sole means "only one"; *sole* also refers to the bottom surface of a foot or shoe. *Soul* refers to the spiritual part of a person.

The monk's *sole* purpose was caring for the dying.

"The *soul* would have no rainbow if the eyes had no tears."
—an Indian chief

493.2 **some, sum**
Some means "an unknown number or part." *Sum* means "an amount."

Some students excel at math.

A few coins—a meager *sum*—lay in his palm.

493.3 **stationary, stationery**
Stationary means "not movable"; *stationery* is the paper and envelopes used to write letters.

493.4 **steal, steel**
Steal means "to take something without permission"; *steel* is a metal.

Early iron makers would *steal* recipes for producing *steel*.

493.5 **than, then**
Than is used in a comparison; *then* tells when.

And *then* he said that being a true friend was more important *than* being cool.

493.6 **their, there, they're**
Their is a possessive pronoun. *There* is an adverb that tells where. *They're* is the contraction for "they are."

Our laptops are over *there*. *They're* the very latest and *their* best feature is the ultraslim monitor.

493.7 **threw, through**
Threw is the past tense of "throw." *Through* means "passing from one side of something to the other."

The ball sliced *through* the strike zone. *Through* his long career in baseball, Nolan Ryan *threw* mostly fastballs.

493.8 **to, too, two**
To is a preposition that means "in the direction of." (*To* also forms an infinitive.) *Too* is an adverb meaning "also," "excessively," or "very." *Two* is the number.

Grandparents who are not *too* familiar with computers are invited *to* the technology fair *to learn* about the school's IT department.

494.1 **vain, vane, vein**
Vain means "worthless" or "conceited." A *vane* is a flat piece of material that shows the direction of the wind. A *vein* is a blood vessel or a mineral deposit.

The prospector made a final *vain* attempt to unearth a *vein* of silver.

Our weather *vane* kept spinning in the wild storm.

494.2 **vary, very**
Vary is a verb that means "to change."

The weather can *vary* from snow to sleet to sunshine in a single day.

Very is an adjective that means "in the fullest sense" or "complete."

Garon's story was the *very* opposite of the truth.

Very is also an adverb that means "extremely."

The story was *very* interesting.

494.3 **waist, waste**
Waist is the part of the body just above the hips. The verb *waste* means "to wear away, decay" or "to use carelessly"; the noun *waste* refers to material that is unused or useless.

Please don't *waste* the water, and put all recyclable *waste* in the right bins.

494.4 **wait, weight**
Wait means "to stay somewhere expecting something." *Weight* is the measure of heaviness.

494.5 **ware, wear, where**
Ware means "a product that is sold"; *wear* means "to have on or to carry on one's body"; *where* asks the question "in what place or in what situation?"

Where can we buy that soft*ware*?

Wear my coat if you're cold.

494.6 **way, weigh**
Way means "path or route." *Weigh* means "to measure weight."

Come this *way* to the scale so the nurse can *weigh* you.

494.7 **weather, whether**
Weather refers to the condition of the atmosphere. *Whether* refers to a possibility.

The *weather* will determine *whether* the space shuttle is launched.

495.1 | **week, weak**
A *week* is a period of seven days; *weak* means "not strong."

495.2 | **which, witch**
Which is a pronoun used to refer to or point out something. A *witch* is a woman believed to have supernatural powers.

Which of the witches in <u>The Wizard of Oz</u> would you like to play?

495.3 | **who, which, that**
Who is used to refer to people. *Which* refers to animals and nonliving things but never to people. *That* can refer to people, animals, or things.

The storm drains *that* dump untreated wastewater into our lake, *which* is already polluted, are a problem. Our mayor, *who* is an environmentalist, has a solution.

495.4 | **who, whom**
Who is used as the subject in a sentence; *whom* is used as the object of a preposition or as a direct object.

Who ordered this pizza?

The pizza was ordered by *whom*?

Note: To test for *who/whom*, arrange the parts of the clause in a subject-verb-object order. (*Who* works as the subject, *whom* as the object.)

495.5 | **who's, whose**
Who's is the contraction for "who is." *Whose* is a possessive pronoun, one that shows ownership.

Who's the first person in history *whose* writing made him or her a billionaire? (J. K. Rowling)

495.6 | **wood, would**
Wood is the material that trees are made of; *would* is a form of the verb "will."

Many earth-concious consumers *would* not buy products made of *wood* from old-growth forests.

495.7 | **your, you're**
Your is a possessive pronoun, one that shows ownership. *You're* is the contraction for "you are."

Understanding **Sentences**

Sentences

496.1 **Sentence**
A sentence is made up of one or more words that express a complete thought. A sentence begins with a capital letter; it ends with a period, a question mark, or an exclamation point.

This book will help you write.

It explains the writing process.

What else does it explain?

Wow, check out the index!

Parts of a Sentence

496.2 **Subject and Predicate**
A sentence must have a subject and a predicate in order to express a complete thought. Either the subject or the predicate (or both) may not be stated, but both must be clearly understood.

(*You*) Click on the instant messenger.
(*You* is the understood subject.)

Who sent you a message?
Joseph (*did*).
(*Did* is the understood predicate.)

What is Joseph's screen name?
(*His name is*) SoccerJoe22.
(*His name* is the understood subject, and *is* is the understood predicate.)

496.3 **Subject**
A subject is the part of a sentence that is doing something or about which something is said.

Instant messaging **is a form of real-time text communication.**

496.4 **Simple Subject**
The simple subject is the subject without the words that describe or modify it.

High-speed wireless *Internet* gives computer owners access to instant messaging.

497.1

Complete Subject
The complete subject is the simple subject and all the words that modify it.

High-speed wireless Internet **gives computer owners access to instant messaging.**

497.2

Compound Subject
A compound subject is composed of two or more simple subjects.

Yahoo, AOL, **and** *Windows* **provide free instant messaging services.**

> See page 86 for information about subject-verb agreement with compound subjects.

497.3

Predicate
The predicate is the part of the sentence that says something about the subject.

My original instant messaging account *expired.*

497.4

Simple Predicate
The simple predicate is the predicate (verb) without the words that describe or modify it.

AOL *launched* **AOL Instant Messenger (AIM) in 1997.**

497.5

Complete Predicate
The complete predicate is the simple predicate with all the words that modify or describe it.

AOL *launched AOL Instant Messenger (AIM) in 1997.*

497.6

Compound Predicate
A compound predicate is composed of two or more simple predicates.

Blog owners *produce* **and** *publish* **their writing on the Internet.**

497.7

Compound Subject and Predicate
A sentence may have a compound subject and a compound predicate.

Michelle **and** *Joseph write* **and** *edit* **their play scripts on a blog.**

> See page 91 for information about combining sentences with compound subjects and predicates.

Sentence . . .

498.1 Direct Object

The direct object is the noun or pronoun that receives the action of the predicate—*directly*. (The direct object answers the question *what?* or *whom?*)

Many young adults use *blogs* as electronic diaries.

The direct object may be compound.

People of all ages publish *diaries, video material,* and *audio podcasts* on blog sites.

498.2 Indirect Object

An indirect object is the noun or pronoun that receives the action of the predicate—*indirectly*. An indirect object names the person *to whom* or *for whom* something is done.

I e-mailed *Joseph* my favorite blog entry.

(*Joseph* is the indirect object because it says to whom the blog entry was e-mailed.)

498.3 Modifier

A modifier is a word or a group of words that changes or adds to the meaning of another word. (See pages 514–516.)

Clauses

A **clause** is a group of related words that has both a subject and a predicate.

498.4 Independent and Dependent Clauses

An independent clause presents a complete thought and can stand as a sentence; a dependent clause does not present a complete thought and cannot stand as a sentence.

In the following sentences, the dependent clauses are in red, and the independent clauses are in **boldface**.

If I couldn't use the Internet, **I would need to change my research habits.**

(Use a comma after a dependent clause at the beginning of a sentence.)

I use the Google search engine when I start my research.

(Usually, do not use a comma before a dependent clause at the end of a sentence.)

Phrases

499.1 **Phrase**
A phrase is a group of related words that lacks either a subject or a predicate (or both).

> **doesn't include any games**
> (This predicate lacks a subject.)

> **this Web site**
> (This subject lacks a predicate.)

> **except for Text Twist**
> (This phrase lacks both a subject and a predicate.)

> **This Web site doesn't include any games except for Text Twist.**
> (Together, the three phrases form a complete thought.)

499.2 **Types of Phrases**
Phrases usually take their names from the main words that introduce them (prepositional phrase, verb phrase, and so on). They are also named for the function they serve in a sentence (adverb phrase, adjective phrase).

> **Michelle's dog blog**
> (noun phrase)
>
> **with videos and podcasts**
> (prepositional phrase)

> **quite frequently**
> (adverb phrase)
>
> **generates hits**
> (verb phrase)

Types of Sentences

499.3 **Simple Sentence**
A simple sentence is a sentence with only one independent clause (one complete thought). It may have either a simple subject or a compound subject. It may also have either a simple predicate or a compound predicate.

> **Michelle's dog barks.** (simple subject; simple predicate)

> **Michelle's dog and cat fight.** (compound subject; simple predicate)

> **Michelle's dog and cat snore and sneeze loudly.**
> (compound subject; compound predicate)

A simple sentence may also contain one or more phrases, but no dependent clauses.

> **Michelle's dog often barks for attention.**
> (simple subject: *dog;* simple predicate: *barks;* phrase: *for attention*)

Sentence . . .

500.1

Compound Sentence

A compound sentence is made up of two or more simple sentences (also called independent clauses) that are joined by a coordinate conjunction, punctuation, or both.

Champ chases his tail, but he never catches it.

He chases flying disks; he retrieves tennis balls.

500.2

Complex Sentence

A complex sentence contains one independent clause (in **boldface**) and one or more dependent clauses (in red).

Even though Michelle's dog is goofy, she still loves him. (dependent clause followed by independent clause)

Michelle disciplines Champ if he does something that upsets a neighbor. (independent clause followed by two dependent clauses)

500.3

Compound-Complex Sentence

A compound-complex sentence contains two or more independent clauses (in **boldface**) and one or more dependent clauses (in red).

The Statue of Liberty was sculpted by Frédéric-Auguste Bartholdi, but the internal framework was designed by Alexandre-Gustave Eiffel, who later designed the Eiffel Tower in Paris.

Kinds of Sentences

500.4

Declarative Sentence

A declarative sentence makes a statement.

Microsoft is the most powerful computer company in the world.

500.5

Interrogative Sentence

An interrogative sentence asks a question.

Why would I want a job with Microsoft?

500.6

Imperative Sentence

An imperative sentence gives a command. It often contains an understood subject (you).

Check this out.

500.7

Exclamatory Sentence

An exclamatory sentence communicates strong emotion.

Microsoft earned $50 billion in 2007! That's a lot of money!

Understanding Our
Language

Noun

A **noun** is a word that names something: a person, a place, a thing, or an idea.

John Ulferts (uncle)	"Star-Spangled Banner" (song)
Mississippi (river)	Labor Day (holiday)

Kinds of Nouns

501.1 **Proper Noun**
A **proper noun** is the name of a specific person, place, thing, or idea. Proper nouns are capitalized.

Brett Favre, Chicago Aquarium, *The Wednesday Wars,* Islam

501.2 **Common Noun**
A **common noun** names a nonspecific person, place, thing, or idea. Common nouns are not capitalized.

man, museum, book, religion

501.3 **Concrete Noun**
A **concrete noun** names a thing that is physical (can be touched or seen). Concrete nouns can be either proper or common.

space shuttle, Wii console, Mount Everest

501.4 **Abstract Noun**
An **abstract noun** names something you can think about but cannot see or touch. Abstract nouns can be either common or proper.

Christianity, Judaism, poverty, wealth, conservation, belief

501.5 **Collective Noun**
A **collective noun** names a group or *collection* of persons, animals, or things.

PERSONS	tribe, congregation, family, class, team
ANIMALS	flock, herd, gaggle, clutch, litter
THINGS	batch, cluster, bunch

Noun . . .

Number of Nouns

Nouns are classified according to their number. The number of a noun tells us whether the noun is singular or plural.

502.1 **Singular Noun**

A **singular noun** names one person, place, thing, or idea.

boy, group, audience, stage, rock concert, hope

502.2 **Plural Noun**

A **plural noun** names more than one person, place, thing, or idea.

boys, groups, audiences, stages, rock concerts, hopes

> **For information on how to create the plural form of nouns, turn to 470–471.**

502.3 **Compound Noun**

A **compound noun** is made up of two or more words.

football (written as one word), **junior high** (written as two words), **brother-in-law** (written as a hyphenated word)

Gender of Nouns

Nouns have **gender,** which means they can be grouped according to sex: *feminine, masculine, neuter,* and *indefinite.*

Turn to page 347 for more information on using gender properly when writing.

502.4 **Gender**

Feminine	**mother, sister, women, cow, hen** (female)
Masculine	**father, brother, men, bull, rooster** (male)
Neuter	**tree, cobweb, closet** (without gender)
Indefinite	**president, doctor** (male or female)

Uses of Nouns

Nouns are classified according to their use in a sentence.

502.5 **Subject Nouns**

A **subject noun** is a noun used as the subject of a sentence. As such, it is either doing something or being talked about.

The young *girl* reached out to touch the salamander. Its *skin* was smooth and wet. (The subject *girl* is "doing something," and the subject *skin* is "being talked about.")

503.1 **Predicate Nouns**

A noun becomes a **predicate noun** when it follows a *be* verb (*is, are, was, were, been*) and repeats or renames the subject.

Salamanders are amphibians. These animals are water-dwellers.
(In these sentences, *amphibians* renames *salamanders,* and *water-dwellers* renames *animals.*)

503.2 **Possessive Nouns**

A noun becomes a possessive noun when it shows possession or ownership.

A *wetland's* population of amphibians is an *insect's* worst nightmare.

> Turn to 464–465 for more about possessive nouns.

503.3 **Object Nouns**

A noun becomes an object noun when it is used as the direct object, the indirect object, or the object of the preposition.

In the wild, a salamander eats *worms, insects,* and *slugs.*
(*Worms, insects,* and *slugs* are direct objects.)

I feed my pet *salamander crickets* from a special *box.*
(*Salamander* is an indirect object, *crickets* is a direct object, and *box* is an object of the preposition *from.*)

Pronoun

A **pronoun** is a word used in place of a noun. Pronouns are used to avoid needless repetition in your writing.

her, it, which, they, who, themselves, this

503.4 **Antecedent**

An **antecedent** is the noun that the pronoun refers to or replaces. Almost all pronouns have antecedents.

The *friends* used binoculars to search the night sky for the *International Space Station.* They knew *it* was passing over *their* city and would look like a fast-moving star.
(*Friends* is the antecedent of *they* and *their; International Space Station* is the antecedent of *it.*)

> All pronouns must agree with their antecedents in number, person, and gender.
> See pages 87–88.

Pronoun . . .

504.1 | Personal Pronouns
These are the basic **personal pronouns.**

> **I, you, he, she, it, we, they**

These are some of the pronouns' other forms.

> **me, him, her, us, them, mine, yours, ourselves, their, its**

Number of Pronouns

504.2 | Singular/Plural
Pronouns can be either singular or plural in **number.**

> SINGULAR .... **I, you, he, she, it**
>
> PLURAL .... **we, you, they**

Note: The pronouns *you, your,* and *yours* may be singular or plural.

Person of a Pronoun

The **person** of a pronoun tells us whether the pronoun is speaking, being spoken to, or being spoken about.

504.3 | First Person
A **first-person pronoun** is used in place of the speaker.

> *I* **see the International Space Station (ISS)!** *We* **see the ISS, too!**

504.4 | Second Person
A **second-person pronoun** is used to name the person or thing spoken to.

> **Jay, did** *you* **spot the ISS? These binoculars will help** *you.*

504.5 | Third Person
A **third-person pronoun** is used to name the person or thing spoken about.

> **NASA uses** *its* **Web site to share information about the space station.**

Uses of Pronouns

A pronoun can be used as a subject, an object, or to show possession.

504.6 | Subject Pronouns
A **subject pronoun** is used as the subject of a sentence (*I, you, he, she, it, we, they*).

> *You* **can even ask one of the crew members questions.**

A subject pronoun is also used after a form of the *be* verb (*am, is, are, was, were, being, been*) if it repeats the subject.

> **It is** *he* **who can tell you what living on the ISS is really like.**

505.1 Object Pronouns

An **object pronoun** can be used as the object of a verb or preposition (*me, you, him, her, it, us, them*).

The stars fascinate *us.* (*Us* is the direct object of the verb *fascinate* because it receives the action of the verb.)

Mr. Short gave *me* a book about space travel. (*Me* is the indirect object of the verb *gave* because it indirectly receives the action of the verb.)

Does being a star traveler appeal to *you*? (*You* is the object of the preposition *to*.)

505.2 Possessive Pronouns

A **possessive pronoun** shows possession or ownership.

my, mine, our, ours, his, her, hers, their, theirs, its, your, yours

Note: Do not use an apostrophe with a personal pronoun to show possession.

Singular Pronouns			
	Subject Pronouns	Possessive Pronouns	Object Pronouns
First Person	I	my, mine	me
Second Person	you	your, yours	you
Third Person	he	his	him
	she	her, hers	her
	it	its	it
Plural Pronouns			
	Subject Pronouns	Possessive Pronouns	Object Pronouns
First Person	we	our, ours	us
Second Person	you	your, yours	you
Third Person	they	their, theirs	them

Note: *My, your, her, his, our, its,* and *their* come before nouns and function as adjectives. (***Our* hamsters escaped.**) The possessive pronouns *his, hers, ours, yours, theirs,* and *mine* do not come before nouns. (**This one is mine. Yours is behind the couch.**)

Pronoun . . .

Other Types of Pronouns

In addition to the commonly used personal pronouns, there are a number of other types of pronouns that you should know about. (See the chart on the next page.)

506.1 **Relative Pronouns**

A **relative pronoun** is both a pronoun and a connecting word. It connects a subordinate clause to the main clause.

China, *which* has the largest population in the world, is home to over 1.3 billion people. (*Which* relates to *China.*)

The Chinese, *who* have worked hard to modernize their country, hosted the 2008 Summer Olympics. (*Who* relates to *Chinese.*)

The country *that* is scheduled to host the Games in 2012 is Great Britain. (*That* relates to *country.*)

> *Who? Which? That?* If you have trouble figuring out which of these pronouns to use when, turn to 495.3.

506.2 **Interrogative Pronouns**

An **interrogative pronoun** asks a question.

We can eat here or go out. *Which* should we do? *Who* can cook? *What* is in the freezer?

I found a ring! *Whom* should we tell? *Whose* is it, do you think?

506.3 **Demonstrative Pronouns**

A **demonstrative pronoun** points out or identifies a noun without naming the noun.

This is a beautiful park!   Are *these* the campsites you wanted?
That was a steep climb.   *Those* are closer to the lake.

Caution: Do not add *here* or *there* to a demonstrative pronoun. Both of the following examples are incorrect.

This here is a beautiful park!   *That there* was a steep climb.

506.4 **Intensive Pronouns**

An **intensive pronoun** emphasizes or *intensifies* the noun or pronoun it refers to. Common intensive pronouns include *itself, myself, himself, herself,* and *yourself.*

Although Leesa is a strong, capable rock climber, she *herself* is very aware of the sport's dangers.

Note: The sentence would be complete without the pronoun *herself,* which simply emphasizes *she.*

507.1 Reflexive Pronouns

A **reflexive pronoun** is a pronoun that throws the action back upon the subject of a sentence or clause.

Leesa joined a climbing club that prides *itself* in an excellent safety record. (direct object)

She gave *herself* plenty of time to train before doing any rock climbing. (indirect object)

Climbers are always dreaming up new challenges for *themselves*. (object of the preposition)

Note: These sentences would not be complete without the reflexive pronouns.

507.2 Indefinite Pronouns

An **indefinite pronoun** is a pronoun that does not specifically name its antecedent (the noun or pronoun it replaces).

Will *anyone* ever visit the stars? Just to reach the nearest *one* (our own sun excepted), *someone* would have to travel at the speed of light for 4.2 years.

> See page 87 for details on using indefinite pronouns properly in a sentence.

507.3 Kinds of Pronouns

Relative
who, whose, whom, which, what, that, whoever, whomever, whatever, whichever

Interrogative
who, whose, whom, which, what

Demonstrative
this, that, these, those

Intensive and Reflexive
myself, himself, herself, itself, yourself, themselves, ourselves

Indefinite Pronouns

all	both	everything	nobody	several
another	each	few	none	some
any	each one	many	no one	somebody
anybody	either	most	nothing	someone
anyone	everybody	much	one	something
anything	everyone	neither	other	such

Verb

A **verb** is a word that shows action or existence (state of being).

Tornadoes *cause* tremendous damage. (action)

The weather *is* often calm before a storm. (existence)

Types of Verbs

508.1 Action Verb

An action verb tells what the subject is doing.

Natural disasters *batter* the globe nearly every day.

508.2 Linking Verb

A **linking verb** connects or links a subject to a noun or an adjective in the predicate.

The 2008 *earthquake* in Sichuan, China, *was a disaster*. (*Disaster* is a predicate noun linked by the verb *was* to the subject *earthquake*.)

I am concerned for the victims of this disaster. (*Concerned* is a predicate adjective linked by the verb *am* to the subject *I*.)

Linking Verbs

The most common linking verbs are forms of the verb *be*—**is, are, was, were, being, been, am**—and verbs such as **smell, look, taste, feel, remain, turn, appear, become, sound, seem, grow, stand.**

508.3 Helping Verb

Helping verbs *help* to form some of the tenses and voice of the main verb. (Helping verbs are also called *auxiliary verbs*.)

Most people *do* know that shooting stars are not stars, but meteors that *are* burning while blasting through Earth's atmosphere.

Helping Verbs

The most common helping verbs are **shall, will, should, would, could, must, can, may, have, had, has, do, did,** and the forms of the verb *be*—**is, are, was, were, am, being, been.**

Number of Verbs

Verbs have **number,** which means they are singular or plural. The number of a verb depends on the number of its subject.

509.1 Singular/Plural

A singular subject needs a **singular verb.** A plural subject needs a **plural verb.**

One wonders if there is life on other planets. (singular)

We wonder if there is life on other planets. (plural)

Person of Verbs

509.2 Point of View

Verbs will also differ in form depending upon the point of view, or *person,* of the pronouns being used with them:

first person *I* write (singular); *we* write (plural)

second person *you* write (singular); *you* write (plural)

third person *he/she/it writes* (singular); *they* write (plural)

Voice of Verbs

The **voice** of a verb tells you whether the subject is doing the action or is receiving the action.

509.3 Active Voice

A verb is in the **active voice** if the subject is doing the action.

We *learned* about dead zones in the earth's oceans.

509.4 Passive Voice

A verb is in the passive voice if the subject is receiving the action.

These dead zones *were discovered* by oceanographers.

TENSE	Active Voice		Passive Voice	
	SINGULAR	PLURAL	SINGULAR	PLURAL
Present Tense	I find	we find	I am found	we are found
	you find	you find	you are found	you are found
	he/she/it finds	they find	he/she/it is found	they are found
Past Tense	I found	we found	I was found	we were found
	you found	you found	you were found	you were found
	he/she/it found	they found	he/she/it was found	they were found
Future Tense	I will find	we will find	I will be found	we will be found
	you will find	you will find	you will be found	you will be found
	he/she/it will find	they will find	he/she/it will be found	they will be found

Verb . . .

Tenses of Verbs

A verb has three principal parts: the *present, past,* and *past participle.* All six of the tenses are formed from these principal parts.

- The past and past participle of regular verbs are formed by adding *-ed* to the present part.
- Irregular verbs are formed with different spellings. (See page 511.)

510.1	**Present Tense**
	A verb is in the **present tense** when it expresses action or existence that is happening *now* or that happens *continually, regularly.*
	An ocean dead zone *is* oxygen deprived. Fish cannot *live* there.

510.2	**Past Tense**
	A verb is in the **past tense** when it expresses action that is completed at a *particular* time in the past.
	Scientists *discovered* why these dead zones *formed.*

510.3	**Future Tense**
	A verb is in the **future tense** when it expresses action that *will* take place.
	Dead zones *will revive* if people *will follow* new practices.

510.4	**Present Perfect Tense**
	A verb is in the **present perfect tense** when it expresses action that *began in the past but continues or is completed in the present.*
	Some bay communities *have been* vigilant about sewage treatment.
	Note: To form this tense, add *has* or *have* to the past participle.

510.5	**Past Perfect Tense**
	A verb is in the **past perfect tense** when it expresses action that *began in the past and was completed in the past.*
	The bay's sewage problems *had begun* in the 1950s.
	Note: To form this tense, add *had* to the past participle.

510.6	**Future Perfect Tense**
	A verb is in the **future perfect tense** when it expresses action that *will begin in the future and will be completed by a specific time in the future.*
	By 2010, scientists *will have known* about the Gulf of Mexico's dead zone for almost 40 years.
	Note: To form this tense, add *will have* to the past participle.

Common Irregular Verbs and Their Principal Parts

The principal parts of common irregular verbs are listed below. The part used with the helping verbs *has, have,* or *had* is called the **past participle**.

PRESENT TENSE	I write.	She hides.
PAST TENSE	I wrote.	She hid.
PAST PARTICIPLE	I have written.	She has hidden.

Present Tense	Past Tense	Past Participle	Present Tense	Past Tense	Past Participle
am, be	was, were	been	lead	led	led
begin	began	begun	lie (recline)	lay	lain
bid (offer)	bid	bid	lie (deceive)	lied	lied
bid (order)	bade	bidden	raise	raised	raised
bite	bit	bitten	ride	rode	ridden
blow	blew	blown	ring	rang	rung
break	broke	broken	rise	rose	risen
bring	brought	brought	run	ran	run
burst	burst	burst	see	saw	seen
catch	caught	caught	set	set	set
come	came	come	shake	shook	shaken
dive	dived	dived	shine		
do	did	done	(polish)	shined	shined
drag	dragged	dragged	(light)	shone	shone
draw	drew	drawn	shrink	shrank	shrunk
drink	drank	drunk	sing	sang, sung	sung
drive	drove	driven	sink	sank, sunk	sunk
drown	drowned	drowned	sit	sat	sat
eat	ate	eaten	slay	slew	slain
fall	fell	fallen	speak	spoke	spoken
fight	fought	fought	spring	sprang, sprung	sprung
flee	fled	fled	steal	stole	stolen
flow	flowed	flowed	strive	strove	striven
fly	flew	flown	swear	swore	sworn
forsake	forsook	forsaken	swim	swam	swum
freeze	froze	frozen	swing	swung	swung
give	gave	given	take	took	taken
go	went	gone	tear	tore	torn
grow	grew	grown	throw	threw	thrown
hang			wake	woke, waked	woken, waked
(execute)	hanged	hanged	wear	wore	worn
(dangle)	hung	hung	weave	wove	woven
hide	hid	hidden, hid	wring	wrung	wrung
know	knew	known	write	wrote	written
lay (place)	laid	laid			

Verb . . .
Uses of Action Verbs

512.1 **Transitive Verbs**

Transitive verbs are verbs that transfer their action to an object. An object must receive the action of a transitive verb for the meaning of the verb to be complete.

> The earthquake *shook* San Francisco with a fury. (*Shook* transfers its action to *San Francisco.* Without *San Francisco,* the meaning of the verb *shook* is incomplete.)

> San Francisco *was shaken* by the earthquake. (The subject of the sentence, *San Francisco,* receives the action of the verb, *was shaken.*)

A transitive verb throws the action directly to a **direct object** and indirectly to an **indirect object.** For a sentence to have an indirect object, it must have a direct object. A sentence can, however, have only a direct object.

Note: Direct and indirect objects are always nouns or pronouns.

> Fires destroyed *San Francisco* after the 1906 earthquake. (direct object: *San Francisco*)

> Our teacher gave *us* the details. (indirect object: *us;* direct object: *details*)

> See 498.1–498.2 for more about direct and indirect objects.

512.2 **Intransitive Verbs**

An **intransitive verb** completes its action without an object.

> Her stomach *felt* queasy. (*Queasy* is a predicate adjective; there is no direct object.)

> She *looked* for a mint. (Again, there is no direct object. *Mint* is the object of the preposition *for.*)

512.3 **Transitive/Intransitive**

Some verbs can be either transitive or intransitive.

> She *read* my note. (transitive)

> She *read* aloud. (intransitive)

Verbals

A **verbal** is a word that is made from a verb, has the power of a verb, but acts as another part of speech. Gerunds, participles, and infinitives are verbals.

513.1 **Gerund**

A **gerund** is a verb form that ends in *-ing* and is used as a noun.

Exercising **is important.** (The noun *exercising* is the subject.)

My grandfather "blames" *exercising* **for his good health.** (The noun *exercising* is the direct object.)

513.2 **Participle**

A **participle** is a verb form that ends in *-ing* or *-ed* and is used as an adjective.

I often see him *running, biking,* **or** *walking* **by our house.** (*Running, biking,* and *walking* modify *him*.)

He never looks *tired*. (*Tired* modifies *he*.)

513.3 **Infinitive**

An **infinitive** is a verb form introduced by *to;* it may be used as a noun, an adjective, or an adverb.

To swim **is fun for Grandpa.** (*To swim* is a noun and is the subject of this sentence.)

He's always ready *to play* **with my little brother.** (*To play* is an adverb and modifies the adjective *ready*.)

Adjective

An **adjective** is a word used to describe a noun or pronoun.

Why did *ancient* dinosaurs become *an extinct* species?

Were they wiped out by *a catastrophic* flood or *a deadly* epidemic?

514.1 **Articles**

The **articles** *a, an,* and *the* are adjectives.

the brontosaurus, *a* huge dinosaur, *an* animal

514.2 **Proper Adjective**

A **proper adjective** is formed from a proper noun, and it is always capitalized.

A *Chicago* museum is home to the skeleton of a dinosaur.
(*Chicago* is a proper adjective describing the noun *museum*.)

514.3 **Common Adjective**

A **common adjective** is any adjective that is not proper, and it is not capitalized (unless it is the first word in a sentence).

Ancient mammoths were *huge, woolly* creatures.

Special Kinds of Adjectives

514.4 **Demonstrative Adjective**

A **demonstrative adjective** is one that points out a particular noun. *This* and *these* point out something nearby; *that* and *those* point out something at a distance.

This mammoth is huge, but *that* mammoth is even bigger.

Note: When a noun does not follow *this, these, that,* or *those,* they are pronouns, not adjectives.

514.5 **Compound Adjective**

A **compound adjective** is made up of two or more words. (Sometimes it is hyphenated.)

Scientists have discovered some *quick-frozen* mammoths.

514.6 **Indefinite Adjective**

An **indefinite adjective** does not tell *exactly* how many or how much. (See page 507.)

Some mammoths were heavier than today's elephants.

515.1   Predicate Adjective

A **predicate adjective** follows a linking verb and describes the subject.

Mammoths were once *abundant,* but now they are *extinct.*

Forms of Adjectives

515.2   Positive Form

The **positive form** describes a noun or pronoun without comparing it to anyone or anything else.

Bullet trains are *fast,* traveling at *incredible* speeds.

515.3   Comparative Form

The **comparative form** *(-er/more/less)* compares two persons, places, things, or ideas.

Magnetic levitation (maglev) trains are *faster* than the bullets, reaching speeds that are even *more incredible.*

515.4   Superlative Form

The **superlative form** *(-est/most/least)* compares three or more persons, places, things, or ideas.

Jets are the *fastest* way to travel, cruising at the *most incredible* speeds of all.

515.5   Two-Syllable Adjective

Some **two-syllable adjectives** show comparisons by the *-er/-est* suffixes, or by modifiers *more/most* and *less/least.*

clumsy, clumsier, clumsiest (or)
clumsy, more clumsy, most clumsy
clumsy, less clumsy, least clumsy

515.6   Adjective of Three or More Syllables

Adjectives of **three or more syllables** usually require the words *more/most* or *less/least* to express comparison.

ridiculous, less ridiculous, least ridiculous

Note: Do not say "ridiculouser" or "ridiculousest."

515.7   Irregular Forms

Some adjectives use completely **different words** to express comparison.

good, better, best   bad, worse, worst

Adverb

An **adverb** is a word used to modify a verb, an adjective, or another adverb. An adverb tells *how, when, where, why, how often,* and *how much.*

Dad snores *loudly*. (*Loudly* modifies the verb *snores*.)

His snores are *really* explosive. (*Really* modifies the adjective *explosive*.)

Dad snores *very* loudly. (*Very* modifies the adverb *loudly*.)

516.1 ### Forms of Adverbs
Adverbs, like adjectives, have three forms: **positive, comparative,** and **superlative.** (See the chart below.)

positive .... describes

comparative .... compares two things

superlative .... compares three or more things

516.2 ### Types of Adverbs
There are four basic types: adverbs of *time, place, manner,* and *degree.*

TIME .... Adverbs of time tell *when, how often,* and *how long.*

tomorrow, often, never

PLACE .... Adverbs of place tell *where, to where,* or *from where.*

there, backward, outside

MANNER ...... Adverbs of manner often end in *-ly* and tell how something is done.

unkindly, gently, well

DEGREE .... Adverbs of degree tell *how much* or *how little.*

scarcely, completely, almost

Note: **Adverbs** often end in *-ly,* but not always, as with *often, there, well, quite,* and many others. Also note that some words that end in *-ly* are **adjectives,** as with *lovely* or *homely.*

Positive	Comparative	Superlative
well	better	best
badly	worse	worst
quietly	more quietly	most quietly
loudly	more loudly	most loudly
dramatically	less dramatically	least dramatically

Preposition

A **preposition** is a word (or group of words) that often shows position or direction and is used to indicate the relationship between two words or ideas. Specifically, a preposition shows how its object is related to some other word in the sentence.

We gathered *near* **the window.** (*Out* shows the relationship between the verb, *looked,* and the object of the preposition, *window.*)

517.1 **Prepositional Phrase**

A **prepositional phrase** includes the *preposition,* the *object* of the preposition, and the *modifiers* of the object.

***Except for a few white clouds,* the sky was blue.**
(preposition: *except for;* object: *clouds;* modifiers: *a, few, white*)

A prepositional phrase may serve as an adjective or an adverb.

The day was perfect *for hiking* (The prepositional phrase, *for hiking,* functions as an adverb and modifies *perfect.*)

517.2 **Object of Preposition**

A preposition always appears with its object.

We grabbed our backpacks *from the table.*

If one of the words listed below appears in a sentence alone, the word is probably an adverb.

We headed *outside.* (*Outside* is an adverb.)

517.3 **Prepositions**

aboard	because of	excepting	of	save
about	before	for	off	since
above	behind	from	on	through
according to	below	from among	on account of	throughout
across	beneath	from between	on behalf of	till
across from	beside	from under	on top of	to
after	besides	in	onto	together with
against	between	in addition to	opposite	toward
along	beyond	in behalf of	out	under
alongside	but	in front of	out of	underneath
alongside of	by	in place of	outside	until
along with	by means of	in regard to	outside of	unto
amid	concerning	in spite of	over	up
among	considering	inside	over to	up to
apart from	despite	inside of	owing to	upon
around	down	instead of	past	with
aside from	down from	into	prior to	within
at	during	like	regarding	without
away from	except	near	round	
back of	except for	near to	round about	

Conjunction

A **conjunction** connects individual words or groups of words. There are three kinds of conjunctions: *coordinating*, *correlative*, and *subordinating*.

Polluted rivers *and* streams can be cleaned up.
(The conjunction *and* connects *rivers* and *streams*.)

518.1 Coordinating Conjunction

A **coordinating conjunction** connects a word to a word, a phrase to a phrase, or a clause to a clause. The words, phrases, or clauses joined by a coordinating conjunction must be equal.

If you want to reduce pollution, ride a bike *or* plant a tree. (Two equal phrases are connected by *or*.)

Planting trees adds oxygen to the atmosphere, *and* riding bikes helps to reduce greenhouse gas emissions. (Two independent clauses are connected by *and*.)

Put on a sweater *and* turn down the thermostat to conserve energy. (Two equal phrases are connected by *and*.)

518.2 Correlative Conjunction

Correlative conjunctions are conjunctions used in pairs.

Either you're part of the problem, *or* you're part of the solution.

518.3 Subordinating Conjunction

A **subordinating conjunction** connects a dependent clause to an independent clause in order to complete the meaning of the dependent clause.

More people may get involved *when they finally realize that Earth is "Home Sweet Home."*
(The clause *when they finally realize that Earth is "Home Sweet Home"* is dependent. It cannot stand alone.)

518.4 Conjunctions

Coordinating: and, but, or, nor, for, so, yet

Correlative: either, or; neither, nor; not only, but also; both, and; whether, or; as, so

Subordinating: after, although, as, as if, as long as, as though, because, before, if, in order that, provided that, since, so, so that, that, though, till, unless, until, when, where, whereas, while

Note: Conjunctive adverbs and relative pronouns can also connect clauses. (See pages 456 and 506.)

Interjection

An **interjection** is a word or phrase used to express strong emotion or surprise. Punctuation (a comma or an exclamation point) is used to separate an interjection from the rest of the sentence.

Wow, would you look at that!

Oh no! He's falling!

Whoops! So am I!

Parts of Speech Review

The chart below lists the eight parts of speech.

■ NOUN: A word that names a person, a place, a thing, or an idea

Alex Moya   Belize   ladder   courage

■ PRONOUN: A word used in place of a noun

I   he   it   they   you   anybody   some

■ VERB: A word that shows action or links a subject to another word in the sentence

sing   shake   catch   is   are

■ ADJECTIVE: A word that describes a noun or a pronoun

stormy   red   rough   seven   grand

■ ADVERB: A word that describes a verb, an adjective, or another adverb

quickly   today   now   bravely   carefully

■ PREPOSITION: A word that often shows position or direction or introduces a prepositional phrase

around   up   under   over   between   to

■ CONJUNCTION: A word that connects other words or groups of words

and   but   or   so   because   when

■ INTERJECTION: A word (set off by a comma or an exclamation point) that shows strong emotion

Good grief!   Hey, how are you?

Student
Almanac

Language

The language lists in this section of your ~~~~~
both interesting and helpful. You can look through ~~
you want to work on your handwriting, when you want to ~~
other languages, or when you need to send a "signed" message ac~
a noisy room.

Manual Alphabet (Sign Language)

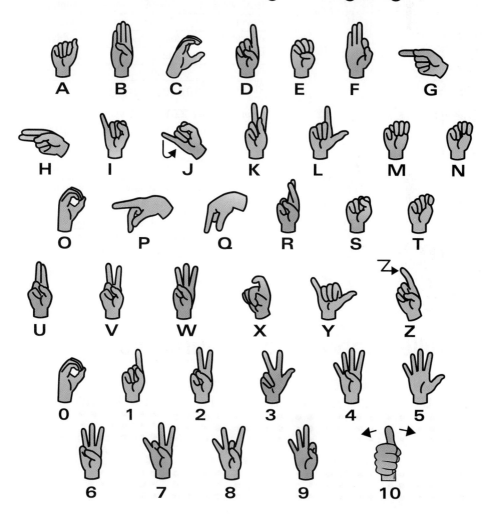

How to Write in Cuneiform

A	⋈	N	⋙
B	丒	O	⟆
C	⟁	P	⊨
D	𒐏	Q	⋈
E	𒀀	R	⋈
F	⟋	S	𒐊
G	𒀹	T	⊢
H	𒐊	U	𒌝
I	⟁	V	𒐊
J	𒐋	W	⋙
K	⊳	X	𒐊
L	𒐊	Y	⋙
M	𒅄	Z	⋈

Foreign Words

Language	HELLO	GOOD-BYE
Chinese (Mandarin dialect)		
	dzǎu	dzàihyàn
Danish	hallo	farvel
Farsi (Iran)	salaam	khoda hafez
	سلام	خدا حافظ
French	bonjour	au revoir
German	Guten Tag	Auf Wiedersehen
Hawaiian	aloha	aloha
Hebrew	shalom	shalom
Italian	buon giorno	addio
Polish	hallo	żegnam
Portuguese	alô	adeus
Russian	Здравствуйте	
pronunciation **ZDRAHST**-vooy-tyeh		
		до свидания
pronunciation		daw svee-**DA**-nee-ya
Spanish	hola	adiós
Swahili	neno la kusalimu rafiki au mtani	kwa heri
Swedish	god dag	adjö
Tagalog (Philippines)		
	kumusta	paalám
Thai	sa wat dee ka	la kone na ka

Braille Alphabet and Numbers

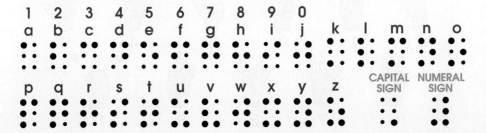

English from Around the World

Words from many languages have been added to English. This chart shows you some English words derived from foreign words.

Old English	man, woman, morning, night, day, month, year, cat, dog, house, red, yellow, at, in, by, from, cow, calf, pig
Scandinavian	they, them, their, knife, sky, ski, happy, scare, egg
French	constitution, city, state, nation, congress, mayor, poetry, art, court, medicine, dance, fashion, tailor, physician, beef, veal, pork
Greek	paragraph, school, alphabet, stomach
Latin	camp, wine, paper, perfume, umbrella, mile, senator, legislator
Native American	canoe, toboggan, opossum, moose, chipmunk, pecan, hickory, igloo, kayak
Spanish	cigar, mosquito, tornado, rodeo, canyon
Italian	spaghetti, pizza, macaroni, balcony, bank, piano, balloon, tarantula, volcano
Dutch	cookie, coleslaw, deck, dock, boss, pump
German	hamburger, kindergarten, pretzel, book
Asian	pepper, panther, shampoo, silk, tea, jungle, ketchup
Australian	kangaroo, boomerang, koala, outback
African	chimpanzee, banana, banjo, okra
Middle Eastern	candy, cotton, coffee, sugar, spinach, tiger
Yiddish	klutz, schlepp, bagel, nosh, chutzpah, glitch, kvetch, schmooze

The History of the English Language

Old English

English is part of the **Indo-European** group of languages. When some of the ancient Indo-Europeans migrated west, they developed a number of Germanic dialects. It was these people who invaded the British Isles about 1,500 years ago, bringing with them what we call Old English—the earliest version of English. These Germanic **Anglo-Saxons** were warriors, but they enjoyed puns and creating compound words. They called the sea the *whaleroad* (hranrad) and combined the word for nose and hole to give us *nostril*.

Half of our everyday words come directly from Old English. Here are some of them: *hand, field, tree, house, sun, day, drink, sit, love,* and *live*.

Invasions

Two more invasions affected English. Beginning in 787, the **Vikings** raided their distant cousins in England, bringing with them most of the words in English that begin with *sk-* (*skin, sky, skirt*) and other common words like *die, freckle,* and *window*. Then in 1066, **William of Normandy** arrived in England, bringing with him knights, clergy, and government officials who spoke French and Latin.

English survived, but it gained a whole new French vocabulary in government (*tax, parliament, royal*), in religion (*sermon, prayer*), in building (*ceiling, porch, curtain*), in law (*judge, attorney, crime*), and so on.

Middle English

English had reasserted itself as a strong language by the time **Geoffrey Chaucer** wrote the *Canterbury Tales* and his other main works (1375–1400). Here are the two opening lines to the *Canterbury Tales* (with a translation in italics):

> Whan that April with his showres soote,
> *(When April's sweet showers)*
> The droughte of March hath perced to the roote,
> *(Have pierced March's drought all the way to the root)*

In Chaucer's day, there began a change in pronunciation. The change is called the **Great Vowel Shift**. Chaucer would have pronounced *hand* with the vowel sound of our word *father* and *ride* like our *reed*.

Early Modern English

The **Renaissance** (1475–1650) brought many new ideas and places into the world of English speakers. English borrowed words from the Americas (*tomato, tobacco, alligator, squash*) and from new learning (*thermometer, hydrant, algebra*). The **printing press** made two great works of Early Modern English available to many English speakers: the English Bible (especially the *King James Version*) and the plays of William Shakespeare (1590–1616).

William Shakespeare had a tremendous vocabulary. He used words in new ways (*assassinate*) and created more than 1,700 new words (*obscene, submerged*) and phrases like "vanished into thin air."

Modern English

English continues to grow and to change. (English has the largest vocabulary of any modern language.) In the United States, Modern English has been influenced by every aspect of the **American experience**. This experience includes the contribution of African Americans: Today, Black English Vernacular is an important variety of English. It also includes the contributions of a constant flow of immigrants and their languages (including Spanish, Yiddish, and many other languages) and modern technology (*radar, astronaut, DVD*).

Is English still changing and developing? Of course it is. The latest source for new words is the vast world of **electronics** and the **media**, from video games to worldwide newscasts to the movie industry.

The Indo-European Family of Languages

Albanian	Armenian	Balto-Slavic ↓	Celtic ↓	Germanic ↓	Greek	Indo-Iranian ↓	Romance ↓
		Bulgarian	Brenton	Dutch		Bengali	French
		Czech	Irish	English		Farsi	Italian
		Latvian	Scots	German		Hindi	Portuguese
		Lithuanian	Welsh	Scandinavian		Pashto	Romanian
		Polish				Urdu	Spanish
		Russian					
		Serbo-Croatian					
		Slovak					
		Slovenian					
		Ukrainian					

Cursive Alphabet

$$Aa\ Bb\ Cc\ Dd\ Ee\ Ff$$
$$Gg\ Hh\ Ii\ Jj\ Kk$$
$$Ll\ Mm\ Nn\ Oo\ Pp$$
$$Qq\ Rr\ Ss\ Tt\ Uu$$
$$Vv\ Ww\ Xx\ Yy\ Zz$$

Editing and Proofreading Marks

agr.	agreement problem		m.m.	misplaced modifier
awk.	awkward expression		n.c.	not clear
cap. (≡)	capitalization		no ¶	no paragraph
⌒	close up space		¶	paragraph
c.f.	comma fault		pro. ref.	pronoun reference
CS	comma splice		?	questionable idea
d.m.	dangling modifier		red.	redundant
✄	delete		RO	run-on sentence
d. neg.	double negative		shift	shift in agreement
frag.	sentence fragment		◯ sp.	spelling
inc.	incomplete		stet.	let it stand
∨ ⁉ ⁉	insert apostrophe or quotation marks		t.	verb tense
			TS	topic sentence
∧ ∧ ∧	insert comma, semicolon, or colon		∩	transpose (switch)
			u.	usage
∧	insert here		⌇	use boldface
⊙	insert period		———	use italics
? ! ∧ ∧	insert question mark or exclamation point		w.c.	word choice
			w.o.	word order
#	insert space		wordy	more words than needed
l.c. (/)	lowercase		X	wrong; correct error

Science

The science facts that follow should be both interesting to use and helpful to have at your fingertips. "Animal Facts," "Periodic Table of the Elements," "The Metric System," and "Planet Profusion" all hold useful information that may be expected of you in other classes at various times.

Animal Facts

Animal	Male	Female	Young	Group	Gestation in days	Longevity in years (*)
Bear	He-bear	She-bear	Cub	Sleuth	180-240	18-20 (34)
Cat	Tom	Queen	Kitten	Clutter/Clowder	52-65	10-17 (30)
Cattle	Bull	Cow	Calf	Drove/Herd	280	9-12 (25)
Chicken	Rooster	Hen	Chick	Brood/Flock	21	7-8 (14)
Deer	Buck	Doe	Fawn	Herd	180-250	10-15 (26)
Dog	Dog	Bitch	Pup	Pack/Kennel	55-70	10-12 (24)
Donkey	Jack	Jenny	Foal	Herd/Pace	340-385	18-20 (63)
Duck	Drake	Duck	Duckling	Brace/Herd	21-35	10 (15)
Elephant	Bull	Cow	Calf	Herd	515-760	30-60 (98)
Fox	Dog	Vixen	Cub/Kit	Skulk	51-60	8-10 (14)
Goat	Billy	Nanny	Kid	Tribe/Herd	135-163	12 (17)
Goose	Gander	Goose	Gosling	Flock/Gaggle	30	25-30
Horse	Stallion	Mare	Filly/Colt	Herd	304-419	20-30 (50+)
Human	Man	Woman	Child (Boy/Girl)	Community	280	70-90 (122)
Lion	Lion	Lioness	Cub	Pride	105-111	10 (29)
Monkey	Male	Female	Boy/Girl	Band/Troop	149-179	12-15 (29)
Rabbit	Buck	Doe	Bunny	Nest/Warren	27-36	6-8 (15)
Sheep	Ram	Ewe	Lamb	Flock/Drove	121-180	10-15 (16)
Swan	Cob	Pen	Cygnet	Bevy/Flock	30	45-50
Swine	Boar	Sow	Piglet	Litter/Herd	101-130	10 (15)
Tiger	Tiger	Tigress	Cub	(None)	105	19
Whale	Bull	Cow	Calf	Gam/Pod/Herd	276-365	37
Wolf	Dog	Bitch	Pup	Pack	63	10-12 (16)

* Record for oldest animal of this type

Periodic Table of the Elements

Legend

- Alkali metals
- Alkaline earth metals
- Transition metals
- Lanthanide series
- Actinide series
- Other metals
- Nonmetals
- Noble gases

Key example

Atomic Number — 2
Symbol — He
Atomic Weight (or Mass Number of most stable isotope if in parentheses) — Helium 4.00260

1a	2a	3b	4b	5b	6b	7b	8	8	8	1b	2b	3a	4a	5a	6a	7a	0
1 **H** Hydrogen 1.00797																	2 **He** Helium 4.00260
3 **Li** Lithium 6.941	4 **Be** Beryllium 9.0128											5 **B** Boron 10.811	6 **C** Carbon 12.01115	7 **N** Nitrogen 14.0067	8 **O** Oxygen 15.9994	9 **F** Fluorine 18.9984	10 **Ne** Neon 20.179
11 **Na** Sodium 22.9898	12 **Mg** Magnesium 24.305											13 **Al** Aluminum 26.9815	14 **Si** Silicon 28.0855	15 **P** Phosphorus 30.9738	16 **S** Sulfur 32.064	17 **Cl** Chlorine 35.453	18 **Ar** Argon 39.948
19 **K** Potassium 39.0983	20 **Ca** Calcium 40.08	21 **Sc** Scandium 44.9559	22 **Ti** Titanium 47.88	23 **V** Vanadium 50.94	24 **Cr** Chromium 51.996	25 **Mn** Manganese 54.9380	26 **Fe** Iron 55.847	27 **Co** Cobalt 58.9332	28 **Ni** Nickel 58.69	29 **Cu** Copper 63.546	30 **Zn** Zinc 65.39	31 **Ga** Gallium 69.72	32 **Ge** Germanium 72.59	33 **As** Arsenic 74.9216	34 **Se** Selenium 78.96	35 **Br** Bromine 79.904	36 **Kr** Krypton 83.80
37 **Rb** Rubidium 85.4678	38 **Sr** Strontium 87.62	39 **Y** Yttrium 88.905	40 **Zr** Zirconium 91.224	41 **Nb** Niobium 92.906	42 **Mo** Molybdenum 95.94	43 **Tc** Technetium (98)	44 **Ru** Ruthenium 101.07	45 **Rh** Rhodium 102.906	46 **Pd** Palladium 106.42	47 **Ag** Silver 107.868	48 **Cd** Cadmium 112.41	49 **In** Indium 114.82	50 **Sn** Tin 118.71	51 **Sb** Antimony 121.75	52 **Te** Tellurium 127.60	53 **I** Iodine 126.905	54 **Xe** Xenon 131.29
55 **Cs** Cesium 132.905	56 **Ba** Barium 137.33	57–71* Lanthanides	72 **Hf** Hafnium 178.49	73 **Ta** Tantalum 180.948	74 **W** Tungsten 183.85	75 **Re** Rhenium 186.207	76 **Os** Osmium 190.2	77 **Ir** Iridium 192.22	78 **Pt** Platinum 195.08	79 **Au** Gold 196.967	80 **Hg** Mercury 200.59	81 **Tl** Thallium 204.383	82 **Pb** Lead 207.19	83 **Bi** Bismuth 208.980	84 **Po** Polonium (209)	85 **At** Astatine (210)	86 **Rn** Radon (222)
87 **Fr** Francium (223)	88 **Ra** Radium 226.025	89–103** Actinides	104 **Rf** Rutherfordium (261)	105 **Db** Dubnium (262)	106 **Sg** Seaborgium (263)	107 **Bh** Bohrium (262)	108 **Hs** Hassium (265)	109 **Mt** Meitnerium (266)	110 **Ds** Darmstadtium (281)	111 **Rg** Roentgenium (272)							

(Of elements 112–121; some are still unknown, and some are recently claimed but unnamed. They have temporary systematic names.)

*Lanthanides

57 **La** Lanthanum 138.906	58 **Ce** Cerium 140.12	59 **Pr** Praseodymium 140.908	60 **Nd** Neodymium 144.24	61 **Pm** Promethium (145)	62 **Sm** Samarium 150.36	63 **Eu** Europium 151.96	64 **Gd** Gadolinium 157.25	65 **Tb** Terbium 158.925	66 **Dy** Dysprosium 162.50	67 **Ho** Holmium 164.930	68 **Er** Erbium 167.26	69 **Tm** Thulium 168.934	70 **Yb** Ytterbium 173.04	71 **Lu** Lutetium 174.967

**Actinides

89 **Ac** Actinium 227.028	90 **Th** Thorium 232.038	91 **Pa** Protactinium 231.036	92 **U** Uranium 238.029	93 **Np** Neptunium 237.048	94 **Pu** Plutonium (244)	95 **Am** Americium (243)	96 **Cm** Curium (247)	97 **Bk** Berkelium (247)	98 **Cf** Californium (251)	99 **Es** Einsteinium (252)	100 **Fm** Fermium (257)	101 **Md** Mendelevium (258)	102 **No** Nobelium (259)	103 **Lr** Lawrencium (260)

The Metric System

Even though the metric system is not the official system of measurement in the United States, it is used in science, medicine, and some other fields.

The metric system is a form of measurement based on the decimal system (units of 10), so there are no fractions. The table below lists the basic measurements in the metric system.

Linear Measure | Length or Distance

1 centimeter	= 10 millimeters	= 0.3937 inch
1 decimeter	= 10 centimeters	= 3.937 inches
1 meter	= 10 decimeters	= 39.37 inches or 3.28 feet
1 dekameter	= 10 meters	= 393.7 inches
1 kilometer	= 1,000 meters	= 0.621 mile

Square Measure | Area

1 square centimeter	= 100 square millimeters	= 0.155 square inch
1 square decimeter	= 100 square centimeters	= 15.5 square inches
1 square meter	= 100 square decimeters	= 1,549.9 sq. inches or 1.196 sq. yards
1 square dekameter	= 100 square meters	= 119.6 square yards
1 square kilometer	= 100 square hectometers	= 0.386 square mile

Capacity Measure

1 centiliter	= 10 milliliters	= 0.338 fluid ounce
1 deciliter	= 10 centiliters	= 3.38 fluid ounces
1 liter	= 10 deciliters	= 1.057 liquid qts. or 0.908 dry qt.
1 kiloliter	= 1,000 liters	= 264.18 gallons or 35.315 cubic feet

Land Measure

1 centare	= 1 square meter	= 1,549.9 square inches
1 hectare	= 100 ares	= 2.471 acres
1 square kilometer	= 100 hectares	= 0.386 square mile

Volume Measure

1 cubic centimeter	= 1,000 cubic millimeters	= 0.061 cubic inch
1 cubic decimeter	= 1,000 cubic centimeters	= 61.023 cubic inches
1 cubic meter	= 1,000 cubic decimeters	= 35.314 cubic feet

Weights

1 centigram	= 10 milligrams	= 0.1543 grain
1 decigram	= 10 centigrams	= 1.5432 grains
1 gram	= 10 decigrams	= 15.432 grains
1 dekagram	= 10 grams	= 0.3527 ounce
1 kilogram	= 1,000 grams	= 2.2046 pounds

American to Metric Table

The following table shows you what the most common U.S. measurements are in the metric system. You probably already know that 1 inch equals 2.54 centimeters. But, did you know that 1 gallon equals 3.7853 liters?

Linear Measure | Length or Distance

1 inch .... = ... 2.54 centimeters
1 foot .... = 12 inches .... = ... 0.3048 meter
1 yard .... = 3 feet .... = ... 0.9144 meter
1 mile .... = 1,760 yards or 5,280 feet .... = ... 1,609.3 meters

Square Measure | Area

1 square inch .... = ... 6.452 square centimeters
1 square foot .... = 144 square inches .... = ... 929 square centimeters
1 square yard .... = 9 square feet .... = ... 0.8361 square meter
1 acre .... = 4,840 sq. yards .... = ... 0.4047 hectare
1 square mile .... = 640 acres .... = ... 259 hectares or 2.59 sq. kilometers

Cubic Measure

1 cubic inch .... = ... 16.387 cubic centimeters
1 cubic foot .... = 1,728 cubic inches .... = ... 0.0283 cubic meter
1 cubic yard .... = 27 cubic feet .... = ... 0.7646 cubic meter
1 cord .... = 8 cord feet .... = ... 3.625 cubic meters

Dry Measure

1 pint .... = ... .5505 liter
1 quart .... = 2 pints .... = ... 1.1012 liters
1 peck .... = 8 quarts .... = ... 8.8096 liters
1 bushel .... = 4 pecks .... = ... 35.2383 liters

Liquid Measure

4 fluid ounces .... = 1 gill .... = ... 0.1183 liter
1 pint .... = 4 gills .... = ... 0.4732 liter
1 quart .... = 2 pints .... = ... 0.9463 liter
1 gallon .... = 4 quarts .... = ... 3.7853 liters

Some Ways to Measure When You Don't Have a Ruler

1. A standard sheet of paper is 8-1/2 by 11 inches (21.59 x 27.94 cms).
2. A quarter is approximately 1 inch wide (2.54 cms).
3. A penny is approximately 3/4 inch wide (1.9 cms).
4. U.S. paper currency is 6-1/8 by 2-5/8 inches (15.56 x 6.67 cms).

Conversion Table

To Change	to	Multiply by
acres	square miles	0.001562
Celsius	Fahrenheit	*1.8
	*(Multiply Celsius by 1.8; then add 32.)	
cubic meters	cubic yards	1.3079
cubic yards	cubic meters	0.7646
Fahrenheit	Celsius	*0.55
	*(Multiply Fahrenheit by .55 after subtracting 32.)	
feet	meters	0.3048
feet	miles	0.0001894
feet/sec.	miles/hr.	0.6818
grams	ounces	0.0353
grams	pounds	0.002205
hours	days	0.04167
inches	centimeters	2.5400
liters	gallons (U.S.)	0.2642
liters	pints (dry)	1.8162
liters	pints (liquid)	2.1134
liters	quarts (dry)	0.9081
liters	quarts (liquid)	1.0567
meters	miles	0.0006214
meters	yards	1.0936
metric tons	tons	1.1023
miles	kilometers	1.6093
miles	feet	5,280
miles/hr.	feet/min.	88
millimeters	inches	0.0394
ounces	grams	28.3495
ounces	pounds	0.0625
pounds	kilograms	0.45359
pounds	ounces	16
quarts (dry)	liters	1.1012
square feet	square meters	0.0929
square kilometers	square miles	0.3861
square meters	square feet	10.7639
square miles	square kilometers	2.5900
square yards	square meters	0.8361
tons	metric tons	0.9072
tons	pounds	2,000
yards	meters	0.9144
yards	miles	0.0005682

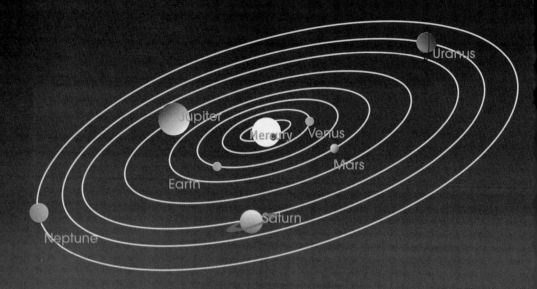

Planet Profusion

There are hundreds of billions of galaxies in the universe. Our solar system is located in the Milky Way galaxy, which is 150,000 light-years in diameter. Even though this galaxy contains an estimated 250 billion to one trillion stars, our solar system contains only one star—the sun. The sun, which is the center of our solar system, has eight planets and a myriad of dwarf planets, asteroids, meteorites, and comets orbiting it. The planets are large, nonluminous bodies that follow fixed elliptical orbits about the sun. (See the illustration above.)

Some of the planets are considered terrestrial planets—Mercury, Venus, Earth, and Mars—which resemble Earth in size, chemical composition, and density. They have rocky bodies and distinct atmospheres. Some planets are considered Jovian planets—Jupiter, Saturn, Uranus, and Neptune—which are much larger in size and have thick, gaseous atmospheres, low densities, and only a small hidden rocky core. The dwarf planets are balls of rock and ice large enough for gravity to make them round, but too small to clear away other objects in their orbits. Some, like Pluto and Eris, have at least one moon. An estimated 200 dwarf planets lie beyond Neptune in the "Kuiper belt." Only Ceres is closer, in the asteroid belt between Mars and Jupiter.

	Sun	Moon	Mercury	Venus	Earth	Mars	Jupiter	Saturn	Uranus	Neptune
Orbital Speed (in miles per second)		0.6	29.8	21.7	18.5	15.0	8.1	6.0	4.2	3.4
Rotation on Axis	25 days 10 hrs. 46 min.	27 days 7 hrs.	59 days	243	23 hrs. 56 min.	24 hrs. 37 min.	9 hrs. 56 min.	10 hrs. 39 min.	17 hrs. 15 min.	16 hrs. 7 min.
Mean Surface Gravity (Earth = 1.00)		0.17	0.38	0.90	1.00	0.38	2.53	1.07	0.92	1.12
Density (times that of water)	150 (core)	3.4	5.4	5.2	5.5	3.9	1.3	0.7	1.3	1.7
Mass (times that of Earth)	333,000	0.01	0.06	0.82	5.98×10^{24} metric tons	0.11	318	95.3	14.6	17.2
Approximate Weight of a 150-Pound Human		26	57	136	150	57	321	161	138	168
Number of Satellites	8 planets	0	0	0	1	2	63	52	27	13
Mean Distance to Sun (in millions of miles)		(234,878 miles from Earth)	36.0	67.24	92.96	141.63	483.7	885.9	1,783.9	2795.1
Revolution Around Sun		(27 days 7 hrs. around Earth)	88 days	227.4 days	365.25 days	687 days	11.86 years	29.46 years	84.0 years	164.8 years
Approximate Surface Temperature (degrees Fahrenheit)	10,000° surface 27,000,000° (center)	−250° to 250°	−279° to 801°	864°	−126° to 136°	−125° to 23°	−234°	−288°	−357°	−353°
Diameter (in miles)	864,949	2,160	3,030	7,521	7,926	4,222	88,846	74,898	31,764	30,776

Additional Units of Measure

Below are some additional units of measure that you may come across in or out of school. They are used to measure everything from boards to light. The ones at the bottom of the page are used in shipbuilding, in the military, and with horses.

Astronomical Unit (A.U.) ▪ 93,000,000 miles, the average distance of the earth from the sun (used in astronomy)

Board Foot (bd. ft.) ▪ 144 cubic inches or 12 in. x 12 in. x 1 in. (used for measuring lumber)

Bolt ▪ 40 yards (used for measuring cloth)

Btu ▪ British thermal unit—amount of heat needed to increase the temperature of one pound of water by one degree Fahrenheit (252 calories)

Gross ▪ 12 dozen or 144

Knot ▪ A rate of speed—one nautical mile per hour (used on boats)

Light, Speed of ▪ 186,281.7 miles per second

Light-year ▪ 5,878,000,000,000 miles—the distance that light travels in a year

Pi (π) ▪ 3.14159265+—the ratio of the circumference of a circle to its diameter

Roentgen ▪ Dosage of unit of radiation exposure produced by X rays

Score ▪ 20 units

Sound, Speed of ▪ Usually placed at 1,088 feet per second at 32° F at sea level

MISCELLANEOUS MEASUREMENTS

3 inches	=	1 palm
4 inches	=	1 hand
6 inches	=	1 span
18 inches	=	1 cubit
21.8 inches	=	1 Bible cubit
2-1/2 feet	=	1 military pace

Mathematics

This section is your guide to the language of mathematics. It lists and defines many of the common (and not so common) mathematical signs, symbols, shapes, and terms. The section also includes helpful math tables and easy-to-follow guidelines for solving word problems.

Common Math Symbols

+	plus (addition)	>	is greater than	″	second (also inch)
−	minus (subtraction)	±	plus or minus	:	is to (ratio)
×	multiplied by	%	percent	π	pi
÷	divided by	$	dollars		
=	is equal to	¢	cents		
≠	is not equal to	°	degree		
<	is less than	′	minute (also foot)		

Advanced Math Symbols

$\sqrt{}$	square root	≅	is congruent to
$\sqrt[3]{}$	cube root	∠	angle
≥	is greater than or equal to	⊥	is perpendicular to
≤	is less than or equal to	‖	is parallel to
{ }	set	∴	therefore

A Chart of Prime Numbers Less Than 500

2	3	5	7	11	13	17	19	23	29
31	37	41	43	47	53	59	61	67	71
73	79	83	89	97	101	103	107	109	113
127	131	137	139	149	151	157	163	167	173
179	181	191	193	197	199	211	223	227	229
233	239	241	251	257	263	269	271	277	281
283	293	307	311	313	317	331	337	347	349
353	359	367	373	379	383	389	397	401	409
419	421	431	433	439	443	449	457	461	463
467	479	487	491	499					

■ Multiplication and Division Table

X	0	1	2	3	4	5	6	7	8	9	10
0	0	0	0	0	0	0	0	0	0	0	0
1	0	1	2	3	4	5	6	7	8	9	10
2	0	2	4	6	8	10	12	14	16	18	20
3	0	3	6	9	12	15	18	21	24	27	30
4	0	4	8	12	16	20	24	28	32	36	40
5	0	5	10	15	20	25	30	35	40	45	50
6	0	6	12	18	24	30	36	42	48	54	60
7	0	7	14	21	28	35	42	49	56	63	70
8	0	8	16	24	32	40	48	56	64	72	80
9	0	9	18	27	36	45	54	63	72	81	90
10	0	10	20	30	40	50	60	70	80	90	100

■ Decimal Equivalents of Common Fractions

1/2	0.5000	1/32	0.0313	3/11	0.2727	6/11	0.5455
1/3	0.3333	1/64	0.0156	4/5	0.8000	7/8	0.8750
1/4	0.2500	2/3	0.6667	4/7	0.5714	7/9	0.7778
1/5	0.2000	2/5	0.4000	4/9	0.4444	7/10	0.7000
1/6	0.1667	2/7	0.2857	4/11	0.3636	7/11	0.6364
1/7	0.1429	2/9	0.2222	5/6	0.8333	7/12	0.5833
1/8	0.1250	2/11	0.1818	5/7	0.7143	8/9	0.8889
1/9	0.1111	3/4	0.7500	5/8	0.6250	8/11	0.7273
1/10	0.1000	3/5	0.6000	5/9	0.5556	9/10	0.9000
1/11	0.0909	3/7	0.4286	5/11	0.4545	9/11	0.8182
1/12	0.0833	3/8	0.3750	5/12	0.4167	10/11	0.9091
1/16	0.0625	3/10	0.3000	6/7	0.8571	11/12	0.9167

■ Roman Numerals

I	1	VIII	8	LX	60	$\overline{V}$	5,000
II	2	IX	9	LXX	70	$\overline{X}$	10,000
III	3	X	10	LXXX	80	$\overline{L}$	50,000
IV	4	XX	20	XC	90	$\overline{C}$	100,000
V	5	XXX	30	C	100	$\overline{D}$	500,000
VI	6	XL	40	D	500	$\overline{M}$	1,000,000
VII	7	L	50	M	1,000		

Math Terms

Addition (+) is combining numbers to get a total, which is called a sum. The sum of 3 plus 5 is 8; 3 + 5 = 8.

An **angle** is made when two rays (lines) share a common endpoint. An angle is measured in degrees.

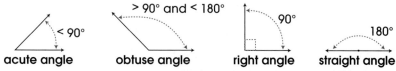

acute angle	obtuse angle	right angle	straight angle
< 90°	> 90° and < 180°	90°	180°

Area is the total surface within a closed figure (circle, square, etc.). The area of a rectangle is figured by multiplying the length by the width. Area is measured in square units such as square inches or square feet.

area is 72 square feet

area

The **average** is found by adding a group of numbers together and then dividing that sum by the number of separate numbers (addends). The average of 7, 8, and 9 is 8, because 7 + 8 + 9 = 24, and 24 ÷ 3 (numbers) = 8. This is also called the mathematical *mean*.

A **circle** is a round, closed figure. All the points on its circumference (edge) are the same distance from the center of the figure.

center

Circumference is the measure of distance around the edge of a circle.

circumference

A **common denominator** is a multiple shared by the denominators of two or more fractions. For example, 6 is a common denominator of $\frac{1}{2}$ and $\frac{1}{3}$ because 6 is a multiple of both 2 and 3. To add or subtract fractions, you must find a common denominator; $\frac{1}{2} + \frac{1}{3} = \frac{3}{6} + \frac{2}{6} = \frac{5}{6}$. The lowest common denominator is also called the least common multiple (LCM) of the denominators.

Congruent ($\cong$) is the term for two figures, angles, or line segments that are the same size and shape.

Data is a set of numbers collected to compare.

congruent triangles

A **decimal** is a fraction written in the decimal number system. (Decimal means "based on the number 10.") Decimals are written using a decimal point and place values—tenths, hundredths, thousandths, and so on. The fraction $\frac{1}{2}$ is 0.5, or $\frac{5}{10}$.

A **degree** is a unit of measurement for angles and arcs. It is written as a small circle [°]. You can write 90° or 90 degrees. There are 360 degrees in a circle.

The **denominator** is the bottom number of a fraction. In the fraction $\frac{1}{3}$, the denominator is 3. It indicates the number of parts needed to make a whole unit.

A **diagonal** is a line from one vertex (corner) of a quadrilateral to the opposite vertex.

The **diameter** is the length of a straight line through the center of a circle.

diameter

A **dividend** is a number to be divided. In the equation 12 ÷ 2 = 6, 12 is the dividend.

Division (÷) is a basic math operation used to determine how many times one quantity is contained in another. Division tells you how many times you have to subtract a number to reach zero. For example, 10 ÷ 5 = 2 because you subtract 5 two times to reach zero (10 − 5 = 5; 5 − 5 = 0).

The **divisor** is the number that divides the dividend. In the statement 12 ÷ 2 = 6, 2 is the divisor.

An **equation** is a statement that says two numbers or mathematical expressions are equal to each other (2 + 10 = 12 or $x + 4 = 9$). Equations use the equal sign (=).

An **estimate** is a reasonable guess at an answer. If you add 6.24 and 5.19, you can estimate the answer will be around 11, because 6 + 5 = 11.

An **even number** is a number that can be divided by 2 without having a remainder (2, 4, 6, and so on). For example, 4 ÷ 2 = 2.

An **exponent** is the small, raised number to the right of the base number that shows how many times the base is to be multiplied by itself. In the expression 2^3, 3 is the exponent (2 is the base). So 2^3 means you need to multiply 2 three times ($2 \times 2 \times 2 = 8$).

A **factor** is a number that is being multiplied. In 4 × 3 = 12, the factors are 4 and 3.

A **fraction** is a number that expresses a part of a whole. In the fraction $\frac{3}{4}$, 4 is the denominator—the number of equal parts that make up the whole. The number 3 is the numerator—the number of parts being talked about.

fraction

Geometry is the study of two-dimensional shapes (circles, triangles), three-dimensional solids (spheres, cubes), and positions in space (points).

A horizontal is a line parallel to the earth's surface, or horizon, going across rather than up and down. A vertical is a line that is straight up and down and perpendicular to the horizon.

A hypotenuse of a right triangle is the side opposite the right angle.

An intersection is the point where two lines in geometry cross each other.

An isosceles triangle is a triangle with two sides of equal length and two equal angles. (See *triangle*.)

Length is the distance along a line from one point to another.

A line is all points formed by extending a line segment both directions, without end.

line

Lowest common denominator (See *common denominator*.)

Mean is another word for average. (See *average*.)

The median is the middle number when a group of numbers is arranged in order from the least to the greatest, or the greatest to the least. In 1, 4, 6 the median (middle number) is 4. In 1, 4, 6, 8 the median is 5, the average of the two middle numbers: 4 + 6 = 10; 10 ÷ 2 = 5.

A multiple is a quantity into which another quantity can be divided, with zero as the remainder (both 6 and 9 are multiples of 3).

Multiplication (×) is like addition because you add the same number a certain number of times (2 × 4 = 4 + 4). When you multiply numbers, the answer is called the product. The product of 2 times 4 is 8 because 2 × 4 = 8. (A raised dot also means multiplication. 2 × 3 is the same as 2 • 3.)

The numerator is the top number of a fraction. In the fraction $\frac{5}{6}$, the numerator is 5.

An obtuse angle is an angle greater than 90 degrees and less than 180 degrees. (See *angle*.)

An odd number is a number that cannot be divided evenly by 2. The numbers 1, 3, 5, 7, and so on, are odd numbers.

Opposite numbers are any two numbers whose sum is zero (−2 and +2 are opposite numbers).

Parallel refers to lines that never intersect.

parallel lines

Percent is a way of expressing a number as a fraction of 100. (*Percent* means "per hundred.") The percent symbol is %. So $\frac{1}{2}$ expressed as a percentage is $\frac{50}{100}$, which is 50%.

3'   3'

3'

perimeter = 9'

The **perimeter** is the distance around the edge of a multi-sided figure. If a triangle has three sides, each 3 feet long, its perimeter is 9 feet (3 + 3 + 3 = 9).

Perpendicular refers to two lines that intersect, forming right angles (90° angles).

Pi (π) is the ratio of the circumference of a circle to its diameter. Pi is approximately 3.14.

perpendicular lines

Place value is the value of the place of a digit depending on where it is in the number.

   3,497   is 3 thousands, 4 hundreds, 9 tens, 7 ones
   0.3497 is 3 tenths, 4 hundredths, 9 thousandths, 7 ten-thousandths

A **point** is an exact location on a plane.

A **positive number** is a number greater than 0.

A **prime number** is a number that cannot be divided evenly (without a remainder) by any number except itself and 1. The number 6 is not a prime number because it can be divided evenly by 1, 2, 3, and 6. The number 5 is a prime number because it can be divided evenly only by itself (5) and 1.

Product is the word used to indicate the result of multiplication. For example, 8 is the product of 2 times 4, because 2 × 4 = 8.

The **quotient** is the number you get when you divide one number by another number. If 8 is divided by 4, the quotient is 2, because 8 ÷ 4 = 2.

radius

The **radius** (r) is the distance from the center of a circle to its circumference. (The radius is half the diameter.)

A **ratio** is a way of comparing two numbers by dividing one by the other. The ratio of 3 to 4 is $\frac{3}{4}$. If there are 20 boys and 5 girls in your class, the ratio of boys to girls is $\frac{20}{5}$ ($\frac{4}{1}$ in lowest terms), or 4:1.

A **rectangle** is a four-sided closed figure with four right angles and with opposite sides parallel and congruent.

A **right angle** is an angle that measures 90 degrees. A right angle is formed when two perpendicular lines meet. (See *angle*.)

Rounding gives you an approximate number if you don't need an exact one. If 2,323 people attended a soccer game, about 2,000 people were there. If 2,857 people attended, about 3,000 were there. Round up if the number is halfway or more to the next highest number (2,500 is halfway between 2,000 and 3,000). Round down if the number is less than halfway.

solid

A **solid** is a three-dimensional figure in geometry, like a cube, a cone, a prism, or a sphere.

A **square** is a rectangle that has four sides of equal length and four right angles. *Square* also refers to the product of a number multiplied by itself. The square of 4 is 16 ($4^2 = 16$; $4 \times 4 = 16$). (See *area* for another use of "square.")

square

The **square root** of a number is a number that, when multiplied by itself, gives the original number as the product. The symbol for square root is $\sqrt{}$. The square root of 4 is 2, because $2 \times 2 = 4$ ($\sqrt{4} = 2$).

Subtraction (−) is the inverse (opposite) of addition. Instead of adding one number to another, you take one number away from another. When you subtract two numbers, you find the difference between them. So $11 - 6 = 5$.

The **sum** is the number you get when you add numbers. For example, 7 is the sum of 4 and 3, because $4 + 3 = 7$.

A **triangle** is a closed figure with three sides. The sum of the angles in every triangle is 180°. Triangles can be classified by *sides:* equilateral, isosceles, or scalene; or by *angles:* right, equiangular, acute, or obtuse.

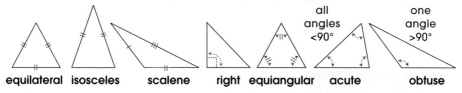

equilateral　isosceles　　scalene　　right　equiangular　acute　　　obtuse

A **vertex** is the point where two sides of a plane (flat) figure meet (corner). The plural of *vertex* is *vertices*.

Vertical (See *horizontal*.)

vertex

Word Problems

To solve word problems, you need strong reading and thinking skills, in addition to good math skills. It is important to solve word problems one step at a time and to show the steps as you work. This way you can explain your solutions.

Steps for Solving Word Problems

1 **Read the problem carefully.**
You may need to read the problem several times to understand it completely. Some problems have two or more parts and ask for more than one answer. Study any maps, charts, graphs, and tables that are part of the problem. To make sure you understand the problem, restate it in your own words, draw it, or even act it out.

2 **Gather the data.**
There are two kinds of data you may need: (1) data that is given in the problem and (2) data that you need to know or look up. Write down the data from the problem that you will use in calculating the solution. Look up (and write down) any other data you need, such as formulas or information.

3 **Set up the equation(s) you will use to solve the problem.**
In this step, you decide how to use the data to solve the problem. This is a good time to check your understanding of the problem by rereading it.

4 **Do the calculations to solve the equation(s).**
If the problem has more than one part, be certain to solve each part.

5 **Check your answers.**
You can solve the problem again (in the same way or in a different way), use a calculator, or start with the answer and work backward.

Helpful Hint

Write an explanation of how you solved the problem, showing the steps you used. This will help you learn from the problem and prepare you to solve more-difficult ones.

Word Problem: Exchanging Money

Imagine that your family is going to Canada. You have saved $35.00 to take with you. How many Canadian dollars will you get when you exchange your American money?

Step 1   **Read and restate the problem.**

"How many Canadian dollars will I get for 35 U.S. dollars?"

Step 2   **Gather the data.**

Data given in the problem: I have 35 U.S. dollars.
Data you need to know or look up: What is the U.S.-to-Canadian exchange rate?

You can find currency exchange rates on the Internet, in the newspaper, or by calling a bank. (Let's say that the U.S.-to-Canadian exchange rate is $1.00 U.S. = $1.46 Canadian.)

Step 3   **Set up the equation you will use to solve the problem.**

$$\frac{\$1.00 \text{ U.S.}}{\$1.46 \text{ Canadian}} = \frac{\$35.00 \text{ U.S.}}{\text{X Canadian}}$$

Step 4   **Do the calculation to solve the equation.**

$$\begin{array}{r} \$1.46 \\ \times\ 35 \\ \hline 730 \\ 438 \\ \hline \$51.10 \end{array}$$

I will get 51.10 Canadian dollars.

Step 5   **Check your answer.**

Divide $51.10 by $1.46 to get the number of U.S. dollars you have (35).

$$\begin{array}{r} \$35. \\ \$1.46_\wedge \overline{)\ \$51.10_\wedge} \\ \underline{438} \\ 730 \\ 730 \end{array}$$

Word Problem: Mixed Numbers

A carpenter needs a total of 15 pieces of lumber to fix a fence. Each piece needs to be $2\frac{2}{3}$ feet long. How many 8-foot boards will she have to buy to get at least 15 pieces $2\frac{2}{3}$ feet long?

Step 1   **Read and restate the problem.**

"How many 8-foot boards will the carpenter have to buy?"

Step 2   **Gather the data.**

Data given in the problem: need 15 pieces $2\frac{2}{3}$ feet long from 8-foot boards.

Step 3   **Set up the problem.**

First you need to know how many $2\frac{2}{3}$-foot pieces can be cut from each 8-foot board (call this number X). Then you need to know how many 8-foot boards must be purchased to get 15 pieces (call this number Y).

$$8 \div 2\frac{2}{3} = X \text{ (number of } 2\frac{2}{3}\text{-foot pieces in one 8-foot board)}$$

$$15 \div X = Y \text{ (number of 8-foot boards needed)}$$

Step 4   **Solve the problem.**

Next, you need to prepare your equation so that you can multiply rather than divide.

$$X = 8 \div 2\frac{2}{3} \ (2\frac{2}{3} = \frac{8}{3}) = 8 \div \frac{8}{3} = 8 \times \frac{3}{8} = \frac{24}{8} = 3$$

$$X = 3 \ (2\frac{2}{3}\text{-foot pieces from each 8-foot board})$$

$$Y = 15 \div X = 15 \div 3 = 5$$

$$Y = 5 \ (8\text{-foot boards})$$

Step 5   **Check your answer.**

Check your answer with a picture and by addition or by multiplication.

$$2\frac{2}{3} + 2\frac{2}{3} + 2\frac{2}{3} = 8$$

3 pieces/board $\times$ 5 boards = 15 pieces

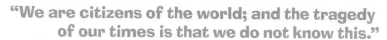

> "We are citizens of the world; and the tragedy
> of our times is that we do not know this."

—Woodrow Wilson

Geography

As global citizens, each of us must stay on top of changes in the world. Just as we try to understand key facts about each of the 50 states, we must also try to understand important information about regions and countries in the world. The section that follows will give you the map skills you need to begin your work.

Using Maps

Finding Direction

Mapmakers use special marks and symbols to show where things are and to give other useful information. Among other things, these marks and symbols show direction (north, south, east, and west). On most maps, north is at the top. But you should always check the **compass rose**, or directional finder, to make sure you know where north is. If there is no symbol, you can assume that north is at the top.

Finding Information

Other important marks and symbols are explained in a box printed on each map. This box is called the legend, or key. It is included to make it easier for you to understand and use the map. Below is the United States map legend. (See page 549.) This legend includes state boundaries.

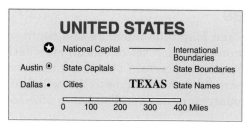

Measuring Distances

0	100	200	300	400 Miles

To measure distances on a map, use the map scale. (See the sample above.) Line up an index card or a piece of paper under the map scale and put a dot on your paper at "0." Put other dots at 100, 200, 300, and so on. You can now measure the approximate distance between points on the map.

Locating Countries

Latitude and longitude lines are another helpful feature of most maps. Latitude and longitude refer to imaginary lines that mapmakers use. Together, these lines can be used to locate any point on the earth.

Latitude

The lines on a map that go from east to west around the earth are called lines of *latitude*. Latitude is measured in degrees, with the equator being 0 degrees (0°). Above the equator, the lines are called *north latitude* and measure from 0° to 90° north (the North Pole). Below the equator, the lines are called *south latitude* and measure from 0° to 90° south (the South Pole). On a map, latitude numbers are printed along the sides.

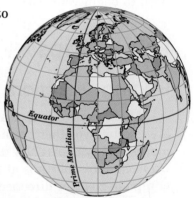

Longitude

The lines on a map that run from the North Pole to the South Pole are lines of *longitude*. Longitude is also measured in degrees. The prime meridian, which runs through Greenwich, England, is 0° longitude. Lines east of the prime meridian are called *east longitude;* lines west of the prime meridian are called *west longitude*. On a map, longitude numbers are printed at the top and bottom.

Coordinates

The latitude and longitude numbers of a country or other place are called its *coordinates*. In each set of coordinates, latitude is given first, then longitude. To locate a certain place on a map using its coordinates, find the point where the two lines cross. (You will find an extensive list of coordinates for countries of the world on pages 557–558.)

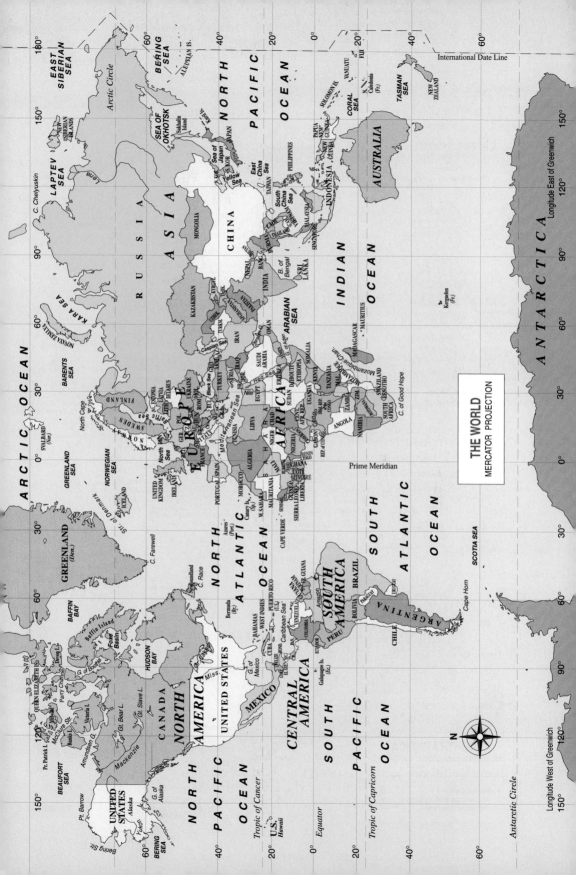

THE WORLD
MERCATOR PROJECTION

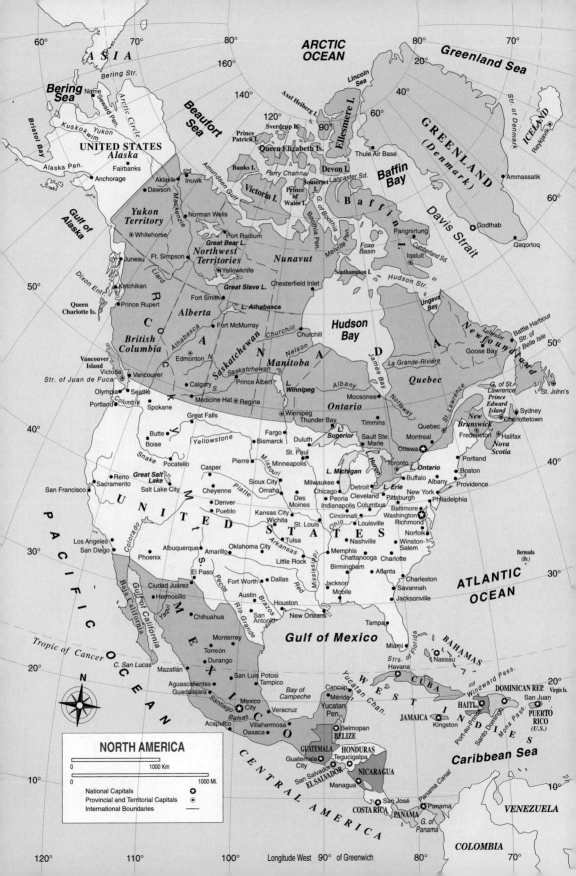

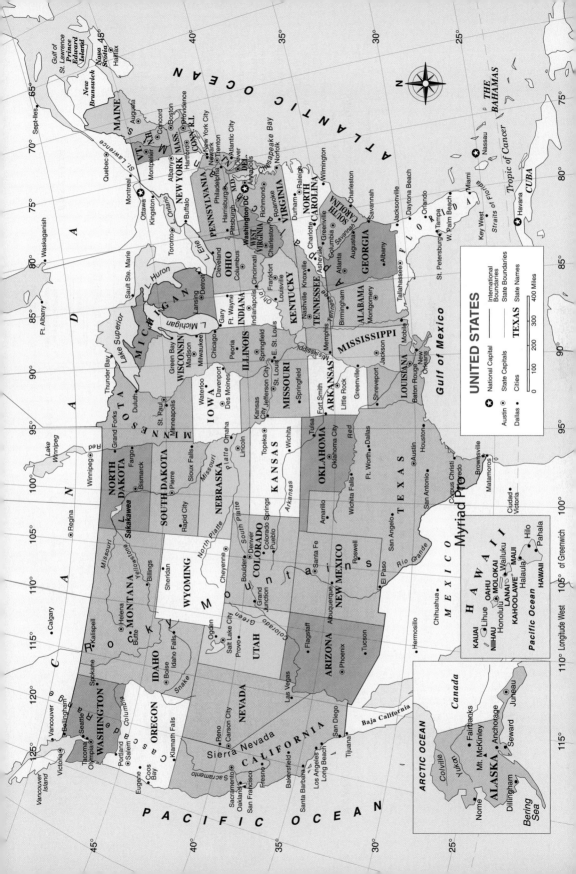

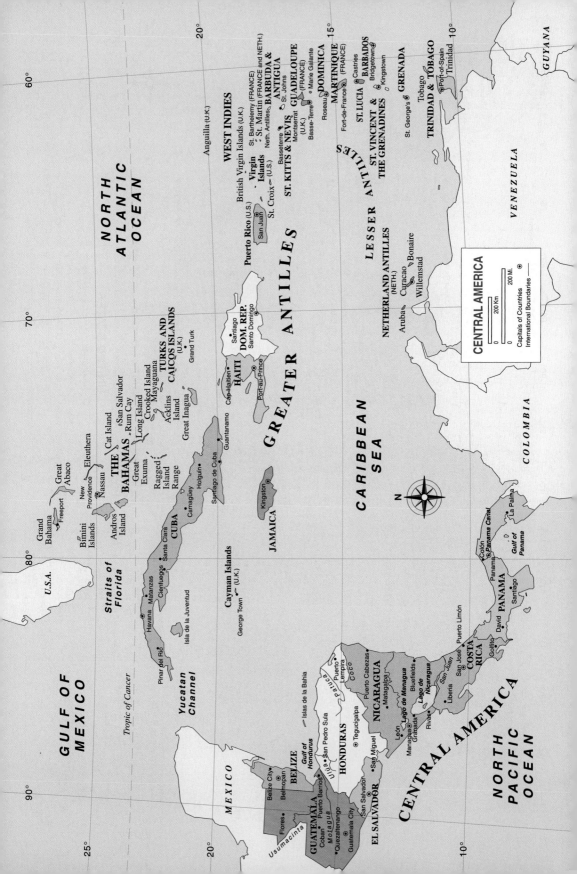

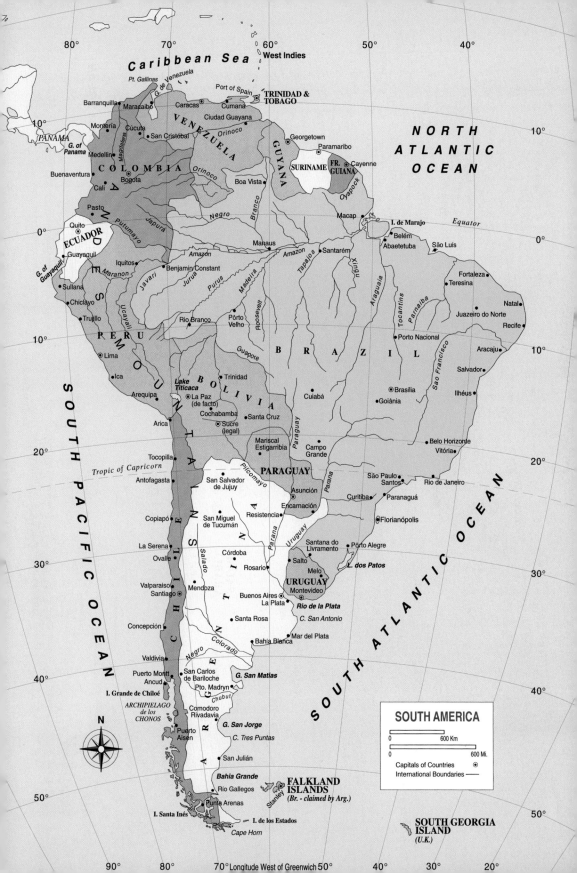

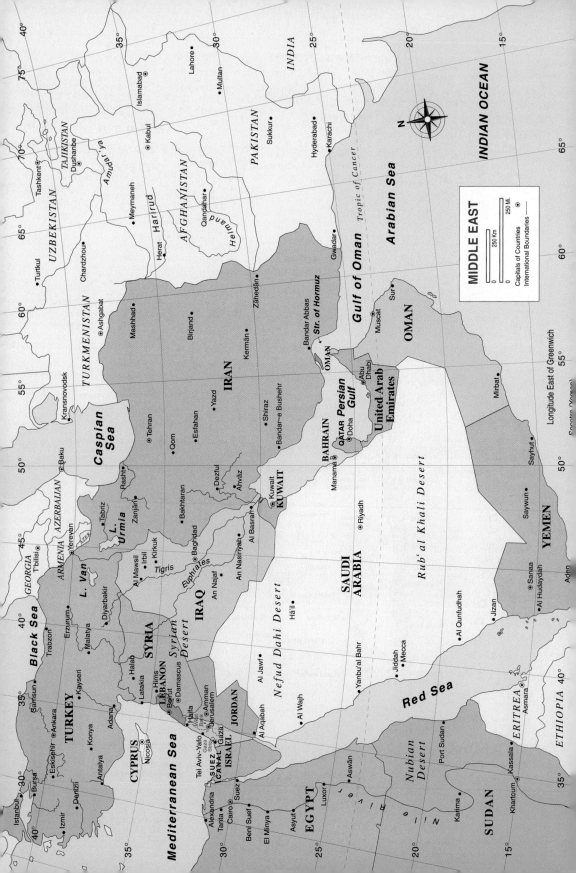

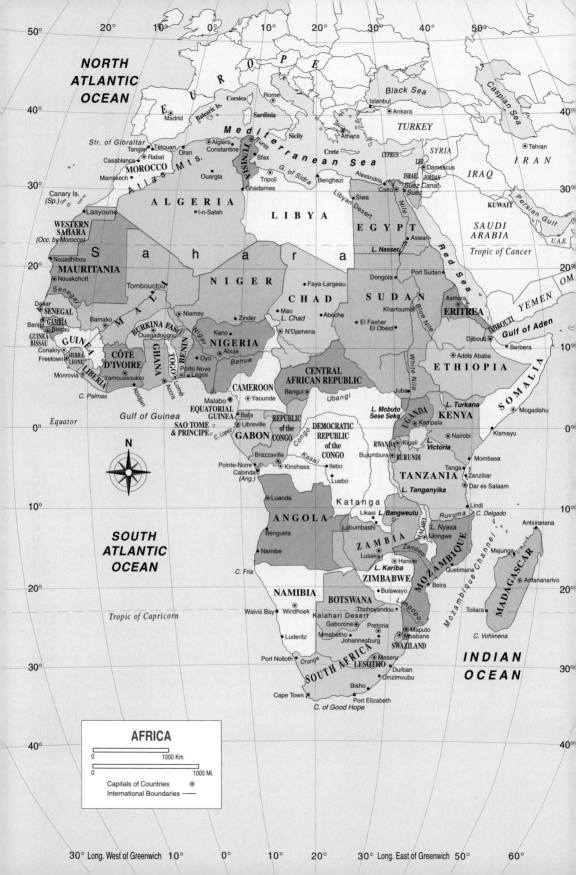

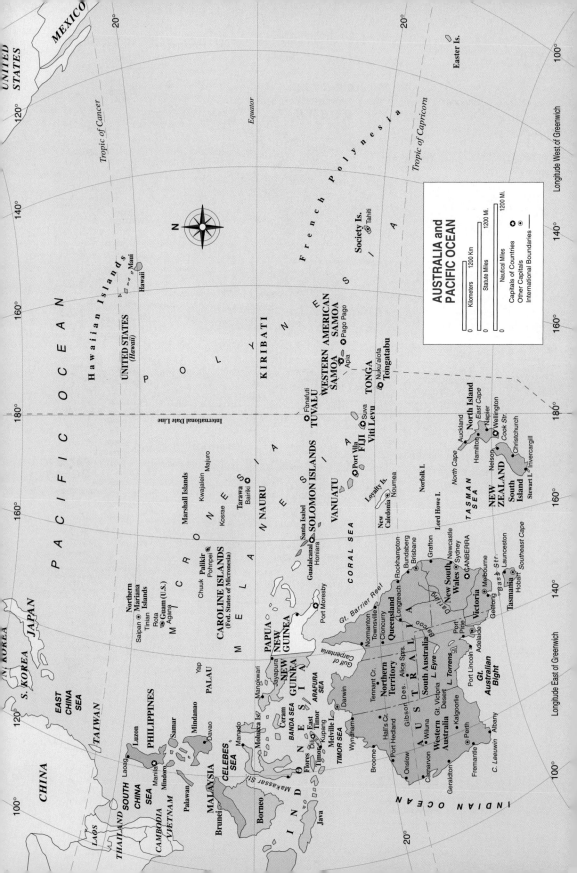

AUSTRALIA and
PACIFIC OCEAN

Kilometers 1200 Km
Statute Miles 1200 Mi.
Nautical Miles 1200 Mi.
0

✪ Capitals of Countries
◉ Other Capitals
— International Boundaries

Index to World Maps

Country	Latitude		Longitude		Country	Latitude		Longitude	
Afghanistan	33°	N	65°	E	France	46°	N	2°	E
Albania	41°	N	20°	E	Gabon	1°	S	11°	E
Algeria	28°	N	3°	E	The Gambia	13°	N	16°	W
Andorra	42°	N	1°	E	Georgia	43°	N	45°	E
Angola	12°	S	18°	E	Germany	51°	N	10°	E
Antigua and Barbuda	17°	N	61°	W	Ghana	8°	N	2°	W
Argentina	34°	S	64°	W	Greece	39°	N	22°	E
Armenia	41°	N	45°	E	Greenland	70°	N	40°	W
Australia	25°	S	135°	E	Grenada	12°	N	61°	W
Austria	47°	N	13°	E	Guatemala	15°	N	90°	W
Azerbaijan	41°	N	47°	E	Guinea	11°	N	10°	W
Bahamas	24°	N	76°	W	Guinea-Bissau	12°	N	15°	W
Bahrain	26°	N	50°	E	Guyana	5°	N	59°	W
Bangladesh	24°	N	90°	E	Haiti	19°	N	72°	W
Barbados	13°	N	59°	W	Honduras	15°	N	86°	W
Belarus	54°	N	25°	E	Hungary	47°	N	20°	E
Belgium	50°	N	4°	E	Iceland	65°	N	18°	W
Belize	17°	N	88°	W	India	20°	N	77°	E
Benin	9°	N	2°	E	Indonesia	5°	S	120°	E
Bhutan	27°	N	90°	E	Iran	32°	N	53°	E
Bolivia	17°	S	65°	W	Iraq	33°	N	44°	E
Bosnia-Herzegovina	44°	N	18°	E	Ireland	53°	N	8°	W
Botswana	22°	S	24°	E	Israel	31°	N	35°	E
Brazil	10°	S	55°	W	Italy	42°	N	12°	E
Brunei Darussalam	4°	N	114°	E	Jamaica	18°	N	77°	W
Bulgaria	43°	N	25°	E	Japan	36°	N	138°	E
Burkina Faso	13°	N	2°	W	Jordan	31°	N	36°	E
Burma	22°	N	96°	E	Kazakhstan	45°	N	70°	E
Burundi	3°	S	30°	E	Kenya	1°	N	38°	E
Cambodia	13°	N	105°	E	Kiribati	0°	N	175°	E
Cameroon	6°	N	12°	E	Kosovo	42°	N	21°	E
Canada	60°	N	95°	W	North Korea	40°	N	127°	E
Cape Verde	16°	N	24°	W	South Korea	36°	N	128°	E
Central African Republic	7°	N	21°	E	Kuwait	29°	N	47°	E
Chad	15°	N	19°	E	Kyrgyzstan	42°	N	75°	E
Chile	30°	S	71°	W	Laos	18°	N	105°	E
China	35°	N	105°	E	Latvia	57°	N	25°	E
Colombia	4°	N	72°	W	Lebanon	34°	N	36°	E
Comoros	12°	S	44°	E	Lesotho	29°	S	28°	E
Congo, Dem. Rep. of the	4°	S	25°	E	Liberia	6°	N	10°	W
Congo, Republic of the	1°	S	15°	E	Libya	27°	N	17°	E
Costa Rica	10°	N	84°	W	Liechtenstein	47°	N	9°	E
Cote d'Ivoire	8°	N	5°	W	Lithuania	56°	N	24°	E
Croatia	45°	N	16°	E	Luxembourg	49°	N	6°	E
Cuba	21°	N	80°	W	Macedonia	43°	N	22°	E
Cyprus	35°	N	33°	E	Madagascar	19°	S	46°	E
Czech Republic	50°	N	15°	E	Malawi	13°	S	34°	E
Denmark	56°	N	10°	E	Malaysia	2°	N	112°	E
Djibouti	11°	N	43°	E	Maldives	2°	N	70°	E
Dominica	15°	N	61°	W	Mali	17°	N	4°	W
Dominican Rep.	19°	N	70°	W	Malta	36°	N	14°	E
Ecuador	2°	S	77°	W	Marshall Islands	7°	N	172°	E
Egypt	27°	N	30°	E	Mauritania	20°	N	12°	W
El Salvador	14°	N	89°	W	Mauritius	20°	S	57°	E
Equatorial Guinea	2°	N	9°	E	Mexico	23°	N	102°	W
Eritrea	17°	N	38°	E	Micronesia	5°	N	150°	E
Estonia	59°	N	26°	E	Moldova	47°	N	28°	E
Ethiopia	8°	N	38°	E	Monaco	43°	N	7°	E
Fiji	19°	S	174°	E	Mongolia	46°	N	105°	E
Finland	64°	N	26°	E	Montenegro	42°	N	19°	E
					Morocco	32°	N	5°	W

Country	Latitude		Longitude	
Mozambique	18°	S	35°	E
Namibia	22°	S	17°	E
Nauru	1°	S	166°	E
Nepal	28°	N	84°	E
The Netherlands	52°	N	5°	E
New Zealand	41°	S	174°	E
Nicaragua	13°	N	85°	W
Niger	16°	N	8°	E
Nigeria	10°	N	8°	E
Northern Ireland	55°	N	7°	W
Norway	62°	N	10°	E
Oman	22°	N	58°	E
Pakistan	30°	N	70°	E
Palau	8°	N	138°	E
Panama	9°	N	80°	W
Papua New Guinea	6°	S	147°	E
Paraguay	23°	S	58°	W
Peru	10°	S	76°	W
The Philippines	13°	N	122°	E
Poland	52°	N	19°	E
Portugal	39°	N	8°	W
Qatar	25°	N	51°	E
Romania	46°	N	25°	E
Russia	60°	N	80°	E
Rwanda	2°	S	30°	E
St. Kitts and Nevis	17°	N	62°	W
Saint Lucia	14°	N	61°	W
Saint Vincent and the Grenadines	13°	N	61°	W
San Marino	44°	N	12°	E
São Tomé and Príncipe	1°	N	7°	E
Saudi Arabia	25°	N	45°	E
Scotland	57°	N	5°	W
Senegal	14°	N	14°	W
Serbia	45°	N	21°	E
Seychelles	5°	S	55°	E
Sierra Leone	8°	N	11°	W
Singapore	1°	N	103°	E
Slovakia	49°	N	19°	E
Slovenia	46°	N	15°	E
Solomon Islands	8°	S	159°	E
Somalia	10°	N	49°	E
South Africa	30°	S	26°	E
Spain	40°	N	4°	W
Sri Lanka	7°	N	81°	E
Sudan	15°	N	30°	E
Suriname	4°	N	56°	W
Swaziland	26°	S	31°	E
Sweden	62°	N	15°	E
Switzerland	47°	N	8°	E
Syria	35°	N	38°	E
Taiwan	23°	N	121°	E
Tajikistan	39°	N	71°	E
Tanzania	6°	S	35°	E
Thailand	15°	N	100°	E
Togo	8°	N	1°	E
Tonga	20°	S	173°	W
Trinidad and Tobago	11°	N	61°	W
Tunisia	34°	N	9°	E
Turkey	39°	N	35°	E
Turkmenistan	40°	N	55°	E
Tuvalu	8°	S	179°	E
Uganda	1°	N	32°	E
Ukraine	50°	N	30°	E
United Arab Emirates	24°	N	54°	E
United Kingdom	54°	N	2°	W
United States	38°	N	97°	W
Uruguay	33°	S	56°	W
Uzbekistan	40°	N	68°	E
Vanuatu	17°	S	170°	E
Venezuela	8°	N	66°	W
Vietnam	17°	N	106°	E
Wales	53°	N	3°	W
Western Samoa	10°	S	173°	W
Yemen	15°	N	44°	E
Yugoslavia	44°	N	19°	E
Zambia	15°	S	30°	E
Zimbabwe	20°	S	30°	E

TOPOGRAPHIC TALLY TABLE

THE CONTINENTS	Area (Sq Km)	Percent of Earth's Land
Asia	44,026,000	29.7
Africa	30,271,000	20.4
North America	24,258,000	16.3
South America	17,823,000	12.0
Antarctica	13,209,000	8.9
Europe	10,404,000	7.0
Australia	7,682,000	5.2

LONGEST RIVERS	Length (Km)
Nile, Africa	6,671
Amazon, South America	6,437
Chang Jiang (Yangtze), Asia	6,380
Mississippi-Missouri, North America	5,971
Ob-Irtysk, Asia	5,410
Huang (Yellow), Asia	4,672
Congo, Africa	4,667
Amur, Asia	4,416
Lena, Asia	4,400
Mackenzie-Peace, North America	4,241

MAJOR ISLANDS	Area (Sq Km)
Greenland	2,175,600
New Guinea	792,500
Borneo	725,500
Madagascar	587,000
Baffin	507,500
Sumatra	427,300
Honshu	227,400
Great Britain	218,100
Victoria	217,300
Ellesmere	196,200
Sulawesi	178,700
South Island (New Zealand)	151,000
Java	126,700

THE OCEANS	Area (Sq Km)	Percent of Earth's Area Water
Pacific	166,241,000	46.0
Atlantic	86,557,000	23.9
Indian	73,427,000	20.3
Arctic	9,485,000	2.6

Government

Every country in the world has a government. The purpose of the government is to make and enforce laws and to protect the rights of its citizens. Every major country in the world also has a constitution, a basic set of laws by which the people are governed.

The U.S. Constitution establishes the form of the United States government and explains the rights and responsibilities of its citizens. This section takes a closer look at those rights and responsibilities, and how the government is organized.

Branches of the Government

Legislative Branch	Executive Branch	Judicial Branch

Duties/Responsibilities

Makes Laws	Enhances Laws Makes Policy	Interprets Laws

Components

Congress	President	Supreme Court

Senate	House of Representatives	Vice President	Circuit Courts

President of the Senate	Speaker of the House	Cabinet	District and Special Courts

President's Cabinet

The Cabinet is a group of advisers appointed by the president to help set policies and make decisions. The Cabinet usually meets weekly with the president.

Department of State

Department of Education

Department of Health and Human Services

Department of Defense

Department of Homeland Security

Department of the Treasury

Department of Veterans Affairs

Department of Commerce

Department of the Interior

Department of Energy

Department of Housing and Urban Development

Attorney General

Department of Labor

Department of Agriculture

Department of Transportation

Individual Rights and Responsibilities

Freedom of Assembly

Freedom to hold meetings. Meetings must be peaceful.

Freedom of Speech

Freedom to express ideas and opinions. No one may say untrue things about other citizens.

Freedom of Petition

Freedom to ask the government to pass laws.

Freedom of the Press

Freedom to print books, newspapers, and magazines. No one may print things that hurt American citizens.

Freedom of Religion

Freedom to practice the religion of your choice.

Equal Justice

All persons accused of a crime must receive fair and equal treatment under law.

Freedom and Security of Citizens

No one may search someone's home without a warrant. People have the right to bear arms to protect themselves.

American citizens must . . .

- serve as jury members when called upon.
- pay taxes to fund the government.
- attend school.
- testify in court.
- obey the law.
- help to defend the nation.

U.S. Presidents and Vice Presidents

1	George Washington	April 30, 1789 – March 3, 1797	John Adams	1
2	John Adams	March 4, 1797 – March 3, 1801	Thomas Jefferson	2
3	Thomas Jefferson	March 4, 1801 – March 3, 1805	Aaron Burr	3
	Thomas Jefferson	March 4, 1805 – March 3, 1809	George Clinton	4
4	James Madison	March 4, 1809 – March 3, 1813	George Clinton	
	James Madison	March 4, 1813 – March 3, 1817	Elbridge Gerry	5
5	James Monroe	March 4, 1817 – March 3, 1821	Daniel D. Tompkins	6
	James Monroe	March 4, 1821 – March 3, 1825		
6	John Quincy Adams	March 4, 1825 – March 3, 1829	John C. Calhoun	7
7	Andrew Jackson	March 4, 1829 – March 3, 1833	John C. Calhoun	
	Andrew Jackson	March 4, 1833 – March 3, 1837	Martin Van Buren	8
8	Martin Van Buren	March 4, 1837 – March 3, 1841	Richard M. Johnson	9
9	William Henry Harrison*	March 4, 1841 – April 4, 1841	John Tyler	10
10	John Tyler	April 6, 1841 – March 3, 1845		
11	James K. Polk	March 4, 1845 – March 3, 1849	George M. Dallas	11
12	Zachary Taylor*	March 5, 1849 – July 9, 1850	Millard Fillmore	12
13	Millard Fillmore	July 10, 1850 – March 3, 1853		
14	Franklin Pierce	March 4, 1853 – March 3, 1857	William R. King	13
15	James Buchanan	March 4, 1857 – March 3, 1861	John C. Breckinridge	14
16	Abraham Lincoln	March 4, 1861 – March 3, 1865	Hannibal Hamlin	15
	Abraham Lincoln*	March 4, 1865 – April 15, 1865	Andrew Johnson	16
17	Andrew Johnson	April 15, 1865 – March 3, 1869		
18	Ulysses S. Grant	March 4, 1869 – March 3, 1873	Schuyler Colfax	17
	Ulysses S. Grant	March 4, 1873 – March 3, 1877	Henry Wilson	18
19	Rutherford B. Hayes	March 4, 1877 – March 3, 1881	William A. Wheeler	19
20	James A. Garfield*	March 4, 1881 – Sept. 19, 1881	Chester A. Arthur	20
21	Chester A. Arthur	Sept. 20, 1881 – March 3, 1885		
22	Grover Cleveland	March 4, 1885 – March 3, 1889	Thomas A. Hendricks	21
23	Benjamin Harrison	March 4, 1889 – March 3, 1893	Levi P. Morton	22
24	Grover Cleveland	March 4, 1893 – March 3, 1897	Adlai E. Stevenson	23
25	William McKinley	March 4, 1897 – March 3, 1901	Garret A. Hobart	24
	William McKinley*	March 4, 1901 – Sept. 14, 1901	Theodore Roosevelt	25
26	Theodore Roosevelt	Sept. 14, 1901 – March 3, 1905		
	Theodore Roosevelt	March 4, 1905 – March 3, 1909	Charles W. Fairbanks	26
27	William H. Taft	March 4, 1909 – March 3, 1913	James S. Sherman	27
28	Woodrow Wilson	March 4, 1913 – March 3, 1917	Thomas R. Marshall	28
	Woodrow Wilson	March 4, 1917 – March 3, 1921		
29	Warren G. Harding*	March 4, 1921 – Aug. 2, 1923	Calvin Coolidge	29
30	Calvin Coolidge	Aug. 3, 1923 – March 3, 1925		
	Calvin Coolidge	March 4, 1925 – March 3, 1929	Charles G. Dawes	30
31	Herbert C. Hoover	March 4, 1929 – March 3, 1933	Charles Curtis	31

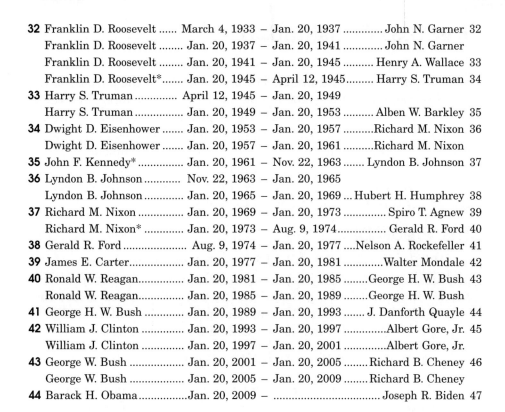

32 Franklin D. Roosevelt ...... March 4, 1933 – Jan. 20, 1937 .... John N. Garner 32

Franklin D. Roosevelt .... Jan. 20, 1937 – Jan. 20, 1941 .... John N. Garner

Franklin D. Roosevelt .... Jan. 20, 1941 – Jan. 20, 1945 .... Henry A. Wallace 33

Franklin D. Roosevelt* .... Jan. 20, 1945 – April 12, 1945 .... Harry S. Truman 34

33 Harry S. Truman .... April 12, 1945 – Jan. 20, 1949

Harry S. Truman .... Jan. 20, 1949 – Jan. 20, 1953 .... Alben W. Barkley 35

34 Dwight D. Eisenhower .... Jan. 20, 1953 – Jan. 20, 1957 ....Richard M. Nixon 36

Dwight D. Eisenhower .... Jan. 20, 1957 – Jan. 20, 1961 ....Richard M. Nixon

35 John F. Kennedy* .... Jan. 20, 1961 – Nov. 22, 1963 .... Lyndon B. Johnson 37

36 Lyndon B. Johnson .... Nov. 22, 1963 – Jan. 20, 1965

Lyndon B. Johnson .... Jan. 20, 1965 – Jan. 20, 1969 ... Hubert H. Humphrey 38

37 Richard M. Nixon .... Jan. 20, 1969 – Jan. 20, 1973 .... Spiro T. Agnew 39

Richard M. Nixon* .... Jan. 20, 1973 – Aug. 9, 1974 .... Gerald R. Ford 40

38 Gerald R. Ford .... Aug. 9, 1974 – Jan. 20, 1977 ....Nelson A. Rockefeller 41

39 James E. Carter................. Jan. 20, 1977 – Jan. 20, 1981 ....Walter Mondale 42

40 Ronald W. Reagan............... Jan. 20, 1981 – Jan. 20, 1985 ....George H. W. Bush 43

Ronald W. Reagan............... Jan. 20, 1985 – Jan. 20, 1989 ....George H. W. Bush

41 George H. W. Bush .... Jan. 20, 1989 – Jan. 20, 1993 .... J. Danforth Quayle 44

42 William J. Clinton .... Jan. 20, 1993 – Jan. 20, 1997 ....Albert Gore, Jr. 45

William J. Clinton .... Jan. 20, 1997 – Jan. 20, 2001 ....Albert Gore, Jr.

43 George W. Bush .... Jan. 20, 2001 – Jan. 20, 2005 .... Richard B. Cheney 46

George W. Bush .... Jan. 20, 2005 – Jan. 20, 2009 .... Richard B. Cheney

44 Barack H. Obama................Jan. 20, 2009 – .... Joseph R. Biden 47

(*Did not finish term)

Order of Presidential Succession

1. Vice president
2. Speaker of the House
3. President pro tempore of the Senate
4. Secretary of state
5. Secretary of the treasury
6. Secretary of defense
7. Attorney general
8. Secretary of the interior
9. Secretary of agriculture
10. Secretary of commerce
11. Secretary of labor
12. Secretary of health and human services
13. Secretary of housing and urban development
14. Secretary of transportation
15. Secretary of energy
16. Secretary of education
17. Secretary of veterans affairs
18. Secretary of homeland security

The U.S. Constitution

The Constitution is made up of three main parts: a **preamble**, 7 **articles,** and 27 **amendments**. The *preamble* states the purpose of the Constitution, the *articles* explain how the government works, and the 10 original *amendments* list the basic rights guaranteed to all American citizens. Together, these parts contain the laws and guidelines necessary to set up and run a successful national government.

Besides giving power to the national government, the U.S. Constitution gives some power to the states and some to the people. Remember this when you study the Constitution.

The Preamble

We the people of the United States, in order to form a more perfect Union, establish justice, insure domestic tranquility, provide for the common defense, promote the general welfare, and secure the blessings of liberty to ourselves and our posterity, do ordain and establish this Constitution for the United States of America.

The Articles of the Constitution

The articles of the Constitution explain how each branch of government works and what each can and cannot do. The articles also explain how the federal and state governments must work together, and how the Constitution can be amended or changed.

Article 1 explains the legislative branch, how laws are made, and how Congress works.

Article 2 explains the executive branch, the offices of the President and Vice President, and the powers of the executive branch.

Article 3 explains the judicial branch, the Supreme Court and other courts, and warns people about trying to overthrow the government.

Article 4 describes how the United States federal government and the individual state governments work together.

Article 5 tells how the Constitution can be amended, or changed.

Article 6 states that the United States federal government and the Constitution are the law of the land.

Article 7 outlines how the Constitution must be adopted to become official.

The Bill of Rights

To get the necessary votes to approve the Constitution, a number of changes (amendments) had to be made. These 10 original amendments are called the Bill of Rights. They guarantee all Americans some very basic rights, including the right to worship and speak freely and the right to have a jury trial.

Amendment 1 People have the right to worship, to speak freely, to gather together, and to question the government.

Amendment 2 People have the right to bear arms.

Amendment 3 The government cannot have soldiers stay in people's houses without their permission.

Amendment 4 People and their property cannot be searched without the written permission of a judge.

Amendment 5 People cannot be tried for a serious crime without a jury. They cannot be tried twice for the same crime or be forced to testify against themselves. Also, they cannot have property taken away while they are on trial. Any property taken for public use must receive a fair price.

Amendment 6 In criminal cases, people have a right to a trial, to be told what they are accused of, to hear witnesses against them, to get witnesses in their favor, and to have a lawyer.

Amendment 7 In cases involving more than $20, people have the right to a jury trial.

Amendment 8 People have a right to fair bail (money given as a promise the person will return for trial) and to fair fines and punishments.

Amendment 9 People have rights that are not listed in the Constitution.

Amendment 10 Powers not given to the federal government are given to the states or to the people.

The Other Amendments

The Constitution and the Bill of Rights were ratified (approved) in 1791. Since that time, more than 7,000 amendments to the Constitution have been proposed. Because three-fourths of the states must approve an amendment before it becomes law, just 27 amendments have been passed. The first 10 are listed under the Bill of Rights; the other 17 are listed below. (The date each amendment became law is given in parentheses.)

Amendment 11 A person cannot sue a state in federal court. (1795)

Amendment 12 The President and Vice President are elected separately. (1804)

Amendment 13 Slavery is abolished, done away with. (1865)

Amendment 14 All persons born in the United States or those who have become citizens enjoy full citizenship rights. (1868)

Amendment 15 Voting rights are given to all [adult male] citizens regardless of race, creed, or color. (1870)

Amendment 16 Congress has the power to collect income taxes. (1913)

Amendment 17 United States Senators are elected directly by the people. (1913)

Amendment 18 Making, buying, and selling alcoholic beverages is no longer allowed. (1919)

Amendment 19 Women gain the right to vote. (1920)

Amendment 20 The President's term begins January 20; Senators' and Representatives' terms begin January 3. (1933)

Amendment 21 (Repeals Amendment 18) Alcoholic beverages can be made, bought, and sold again. (1933)

Amendment 22 The President is limited to two elected terms. (1951)

Amendment 23 District of Columbia residents gain the right to vote. (1961)

Amendment 24 All voter poll taxes are forbidden. (1964)

Amendment 25 If the Presidency is vacant, the Vice President takes over. If the Vice Presidency is vacant, the President names someone and the Congress votes on the choice. (1967)

Amendment 26 Citizens 18 years old gain the right to vote. (1971)

Amendment 27 No law changing the pay for members of Congress will take effect until after an election of Representatives. (1992)

History

A famous American author, Oliver Wendell Holmes, once said, "When I want to understand what is happening today or try to decide what will happen tomorrow, I look back." In other words, we can learn a lot about the world around us by looking at what has happened in the past—by studying history.

Historical Time Line

The historical time line included on the next 11 pages will help you look back. The time line begins with Columbus's arrival in the New World and covers the period from 1492 to the present. The time line is divided into three main parts: United States History, Science and Inventions, and Literature and Life. You'll find many interesting facts in the time line—when watches were invented (1509), when paper money was first used in America (1690), and who developed the first pair of blue jeans (Levi Strauss in 1850).

But even before the first European settlers arrived in the United States, there were many Native American tribes living here. As you can see on the map below, each tribe lived in one of five major regions. American history really begins with the Native Americans.

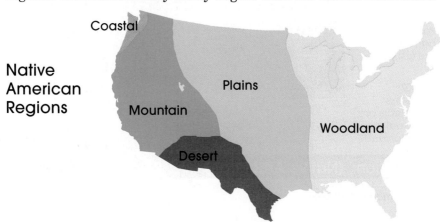

Native American Regions

Coastal

Mountain

Plains

Woodland

Desert

1500	1520	1540	1560	1580

United States History

1492 Columbus reaches the West Indies.

1513 Ponce de León explores Florida.

1519 Magellan begins three-year voyage around the world.

1519 Aztec empire dominates Mexico.

1521 Cortez defeats Aztecs and claims Mexico for Spain.

1559 Spanish colony of Pensacola, Florida, lasts two years.

1565 Spain settles St. Augustine, Florida, first permanent European colony.

1570 League of the Iroquois Nations formed.

1588 England defeats the Spanish Armada and rules the seas.

1590 English colony of Roanoke vanishes.

Science and Inventions

1507 Book on surgery is developed.

1509 Watches are invented.

1530 Bottle corks are invented.

1531 Halley's comet appears and causes panic.

1543 Copernicus challenges beliefs by claiming sun-centered universe.

1545 French printer Garamond sets first type.

1558 Magnetic compass invented by John Dee.

1565 Pencils invented in England.

1585 Decimals introduced by Dutch mathematicians.

1590 First paper mill is used in England.

1596 Thermometer is invented.

Literature and Life

1500 Game of bingo developed.

1503 Pocket handkerchiefs are first used.

1507 Glass mirrors are greatly improved.

1536 First songbook used in Spain.

1538 Mercator draws map with America on it.

1541 Michelangelo completes largest painting, *The Last Judgement*.

1564 First horse-drawn coach used in England.

1580 First water closet designed in Bath, England.

1582 Pope Gregory XIII introduces the calendar still in use today.

1599 First copper coins are made.

U.S. Population: (Native American)   (Spanish)

approximately 1,100,000   1,021

| 1600 | 1620 | 1640 | 1660 | 1680 | 1700 |

1619
House of Burgesses in Virginia establishes first representative government in colonies.

1607
England establishes Jamestown, Virginia, first English settlement.

1620
Pilgrims found Plymouth Colony.

1629
Massachusetts Bay Colony is established.

1609
Henry Hudson explores the Hudson River.

1634
Colony of Maryland is founded.

1664
The Dutch colony of New Netherlands becomes the English colony of New York.

1690
Paper money first used in America.

1673
Marquette and Joliet explore Mississippi River for France.

1682
William Penn founds Pennsylvania.

1608
Telescope is invented.

1629
Human temperature measured by physician in Italy.

1641
First cotton factories begin operating in England.

1609
Galileo makes first observations with telescope.

1643
Torricelli invents the barometer.

1668
Reflecting telescope invented by Sir Isaac Newton.

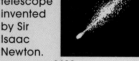

1682
Halley's comet is studied by Edmund Halley and named for him.

1671
First calculation machine invented.

1600
William Shakespeare's plays are performed at Globe Theatre in London.

1630
Popcorn is introduced to Pilgrims by Quadequina.

1622
January 1 accepted as beginning of the year (instead of March 25).

1609
The song "Three Blind Mice" is written.

1653
First postage stamps used in Paris.

1685
First drinking fountain used in England.

1658
First illustrated book for children, *World of Visible Objects in Pictures*, created by John Comenius.

1697
Tales of Mother Goose written by Charles Perrault.

(English)

| 350 | 2,302 | 26,634 | 75,058 | 151,507 |

1700 1710 1720 1730 1740

United States History

1700
France builds forts at Mackinac and Detroit and controls fur trade.

1705
Virginia Act establishes public education.

1707
England (English) and Scotland (Scots) unite and become Great Britain (British).

Scotland

England

1718
New Orleans founded by France.

1733
James Oglethorpe founds Georgia.

1733
British Molasses Act places taxes on sugar and molasses.

1735
Freedom of the press established during trial of John Peter Zenger.

1747
Ohio Company formed to settle Ohio River Valley.

Science and Inventions

1701
Seed drill that plants seeds in a row is invented by Jethro Tull.

1712
Thomas Newcomen develops first practical steam engine.

1709
The pianoforte (first piano) is invented by Christofori Bartolommeo.

1728
First dental drill is used by Pierre Fauchard.

1732
Sedatives for operations discovered by Thomas Dover.

1735
Rubber found in South America.

1738
First cuckoo clocks invented in Germany.

1742
Benjamin Franklin invents efficient Franklin stove.

Literature and Life

1700
The Selling of Joseph by Samuel Sewall is first protest of slavery.

1704
First successful newspaper in colonies, *Boston News-Letter*, is published.

1716
First hot-water home heating system is developed.

1719
Robinson Crusoe written by Daniel Defoe.

1726

Gulliver's Travels written by Jonathan Swift.

1731
Ben Franklin begins first subscription library.

1736
First American cookbook written by Mrs. E. Smith.

1744
John Newbery publishes children's book, *A Little Pretty Pocket-Book*.

U.S. Population: (English Colonies)

250,888	331,711	466,185	629,445	905,563

1750 1760 1770 1780 1790 1800

1750
The French and Indian War begins.

1763
Britain defeats France in French and Indian War.

1775
First battles of the Revolutionary War are fought.

1781
British surrender at Yorktown Oct. 19.

1781
United colonies adopt Articles of Confederation as first government.

1797
U.S.S. Constitution is launched.

1765
Stamp Act tax imposed on colonies by Britain.

1787
The United States Constitution is signed.

1750
Flatbed boats and Conestoga wagons begin moving settlers west.

1776
Declaration of Independence signed at Second Continental Congress on July 4.

1789
George Washington elected president of the United States.

1752
Benjamin Franklin discovers lightning is a form of electricity.

1764
James Hargreaves invents spinning jenny for making thread.

1781
Uranus, first planet not known to ancient world, is discovered.

1793
Eli Whitney invents cotton gin that takes seeds out of cotton.

1770
First steam carriage is invented by French engineer Nicholas Cugnot.

1758
Sextant for navigation is invented by John Bird.

1783
First balloon is flown by Frenchmen Joseph and Jacques Montgolfier.

1798
Eli Whitney invents mass production.

1752
First general hospital is established in Philadelphia.

1764
Mozart writes first symphony.

1780
The waltz becomes popular dance.

1790
Official U.S. census begins.

1782
The American bald eagle is first used as symbol of the United States.

1795
Food canning is introduced.

1769
Venetian blinds are first used.

1757
Streetlights are installed in Philadelphia.

1786
First ice-cream company in America begins production.

1,170,760   1,593,625   2,148,076   2,780,369   3,929,157

| 1800 | 1810 | 1820 | 1830 | 1840 |

United States History

1800
Washington, D.C., becomes U.S. capital.

1812-1814
War of 1812 fought between U.S. and Britain.

1830
Indian Removal Act forces Native Americans west of Mississippi River.

1846
Mexican War gives U.S. Southwestern territories.

1803
Louisiana Purchase from France doubles U.S. size.

1819
U.S. acquires Florida from Spain.

1836
Texans defend the Alamo.

1846
Britain cedes Oregon Country to U.S.

1803
Lewis & Clark explore Louisiana Territory & the Northwest.

1821
Sierre Leone established by U.S. for freed slaves.

1838
Cherokee Nation forced west on "Trail of Tears."

1848
Gold discovered in California.

Science and Inventions

1800
The battery is invented by Count Volta.

1816
Stethoscope invented by René Laënnec.

1836
Samuel Morse invents telegraph.

1849
Safety pin is invented.

1802
Steamboat is built by Robert Fulton.

1817
The Erie Canal is begun.

1839
Bicycle is invented by Kirkpatrick Macmillan.

1844
Safety matches produced.

1808
Chemical symbols are developed by Jöns Berzelius.

1819
Electromagnetism discovered by Hans Christian Oestad.

1846
Elias Howe invents sewing machine.

Literature and Life

1804
First book of children's poems is published.

1812
Army meat inspector, "Uncle Sam" Wilson, becomes U.S. symbol.

1820
Rip Van Winkle is written by Washington Irving.

1834
Louis Braille perfects a letter system for the blind.

1849
Elizabeth Blackwell becomes first woman doctor.

1806
Gas lighting used in homes.

1814
Francis Scott Key writes "The Star-Spangled Banner."

1827
Audubon's *Birds of America* is published.

1835
Hans Christian Anderson publishes *Tales Told to Children.*

1816
J. Niepce takes first photograph.

1828
Webster's Dictionary is published.

1849
Thoreau writes "Civil Disobedience."

U.S. Population: (Multicultural)

| 5,308,080 | 7,240,102 | 9,638,453 | 12,860,702 | 17,063,353 |

1850   1860   1870   1880   1890   1900

1853
National Council of Colored People is founded.

1860
Abraham Lincoln elected 16th president of the U.S.

1861
Civil War begins when Confederates fire on Fort Sumter.

1862
Lincoln proclaims abolition of slavery in U.S.

1876
Custer defeated at Battle of Little Big Horn.

1876
U.S. Centennial celebrated.

1869
Coast-to-coast railroad is finished in Utah.

1898
U.S. defeats Spain in Spanish-American War.

1889
Jane Addams founds Hull House in Chicago to help immigrants.

1851
Isaac Singer produces sewing machine.

1860
Internal combustion engine built by Jean Lenoir.

1852
Elisha Otis invents first elevator with a safety brake.

1865
Antiseptic practices are introduced by Joseph Lister.

1857
Atlantic cable is completed.

1874
Barbed wire introduced by Joseph Glidden.

1876
Alexander Graham Bell invents telephone.

1877
Thomas Edison invents phonograph.

1879
Edison makes incandescent lightbulb.

1887
Radio waves produced by Hertz.

1893
Charles and Frank Duryea build first successful U.S. gasoline automobile.

1896
Marconi invents wireless radio.

1850
Levi Strauss produces blue jeans.

1852
Uncle Tom's Cabin by Harriet Beecher Stowe strengthens antislavery movement.

1855
Alexander Parks produces first synthetic plastic.

1864
Red Cross is established.

1873
Zipper invented by Whitcomb Judson.

1869
Chewing gum is patented.

1876
National Baseball League established.

1882
Malted milk produced by William Horlick.

1883
Four U.S. time zones are established.

1886
Dr. Penberton invents Coca-Cola.

1892
The first basketball game is played.

1889
Roll film produced by George Eastman.

23,191,876   31,443,321   38,558,371   50,189,209   62,979,766

1900   **1905**   **1910**   **1915**   **1920**

United States History

1900
First Olympics involving women held in Paris.

1903
Orville and Wilbur Wright fly first successful airplane.

1909
National Association for the Advancement of Colored People (NAACP) is founded.

1913
Income Tax Amendment establishes a tax on wages people make.

1914
Panama Canal opens.

1914
World War I in Europe begins.

1917
United States enters World War I.

1918
World War I ends in Europe.

1920
Prohibition of alcoholic beverages begins.

1920
Women given right to vote.

Science and Inventions

1901
Walter Reed discovers yellow fever is carried by mosquitoes.

1905
Albert Einstein announces theory of relativity $(E=mc^2)$ of time and space.

$$E=mc^2$$

1900
Zeppelin airships developed.

1904
New York City opens its subway system.

1913
Henry Ford establishes assembly line for automobiles.

1915
Coast-to-coast telephone system established.

1921
Vaccine for tuberculosis is discovered.

1922
Philo T. Farnsworth develops electron scanner for television.

Literature and Life

1900
American Baseball League established.

1900
Hot-dog sausages created in New York City.

1903
First World Series played.

1905
First nickelodeon movie theater established in Pittsburgh.

1907
Artists Picasso and Braque create cubism.

1903
Call of the Wild written by Jack London.

1913
Boy's Life magazine is published by Boy Scouts.

1917
Doughnuts created for the soldier "doughboys" fighting in World War I.

1917
The American Girl magazine published by Girl Scouts.

1920
First radio station, KDKA, founded in Pittsburgh.

U.S. Population: (Multicultural)

| 76,212,168 | 92,228,496 | 106,021,537 |

| 1925 | 1930 | 1935 | 1940 | 1945 | 1950 |

1927
Charles Lindbergh flies solo across the Atlantic Ocean.

1931
The 102-story Empire State Building completed as tallest in the world.

1939
Germany invades Poland to begin World War II.

1945
World War II ends.

1933
President Franklin Roosevelt inaugurated and begins New Deal to end Great Depression.

1941
Japanese bomb Pearl Harbor Dec. 7, and U.S. enters World War II.

1929
Wall Street Stock Market crashes.

1933
Prohibition of alcoholic beverages repealed.

1945
United States becomes a member of the United Nations.

1926
John Baird demonstrates his television system.

1935
Radar is invented.

1938
Modern-type ballpoint pens developed.

1947
Edwin Land invents Polaroid camera.

1928
Alexander Fleming develops penicillin.

1938
First photocopy machine produced.

1947
Bell Lab scientists invent transistor.

1929
Clarence Birdseye introduces frozen foods.

1940
Enrico Fermi develops nuclear reactor.

1947
Raytheon invents the microwave oven.

1930
First analog computer invented by Vannevar Bush.

1925
Potato chips are produced in New York City.

1931
"The Star-Spangled Banner" becomes U.S. national anthem.

1937
First full-length animated film, *Snow White and the Seven Dwarfs,* is made.

1946
Highlights for Children magazine published.

1925
First National Spelling Bee is held.

1938
Superman "Action Comics" created.

1947
Jackie Robinson becomes the first black major league baseball player.

1927
First "talking movie," *The Jazz Singer,* is made.

1939
Nestlés chocolate chips are produced.

1928
My Weekly Reader magazine is founded.

1947
Anne Frank's *Diary of a Young Girl* is published.

123,202,624   132,164,569

1950 1955 1960 1965 1970

United States History

1950
United States enters Korean War.

1954
Korean War ends.

1955
Rosa Parks refuses to follow segregation rules on Montgomery bus.

1955
Martin Luther King, Jr., begins organizing protests against black discrimination.

1959
Alaska becomes 49th state.

1959
Hawaii becomes 50th state.

1961
Alan Shepard becomes first U.S. astronaut in space.

1963
President John F. Kennedy assassinated in Dallas, TX.

1965
U.S. combat troops sent to Vietnam.

1968
Martin Luther King, Jr., is assassinated.

1969
Neil Armstrong and Buzz Aldrin are first men to walk on moon.

1974
President Richard Nixon resigns.

1971
Eighteen-year-olds are given right to vote.

Science and Inventions

1951
Fluoridated water introduced to prevent tooth decay.

1953
Watson and Crick map the DNA molecule.

1954
Jonas Salk discovers polio vaccine.

1957
Russia launches first satellite, *Sputnik 1*, beginning Space Age.

1958
Stereo long-playing records produced.

1960
First laser invented by Theodore Maiman.

1963
Cassette music tapes developed.

1967
Cholesterol discovered as cause of heart disease.

1968
First U.S. heart transplant is performed by surgeon Norman Shumway.

1971
Space probe *Mariner* maps surface of Mars.

1974
Sears Tower (110 stories) built in Chicago.

1975
VCR's introduced for home use.

Literature and Life

1950
Peanuts comic strip produced by Charles Schulz.

1951
Fifteen million American homes have television.

1952
Charlotte's Web is published.

1957
Theodor "Dr. Seuss" Geisel's *Cat in the Hat* is published.

1957
Elvis Presley is the most popular rock 'n' roll musician in U.S.

1961
Peace Corps is established, helping others around the world.

1964
The Beatles appear on *The Ed Sullivan Show* and change American music.

1970
First Earth Day begins a focus on protecting the environment.

1970
Sounder by William Armstrong wins Newbery Award for children's literature.

1970
Sesame Street television show with Jim Henson's Muppets begins.

U.S. Population:: (Multicultural)

| 151,325,798 | 179,323,175 | 203,302,031 |

1975 · · · · · 1980 · · · · · 1985 · · · · · 1990 · · · · · 1995 · · · · · 2000

1975
Vietnam
War ends.

1978
Camp
David
Accords
signed
by Egypt
& Israel.

1979
Iran
seizes U.S.
hostages.

1981
Sandra Day
O'Connor
becomes first
woman on
Supreme Court.

1981
U.S. hostages returned
from Iran after 444 days.

1983
Sally Ride
becomes first U.S. female
astronaut in space.

1986
Challenger space shuttle
explodes, killing entire
crew.

1989
Berlin Wall
separating
East and West
Germany is
torn down.

1991
Persian Gulf War "Operation
Desert Storm" begins.

1994
NATO (North Atlantic
Treaty Organization)
expands to include
Eastern European
nations.

1994
Earthquake
rocks
Los Angeles,
California, killing
more than 50
people.

1976
Concorde
becomes
world's first
supersonic
passenger jet.

1977
Apple
Computers
produces
first personal
computer.

1981
Scientists identify
AIDS (acquired
immune
deficiency
syndrome).

1983
Pioneer 10 space probe
passes Neptune and
leaves solar system.

1984
Compact disk
(CD) music players
developed.

1988
NASA reports greenhouse effect on
Earth's atmosphere is caused by
destruction of forests.

1991
Environmental Protection
Agency cites growing danger
of hole in Earth's ozone layer.

1991
World Wide Web is launched.

1997
Scottish
scientists
clone an
adult sheep.

1976
Alex Haley's African-American
saga *Roots* published.

1976
United States
celebrates Bicentennial.

1977
Star Wars becomes one
of the highest-grossing
movies of all time.

1979
Yellow ribbons displayed
in support of return of
U.S. hostages in Iran.

1986
Martin Luther King
Day proclaimed
national holiday.

1987
The Whipping Boy
by Sid Fleischman
wins Newbery
Award.

1988
Thirty million U.S.
schoolchildren have
access to computers.

1998
The Chicago Bulls win their
sixth NBA Championship.

1998
Titanic becomes
the top money-
making film in
history.

2000　　　　　　　　　2005　　　　　　　　　2010

United States History

2000
Mad cow disease raises concern in Europe.

2001
Al-Qaeda attacks United States with hijacked airplanes on September 11.

2001
United States declares the War on Terror and invades Afghanistan.

2003
United States goes to war against Iraq.

2005
REAL ID Act passed into United States law.

2005
Hurricane Katrina devastates the Gulf Coast, followed by Hurricane Rita.

2006
U.S. population officially reaches 300 million.

2007
Former vice president Al Gore and UN Intergovernmental Panel on Climate Change receive the Nobel Peace Prize.

2008
Barack Obama is voted first African American U.S. president.

Science and Inventions

2000
Joint U.S./Russian team boards the International Space Station (I.S.S.) as first full-time crew.

2000
Human genome is deciphered.

2003
American scientists clone a white-tailed deer.

2003
Space shuttle *Columbia* is destroyed during re-entry.

2004
SpaceShipOne, the first privately held spacecraft, leaves Earth's atmosphere.

2005
Space probes land on Titan, Saturn's largest moon.

2006
International Astronomical Union reclassifies Pluto as a dwarf planet.

2007
Fossil finds suggest *Homo habilis* and *Homo erectus* coexisted for 500,000 years.

2008
NASA's *Phoenix Lander* discovers ice on Mars.

Literature and Life

2000
Survivor inspires "reality television" in the United States.

2001
Dennis Tito is first "space tourist" to visit International Space Station.

2003
Hispanics become largest American minority group.

2004
Cell phone users exceed 171 million.

2004
Boston Red Sox win the World Series for the first time since 1918.

2005
YouTube video Web site goes online.

2006
Google buys YouTube for $1.65 billion.

2008
With 8 gold medals in one Olympics, Michael Phelps breaks previous record.

2007
Apple introduces the iPhone.

2007
The final book of the Harry Potter series sells 11 million copies in 24 hours.

U.S. Population:: (Multicultural)

281,421,906

303,763,031 (2008 est.)

Credits

Page 336: The artist's image of a climber on the space elevator is used courtesy of the National Aeronautics and Space Administration (NASA).

Page 391: Copyright © 2207 by Houghton Mifflin Harcourt Publishing Company. Reproduced by permission from *The American Heritage Student Dictionary.*

Shutterstock: pages 157, 176, 226, 320, 321, 365, 368, 372, 404, 406, 420

Index

This index is your personal guide to using the *Write on Course* handbook. For example, if your teacher asks you to review your writing with several of your classmates, you may not remember that the guidelines for reviewing are found in the "Peer Responding" chapter. Fortunately, the index lists those same guidelines under several entries: **Advising** in groups; **Discussion** group, writing; **Group** skills, Writing; **Responding** to writing; and **Writing** group guidelines. If you don't find what you are looking for the first time you try, think of other "keywords" that may get you to the same information. Learning how to use an index will prove to be a valuable lifelong skill.

H

I

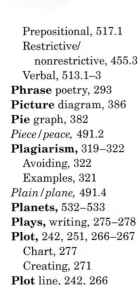

Y